“One of my colleagues in the Old Testament department likes to q

of the gods, but Hebrew is the language of God. If he’s right, that may explain why Hebrew is so challenging to learn! But fear not, for expert help is at hand. Bill Fullilove’s mission is to make learning Biblical Hebrew as painless, productive, and pastorally relevant as it can be. I’m delighted that he has now written an introductory text based on his many years of teaching experience and his sympathetic attention to students’ needs. It will be an invaluable resource not only for seminarians but for any other lover of God’s Word who desires to read Jesus’ own Bible in its original language. I highly recommend it.”
—**James N. Anderson**, Academic Dean, Reformed Theological Seminary Global Campus; Associate Professor of Theology and Philosophy, Reformed Theological Seminary, Charlotte

“Bill Fullilove’s new grammar of Biblical Hebrew is an outstanding introduction to the language for beginning students. The author presents the basic material clearly and cogently, while deftly incorporating insights gleaned from the latest research. Beginners will enjoy starting to read actual excerpts from the Bible at an early stage; and by the end, they will be well equipped for the task of Old Testament exegesis. I warmly and enthusiastically recommend this fine new textbook.”
—**Ed Cook**, Chairman, Department of Semitic and Egyptian Languages and Literatures; Associate Professor, The Catholic University of America

“Learning biblical languages can be tedious, but it does not have to be; it is much more enjoyable when guided by a gifted teacher. Therefore, I am happy to commend this distinctive textbook written by a trustworthy guide. William Fullilove not only shepherds students through the rudiments of Hebrew grammar, but also introduces sound exegetical method. Each chapter contains “live” examples of Biblical Hebrew, which provides encouragement for students to persevere in their studies, and demonstrates the need for diligence to be faithful stewards of the Word of God. This is an excellent choice for an introductory Hebrew grammar.”
—**Brandon Crowe**, Associate Professor of New Testament, Westminster Theological Seminary

“From beginning to end, Fullilove keeps in mind that the ultimate goal of biblical language-learning is to grasp the message of Scripture so that the text can master us. This is an exegetically oriented beginning Hebrew grammar. It sets itself apart by teaching not only what morphology and clause syntax are but how our knowledge of Hebrew helps us understand God’s Book. Fullilove gets students into the biblical text early and then uses creative paths to nurture discovery and to point forward toward application. The chapters are well structured and clear, and the overall work is highly creative. This is a guidebook that will motivate students to learn, so I joyfully recommend this grammar.”
—**Jason S. DeRouchie**, Professor of Old Testament and Biblical Theology, Bethlehem College & Seminary; Coauthor, *A Modern Grammar for Biblical Hebrew*

"Bill Fullilove is a former student of mine and served as an excellent teaching assistant in my courses. Clearly, his interest in Hebrew is not merely academic. He wants his students to understand the language and to use it in teaching the Bible, more than is common among seminary graduates. I am not an expert in Hebrew grammar, but I share Bill's concern for its use in ministry. The book seems to be very complete, going beyond the text I perused in seminary. Bill presents not only the Hebrew vocabulary and forms, but much on the actual practice of textual criticism, semantic range of terms, and continuing differences among translators. He is much aware of the tendency of beginning Hebrew students to claim more knowledge than they actually have, and he issues appropriate warnings. I hope the book gets a wide usage so that it might enrich the church's teaching of the Word of God."
—**John Frame**, Professor of Systematic Theology and Philosophy, Reformed Theological Seminary, Orlando

"In my experience, students work incredibly hard to learn Hebrew. But since they don't experience firsthand the value of reading Hebrew for exegesis, a regrettable number of them don't maintain their Hebrew and therefore never get to see its payoff. Or else they are daunted by the process of using the exegetical reference tools that could help them capitalize on the skills they worked so hard to acquire.

"*Introduction to Hebrew* by Bill Fullilove, a great new resource for Hebrew teachers and students, was designed to solve that problem. Its chief brilliance lies in showing students the value of Hebrew for exegesis from the very beginning of their study. Every chapter guides the students through an exegetical exercise based on the material just learned. (Even if all they know is the alphabet!) It teaches them to use reference tools and to draw conclusions *based on their understanding of Hebrew*. This not only shows them the value of knowing Hebrew, but trains them to use those reference tools so that they come out equipped rather than intimidated by them. Hurray!

"At the same time that the book builds students' confidence in finding answers, it encourages humility in interacting with others and cautions them not to assume, as beginning students, that they *have* all the answers. That gracious word is as valuable as the skills imparted.

"Of course, many specific aspects of the book are well thought out, too: introducing verbs early; familiarizing students with morphological tendencies, such as assimilating *nuns*, but waiting to teach weak verbs until the strong verb is well learned; and drawing the practice exercises from Scripture. But its greatest benefit lies in simultaneously training students in Hebrew and in exegesis—and building their confidence in both."
—**Elizabeth Groves**, Lecturer in Biblical Hebrew, Westminster Theological Seminary

"This is the best teaching grammar of Biblical Hebrew available today. It has no rival. Fullilove combines his expert knowledge of the language with clear and concise explanations that are oriented toward beginning students. What sets this grammar apart is its exegetical focus, showing at every turn the relevance of the language for biblical interpretation. This is the ideal textbook for college and seminary students who are preparing for Christian ministry."
—**Scott C. Jones**, Professor of Biblical Studies, Covenant College; Author, *Rumors of Wisdom: Job 28 as Poetry*

"It is a joy to commend Bill Fullilove's *Introduction to Hebrew* to present and future pastors and to serious readers of the Scripture. He has found ways to make the language so accessible and yet filled with such accuracy that many who thought Hebrew was beyond their reach will find it readily and comfortably right at hand."
—**Walter C. Kaiser Jr.**, President Emeritus, Gordon-Conwell Theological Seminary

"Here's the book that I wish I had been given—and from which I wish I had been instructed—when I was a student of Hebrew. Ministry students are frankly goal-oriented when it comes to language study. We want our language knowledge to directly and continually enable us to interpret God's Word. Bill Fullilove's *Introduction to Hebrew* never loses sight of this goal. I highly recommend it."
—**Tim Keller**, Redeemer Presbyterian Church, New York City

"Dr. Bill Fullilove has successfully produced a new grammar that demonstrates the benefits of Biblical Hebrew for exegetical matters. From something as basic as the alphabet to more sophisticated linguistic concepts, he provides practical steps in gaining a knowledge of Hebrew as an essential tool to understand the message of Scripture. Diligent students will find this grammar rewarding and see immediate fruits of their labors."
—**Peter Lee**, Associate Professor of Old Testament, Reformed Theological Seminary, Washington, DC

"Many students begin their study of Biblical Hebrew with enthusiasm, but lose their zeal because they see no practical benefit. Dr. Fullilove shows beginning students the value of learning Hebrew every step of the way. His approach will encourage students to keep moving forward until they master the basic grammar of Biblical Hebrew."
—**Richard L. Pratt Jr.**, President, Third Millennium Ministries

"In my years of teaching biblical studies, I have increasingly come to understand the need to help students discern the weightier matters of the languages without neglecting the finer points. So organization and clarity are absolutely imperative. The better a professor can help students clearly see the organizational patterns of the language, the more encouraged they are to continue—and the more likely they are to succeed. Bill Fullilove's Hebrew grammar accomplishes just that. The organization is shrewd and helpful. The clarity is unsurpassed. I look forward to using it with my own students."
—**Nicholas G. Piotrowski**, Director of Biblical and Theological Studies and Associate Dean of Academics, Crossroads Bible College

"Fullilove accomplishes what every student, not to mention every teacher, of Biblical Hebrew wants to accomplish as quickly as possible: introducing the learner to the ancient text of Scripture. While many grammars succeed in teaching the structure and lexicon of Biblical Hebrew, this well-designed grammar reminds us early and often of the reason why we study the language and of the rich teaching we can glean from a robust exegesis of the Holy Scriptures."
—**John Scott Redd Jr.**, President and Associate Professor of Old Testament, Reformed Theological Seminary, Washington, DC

"The product of many years of careful study and of sustained engagement with students studying Hebrew for the first time, William Fullilove's *Introduction to Hebrew* offers a wonderful balance between detailed language instruction and exegetical engagement with the Hebrew Bible. Students will gain a strong foundation in Hebrew from this book while immediately experiencing the benefits of that study for interpreting the Bible. This combination of features will aid instructors in teaching their students and help students to sustain their motivation to study the language, two areas in which so many other grammars fail to serve their primary audiences. *Introduction to Hebrew* can and will initiate students into a lifetime of enriching interaction with the Hebrew text of the Bible."
—**C. A. Strine**, Vice-Chancellor's Fellow and Lecturer in Hebrew Bible, University of Sheffield; Author, *Sworn Enemies: The Divine Oath, the Book of Ezekiel, and the Polemics of Exile*

"I wish I had been given this book forty years ago! Dr. Fullilove's Hebrew grammar is much more than a primer; it is a veritable treasure that takes students by the hand and demonstrates how we might now use what we know without overblown and self-confident claims of 'new insights' or 'errors in the translation.' An impressive and much-needed book that will help every student of Scripture profit from the original language. Enthusiastically recommended."
—**Derek W. H. Thomas**, Robert Strong Professor of Systematic and Pastoral Theology, Reformed Theological Seminary, Atlanta; Senior Minister, First Presbyterian Church, Columbia, SC

INTRODUCTION TO

HEBREW

A Guide for Learning and *Using* Biblical Hebrew

WILLIAM FULLILOVE

FOREWORD BY BRUCE K. WALTKE

P&R

PUBLISHING

P.O. BOX 817 • PHILLIPSBURG • NEW JERSEY 08865-0817

Unless otherwise indicated, all Scripture quotations are the author's own translation.

Italics within Scripture quotations indicate emphasis added.

ISBN: 978-1-62995-271-0 (pbk)

Printed in the United States of America

To the many men and women who have patiently taught me Hebrew.

Far more, to Jill, without doubt an אֵ֫שֶׁת חַ֫יִל, and the one who has patiently walked beside me each step of the way.

Additional Aids for Teachers or Students

at www.introductiontohebrew.com:

- **Answer Key**
- **Free YouTube Curriculum**
- **Errata List**

Contents

Foreword

Writing a grammar to teach Biblical Hebrew is difficult. This is due in part to the historical development of the Hebrew text: its consonantal text was later supplemented with *matres lectionis* (consonants to represent vowels) and then even later was also provided with the Masoretic vocalization. The task of teaching such a language is simply complex. All languages consist of a subject, predicate, modifiers, and particles, such as prepositions, connecting them. But the Semitic family of languages, of which Biblical Hebrew is a member, differs significantly from the Indo-European family of languages, of which English is a member. For example, the Semitic family, unlike the Indo-European family, contains an extensive verbal system to signify causation in connection with voice. Beyond this, in the college, seminary, or university environment, Biblical Hebrew often is not taught for the value of learning the language in its own right   though it certainly has such value! Instead, Biblical Hebrew is taught to enable strong, solid exegetical work, to enable students to read the Hebrew Bible/Old Testament and grasp more fully its meaning and nuance. To expect a grammar to do all of this well is simply a lot to ask.

Nevertheless, William Fullilove's *Introduction to Hebrew* succeeds admirably. This book is the best introductory option for teaching Hebrew in a seminary, college, or university setting because it combines an expert understanding of the language with clear explanations that a beginning student can easily grasp. Dr. Fullilove's teaching grammar combines several admirable features that make it so pedagogically successful:

- All its examples are from the biblical text, thereby keeping students constantly aware of their progress in reading and their growing capability.
- It quickly introduces the basic forms of the verb (Qal perfect and imperfect) in chapters 3 and 5, thereby introducing the linguistic center of the sentence as early as possible and maximizing students' practice in parsing and translating verbs.
- The full paradigm of the strong verb is taught first, enabling students to gain a basic conception of the Hebrew verbal system before being weighed down by the myriad complexities of parsing forms built from weak verbal roots.
- Weak roots are held until the second half of the grammar and then introduced by type, enabling the student to see how the phonological impact of a weak consonant carries through the verbal system in a relatively regular way. Instead of overwhelming the

student who has just been introduced to the Qal perfect, this method vastly simplifies teaching weak roots.

- Skills such as the proper use of a lexicon, the basics of word studies, and the use of the apparatus—skills that professors must usually teach in a supplemental way—are instead integrated into the grammar.
- With all of this, the grammar is not overlong, and it can easily be completed in two semesters of introductory language study.

Beyond all these features, however, what really makes this grammar sparkle is the final section of each chapter. Based on years of classroom teaching, Dr. Fullilove has crafted each final section as a set of exegetical exercises that require students to immediately apply the skills learned in that chapter to better understanding the Hebrew text. Even in chapter 1, for example, having learned only the alphabet, students are introduced to the acrostic poem and are asked (and able!) to analyze an incomplete acrostic and consider how the text of the poem is to be understood.

No better grammar is currently available to teach the beginning Hebrew student, especially the one interested in using Hebrew for the sake of biblical exegesis. In an age of slipshod preparation for ministry and exegesis, we need better-trained students who will become superior exegetes, both in the academy and in the church. This grammar is a welcome contribution to exactly that endeavor and a superb choice for the classroom teaching of Hebrew.

Bruce K. Waltke

July 2016

Preface

Why another Hebrew grammar? Simply put, many of today's Hebrew students need to be convinced of the value of their task. The common query is this: "Can't I just look it up in Bible software? Why do I bother learning the original languages?" Having devoted decades to studying Biblical Hebrew (and other Semitic languages), I remain among those who see that these languages have value simply for their own sake—learning *is* a value. Nonetheless, I recognize that the educational climate of the day requires a continually goal-oriented approach to language study. Modern students rarely do well with an approach that says, in essence, "Just learn it now, and next year we'll show you why it's relevant." Instead, the strength to press on has to come from a continual reminder of *why* the difficult study of an ancient language is valuable.

I began my career in business, and I still remember a study done by one team at our firm. It was an attempt to answer a question about forecasting: which is more accurate in predicting future trends—experts or computer models? Sometimes the answer was "the experts" and other times "the computer models." Unsurprisingly, though, by far the most effective forecasting was done by neither the experts nor the computer models, but instead by experts using computer models. By analogy with Hebrew, computer software can be exceptionally valuable and helpful, and I use it regularly. True strength in study and exegesis, however, will come from experts—students who have deeply learned the language—as they use that computer software. Such learning takes time and effort, and such effort, when given, produces great fruit.

While much of this grammar follows traditional methods, those methods are put to use in the final section of each chapter, a set of *exegetical* exercises that give the student the opportunity to immediately apply the skills developed from his or her study to the biblical text, in order to gain insights that have a practical payoff of understanding the biblical text more clearly. Along with these exercises, this grammar serves as a primer on the use of Hebrew for interpretation, introducing the use of secondary resources such as a lexicon, word-study resources, and the critical apparatus. The skills typically taught in Hebrew III or IV are instead brought forward into Hebrew I and II so that the student sees the value of his or her hard work. For many students, this is the payoff that makes the hard work of learning Biblical Hebrew worth it, the reason to return another day to the paradigms and vocabulary drills and puzzling phrases that they seek to understand. People do what they want to do. We are largely guided by our loves, and if students love Hebrew (or even like it), they will continue to use it. If they simply "grind it out," they will soon drop it and forget it, and all the effort—by students and professors alike—will have been for naught.

In that regard, this book has been both a love and a labor, both given to the Lord. My deep thanks are due to so many who labored with me on it. As two of my teachers, Drs. Waltke and O'Connor, often observed, all language study is cumulative. I have been blessed in life with outstanding teachers of Hebrew, and my deep thanks, both for their teaching and even more for their patience, go to Dr. Edward Chandler, Dr. Bruce Waltke, Dr. Douglas Gropp, Dr. Michael Patrick O'Connor, Dr. Adele Berlin, Dr. Edward Cook, and Dr. Andrew Gross, each of whom taught me Hebrew at one stage. No human being should be so fortunate to study with all of them. Special thanks go to Katie Kelley, who edited early drafts of this book; to my 2015–16 Hebrew class at Reformed Theological Seminary Atlanta, who worked through these materials week by week as they were formed into chapters; and to the 2016-2017 Hebrew classes at Reformed Theological Seminary Atlanta, Reformed Theological Seminary New York, and Covenant College, who endured my countless typos among the page proofs of this book. Further thanks go to the many at P&R Publishing who shepherded this book through various stages—each was a delight in interaction and expertise: Natalie Nyquist, who edited these chapters; Karen Magnuson, who patiently proofread every page; Amanda Martin, a continual resource for questions; Ian Thompson, under whose encouragement this project went forward; and John J. Hughes, who believed in this grammar and without whom it would not exist. Most importantly, thanks go to Dr. Scott Jones of Covenant College, who edited each chapter—many times twice or even three times. Quite literally, each page is better because of his work, friendship, and encouragement. (Any errors and flaws, of course, remain entirely my responsibility.) Scott is a blessing beyond measure, an expert with a gentle spirit and a dear friend. Finally, thanks go to the German Bible Society for its permission to include the reproduction of a page of *Biblia Hebraica Stuttgartensia* (*BHS*) in this volume.

One cannot make the study of Hebrew easy, but I hope that, by grace, this book will make it "less hard." May יהוה be blessed if that is so.

SDG

William Fullilove

July 2016

א (1) Learning to Speak, Part 1

1.1 The Alphabet

Hebrew is written from right to left. The Hebrew alphabet consists of twenty-three consonants:

Letter	Final Form	Name	Transliteration	Pronunciation
א		*aleph*	ʾ	None (silent)
בּ (ב)		*bet*	b (ḇ)	b as in “but” (v as in “vat”)
גּ (ג)		*gimel*	g (ḡ)	g as in “god” (g as in “god”)
דּ (ד)		*dalet*	d (ḏ)	d as in “dog” (d as in “dog”)
ה		*heh*	h	h as in “hay”
ו		*waw*	v	v as in “vet”
ז		*zayin*	z	z as in “zip”
ח		*ḥet*	ḥ	ch as in “loch”
ט		*ṭet*	ṭ	t as in “tamp”
י		*yod*	y	y as in “yet”
כּ (כ)	ך	*kaph*	k (ḵ)	k as in “kit” (ch as in “loch”)
ל		*lamed*	l	l as in “lamp”
מ	ם	*mem*	m	m as in “mom”
נ	ן	*nun*	n	n as in “noun”
ס		*samek*	s	s as in “sat”
ע		*ayin*	ʿ	None (but see below)
פּ (פ)	ף	*pe(h)*	p (p̄)	p as in “pet” (ph as in “phone”)

Letter	Final Form	Name	Transliteration	Pronunciation
צ	ץ	*ṣade*	ṣ	ts as in "bats"
ק		*qoph*	q	k as in "king"
ר		*resh*	r	r as in "rat"
שׂ		*sin*	ś	s as in "sip"
שׁ		*shin*	š	sh as in "ship"
תּ (ת)		*taw*	t (ṯ)	t as in "tamp" (t as in "tamp")

Notes:

- As will be discussed in the next chapter, these **letter forms** are called the **Aramaic square script**, which was adopted for writing Hebrew after the Babylonian exile.[1] Note the danger of confusion between the following letters:
  - *bet* (בּ) and *kaph* (כּ)
  - *gimel* (גּ), *waw* (ו), and *nun* (נּ)
  - *dalet* (ד), *resh* (ר), and final *kaph* (ך)
  - *waw* (ו), *zayin* (ז), *gimel* (גּ), and final *nun* (ן)
  - *heh* (ה) and *ḥet* (ח)
  - *ḥet* (ח) and *taw* (ת)
  - *samek* (ס) and final *mem* (ם)
  - *ayin* (ע) and *ṣade* (צ)
- As seen in the chart above, five letters have **final forms**: they are written slightly differently when appearing as the last letter of a word. No change in sound occurs when a letter is written in its final form. The usual form, used when the letter occurs on its own or in the midst of a word, is the **medial form**.

---

[1] The script commonly in use for Aramaic was "borrowed" and used to write Hebrew. Any language can be written in more than one script, as a script is merely the graphical system used to represent the sounds of the language. For example, one could write English words in the Aramaic square script: "My name is Bill." would be מי נם אס בלל.

- Both *aleph* (א) and *ayin* (ע) represent what linguists call **glottal stops**, when the flow of air is interrupted.[2] *Aleph* is voiceless—no sound is made. *Ayin* is technically voiced ("with sound"), but its sound is difficult for English speakers to make. Therefore, most Hebrew students whose native language is English do best to treat *ayin* as silent. Remember, however, that *aleph* (א) and *ayin* (ע) are different letters.
- **Transliteration** is *writing the same sounds with different symbols*. For example, the English name *Bill* could be written in Hebrew letters using the consonants בלל plus *an i*-class vowel (see 1.3 below). It is important to be aware of transliteration values because many reference works, especially those from earlier eras, will write Hebrew words in transliteration instead of the Aramaic square script. You are not required to memorize the transliteration symbols, but you should be able to use the chart above to recognize the word being represented in transliteration.
- The **pronunciations** given here follow the modern system. The classical system, sometimes still used in academic settings, differs in the pronunciation of a few letters (see also 1.2). You should learn the modern pronunciation, but the classical pronunciation differences are noted here for completeness:

Letter	Modern Pronunciation	Classical Pronunciation
ו	v as in "vet"	w as in "wait"
ט	t as in "tamp"	t as in "top"
ק	k as in "king"	ck as in "lack"

Your instructor will detail both the best way to write the letters and his or her preference regarding modern versus classical pronunciation.

1.2 ב ג ד כ פ ת (The *Begadkephat* Letters)

As indicated above, six letters—*bet* (ב), *gimel* (ג), *dalet* (ד), *kaph* (כ), *pe(h)* (פ), and *taw* (ת) —were originally capable of two distinct pronunciations. These six letters could be pronounced either as a **stop**, when the flow of air is interrupted, or as a **spirant**, when air

[2] For example, consider the English phrase "an ice man" as opposed to "a nice man." The placement of the stoppage of air determines the correct understanding of the words in question.

flows out of the mouth during the pronunciation of the letter. Collectively, they are known by the mnemonic "the *begadkephat* letters."[3]

The *begadkephat* letters are pronounced as a stop when they follow another consonant and as a spirant when they follow a vowel. The stop, which is a "hard" sound, is indicated by a dot called the ***dagesh lene*** placed in the letter. For more on the *dagesh*, see 2.1.

The distinction in pronunciation between a stop and a spirant is preserved in modern pronunciation only for *bet* (בּ), *kaph* (כּ), and *pe(h)* (פּ) (see 1.1). The classical differences between the other three letters, again noted here only for completeness, are:

Letter	Modern Pronunciation	Classical Pronunciation
גּ	g as in "god"	g as in "log"
ד	d as in "dog"	th as in "that"
תּ	t as in "tamp"	th as in "thunder"

1.3 Vowels

As seen in 1.1, the Hebrew alphabet has no vowel letters. The original Hebrew text of the Old Testament was a **consonantal text** (written only in consonants). While this may seem strange to an English speaker, many languages of antiquity (and today) are written without vowel letters. In practice, a fluent speaker can usually determine and supply the necessary vowels:

Y knw ths bcs y snd txt mssgs n yr phn.

However, due to both potential ambiguities and the eventual loss of Hebrew as an everyday language, it was eventually deemed necessary to indicate the vowels traditionally used with the consonantal text. At the time—the late first millennium A.D.—there was a strong reluctance among scribes to change in any way the consonantal text that they had received. Accordingly, the graphical representation of vowels was accomplished not by letters but by a system of **diacritics**—marks added above and below the consonants. The system of diacritics in the Hebrew Bible used by students today is from the Masoretes (for more information on the Masoretes and the Masoretic system, see 8.12.A).

---

[3] This mnemonic is formed by the addition of vowels to these six Hebrew consonants. The vowels themselves have no value other than making it possible to pronounce (and therefore remember) these six consonants together.

The vowel system includes the following vowels in three classes, or vowel types:

Class	Sign	Name	Length	Transliteration	Pronunciation
a	בַ	*pataḥ*	short	a	a as in "what"
	בָ	*qameṣ*	long	ā	a as in "father"
i	בֶ	*segol*	short	e	e as in "bet"
	בֵ	*ṣere*	long	ē	e as in "they"
	בִ	*ḥireq*	short or long	i or ī	i as in "hit" (short)
					i as in "unique" (long)
u	בָ	*qameṣ ḥatup̄*	short	o	o as in "pot"
	בֻ	*qibbuṣ*	short or long	u or ū	u as in "put" (short)
					u as in "rule" (long)
	בֹ	*ḥolem*	long	ō	o as in "pole"

Notes:

- The vowel signs are represented with the letter ב, which is conventional when teaching Hebrew. Only the vowel's sound is represented in the pronunciation column.
- The *i*-class vowels subsume the English *e*-class vowels, and the *u*-class vowels subsume the English *o*-class vowels.
- Vowels are pronounced after the letter on which their sign is written (e.g.: בַ is pronounced "ba").[4]
- Though the *pataḥ* and *qameṣ* are, respectively, short and long vowels, their pronunciation in practice is often indistinguishable.
- For space considerations, a vowel following a final *kaph* (ך) or *nun* (ן) is written just to its left (e.g.: ךָ).

[4] For the one exception, see 5.5.

- When written over a *sin* (שׂ) or a *shin* (שׁ), the *ḥolem* may merge with the supralinear dot on the consonant.
- The *qameṣ* and the *qameṣ ḥatup̄* are graphically indistinguishable. The rules for distinguishing the two are covered in 2.5.

1.4 *Shewa*

The symbol ְ placed under a consonant (e.g.: בְ) is called ***shewa***. There are two types of *shewa* in Hebrew: the **silent *shewa*** and the **vocal *shewa***. The silent *shewa* has no phonetic value (no pronunciation) and therefore is not transliterated. The vocal *shewa* is pronounced with a "scooped" vowel, sounding much like the first sound in the English word *abuse*.[5] It is transliterated with an inverted *e* (e.g.: *bə*), a superscript *e* (e.g.: b^e), or the symbol ĕ. The rules for distinguishing the silent *shewa* from the vocal *shewa* will be covered in 2.3.

1.5 Syllables

Hebrew words may be divided into syllables by the application of two rules:

1. Each syllable begins with one consonant. The only exception is the conjunction וּ (û), which will be introduced later.
2. Each syllable contains one, and only one, vowel. (A vocal *shewa* is considered a vowel for syllabification.)

Syllables can end in either a vowel or a consonant. A syllable ending in a vowel is called an **open syllable**, and a syllable ending in a consonant is called a **closed syllable**. Open syllables are sometimes noted in grammars as being the CV (Consonant + Vowel) pattern, and closed syllables are noted as being the CVC (Consonant + Vowel + Consonant) pattern.

Thus the Hebrew word מֶלֶךְ (*meleḵ* = "king") has two syllables: לֶךְ | מֶ (*me*| *leḵ*).

[5] The vocal *shewa* is sometimes termed a "half vowel" because it has a shorter pronunciation than the vowels introduced in 1.3.

1.6 Stress

Most Hebrew words have their accent (stress) on the final syllable. Developing this stress pattern in speech is often difficult for English speakers, since English more often stresses the first syllable of a word. If a word is stressed on the final syllable, no accent mark will be given in the vocabulary section. If a word is normally stressed on a syllable other than the final syllable, the stress will be marked. For example, מֶלֶךְ, given above, is stressed on the first syllable and will appear in the vocabulary as מֶ֫לֶךְ (*mé*| *leḵ*).

1.7 Vocabulary

As will be discussed in later chapters, the English provided after each Hebrew word is technically not a definition of that word; it is a **gloss**, an English summary that corresponds (though imperfectly) to a meaning of the Hebrew word. These glosses must be memorized. The *shewa* in the word מְאֹד below is vocal, while the *shewa* in מַלְאָךְ is silent.[6]

אָדָם	man, mankind; Adam
אֶל	(prep.) to, toward
אֵל	god; God
אִם	(conj.) if
אֶ֫רֶץ	earth, ground; land; country
אֵשׁ	fire
גַּם	also, even; as well as
דָּבָר	word; thing, affair, matter
דָּם	blood
הַר	hill, hill country, mountain
חַי	living, alive
יָם	sea, lake
לֹא	no, not
לָכֵן	(adv.) therefore
מְאֹד	(adv.) very, exceedingly
מַלְאָךְ	angel, messenger
מִן	(prep.) from
רֹאשׁ	head, top, chief
שָׁם	(adv.) there; then

[6] The glosses in this grammar were derived by consulting and comparing three major English language lexica: Brown Driver Briggs (BDB), Dictionary of Classical Hebrew (DCH), and the Hebrew and Aramaic Lexicon of the Old Testament (HALOT).

1.8 Language Exercises

A. Write the Hebrew alphabet in order, from right to left. Practice until you can do so easily.

B. Divide each word into syllables. Then, using your knowledge of the Hebrew alphabet, look up the following words in the lexicon assigned by your instructor. Write down the first gloss provided for each word.

1. דֶּ֫רֶךְ
2. כֹּהֵן
3. כֶּ֫סֶף
4. זָהָב
5. מֶ֫לֶךְ
6. מִנְחָה
7. לָכֵ֫ן
8. חָזָק
9. זָקֵן
10. פָּרֹ֫כֶת

C. Practice reading the following sentences aloud. (Verse numbers are provided if you wish to know what you are reading.)

Any instance of *shewa* in this section is vocal. Marks other than the vowel diacritics you have learned are part of the Masoretic accentual system and will be explained later. In the last example, יְהוָה is the Tetragrammaton, the divine name, which is always pronounced *"adonai."*[7]

Gen. 1:1	בְּרֵאשִׁ֖ית בָּרָ֣א אֱלֹהִ֑ים אֵ֥ת הַשָּׁמַ֖יִם וְאֵ֥ת הָאָֽרֶץ׃
Gen. 2:10a	וְנָהָר֙ יֹצֵ֣א מֵעֵ֔דֶן
Gen. 2:17a (alt.)	וּמֵעֵ֗ץ הַדַּ֙עַת֙ טֹ֣ב וָרָ֔ע לֹ֥א תֹאכַ֖ל מִמֶּ֑נּוּ
Gen. 3:1 (alt.)	וְהַנָּחָשׁ֙ הָיָ֣ה עָר֔ם מִכֹּל֙ חַיַּ֣ת הַשָּׂדֶ֔ה אֲשֶׁ֥ר עָשָׂ֖ה יְהוָ֣ה אֱלֹהִ֑ים וַיֹּ֙אמֶר֙ אֶל־הָ֣אִשָּׁ֔ה אַ֚ף כִּֽי־אָמַ֣ר אֱלֹהִ֔ים לֹ֣א תֹאכְל֔ מִכֹּ֖ל עֵ֥ץ הַגָּֽן׃

[7] *Adonai* is the addition of the possessive suffix *-ay* ("my") to אָדוֹן from the vocabulary list for chapter 2. When reading the text *adonai* is substituted for יהוה out of deference to the traditional reticence to speak the personal name of God.

1.9 Exegetical Exercises—The Acrostic

A. Acrostic Poems. An **acrostic** is a Hebrew poem in which each successive verse or stanza begins with the next successive letter of the Hebrew alphabet. Psalm 119 is a famous example; each stanza of the poem is composed of verses that begin with the letter of the Hebrew alphabet corresponding to that stanza.

1. Look up Psalm 119 in your Hebrew Bible. Which verses start with *gimel* (ג)? How many are there? Which verses start with *ayin* (ע)? How many are there?

2. Look at Psalm 145 in your *Biblica Hebraica Stuttgartensia* (BHS) or *Biblica Hebraica Quinta* (BHQ). This chapter is also an acrostic.

   a. How many verses are in the psalm? How does this compare to the number of letters in the Hebrew alphabet? What letters are missing?

   b. One letter is missing because verse 20 covers both *sin* and *shin*, which is unsurprising since the dot that distinguishes these letters is probably a later diacritical mark, not an original consonantal distinction. (The symbol ש most likely stood for both *s* and *sh*.) The other missing letter has a more complex explanation. Which other letter is missing?

c. Look at Psalm 145 in the NIV and ESV. Notice that all the verses, except one, are similar in length and fall easily into halves. Which verse in the English translation does not fit this pattern? Why?

d. If you compare the English verse 13 to the Hebrew, you will find that the English translation includes two lines of poetry not present in BHS: "The LORD is faithful in all his words and kind in all his works" (ESV). How would you justify this seeming addition to the Hebrew text? The copy of Psalm 145 found among the Dead Sea Scrolls at Qumran (11QPs[a]) has an additional line of poetry:

נאמן אלוהים בדבריו וחסיד בכול־מעשיו

Likewise, the Septuagint translation of the Hebrew Bible into Greek, made in the last centuries B.C., contains an extra line labeled as verse 13a: *πιστὸς κύριος ἐν τοῖς λόγοις αὐτοῦ καὶ ὅσιος ἐν πᾶσι τοῖς ἔργοις αὐτοῦ*. If one were to back-translate this into Hebrew, it would likely have been written as:

נֶאֱמָן יהוה בְּכָל־דְּבָרָיו וְחָסִיד בְּכָל־מַעֲשָׂיו

Both the Greek and the Hebrew would be translated as the ESV has done. What letter begins this proposed line of poetry in Hebrew?

e. Given the witness of the Septuagint translation, the presence of the *nun* line in manuscripts from the Dead Sea Scrolls, and its presence in the Syriac translation of the Hebrew, most interpreters surmise that a copyist accidentally skipped the *nun* line of the poem, leaving the manuscript that is reproduced in BHS with a copyist error. Accordingly, most major English translations restore this line and consider it part of Psalm 145. The NIV, ESV, and other translations have not misled you when they add a line to verse 13; they are restoring what they believe to be the original composition.

B. Hebrew Bible Book Names and Order. The Hebrew Scriptures are grouped into three sections: the תּוֹרָה ("Torah"), the נְבִיאִים ("Prophets"), and the כְּתוּבִים ("Writings"), hence the common designation of the Hebrew Scriptures as the תנ״ך (often written in English as "Tanakh"). The order here is that used by BHS.

כְּתוּבִים (Writings)	נְבִיאִים (Prophets)		תּוֹרָה (Torah)
	אַחֲרוֹנִים (Latter)	רִאשׁוֹנִים (Former)	
תְּהִלִּים (Psalms)	יְשַׁעְיָהוּ (Isaiah)	יְהוֹשֻׁעַ (Joshua)	בְּרֵאשִׁית (Genesis)
אִיּוֹב (Job)	יִרְמְיָהוּ (Jeremiah)	שֹׁפְטִים (Judges)	שְׁמוֹת (Exodus)
מִשְׁלֵי (Proverbs)	יְחֶזְקֵאל (Ezekiel)	שְׁמוּאֵל א (1 Samuel)	וַיִּקְרָא (Leviticus)
רוּת (Ruth)	הוֹשֵׁעַ (Hosea)	שְׁמוּאֵל ב (2 Samuel)	בְּמִדְבַּר (Numbers)
שִׁיר הַשִּׁירִים (Song of Songs)	יוֹאֵל (Joel)	מְלָכִים א (1 Kings)	דְּבָרִים (Deuteronomy)
קֹהֶלֶת (Ecclesiastes)	עָמוֹס (Amos)	מְלָכִים ב (2 Kings)	
אֵיכָה (Lamentations)	עֹבַדְיָה (Obadiah)		
אֶסְתֵּר (Esther)	יוֹנָה (Jonah)		
דָּנִיֵּאל (Daniel)	מִיכָה (Micah)		
עֶזְרָא (Ezra)	נַחוּם (Nahum)		
נְחֶמְיָה (Nehemiah)	חֲבַקּוּק (Habakkuk)		
דִּבְרֵי הַיָּמִים א (1 Chronicles)	צְפַנְיָה (Zephaniah)		
דִּבְרֵי הַיָּמִים ב (2 Chronicles)	חַגַּי (Haggai)		
	זְכַרְיָה (Zechariah)		
	מַלְאָכִי (Malachi)		

Note that BHS, which follows the Leningrad Codex for its text, has a different order of books within the כְּתוּבִים than many other editions of the תנ״ך. BHS also gives book titles in Latin on the facing pages. Using the chart above, find each of the following books in BHS and write its corresponding Latin title and English name.

Hebrew Book Name	Latin Book Name	English Book Name
וַיִּקְרָא		
מִשְׁלֵי		
דִּבְרֵי הַיָּמִים א		
מְלָכִים א		
מַלְאָכִי		
שִׁיר הַשִּׁירִים		
קֹהֶלֶת		

ב (2) Learning to Speak, Part 2; Adjectives

2.1 The *Dagesh Forte*

We have already learned one use of the *dagesh*, the *dagesh lene*, which marks the hard sound (the stop) in a *begadkephat* letter. A second type of *dagesh*, the ***dagesh forte***, is graphically identical, also written as a dot inside the letter form.

The *dagesh forte* indicates that the consonant in which it is placed is doubled so that, although the letter is written only once to save space, it is pronounced twice. Therefore, מּ would be transliterated as *mm*, זּ as *zz*, etc. Regarding syllabification, because the presence of a *dagesh forte* indicates the presence of a double consonant in a word, a new syllable will usually begin with the second instance of the doubled letter:

שִׁבַּר is divided into syllables as *shib | bar*, **not** *shi | bar*

A *dagesh* in any letter other than a *begadkephat* letter can be only a *dagesh forte*. In the *begadkephat* letters it can be either a *dagesh forte* (indicating doubling) or a *dagesh lene* (indicating the stop pronunciation). In the *begadkephat* letters the following rules distinguish the type of *dagesh* present:

- Only stops can double, not spirants. Therefore, פּ could indicate a *peh* with a *dagesh forte* (transliterated *pp*) or a *peh* with a *dagesh lene* (transliterated *p*). It cannot, however, indicate a *peh* with the spirantized vocalization of *p̄*.
- Because *begadkephat* letters are normally pronounced as spirants when they follow a vowel sound, if the *begadkephat* letter follows a vowel and is written with a *dagesh*, that *dagesh* must be a *dagesh forte*, doubling the consonant.
- If the *begadkephat* letter containing the *dagesh* follows another consonant, it will usually be a *dagesh lene*, indicating the stop pronunciation but no doubling (though exceptions do occur).

2.2 Assimilation of *nun*

The *n* sound of the letter *nun* is a very weak sound and therefore often assimilated into the following consonant. When a *nun* is thus assimilated it is no longer pronounced, but the letter into which it assimilates is doubled. This doubling is indicated with a *dagesh forte.*

מִן+זָהָב > מִזָּהָב (min + zāhāḇ > mizzāhāḇ)

This same linguistic pattern is common in many English words. For example, *illiterate* in English comes from combining the Latin *in* ("not") and *litteratus* ("literate"). The English word *illiterate* is simply an inherited Latin form with the assimilation of /n/:

Latin: *in-* + *litteratus* > *illiteratus* → English: illiterate (cf. "illegible," etc.)

2.3 Vocal and Silent *Shewa*

Section 1.4 introduced the difference between a vocal and a silent *shewa*. The following rules distinguish when a *shewa* is vocal or silent. At first the rules require persistence to carefully apply, but they will eventually become second nature to you.

Shewa is vocal when:

- It is placed on a consonant that begins a word, e.g.: בְּרָכָה (*bərākâh*).
- It is the second of two *shewas* that immediately follow each other, e.g.: יִקְטְלוּ (*yiqṭəlû*).
- It is placed on a consonant with a *dagesh forte*, e.g.: מַמְּרֹרִים (*mammərōrîm*).
- It is placed on a consonant that immediately follows a long vowel, e.g.: שֹׁמְרִים (*shōmərîm*).

Note that in each case the vocal *shewa* is the vowel sound in an open syllable.

Shewa is silent when:

- It is placed on a consonant that follows a short vowel, e.g.: מִצְרִי (*miṣrî*).
- It is the first of two *shewas* that immediately follow each other, e.g.: יִקְטְלוּ (*yiqṭəlû*).
- It is at the end of a word (even if it immediately follows another *shewa*), e.g.: קָטַלְתְּ (*qātalt*).

Note that in each case the silent *shewa* comes at the end of a closed syllable.

A silent *shewa* comes at the end of a closed syllable, while a vocal *shewa* exists only in an open syllable. The rule of thumb is to look for a preceding short vowel. If the *shewa* follows a short vowel, it is almost always silent; in most other cases it is vocal.

2.4 Compound *Shewa*

Four Hebrew consonants—*aleph* (א), *heh* (ה), *ḥet* (ח), and *ayin* (ע)—are pronounced back in the throat and are therefore called **gutturals** (Latin *guttur* = "throat"). Because of their sound, these letters do not take a vocal *shewa* and instead are pronounced with a reduced vowel, called a **compound** or **composite *shewa***. The three compound *shewas* are:

Class	Sign	Name	Transliteration	Pronunciation
a	חֲ	*ḥatep̄-pataḥ*	ă	a as in "sat"
i	חֱ	*ḥatep̄-segol*	ĕ	e as in "bet"
u	חֳ	*ḥatep̄-qameṣ*	ŏ	o as in "pot"

The pronunciation of each compound *shewa* is basically the same as its corresponding short vowel, though a bit more hurried and scooped.

2.5 *Qameṣ* and *Qameṣ ḥatup̄*

Section 1.3 noted that the *qameṣ* and the *qameṣ ḥatup̄* are graphically indistinguishable, being written with the same sign. Two rules will help distinguish the two:

- *Qameṣ ḥatup̄* can occur only in a **closed and unaccented syllable**. Recall that, unless marked otherwise, Hebrew words take their stress on the final syllable. Accordingly, the word for "wisdom," חָכְמָה (*ḥok̲ / māh*), is stressed on its last syllable, and therefore the vowel in the first syllable is the *qameṣ ḥatup̄.*
- The presence of a small vertical line, called a ***metheg***, indicates that the vowel represented is a *qameṣ.* שָֽׁמְרָה (*shā / m^e / rāh*) therefore contains a *qameṣ* in its first syllable.

2.6 *Matres Lectionis*

The vowel system that you began learning in chapter 1 was not the first attempt to represent vowels in Hebrew writing. A much older tradition involves ***matres lectionis***, "mothers of reading." *Matres* (singular: *mater*) were an initial indication of vowel letters on some Hebrew words. Unlike the Masoretic vowel pointing, the presence of *matres* varies by word and is not systematic. *Matres* are more common with some words than with others, but there is no discernibly consistent pattern of where and when they occur.

Marking vowels with *matres lectionis* involves writing three key consonants—*heh* (ה), *waw* (ו), and *yod* (י)—to indicate a vowel sound instead of the consonantal sound with which they are associated. For example, if English had no vowel letters and a scribe wished to indicate the *i* sound, he could write an extra *y* in the middle of the word. Thus the clause "Tip your hat" could be written:

with a purely consonantal text as "tp yr ht" OR

with a *y mater* as "typ yr ht"

The English letter *y* in fact functions similarly. Though usually classified as a consonant, as in the word *beyond*, the *y* can also mark a vowel sound, as in the word *tyrant*.

Remember that when the *heh* (ה), *waw* (ו), and *yod* (י) are used this way, they are **not consonants; they are vowel markers**.

The following *matres* frequently occur:

a class: ה for ā

i class: י for ī, e, ē; ה for e, ē

u class: ו for ō, ū; ה for ō

When the Masoretic vowel system was superimposed on the text the *matres* **were not removed**. Instead the corresponding Masoretic vowel pointing was added to them, producing the following possibilities:

Class	Sign	Name	Transliteration	Pronunciation
a	בָה	*qameṣ heh*	â	a as in “father”
i	בִי	*ḥireq yod*	î	i as in “unique”
	בֶי	*segol yod*	ê	e as in “bet”
	בֵי	*ṣere yod*	ê	e as in “they”
	בֶה	*segol heh*	ê	e as in “bet”
	בֵה	*ṣere heh*	ê	e as in “they”
u	בוֹ	*ḥolem waw*	ô	o as in “pole”
	בוּ	*shureq*	û	u as in “rule”
	בֹה	*ḥolem heh*	ô	o as in “pole”

Notes:

- As before, the vowel signs are represented with the letter ב, which is conventional when teaching Hebrew.
- With the exception of the *shureq*, the name of each *mater* is simply the name of the vowel plus the name of the letter used as a *mater*.
- *heh* (ה) serves only as a *mater* at the end of a word, whereas *waw* (ו) and *yod* (י) can serve as *matres* in the middle or at the end.
- Because *heh* (ה) is often a *mater* at the end of a word, when a word-ending *heh* is a consonant it will often have a dot—called a ***mappîq***—placed in it, as in גֹּבַהּ (“height”).
- If a letter commonly used as a *mater* is pointed with a vowel sound not listed above, the letter represents a consonant, as in מָוֶת (*ma / vet*).
- This system of doubly marking vowel sounds was intended to clarify the text, and it usually does so. Sometimes, however, the system creates confusion for the beginning reader, e.g.: מִצְוֹת may appear to be *mi / ṣôt*, but it is actually *miṣ / vôt*. Though this may be frustrating, such ambiguities are a feature of most writing systems, and they can be learned with repetition.

Remember that the presence or absence of a *mater* does not affect a word’s meaning. Writing a word with *matres* is termed **full spelling** or **full writing**. The writing of the same word without *matres* is termed **defective spelling** or **defective writing**. Even though the terms seem to imply a value judgment, there is no difference in meaning between full and defective spellings.

2.7 Adjectives

The Hebrew adjective is inflected for both gender and number. In the chart below, the adjective טוֹב ("good") demonstrates the addition of endings to indicate this inflection:

	Adjective		Endings	
	Singular	Plural	Singular	Plural
Masculine	טוֹב	טוֹבִים	--	ִים
Feminine	טוֹבָה	טוֹבוֹת	ָה	וֹת

(The rules for the agreement of an adjective with the noun it modifies will be covered in 4.6.)

The presentation of inflectional endings on a word is called a **paradigm**. **This adjective paradigm must be memorized**.

2.8 Verbless Clauses

A clause can be formed in Hebrew simply by placing two nouns (or a noun and an adjective) adjacent to each other. Unlike in English, a form of the verb *to be* is not required to produce a complete sentence. The tense, or time signature, of the verbal idea must be inferred from the context.

וְאַבְרָהָם זָקֵן ("and Abraham was old"—Gen. 24:1)

וְעֵץ הַחַיִּים בְּתוֹךְ הַגָּן ("and the tree of life was in the middle of the garden"—Gen. 2:9)

מְרַגְּלִים אַתֶּם ("You are spies."—Gen. 42:9)

For more on verbless clauses, see 15.8.

2.9 Vocabulary[1]

אָדוֹן	lord, master; the Lord
אוֹ	(conj.) or
אָמֵן	"surely!"
אֵת	an untranslatable particle that can be used to mark the definite direct object of a verb
גּוֹי	people, nation (pl. = nations other than Israel)
הַרְבֵּה	much, many; (adv.) very much
וּ or וְ	(conj.) and; but
זָקֵן	old
חָזָק	firm, hard; strong, powerful
טוֹב	good
יוֹם	day, daylight
יוֹמָם	(adv.) daily, by day
כֹּה	(adv.) here; now; thus
כְּלִי	vessel; instrument; weapon
כֵּן	(adv.) thus, so; then, afterwards
מָלֵא	full, filled, full of
נֶגֶד	(prep.) opposite, in front of, before
עוֹלָם	long time, duration; eternity
פֶּן	(conj.) lest, so that not
צֹאן	flocks, herds (collective noun)
קוֹל	voice, sound, noise

[1] Now that the rules for distinguishing vocal and silent *shewas* have been explained, the vocabulary sections will no longer mark this distinction. Applying 2.3 will enable you to determine the appropriate pronunciation of each *shewa*.

2.10 Language Exercises

A. Indicate whether the following adjectives are masculine or feminine and singular or plural.

At times the first vowel in the word will differ from the form given in the vocabulary, but you should still be able to recognize the word.

Form	Gender	Number
חֲזָקִים	masc.	pl.
חֲזָקָה		
חָזָק		
זְקֵנָה		
זְקֵנִים		
זָקֵן		
זְקֵנוֹת		
טוֹב		
טוֹבִים		
טוֹבוֹת		
טוֹבָה		

B. Translate the following verbless clauses.

To aid the beginning student, names will be given in gray text for the first few chapters. Say them aloud and attempt to identify them. As in 1.8.C (and so through the remainder of this book) marks other than the diacritics you know are part of the Masoretic accentual system, which will be further explained in section 11.8. You should place the accentual stress (see section 1.6) on the syllable marked with the Masoretic accent.

מֹשֶׁה גָּדוֹל מְאֹד

דָּוִד֙ זָקֵ֔ן

יוֹסֵ֖ף חָ֔י

זָקֵ֖ן יִצְחָ֔ק

C. Translate the following verbless clauses. You will need to use your lexicon to look up the glosses for many of these words.

The high vertical dash in several of these examples is called a ***maqqēp̄***. It indicates that the two words are bound together for purposes of pronunciation and should be pronounced as one word.

2 Chron. 12:6	צַדִּ֖יק יְהוָֽה[2]
Eccl. 2:19	גַּם־זֶ֖ה הָֽבֶל
Gen. 48:8	מִי־אֵ֫לֶּה
Deut. 4:31	רַח֙וּם יְהוָ֣ה
Judg. 9:28	מִֽי־אֲבִימֶ֑לֶךְ
Mic. 6:8	מַה־טּ֑וֹב

[2] Pronounce as "*adonai*" (see 1.8.C and 8.12.B).

D. Practice reading the following text (Gen. 1:1–5) aloud.

בְּרֵאשִׁית בָּרָא אֱלֹהִים אֵת הַשָּׁמַיִם וְאֵת הָאָרֶץ׃ וְהָאָרֶץ הָיְתָה תֹהוּ וָבֹהוּ וְחֹשֶׁךְ עַל־פְּנֵי
תְהוֹם וְרוּחַ אֱלֹהִים מְרַחֶפֶת עַל־פְּנֵי הַמָּיִם׃ וַיֹּאמֶר אֱלֹהִים יְהִי אוֹר וַיְהִי־אוֹר׃ וַיַּרְא
אֱלֹהִים אֶת־הָאוֹר כִּי־טוֹב וַיַּבְדֵּל אֱלֹהִים בֵּין הָאוֹר וּבֵין הַחֹשֶׁךְ׃ וַיִּקְרָא אֱלֹהִים ׀ לָאוֹר
יוֹם וְלַחֹשֶׁךְ קָרָא לָיְלָה וַיְהִי־עֶרֶב וַיְהִי־בֹקֶר יוֹם אֶחָד׃

2.11 Exegetical Exercises—Letter Confusion and Text Criticism

A. The Concept of Text Criticism. **Text criticism** attempts to be certain that the text used today is the same as the original composition. A robust doctrine of inspiration does not imply that God protected copies of that original composition from copyist errors or other changes over millennia. (The technical term for these changes is **corruptions**.) In fact, the existence of biblical manuscripts with differing readings for the same verse provides prima facie evidence that copyist errors occurred. Two manuscripts with differing readings cannot both be faithful copies (in the same sense of the term) of the same original. Text criticism is the attempt to "get the text right," by accurately reflecting a biblical text as it was originally composed before the millennia of copying and recopying.

Text criticism is a complex endeavor, and the explanation offered above embarrassingly oversimplifies. It must account for the differences between accidental errors (of many types) and intentional changes introduced by copyists. Further, it must evaluate and address the concept of redaction. This *Introduction* will return to text criticism once you have more experience in the language. Here the focus is only on the issue of copyists accidentally confusing letters.

Recall the list of commonly confused letter pairs from 1.1. Consider copyists working entirely by hand, in poor lighting, possibly while tired, sometimes while taking dictation, and at times with a very poor grasp of the language they were copying. The error-checking of copied manuscripts was often rigorous, but errors could still appear. For example, one common challenge in reading ancient manuscripts is the distinction between *waw* (ו) and *yod* (י). While the letters seem distinct in a typeface, imagine the slightly elongated *yod* if a scribe's pen stayed on the parchment too long. Likewise imagine the slightly shortened *waw* if a scribe's pen came off the parchment too quickly. The two might be indistinguishable, and at times they basically are. The difficulty of distinguishing *waw* and *yod* in some ancient documents (e.g.: portions of the Dead Sea Scrolls) can be substantial.

An example from the Old Testament is Genesis 10:28 compared with 1 Chronicles 1:22. Genesis 10:28 includes the names עוֹבָל (Obal) and אֲבִימָאֵל (Abimael) in its genealogical record, but 1 Chronicles 1:22 lists the names as עֵיבָל (Ebal) and אֲבִימָאֵל (Abimael). Notice the letter change, with the only consonantal distinction being the question of *waw* versus *yod*. This type of interchange is most common in later biblical books, likely because the letters *waw* and *yod* became more similar graphically in the later centuries B.C.

B. Ruth 4:5.[3] Find Ruth 4:5 in your Hebrew Bible. Boaz is talking to the "nearer kinsman redeemer," who has indicated his willingness to take on the property of Elimelech, Naomi's dead husband. Boaz states:

בְּיוֹם־קְנוֹתְךָ הַשָּׂדֶה מִיַּד נָעֳמִי וּמֵאֵת רוּת הַמּוֹאֲבִיָּה אֵשֶׁת־הַמֵּת...

Read this text aloud to continue practicing your reading.

Woodenly, this would be translated "On the day you acquire the field from Naomi **and from with** Ruth the Moabitess, the wife of the dead man . . . ."

1. The word in question is וּמֵאֵת. As written, it is the combination of three Hebrew vocabulary words from this chapter. What are they? (Review 2.2 and 2.9 above if necessary.)

[3] For more detail, see P. Kyle McCarter, *Textual Criticism: Recovering the Text of the Hebrew Bible*, GBS Old Testament Series (Minneapolis: Augsburg Fortress, 2001), 45.

2. If the text is correct, this phrasing would result in "and from with." One could understand the sense of the text, but it seems awkward Hebrew. Most translators and interpreters suggest that this should be read as two words with a space between them: גַּם אֶת. Looking at the letter confusions in 1.1, which confusions might explain their reasoning?

3. If reading this as two words is correct (and evidence from the Vulgate suggests that it is), what would be the better translation of this verse?

C. Isaiah 11:15.[4]

1. Now consider Isaiah 11:15, which reads (BHS):

וְהֵנִיף יָדוֹ עַל־הַנָּהָר בַּעְיָם רוּחוֹ

The text reads "And he will brandish his hand over the river ______ his wind." The challenge is the word בַּעְיָם, formed from the combination of the preposition בְּ and the noun עְיָם. Most translations read this as some variation of "with the scorching of." The challenge with this reading is that עְיָם has no other occurrences in the Old Testament, and the word can be only questionably connected to *heat* via the Arabic *ġāma* ("to be overcast or tormented by a burning thirst"[5]).

---

[4] For more detail, see Emanuel Tov, *Textual Criticism of the Hebrew Bible* (Minneapolis: Augsburg Fortress, 2001), 358–59.
[5] See HALOT, 2:817.

Some scholars accept a reading not as בַּעְיָם but as בְּעֹצֶם, changing the *yod* (י) to a *ṣade* (צ). Look at 1.1 again. Is there any plausible confusion between these letter shapes, or are the scholars stretching credibility?

2. Recall from 1.1 that the script used here is the Aramaic square script. Much of the Old Testament would have been originally written in an older Hebrew script, often called the Paleo-Hebrew script. Here are its letter forms:

You are *not* expected to learn these forms, but a quick perusal shows that the potential letter confusions differ between the Paleo-Hebrew script and the Aramaic square script. The common letter confusions in the Paleo-Hebrew script also include *aleph* and *taw, yod* and *ṣade*, and *peh* and *nun.*

Given this knowledge, what may have seemed an offbeat and baseless suggestion bears strong consideration, and most scholars accept the proposal of בְּעֹצֶם as the correct reading of Isaiah 11:15. It would then be translated as "and he will brandish his hand over the river with the might of his wind," treating this as a *yod/ṣade* confusion in the Paleo-Hebrew script. The takeaway: to evaluate cases of potential letter confusion in the copying of Old Testament Hebrew manuscripts, you cannot simply consider the possible letter confusions in the currently used script; you must also be aware of the more ancient script and its impact on the copying process.

ג (3) Qal Perfect

3.1 Triconsonantal Roots and Patterns

The vast majority of Hebrew words are built on a three-letter **root**. Various patterns of vowels (and sometimes consonants) are applied to this root to produce different parts of speech related to the same idea. For example:

זָבַח —verb: to slaughter, sacrifice

מִזְבֵּחַ —noun: altar

זֶבַח —noun: communal sacrifice

You can quickly see that these three words are related, with the commonality being the three letters *zayin* (ז), *bet* (ב), and *ḥet* (ח).

Similarly, consider the commonality in the following words:

שֹׁפֵט —judge, one who judges

שֹׁמֵר —guard, one who guards

יֹשֵׁב —inhabitant, one who dwells

You can quickly see that these three words are related not in their meaning but in their function, that they are all participles, a type of verbal noun (see ch. 9 for more on participles). Here the commonality is not the consonants but the vowel pattern *ḥolem* and *ṣere.*

Patterns like these are pervasive in Biblical Hebrew and a great help in understanding the language. They will form the backbone of learning Hebrew. But with this observation comes an immediate caution. There is a proverb in linguistics research, most likely coined by Edward Sapir: "All grammars leak." Languages are living things, continually changing. Patterns are almost always just that—patterns, not ironclad rules. Exceptions happen.

3.2 Qal Perfect

The Hebrew verbal system is composed of seven major stems (*binyanim*; sing. *binyan*). These stems provide a vowel pattern and affix various prefixes and suffixes to the Hebrew consonantal root. Of these, the Qal is the basic verbal stem, covering approximately two-thirds of all verbs in the Old Testament. (In fact, קַל typically glosses as "easy" in a modern Hebrew lexicon.)

The **lexical form** (the form that one would look up in a lexicon) of a Hebrew verb is the third-person masculine singular. The **perfect conjugation** of the verb is accomplished by adding suffixes to the lexical form. Because it is dominated by the suffixes, the perfect conjugation is sometimes termed the **suffix conjugation**. Verbal paradigms are typically illustrated with the root קטל ("to kill"):

Qal Perfect Paradigm

	Verbal Form	Suffix	Gloss*
3ms	קָטַל	--	he killed
3fs	קָטְלָה	ָה	she killed
2ms	קָטַ֫לְתָּ	תָּ	you (ms) killed
2fs	קָטַלְתְּ	תְּ	you (fs) killed
1cs	קָטַ֫לְתִּי	תִּי	I killed
3cp	קָטְלוּ	וּ	they killed
2mp	קְטַלְתֶּם	תֶּם	you (mp) killed
2fp	קְטַלְתֶּן	תֶּן	you (fp) killed
1cp	קָטַ֫לְנוּ	נוּ	we killed

*Regarding the translation of the perfect, see 3.7 below.

This paradigm must be memorized.

Notes:

- This paradigm is for the so-called "strong verb." Certain letters (e.g.: *nun,* see 2.2; gutturals, see 2.4; etc.) have peculiarities or "weaknesses" that change how they interact with vowels or other consonants. קטל is typically used to illustrate verbal paradigms because none of its three root letters have such a weakness. The weaknesses and their impact on the verbal paradigms will be introduced later.

   - Exception: You have already learned that gutturals cannot take a vocal *shewa* and instead take a compound *shewa*. This will impact the 2mp and 2fp perfect forms.
- The Hebrew verb does not require an explicit subject. קָטַל could be a complete sentence by itself—"He killed."
- Unlike Romance languages and English, in which verbal paradigms are learned in order from first to third person, Hebrew verbal paradigms are taught beginning with the third-person masculine singular form. As stated above, this 3ms form is the lexical form of the verb; it shows no addition of prefixes and suffixes, and the three-letter verbal root is most easily identified from it.
- The third-person singular (3ms and 3fs), second-person singular (2ms and 2fs), and second-person plural (2mp and 2fp) forms differ by gender, being marked masculine and feminine. The first-person singular (1cs), third-person plural (3cp), and first-person plural (1cp) forms are not marked for differing gender and are termed "common."
- These suffixes can be applied to any verbal root to create the perfect conjugation for that verb. (This will even be true for the perfect conjugation of the **derived stems**, which begin in ch. 14.) For strong roots, the Qal perfect conjugation will match the paradigm above, simply with different root letters in place of קטל.
- If the third letter of the root is the same as the first letter of the suffix, however, the letter will be written only once, with the doubling indicated by a *dagesh forte*. For example, consider the addition of the perfect suffixes to the verb כרת ("to cut"):

Qal Perfect Paradigm of כרת

	Verbal Form	Suffix
3ms	כָּרַת	--
3fs	כָּרְתָה	ָה
2ms	כָּרַ֫תָּ	תָּ
2fs	כָּרַתְּ	תְּ
1cs	כָּרַ֫תִּי	תִּי
3cp	כָּרְתוּ	וּ
2mp	כְּרַתֶּם	תֶּם
2fp	כְּרַתֶּן	תֶּן
1cp	כָּרַ֫תְנוּ	נוּ

- Also remember that *nun*, unless followed by a vowel, regularly assimilates into a following consonant and doubles it, with the doubling indicated by a *dagesh forte* (see 2.2). For example, consider the addition of the perfect suffixes to the verb נתן ("to give"):

Qal Perfect Paradigm of נתן

	Verbal Form	Suffix
3ms	נָתַן	--
3fs	נָתְנָה	ָה
2ms	נָתַתָּ	תָּ
2fs	נָתַתְּ	תְּ
1cs	נָתַתִּי	תִּי
3cp	נָתְנוּ	וּ
2mp	נְתַתֶּם	תֶּם
2fp	נְתַתֶּן	תֶּן
1cp	נָתַנּוּ	נוּ

3.3 Parsing Verbs

To **parse** a verb is to give a grammatical description of it, identifying the information communicated by its form. Always parse verbs in the following order:

Verbal Stem, Conjugation, Person, Gender, Number, Root, Gloss

- The **stem**, as indicated in 3.2, is the verbal pattern—the *binyan*—applied to the root. At this stage you know only one stem: the Qal.
- The **conjugation** is the verb form. Each stem can be put into each conjugation. At this stage, you know only one conjugation: the perfect.
- **Person** indicates the subject of the verb. There are three possible values for the category of person: first (I, we), second (you, sing. and pl.), and third (he, she, they).
- **Gender** indicates the **grammatical** gender of the verb's subject.[1] There are three possible genders for the Hebrew verb: masculine, feminine, and common.
- **Number** indicates the counting of the subject with which the verb agrees. There are two numbers for the Hebrew verb: singular and plural.

[1] As discussed in 4.1, gender in this sense is a grammatical, not biological, category.

- The **root** is the three-letter base of the word, as discussed in 3.1.
- Finally, the **gloss** is a "rough and ready" translation or explanation of the meaning of the verb.

For example, קָטַלְתָּ is parsed:

Verbal Stem	Conjugation	Person	Gender	Number	Root	Gloss
Qal	Perfect	2	m	s	קטל	you (ms) killed

While providing a gloss is not technically part of parsing a verb, it is a good discipline to include. The goal of parsing is achieving certainty that you are correctly interpreting the word in question. In this case repetition is the mother of learning, and *there is considerable value in keeping your parsing order consistent*. The order guards against careless mistakes and forces you to carefully analyze the actual word in front of you—not jump too quickly to what you think it means.

3.4 Syllables, Part 2

We have previously covered the division of a word into syllables (1.5) and the idea of stress (1.6). While Hebrew words are most commonly stressed on their final syllable, this is not always the case, and the movement of the stressed syllable can impact the formation of words and the vowels used in them. Two terminologies are often used to discuss Hebrew syllables. Both are commonly used in secondary literature about the Old Testament, so they need to be understood:

- **Tonic/pretonic/propretonic:** In this system, the accented syllable of a word is termed the **tonic** syllable. The **pretonic** syllable is the syllable that precedes the accented syllable, and the **propretonic** syllable is the syllable that precedes the pretonic syllable.
- **Ultima/penultima/antepenultima:** In this system, the last syllable of a word is termed the **ultima**, the next-to-last is the **penultima**, and the third-to-last is the **antepenultima**.

The first system names syllables based on their position relative to the word's accent, whereas the second system names syllables based on their position in the word.

For example, טְבַלְיָ֫הוּ divides into syllables as:

הוּ	יָ֫	בַלְ	טְ
	tonic	pretonic	propretonic
Ultima	penultima	antepenultima	

3.5 Vowel Reduction

Note the vowel under the *qoph* in the Qal perfect paradigm. While usually a *qameṣ*, it is a vocal *shewa* in both the 2mp and 2fp forms. Why? Certain vowels in Hebrew usually **reduce**—become a *shewa*—in the following situations:

- In the propretonic syllable, either a *qameṣ* (ָ) or a *ṣere* (ֵ) will reduce to a vocal *shewa* if the syllable is open (CV).
- If there is no vowel reduction in the propretonic syllable, a *ṣere* (but **not** a *qameṣ*) in a pretonic open (CV) syllable will reduce to a vocal *shewa*.
- If the consonant in the syllable is a guttural, the *qameṣ* or *ṣere* will reduce to its corresponding compound *shewa*—*ḥatep̄-pataḥ* or *ḥatep̄-segol*, respectively.

Thus, in the verbal paradigm above, the reduction is:

* קָטַלְתֶּם > קְטַלְתֶּם

Because the first syllable is both propretonic and open, the *qameṣ* reduces to a vocal *shewa*.

Note: The asterisk (*) marker denotes a hypothetical or reconstructed form—in this case, the form before vowel reduction would have occurred.

3.6 Stative Verbs

Most Qal perfect verbs are **dynamic**—they indicate an action. A significant subclass of Qal perfects, however, indicate not an action but a state of being, essentially functioning as adjectives. These are called **stative verbs**. In the Qal perfect, stative verbs most commonly follow a vowel pattern with a *ṣere* instead of a *pataḥ* in the second vowel position (known as the **theme vowel**). For example, the root יבשׁ ("to be dry"):

Qal Perfect Paradigm of יבשׁ

	Verbal Form	Suffix
3ms	יָבֵשׁ	--
3fs	יָבְשָׁה	ָה
2ms	יָבַשְׁתָּ	תָּ
2fs	יָבַשְׁתְּ	תְּ
1cs	יָבַשְׁתִּי	תִּי
3cp	יָבְשׁוּ	וּ
2mp	יְבַשְׁתֶּם	תֶּם
2fp	יְבַשְׁתֶּן	תֶּן
1cp	יָבַשְׁנוּ	נוּ

The *ṣere* is evident only in the 3ms form of the paradigm and when the stative verb is in a pausal form (see 13.5).

Avoid leaning on the *ṣere* theme vowel as more than a rule of thumb because several variations occur. Some verbs with a *ṣere* theme vowel seem to have a more dynamic sense, and other verbs with a *pataḥ* theme vowel have a more stative sense. Further, a smaller class of stative verbs have a *ḥolem* theme vowel.

The verb הָיָה ("to be") is doubly weak (see section 3.2) and therefore will be formally introduced in chapter 24. However, given its gloss, you can see that it is particularly important. The Qal perfect of היה, then, is provided here for reference, but not for memorization:

Qal Perfect Paradigm of היה

	Verbal Form	Suffix
3ms	הָיָה	--
3fs	הָיְתָה	ָה
2ms	הָיִ֫יתָ	תָ
2fs	הָיִית	תְ
1cs	הָיִ֫יתִי	תִי
3cp	הָיוּ	וּ
2mp	הֱיִיתֶם	תֶם
2fp	הֱיִיתֶן	תֶן
1cp	הָיִ֫ינוּ	נוּ

3.7 Meaning and Translation of the Perfect Conjugation

Beginning Hebrew students often translate the perfect as a past tense. This is acceptable as an initial working default when doing grammar exercises, but understand that the Hebrew verbal system is not tensed in the same sense as the English verbal system.

The most common opinion holds that the perfect conjugation and its counterpoint, the imperfect (see ch. 5), relate to the question of **aspect**—the viewpoint of the speaker relative to the situation. In this understanding the Hebrew perfect expresses a completed action or state of being as seen from the outside. Important minority positions dispute this formulation, however, because the exact nuances of the Hebrew verbal system remain an area of contention among grammarians.

Regardless of how you evaluate these debates, which belong in a venue other than an introductory grammar, it is doubtless true that the perfect can indicate more than simply past action:[2]

אָהַ֫בְתִּי ("I love"—Gen. 27:4)

זָקַ֫נְתִּי ("I am old"—Gen. 18:13)

[2] For more examples, see P. Joüon and T. Muraoka, *A Grammar of Biblical Hebrew*, 2nd ed., SubBi 27 (Rome: Pontifical Biblical Institute, 2008), 112a.

In fact, the Hebrew perfect can have multiple contextual meanings depending on the context in which it is employed:

1. Simple past tense—indicating an action in the past:

    בְּרֵאשִׁית בָּרָא אֱלֹהִים אֵת הַשָּׁמַיִם וְאֵת הָאָרֶץ ("In the beginning, God *created* the heavens and the earth."—Gen. 1:1)

2. Present perfect—indicating an action that remains true:

    הִנֵּה נָתַתִּי אֶת־הָאָרֶץ בְּיָדוֹ ("See, I *have given* the land into his hand."—Judg. 1:2)

3. Pluperfect—indicating an action *before* an action that is itself in the past:

    כַּאֲשֶׁר נָתַן לָהֶם מֹשֶׁה ("which Moses *had given* them"—Josh. 13:8)

4. Stative—indicating a state of being, whether present or past:

    לָמָּה חָרָה לָךְ ("why *are* you *angry*?"—Gen. 4:6)

Several further contextual meanings are possible but much more rare. For these, consult an intermediate syntax or grammar.

3.8 Vocabulary

Note: As noted in 3.2, Hebrew verbs are listed in the lexicon under their Qal Perfect 3ms form, not their infinitive form (as in many languages) or their 1cs form (as in Biblical Greek and others). The glosses in this grammar are given ***as if*** *the form were an infinitive, though it is, in fact, a Qal Perfect 3ms. For example, the form* אָבַד*, the first vocabulary item below, would actually be translated as "he died, perished; became lost; went astray." The gloss "to die, perish; become lost; go astray" is given because English speakers are used to verbal glosses given as infinitive forms.*

אָבַד	to die, perish; become lost; go astray
אָהַב	to love
אָכַל	to eat, feed
אָמַר	to say
גָּדַל	to grow up, become strong, become great
הָלַךְ	to go, walk
זָכַר	to remember, call to mind
חָזַק	to be strong, become strong, have courage
כָּרַת	to cut; cut off, exterminate (with בְּרִית = to make a covenant)
לָקַח	to take, seize, grasp
מָלַךְ	to rule, reign, be king; become king
נָתַן	to give, set, put
עָבַד	to serve, work
עָבַר	to pass over, pass by, move through
עָמַד	to stand, stand before
פָּקַד	to visit, appoint, inspect
שָׁלַח	to send, send out, stretch out
שָׁמַע	to hear, listen, obey
שָׁמַר	to guard, watch over
שָׁפַט	to judge (mainly military sense), pass judgment, rule

3.9 Language Exercises

A. Write out the Qal perfect paradigm for קטל from memory. Remember to begin with the 3ms form of the verb.

3ms

3fs

2ms

2fs

1cs

3cp

2mp

2fp

1cp

B. Apply the paradigm from (A) to write out the Qal perfect forms of the following verbs, again beginning with the 3ms form.

מלך שׁמר אמר זכר כרת

C. Parse the following verbal forms. Appendix 1 contains a blank parsing grid, which can be photocopied for use in this and future parsing sections.

Example: גָּדַ֫לְתָּ

Verbal Stem	Conjugation	Person	Gender	Number	Root	Gloss
Qal	Perfect	2	m	s	גדל	you (ms) grew up

קָטַ֫לְתִּי

קְטַלְתֶּן

גָּֽדְלוּ

אָבַ֫דְתָּ

זְכַרְתֶּם

עָבַ֫דְתָּ

אָכַלְתָּ

שָׁמַ֫רְנוּ

לָקַחְתָּ

כְּרַתֶּם

D. Translate the following sentences and parse each verb. Use your lexicon to look up the glosses for any words you do not know from your vocabulary.

Remember that from this chapter onward any diacritical marks that have not already been introduced are accents from the Masoretic accentual system. These will be explained later. For now, simply note that the accent is placed on the stressed syllable in each word.

2 Kings 8:25 מָלַ֣ךְ אֲחַזְיָ֣הוּ

Gen. 26:13	גָּדַל מְאֹד
Gen. 13:12	אַבְרָם יָשַׁב
Josh. 13:8, altered	נָתַן מֹשֶׁה
Judg. 8:34, altered	וְלֹא זָכְרוּ אֶת־יְהוָה
Ps. 6:10	שָׁמַע יְהוָה
Jer. 23:21	לֹא־שָׁלַחְתִּי
Josh. 9:16, altered	כָּרְתוּ בְּרִית
Ex. 31:6	נָתַתִּי חָכְמָה
Gen. 2:20	לֹא־מָצָא[3] עֵזֶר
Gen. 3:1	עָשָׂה[4] יְהוָה אֱלֹהִים

---

[3] The paradigm form of this verb has a *pataḥ* instead of a *qameṣ* for the second vowel. Changes in vowel length are relatively common due to various linguistic circumstances.

[4] This is the same vowel length change as in **מָצָא** above.

אָמַר אֱלֹהִים	Gen. 17:19, altered
עָלָה בָּרָק	Judg. 4:12
שָׁלַחְתִּי כֶּסֶף וְזָהָב	1 Kings 15:19, altered
מָכְרָה נָעֳמִי	Ruth 4:3
לֹא־יָדַע יַעֲקֹב	Gen. 31:32
שָׁכַח אֵל	Ps. 10:11
אִישׁ הָרַגְתִּי	Gen. 4:23
וְגַם יָלַדְתִּי	Ruth 1:12

E. Practice reading the following text (Gen. 1:6–10) aloud:

וַיֹּאמֶר אֱלֹהִים יְהִי רָקִיעַ בְּתוֹךְ הַמָּיִם וִיהִי מַבְדִּיל בֵּין מַיִם לָמָיִם׃ וַיַּעַשׂ אֱלֹהִים אֶת־
הָרָקִיעַ וַיַּבְדֵּל בֵּין הַמַּיִם אֲשֶׁר מִתַּחַת לָרָקִיעַ וּבֵין הַמַּיִם אֲשֶׁר מֵעַל לָרָקִיעַ וַיְהִי־כֵן׃
וַיִּקְרָא אֱלֹהִים לָרָקִיעַ שָׁמָיִם וַיְהִי־עֶרֶב וַיְהִי־בֹקֶר יוֹם שֵׁנִי׃ וַיֹּאמֶר אֱלֹהִים יִקָּווּ הַמַּיִם
מִתַּחַת הַשָּׁמַיִם אֶל־מָקוֹם אֶחָד וְתֵרָאֶה הַיַּבָּשָׁה וַיְהִי־כֵן׃ וַיִּקְרָא אֱלֹהִים ׀ לַיַּבָּשָׁה אֶרֶץ
וּלְמִקְוֵה הַמַּיִם קָרָא יַמִּים וַיַּרְא אֱלֹהִים כִּי־טוֹב׃

3.10 Exegetical Exercises

Look at Judges 5:7b:

עַד שַׁקַּ֫מְתִּי דְּבוֹרָ֔ה שַׁקַּ֥מְתִּי אֵ֖ם בְּיִשְׂרָאֵֽל׃

קַמְתִּי in the phrase שַׁקַּמְתִּי is a verbal form, a Qal perfect from the root קוּם. This type of root is called a **hollow root** and will be explained more fully in chapter 26. Look up the root in your lexicon. What does it mean in the Qal?

Given your knowledge of the Qal paradigm's suffixes, how would you parse קַמְתִּי?

Now consider how Judges 5:7b reads in the following translations:

ESV—"until I arose; I, Deborah, arose as a mother in Israel"

NIV—"until I, Deborah, arose, until I arose, a mother in Israel"

KJV—"until that I Deborah arose, that I arose a mother in Israel"

CEB—"until you, Deborah, arose, until you arose as a mother in Israel"

HCSB—"until I, Deborah, arose, a mother in Israel"

RSV—"until you arose, Deborah, arose as a mother in Israel"

Given your parsing, what would you say about the accuracy of these translations?

How would you teach this text in a context in which most people use the CEB or RSV? How has Hebrew helped you in preparing to teach?

Judges 5 represents one of the oldest pieces of poetry in the entire Old Testament. Add to that a piece of information you may not yet know about Hebrew: there is an archaic, 2fs ending תִּי־. (For evidence of this ending, see Jer. 2:33; 31:21; Ezek. 16:18.) How does this change your answers above?

The moral of the story: a little knowledge of Hebrew can be a dangerous thing! Beginning students often start correcting Bible translations based on a very rudimentary knowledge of the language. Be careful; you can easily run ahead of your actual knowledge. A time will come to comment on the weaknesses of various Bible translations, but that time is *not* during your first year of language learning!

All the translations quoted above (and many more) have been produced by groups of translators, each of whom has far more experience in Hebrew than you do at this stage in your study. If those individuals together have translated a verse in a certain way, there is probably at least an argument to be made for their translation. (In fact, the case of Judges 5:7 is ambiguous. The point of this exercise is not to argue for one translation over the other, but to warn you about assuming too much when you are just beginning your language study.) Walk softly and avoid blanket pronouncements until you have gained much more experience!

ד (4) Basic Nouns; The Definite Article

4.1 The Noun Paradigm

The basic Hebrew noun paradigm is closely related to that of the Hebrew adjective learned in chapter 2. Consider the forms of the noun סוּס ("horse"):

	Noun			Endings		
	Singular	Dual	Plural	Singular	Dual	Plural
Masculine	סוּס	סוּסַ֫יִם	סוּסִים	--	ַ֫יִם	ִים
Feminine	סוּסָה	סוּסָתַ֫יִם	סוּסוֹת	ָה	ַ֫יִם	וֹת

Notes:

- The **lexical form** of a noun is the masculine or feminine singular form. The standard ending for a feminine singular noun is *qameṣ heh* (ָה), as in the paradigm. It is common, however, for feminine nouns to also end in *taw*, as ִית , וּת , ֶת , or ַת .
- A noun's gender determines its plural form. Gender in this sense is a grammatical term. Grammatical gender, while often aligning with biological gender, need not do so. (The classic example of this difference is in French, which treats *professeur* as masculine for grammatical gender, using the masculine form of the French definite article [*le*]. Accordingly, a female professor will be addressed in French as *madame le professeur*.)
- Exceptions do occur, particularly cases of feminine nouns without a *heh* or *taw* ending in the feminine singular. For example:

  אֶ֫רֶץ (land, earth—fs) יָד (hand—fs)

  Such feminine nouns are grammatically *unmarked* for gender in the feminine singular, but they usually show their feminine gender in their plural form:

  אֲרָצוֹת (lands—fp) יָדוֹת (hands—fp)

Nouns ending in *heh* or *taw* should be considered feminine and nouns ending in any other consonant considered masculine ***unless otherwise marked in the vocabulary sections***.

- The **dual** form still existed at the time of Biblical Hebrew, though its use was declining. It indicates two of the noun. The dual form in Biblical Hebrew is usually used for items that are natural pairs (e.g.: hands, feet) or for measurements (e.g.: two days, two hundred).[1] However, a few prominent nouns exist exclusively in the dual, especially מַ֫יִם (water) and שָׁמַ֫יִם (heaven, the heavens).[2]
- In the formation of the feminine dual and plural, the *qameṣ heh* (ָה) ending of the feminine singular is removed or altered. For the feminine plural, it is replaced by וֹת, and for the feminine dual, it changes to ָת before the addition of the dual ending ַ֫יִם.
- Be aware of the possibility of defective spellings, particularly of the feminine plural ending. Remember that סוּסוֹת and סוּסֹת are different spellings of the *same* feminine plural noun.
- Note that propretonic and pretonic vowel reduction (see 3.5) can occur with nouns when the addition of an ending changes the number of syllables in the word:

  זָקֵן (ms), but:

  *זָקֵנָה > זְקֵנָה (fs)

  *זָקֵנִים > זְקֵנִים (mp)

  *זָקֵנוֹת > זְקֵנוֹת (fp)

  חָזָק (ms), but:

  *חָזָקָה > חֲזָקָה (fs)

  *חָזָקִים > חֲזָקִים (mp)

  *חָזָקוֹת > חֲזָקוֹת (fp)

---

[1] Certain nouns can appear in either the dual or plural form depending on whether a speaker or writer intends to indicate two of the nouns *in particular* (e.g.: יָדַ֫יִם "a pair of hands") or more than one *in general* (e.g.: יָדוֹת "hands").

[2] These forms are *morphologically* dual, but they show no *semantic* usage that corresponds with their dual form, leading to debate about whether they should be classified differently.

4.2 Contraction

Vowel contraction is relatively rare in Hebrew, but two cases should be noted. Each impacts the pluralization of certain nouns that contain a diphthong, which is a cluster of vowels acting as a single unit.

- When the *pataḥ* is stressed in the combination *ayi* (ַ֫יִ), the removal of the stress causes it to contract to *ṣere yod* (ֵי):
  עַ֫יִן (eye, spring—fs) and עֵינוֹת (eyes, springs—fp)

- Similarly, when the *qameṣ* is stressed in the combination *āwe* (ָ֫וֶ), the removal of the stress causes it to contract to a *ḥolem waw* (וֹ):
  אָ֫וֶן (trouble, disaster—ms) and אוֹנִים (troubles, disasters—mp)

4.3 Parsing Nouns and Adjectives

Because less information is conveyed by the noun or adjective form, parsing a noun or adjective involves fewer elements. You should always parse nouns and adjectives in the following order:

Gender, Number, Lexical Form, Gloss

For example: נְבִיאִים

Gender	Number	Lexical Form	Gloss
m	p	נָבִיא	prophets

4.4 The Definite Article

The Hebrew definite article is indicated by prefixing הַ and doubling the following consonant:

Noun	Definite Article + Noun
מֶ֫לֶךְ (king, a king)	הַמֶּ֫לֶךְ (the king)
סוּס (horse, a horse)	הַסּוּס (the horse)
קוֹל (sound, a sound)	הַקּוֹל (the sound)
כֶּ֫סֶף (silver, money)	הַכֶּ֫סֶף (the silver, the money)

Notes:

- English can mark nouns with both the definite article ("the") and an indefinite article ("a, an"). Hebrew, however, marks nouns only with a definite article. A Hebrew noun without the definite article can be either indefinite or anarthrous (e.g.: סוּס = "a horse" or "horse"). The presence of the article marks the item in question as definite in some sense (e.g.: הַסּוּס = "the horse").
- If the first letter of the noun to which the definite article is attached is a *begadkephat* letter, it will usually already have a *dagesh lene* present to indicate the stop pronunciation. The addition of the definite article changes the *dagesh lene* to a *dagesh forte* because the letter is now doubled.
- The article and the initial consonant following it form an initial CVC syllable at the beginning of the word:

  הַסּוּס (has | sûs) הַקּוֹל (haq | qôl)
- Both mem (מ) and yod (י) will often drop the *dagesh forte* when their vowel is a vocal *shewa*. When they do so, the *shewa* remains vocal, and the article is still considered its own syllable. (Though less common, this loss of the *dagesh* can occur with other consonants as well.)

  הַיְבוּסִי (hay | y^e| ḇû |sî) הַמְזִמָּתָה (ham | m^e | zim | mā | tâ)

4.5 Gutturals and Doubling

As mentioned in 2.4, four Hebrew consonants—*aleph* (א), *heh* (ה), *ḥet* (ח), and *ayin* (ע)—are pronounced back in the throat and therefore called gutturals. Not only do the guttural consonants take a compound vocal *shewa*, but they also resist doubling because their pronunciation is in the back of the throat (i.e.: They do not accept a *dagesh forte*). In this regard, *resh* (ר) behaves similarly to a guttural, since it also resists the *dagesh forte*.

When a word's normal formation would require the doubling of a guttural or *resh*, such doubling does not occur. Instead, you find either:

- **Compensatory Lengthening:** With the gutturals *aleph* (א) and *ayin* (ע) and with *resh* (ר), the rejection of the *dagesh forte* is compensated for by lengthening the preceding vowel:

אֵשׁ + הַ > הָאֵשׁ ("the fire"—Gen. 22:6)

עִבְרִי + הַ > הָעִבְרִי ("the Hebrew"—Gen. 14:13)

רֹאשׁ + הַ > הָרֹאשׁ ("the head"—Lev. 1:8)

- **Virtual Doubling:** With the gutturals *heh* (ה) and *ḥet* (ח), there is no compensating response for the rejection of the *dagesh forte*:

  הֵיכָל + הַ > הַהֵיכָל ("the temple"—1 Kings 7:21)

  חֲמוֹר + הַ > הַחֲמוֹר ("the donkey"—Judg. 19:28)

This is a strong tendency in Biblical Hebrew, but exceptions occur—for example, *heh* with compensatory lengthening, as in:

הָר + הַ > הָהָר ("the mountain"—Ex. 19:3)

4.6 Adjective Agreement Rules

With the noun and adjective paradigms mastered, you can address the rules of agreement between adjectives and the nouns they modify. Hebrew adjectives always agree in gender and number with the nouns they modify. Depending on their use, they **may or may not** agree with the nouns in definiteness.

Adjectives can be used in one of three ways:

- **Attributive Use:** An attributive adjective gives a characteristic or description of the noun it modifies. English examples are "the good boy," "the fast runner," etc. The attributive adjective usually comes after the noun it modifies and agrees with it in gender, number, and definiteness. For example:

  אִישׁ טוֹב ("a good man"—Prov. 14:14)

  אֶרֶץ טוֹבָה ("a good land"—Ex. 3:8)

  הַדֶּרֶךְ הַטּוֹבָה ("the good way"—2 Chron. 6:27)

- **Predicative Use:** A predicate adjective makes a statement about a noun. English examples would be "The boy is good," "The runner is fast," etc. In prose, the predicative adjective usually precedes the noun and agrees with it in gender and number. Hebrew predicate adjectives do not take the definite article. For example:

  טוֹב־הַדָּבָר ("The thing is good."—Deut. 1:14)

  טוֹבָה הָאָרֶץ ("The land is good."—Deut. 1:25)

- **Substantive Use:** A substantivized adjective is an adjective used as a noun. English examples would be "the good," "the fast (one)," etc. Here the adjective no longer modifies a noun. Gender, number, and definiteness are determined by the context of the phrase or clause in which it is used. For example:

  טוֹב ("a good man"—Prov. 12:2)

  הַטּוֹב ("the good"—Deut. 12:28)

A Hebrew noun is considered definite for purposes of agreement if it (1) is marked by the definite article, (2) is a proper noun, or (3) has a possessive pronoun attached.

4.7 Vocabulary

אֹיֵב	enemy
אַמָּה	forearm, cubit
אֲרוֹן	ark, money chest
זָהָב	gold
חַ֫יִל	power, strength
כָּבוֹד	glory, splendor, reputation
לֵב	heart, mind, will (alt. spelling = לֵבָב)
מַ֫יִם	water (always dual)
מִנְחָה	gift, present, offering
מַעֲשֶׂה	work, labor, deed
מִצְוָה	command, commandment
מָקוֹם	place, location
נָשִׂיא	leader, chieftain
סוּס	horse
סוּסָה	mare
עִיר	city, town (fem.; pl. = עָרִים)[3]
עֹלָה	burnt offering
עַמּוּד	pillar, tent pole
צוּר	rock
שָׁמַ֫יִם	heaven, sky (always dual)

[3] Note that עָרִים, though appearing as if it is a masculine plural form, is still a feminine plural noun. This irregularity simply must be memorized.

4.8 Language Exercises

A. Reproduce the noun paradigm for סוּסָה / סוּס.

	Singular	Dual	Plural
Masculine			
Feminine			

B. Parse the following nouns and adjectives. Appendix 1 contains a blank parsing grid, which can be photocopied for use in this and future parsing sections.

Example: דְּבָרִים

Gender	Number	Lexical Form	Gloss
m	p	דָּבָר	words, things

אֲדֹנִים

מְלָאכִים

זְקֵנָה

יוֹמַיִם

הָרִים

גּוֹיִים

זֵיתִים

קֹלֹת

חֲזָקִים

C. Translate the following clauses and phrases. Parse each verb. Use your lexicon to look up the glosses for any words you do not know from your vocabulary.

Gen. 2:11	שָׁ֥ם הַזָּהָֽב
Deut. 12:2	עָֽבְדוּ־שָׁ֤ם הַגּוֹיִ֔ם
Isa. 17:10, altered	הַצּוּר לֹ֣א זָכָ֑רְתְּ
Josh. 4:22	עָבַ֤ר יִשְׂרָאֵ֔ל אֶת־הַיַּרְדֵּ֖ן
Gen. 1:5, altered	וְהַחֹ֖שֶׁךְ קָ֣רָא לָ֑יְלָה
1 Sam. 13:13, altered	לֹ֥א שָׁמַ֛רְתָּ אֶת־הַמִּצְוָ֖ה
Gen. 3:6	ט֥וֹב הָעֵ֨ץ
Josh. 7:11, altered	לָֽקְחוּ֙ אֶת־הַחֵ֔רֶם
Gen. 38:23	שָׁלַ֙חְתִּי֙ הַגְּדִ֣י
1 Sam. 7:17	וְשָׁ֥ם שָׁפָ֖ט אֶת־יִשְׂרָאֵ֑ל

D. Practice reading the following text (Gen. 1:11–15) aloud:

וַיֹּ֣אמֶר אֱלֹהִ֗ים תַּֽדְשֵׁ֤א הָאָ֙רֶץ֙ דֶּ֗שֶׁא עֵ֚שֶׂב מַזְרִ֣יעַ זֶ֔רַע עֵ֣ץ פְּרִ֞י עֹ֤שֶׂה פְּרִי֙ לְמִינ֔וֹ אֲשֶׁ֥ר
זַרְעוֹ־ב֖וֹ עַל־הָאָ֑רֶץ וַֽיְהִי־כֵֽן׃ וַתּוֹצֵ֨א הָאָ֜רֶץ דֶּ֠שֶׁא עֵ֣שֶׂב מַזְרִ֤יעַ זֶ֙רַע֙ לְמִינֵ֔הוּ וְעֵ֧ץ עֹֽשֶׂה־
פְּרִ֛י אֲשֶׁ֥ר זַרְעוֹ־ב֖וֹ לְמִינֵ֑הוּ וַיַּ֥רְא אֱלֹהִ֖ים כִּי־טֽוֹב׃ וַֽיְהִי־עֶ֥רֶב וַֽיְהִי־בֹ֖קֶר י֥וֹם שְׁלִישִֽׁי׃
וַיֹּ֣אמֶר אֱלֹהִ֗ים יְהִ֤י מְאֹרֹת֙ בִּרְקִ֣יעַ הַשָּׁמַ֔יִם לְהַבְדִּ֕יל בֵּ֥ין הַיּ֖וֹם וּבֵ֣ין הַלָּ֑יְלָה וְהָי֤וּ לְאֹתֹת֙
וּלְמ֣וֹעֲדִ֔ים וּלְיָמִ֖ים וְשָׁנִֽים׃ וְהָי֤וּ לִמְאוֹרֹת֙ בִּרְקִ֣יעַ הַשָּׁמַ֔יִם לְהָאִ֖יר עַל־הָאָ֑רֶץ וַֽיְהִי־כֵֽן׃

4.9 Exegetical Exercises—Transcription

Reading Commentaries: Practice the skill of recognizing Hebrew words in transliteration, referring to 1.1 when necessary. The following are quotations from commentaries on Old Testament books. Write the Hebrew spelling of the transliterated words that the commentator is discussing. Note also that there is no single system of transcription agreed upon by all scholars, so various commentaries will use differing transcription systems (e.g.: שׁ may be š or *sh*). Look up the boldfaced words in your lexicon and list the different glosses provided for each word.

A. "The structure of the chapter is balanced between male and female cases to show the unity of the human predicament. Each of the four sections begins with 'if a man' (***ʾîš*** *kî*; 15:2, 16) or 'if a woman' (***ʾiššâ*** *kî*; 15:19, 25)."[4]

B. "For uses of the verb 'discipline' (***yāsar***) in Deut., to which the noun (***mûsar***) employed here is related, see 4:36; 8:5; 21:18; 22:18."[5]

---

[4] Allen P. Ross, *Holiness to the Lord: A Guide to the Exposition of the Book of Leviticus* (Grand Rapids: Baker Academic, 2006), 304.
[5] Peter C. Craigie, *Deuteronomy*, 2nd ed., NICOT (Grand Rapids: Eerdmans, 1976), 208.

C. "The text of verse 11 is somewhat difficult, but I am assuming that a form of the verb ***yasha***^{c} (to save), which does occur in verse 12, is implicit in verse 11."[6]

D. "From the very start, as verse 25 shows, the monarchy was constitutional: the kings would have both *rights and duties*. We might see in the document mentioned here a sort of bill of rights for the people, held in the very safe keeping of a sanctuary (that is the meaning of the phrase *before the Lord*). Here was an important brake upon the development of absolute power. Strictly speaking, *rights and duties* is used to translate a single word (***mishpat***) in Hebrew, which in other contexts might mean 'custom' or 'ways' as in 8:11."[7]

E. "A rendering that better brings out the ambiguities of the verse would be: '. . . to serve (Hb. ^{c}*mḏ lipnê*) the king and be of use to him (***skn***) . . . lie in his (Hb. 'your') arms . . . .'"[8]

---

[6] Dale Ralph Davis, *Judges*, Expositor's Guide to the Historical Books (Grand Rapids: Baker Academic, 1990), 134.
[7] David F. Payne, *1 and 2 Samuel*, Daily Study Bible (Louisville: Westminster John Knox, 1982), 53.
[8] Iain W. Provan, *1 & 2 Kings*, NIBCOT 7 (Peabody, MA: Paternoster, 2000), 27.

ה (5) Qal Imperfect

5.1 The Qal Imperfect

The **imperfect conjugation** is accomplished by adding both prefixes and (in some cases) suffixes to the verbal root. Because it is dominated by these prefixes, it is sometimes termed the **prefix conjugation**.

Qal Imperfect Paradigm

	Verbal Form	Suffix...Prefix	Gloss*
3ms	יִקְטֹל	--- יִ	he will kill
3fs	תִּקְטֹל	--- תִּ	she will kill
2ms	תִּקְטֹל	--- תִּ	you (ms) will kill
2fs	תִּקְטְלִי	ִי --- תִּ	you (fs) will kill
1cs	אֶקְטֹל	--- אֶ	I will kill
3mp	יִקְטְלוּ	וּ --- יִ	they (mp) will kill
3fp	תִּקְטֹלְנָה	נָה --- תִּ	they (fp) will kill
2mp	תִּקְטְלוּ	וּ --- תִּ	you (mp) will kill
2fp	תִּקְטֹלְנָה	נָה --- תִּ	you (fp) will kill
1cp	נִקְטֹל	--- נִ	we will kill

*Regarding the translation of the imperfect, see 5.2 below.

This paradigm must be memorized.

Notes:

- Unlike the perfect, the imperfect conjugation has distinct masculine and feminine forms in the third-person plural.
- The 3fs and 2ms forms are identical, as are the 3fp and 2fp forms. In practice they are almost always easily distinguished by context.
- The theme vowel is reduced to *shewa* when appearing in an unstressed syllable, e.g.: יִקְטְלוּ (not * יִקְטֹלוּ).

- There are two potential **theme vowels** for the imperfect conjugation, ō (e.g.: יִקְטֹל) and *a* (e.g.: יִכְבַּד). Dynamic verbs generally take an ō theme vowel, while verbs with an *a* theme vowel may be stative or dynamic.

	Qal Perfect	Qal Imperfect
Dynamic	קָטַל	יִקְטֹל
Stative or Dynamic	כָּבֵד	יִכְבַּד

  Other vowels, such as a *ṣere*, can also appear in certain contexts.
- Sometimes an additional *nun* follows the 3mp and 2mp forms. This is called a **paragogic *nun*** (from the Greek ἡ *παραγωγή*, meaning "a variation or deviation"), and it does not impact either the parsing or the meaning of a verbal form. יִקְטְלוּ and יִקְטְלוּן are both parsed as Qal Imperfect 3mp of קטל, and both are glossed as "they (mp) will kill."

While weak consonants are generally left for later discussion after you have mastered the basics of the verbal system, two letter peculiarities with which you are already familiar will impact the formation of the Qal imperfect:

- The Assimilation of *Nun*: Recall that *nun* assimilates to a following consonant if no vowel intervenes (2.2). Therefore, a verb such as נָתַן (vocabulary, ch. 3) will often not show its first root letter in the imperfect form:
  - * יִנְתֵּן > יִתֵּן (Qal imperfect 3ms of נתן; the *nun* of the root is assimilated into the *taw*, and the *dagesh* becomes a *dagesh forte.*)
  - * נִנְתֵּן > נִתֵּן (Qal imperfect 1cp of נתן; the *nun* of the root is assimilated into the *taw*, and the *dagesh* becomes a *dagesh forte*. The visible *nun* at the beginning of the word is from the prefix, not the root.)

- Gutturals and Compound *Shewa*: Recall that gutturals do not take a simple vocal *shewa* (except for rare cases), taking a compound *shewa* instead (2.4) Therefore, a verb like עָמַד (vocabulary, ch. 3) will have a compound *shewa* under the first root letter in the imperfect:
  - * יַעְמֹד > יַעֲמֹד (Qal imperfect 3ms of עמד; the *shewa* under *ayin* is compound.)

One more observation should be added: guttural consonants have a strong preference for an *a* class vowel. This not only pertains to the vowel sound of the compound *shewa* but also often influences the vowel that precedes it. Note that the vowel under the *yod* prefix of יַעֲמֹד is a *pataḥ*, not a *ḥireq*.

➢ The parsing of verbs follows the same order given in chapter 3, regardless of the conjugation:

Verbal Stem, Conjugation, Person, Gender, Number, Root, Gloss

The imperfect is simply a second conjugation, so תִּקְטְלִי would be parsed as:

Verbal Stem	Conjugation	Person	Gender	Number	Root	Gloss
Qal	Imperfect	2	f	s	קטל	you (fs) will kill

Two irregularities that occur in common verbs should also be noted:

- הָלַךְ loses its first radical in the imperfect. The vowel under the prefix lengthens to a *ṣere*, and the theme vowel often becomes *ṣere* as well:

***Qal Imperfect of* הלך**

	Verbal Form	Prefix...Suffix	Gloss*
3ms	יֵלֵךְ	--- יֵ	he will go
3fs	תֵּלֵךְ	--- תֵּ	she will go
2ms	תֵּלֵךְ	--- תֵּ	you (ms) will go
2fs	תֵּלְכִי	ִי --- תֵּ	you (fs) will go
1cs	אֵלֵךְ	--- אֵ	I will go
3mp	יֵלְכוּ	וּ --- יֵ	they (mp) will go
3fp	תֵּלַכְנָה	נָה --- תֵּ	they (fp) will go
2mp	תֵּלְכוּ	וּ --- תֵּ	you (mp) will go
2fp	תֵּלַכְנָה	נָה --- תֵּ	you (fp) will go
1cp	נֵלֵךְ	--- נֵ	we will go

- The *lamed* of לָקַח acts like a *nun* in the imperfect, assimilating into the following consonant. This assimilation is often (but not always) indicated by a *dagesh forte*:

  * יִלְקַח > יִקַּח ("he will take")

As mentioned in section 3.6, the verb הָיָה ("to be") is doubly weak (see section 3.2) and therefore will be formally introduced in chapter 24. The Qal imerfect of היה is provided here, again for reference, not memorization.

***Qal Imperfect of* היה**

	Verbal Form	Prefix...Suffix	Gloss*
3ms	יִהְיֶה	--- יִ	he will be
3fs	תִּהְיֶה	--- תִּ	she will be
2ms	תִּהְיֶה	--- תִּ	you (ms) will be
2fs	תִּהְיִי	תִּ --- ִי	you (fs) will be
1cs	אֶהְיֶה	--- אֶ	I will be
3mp	יִהְיוּ	יִ --- וּ	they (mp) will be
3fp	תִּהְיֶינָה	תִּ --- נָה	they (fp) will be
2mp	תִּהְיוּ	תִּ --- וּ	you (mp) will be
2fp	תִּהְיֶינָה	תִּ --- נָה	you (fp) will be
1cp	נִהְיֶה	--- נִ	we will be

5.2 Translation of the Qal Imperfect

The imperfect conjugation has a large range of translational values depending on its context. As a complement to their treatment of the perfect, beginning students tend to translate the imperfect as a future (e.g.: "he will kill"), but this is only a convenience when parsing and should not even be a rule of thumb. The imperfect can have the following contextual meanings:

1. Simple future tense—indicating an action in the future:
   מָחָר אֶשְׁלַח אֶת־עֲבָדַי אֵלֶיךָ ("Tomorrow I *will send* my servants to you."—1 Kings 20:6)

אֶל־אֲשֶׁר תֵּלְכִי אֵלֵךְ ("Where you *will go*, I *will go*."—Ruth 1:16)

2. Modals (usually translated as English helping verbs, e.g.: *must*, *should*, *would*, *may*, *might*)—indicating likelihood, permission, obligation, etc.:

    דֶּרֶךְ שְׁלֹשֶׁת יָמִים נֵלֵךְ בַּמִּדְבָּר ("We *must go* three days' journey into the wilderness."—Ex. 8:23)

    מִי יַעֲלֶה־לָּנוּ אֶל־הַכְּנַעֲנִי ("Who *should go up* for us against the Canaanites?"—Judg. 1:1)

    וְאֶת־בִּנְיָמִן תִּקָּחוּ ("And you *would take* Benjamin . . . ."—Gen. 42:36)

    אֵיךְ תֹּאמַר אֲהַבְתִּיךְ ("How *can you say*, 'I love you' . . . ?"—Judg. 16:15)

    מִכֹּל עֵץ־הַגָּן אָכֹל תֹּאכֵל ("You certainly *may eat* from any tree of the garden."—Gen. 2:16)

    מָחָר יֹאמְרוּ בְנֵיכֶם לְבָנֵינוּ ("In the future, your children *might say* to our children . . . ."—Josh. 22:24)

3. Iterative past—indicating a regular or continuous action in the past:

    יִבְחַר אֱלֹהִים חֲדָשִׁים ("He [Israel] *was choosing* new gods."—Judg. 5:8)

Several further contextual meanings are possible, though more rare. For these, consult an intermediate syntax or grammar.

5.3 Quiescent *Aleph*

As you learned in chapter 1, when *aleph* occurs with a vowel, the vowel sound is pronounced but *aleph* itself is voiceless. When *aleph* occurs without a vowel, it is *quiescent*—quiet (i.e., it makes no sound)—and not considered a consonant when dividing a word into syllables. Because of this, *aleph* never takes the vocal *shewa*:

צֹאן ("flocks, herds"—vocabulary, ch. 2) and רֹאשׁ ("head, top, chief"—vocabulary, ch. 1), therefore, are both one-syllable words.

5.4 The Furtive *Pataḥ*

When a Hebrew word ends in an *ayin* (ע) or *ḥet* (ח), a *pataḥ* (the short *a* vowel) may appear under it to aid pronunciation. While by rule a Hebrew vowel is pronounced after the consonant on which it is placed, this **furtive *pataḥ*** is the one exception. It is pronounced before the letter on which it is placed (and therefore is also transcribed before it). Note the pronunciation of Noah's name with the **furtive *pataḥ*** (נֹחַ, *nōaḥ*) versus the more difficult pronunciation (נֹח, *nōḥ*).

This furtive *pataḥ* is not considered a vowel for the sake of syllabification. מִזְבֵּחַ is therefore *mizbēaḥ* and considered a two syllable word: *miz | bēaḥ*

5.5 Vocabulary

בָּטַח	to trust; have confidence
גָּאַל	to redeem, reclaim
זָבַח	to slaughter, sacrifice
חָשַׁב	to think, assume, plan
כָּבֵד[1]	to be heavy, weigh heavily upon; be honored
כָּבֵד	(adj.) heavy, thick, oppressing
לָבַשׁ	to put on, clothe
לְבוּשׁ	garment
לָכַד	to catch, overthrow
מַדּוּעַ	why, on what account?
מִזְבֵּחַ	altar
מִסְפָּר	number, quantity
נָבִיא	prophet
נָגַע	to touch, strike
נָגַשׁ	to approach, draw near, step forward
נָסַע	to tear out, pull up; to journey further on
נָפַל	to fall
סָבִיב	surrounding, on all sides (noun = surroundings)
סָפַר	to count, record

[1] Note from section 3.6 that this vowel pattern typically indicates a stative verb.

5.6 Language Exercises

A. Write out the Qal imperfect paradigm for קטל from memory. Remember to begin with the 3ms form of the verb.

B. Apply the paradigm from (A) to write out the Qal imperfect forms of the following verbs, again beginning with the 3ms form.

מלך שׁמר עבר זכר כרת

C. Parse the following verbal forms. Appendix 1 contains a blank parsing grid, which can be photocopied for use in this and future parsing sections.

Example: יִגְדַּל

Verbal Stem	Conjugation	Person	Gender	Number	Root	Gloss
Qal	Imperfect	3	m	s	גדל	He will be(come) great

אֶזְכֹּר

כָּרַ֫תִּי

נִקַּח

תִּשְׁמְעוּ

אָמַ֫רְתִּי

לָבַ֫שְׁתָּ

יִבְטַח

תִּלְכְּדוּ

סְפַרְתֶּם

יִזְבְּחוּ

D. Translate the following sentences and parse each verb. Use your lexicon to look up the glosses for any words you do not know from your vocabulary.

Num. 22:18, altered — אִם־יִתֶּן בָּלָק כֶּסֶף וְזָהָב

Judg. 6:34, altered — וְרוּחַ לָבְשָׁה אֶת־גִּדְעוֹן

1 Sam. 20:21	אֶשְׁלַ֣ח אֶת־הַנַּ֔עַר
Deut. 16:6	שָׁ֛ם תִּזְבַּ֥ח אֶת־הַפֶּ֖סַח
Deut. 13:12 [Engl. 13:11]	יִשְׂרָאֵ֕ל יִשְׁמְע֖וּ
Ex. 15:18, altered	יְהוָ֥ה יִמְלֹ֖ךְ עֹלָֽם
2 Sam. 1:19	אֵ֖יךְ נָפְל֥וּ גִבּוֹרִֽים
Gen. 16:5	יִשְׁפֹּ֥ט יְהוָ֖ה
Ruth 3:13, altered	אִם־יִגְאַל טוֹב֙ יִגְאָ֔ל
Isa. 13:17	אֲשֶׁר־כֶּ֙סֶף֙ לֹ֣א יַחְשֹׁ֔בוּ וְזָהָ֖ב לֹ֥א יַחְפְּצוּ

5.7 Exegetical Exercises—Semantic Range

It is important to understand that words have meaning based on their usage, not some inherent meaning. For example, take the English word *funny*. The meaning of the word is vastly different in each of the following sentences:

That was a funny joke.

This milk tastes funny.

When translating, one of the first tasks is to determine the **semantic range** of the word in question. A word's semantic range is the set of meanings that it could *potentially* have. The meaning of the word in a particular usage will be within that semantic range and must be determined by its context.

A. Consider the Hebrew verb רצח. The negated form of this verb constitutes the sixth commandment in both Exodus 20:13 and Deuteronomy 5:17:

לֹא תִּרְצָח

In the Qal this word occurs in the following verses:

- Num. 35:6, 11, 12, 16, 17, 18, 19, 21, 25, 26, 27, 28, 30, 31
- Deut. 4:42; 19:3, 4, 6; 22:26
- Josh. 20:3, 5, 6; 21:13, 21, 27, 32, 38
- 1 Kings 21:19
- Job 24:14
- Jer. 7:9[2]
- Hos. 4:2

It also occurs in other stems (which are covered in later chapters) in the following verses:

- Judg. 20:4
- 2 Kings 6:32
- Pss. 62:4; 94:6
- Prov. 22:13
- Isa. 1:21
- Hos. 6:9

[2] The form in both Jeremiah 7:9 and Hosea 4:2 is an infinitive absolute (see 13.1).

Survey these verses in at least two English translations. Use your Hebrew Bible to locate the form of רצח in each verse. Parse the Qal forms to ensure that the English translation of the verb you identified corresponds to the Hebrew. What is common about the uses of רצח in these verses? What differs?

Using these observations, make a preliminary judgment about the semantic range of the root רצח.

B. How would you then translate the first use of this root in the sixth commandment?

Comment on the famous translation of this commandment in the KJV (also RSV, etc.) as "Thou shalt not kill."

Comment on the alternative translation (NRSV, NJPS, etc.) of this commandment as "Thou shalt not murder."

C. Compare your findings to the entries for רצח in as many of the following resources as you can access, either via a library or via a software package:
   - Lexica (sing.: lexicon): *Brown Driver Briggs* (BDB), *Hebrew and Aramaic Lexicon of the Old Testament* (HALOT), and *Dictionary of Classical Hebrew* (DCH).
   - Word-study resources: *Theological Wordbook of the Old Testament* (TWOT), *Theological Dictionary of the Old Testament* (TDOT), and *New International Dictionary of Old Testament Theology and Exegesis* (NIDOTTE).

   How do the results of your study compare to the lexical analyses in these resources?

D. Using these same resources, compare the use of רצח to the related word הרג. Draw a Venn diagram to show the relationship of these terms.

If an author chose to use the word רצח instead of הרג, what do you think that choice would indicate? Why?

If an author chose to use the word הרג instead of רצח, what do you think that choice would indicate? Why?[3]

[3] For more information, see Patrick D. Miller, *The Ten Commandments*, Interpretation: Resources for the Use of Scripture in the Church (Louisville: Westminster John Knox Press, 2009), 223ff.

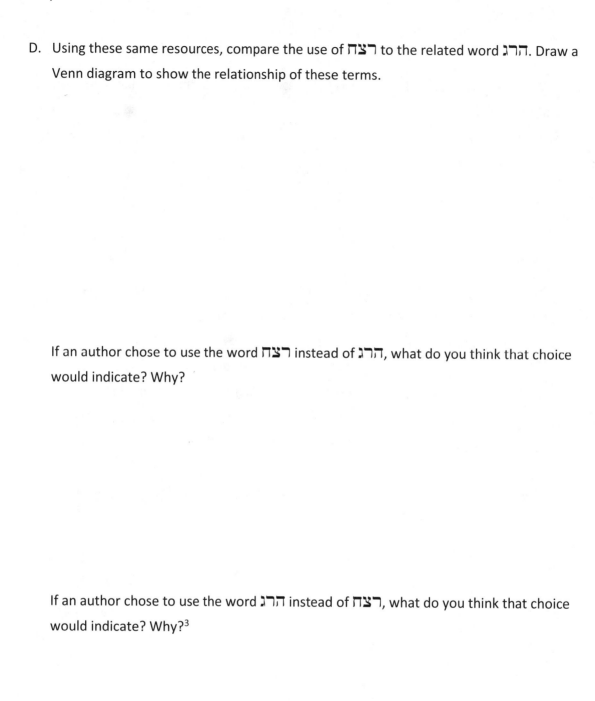

ו (6) Segolate and Geminate Nouns; Prefixed Prepositions

6.1 Segolate Nouns

Segolate nouns are two-syllable Hebrew nouns with the accent on the first syllable. We have already introduced a few segolate nouns in the vocabulary (e.g.: אֶ֫רֶץ in ch. 1). In their current forms, segolate nouns are dominated by the short vowels *segol* (hence their name) and *pataḥ.*

For reasons that will become apparent in later chapters, note that the current form of segolate nouns represents the collapsing of three different historical forms. Consider three body parts in the singular, dual, and plural forms:[1]

	Singular	Dual	Plural
foot (qaṭl)	רֶ֫גֶל	רַגְלַ֫יִם	רְגָלִים
knee (qiṭl)	בֶּ֫רֶךְ	בִּרְכַּ֫יִם	(Not attested)
ear (qoṭl)[2]	אֹ֫זֶן	אָזְנַ֫יִם	(Not attested)

The dual forms of these nouns imply that segolate nouns originally had one of three vowel patterns: *a* pattern, *i* pattern, and *o* pattern. Earlier in the history of Hebrew, these were one-syllable nouns. For example, מֶ֫לֶךְ, a common segolate noun, probably emerged from an earlier form, *malk*. The *segol* developed as an **anatyptic vowel**, a vowel inserted between two consonants to aid pronunciation.

*מַלְךְ > *מַלֶךְ > מֶ֫לֶךְ

For now, it will suffice to be aware that segolate nouns hide three different vowel patterns that may reappear in certain linguistic contexts.

---

[1] Adapted from C. L. Seow, *A Grammar for Biblical Hebrew*, rev. ed. (Nashville: Abingdon, 1995), 43.

[2] Originally quṭl.

6.2 Geminate Nouns

Geminate nouns have the same consonant for their second and third root letters.[3] One such noun (לֵבָב) was introduced in the vocabulary of chapter 4. In most cases, unlike לֵבָב, the duplicated root letter is only written once. The marking of doubling by the *dagesh forte* typically occurs only in the plural form:

	Singular	Plural
qaṭl	עַם (people/a people)	עַמִּים (peoples)
qiṭl	אֵם (mother/a mother)	אִמּוֹת (mothers)
qoṭl	חֹק (statute/a statute)	חֻקִּים (statutes)

The differing vowels in these plurals show that geminate nouns also have three different vowel types obscured in the singular forms: *a* type, *i* type, and *u* type. The vowel of the plural is not identifiable from the lexical form of the noun. Fortunately, the lexical form of the noun can usually be discerned when confronted with the plural.

Gutturals and *resh* cannot be doubled with a *dagesh forte*, leading to the possibility of virtual doubling or compensatory lengthening in plural forms (see 4.5).

6.3 Irregular Plurals

In most languages, irregularities are more likely to be present in common words. Hebrew is no exception, and certain common nouns have irregular plurals. The causes of these irregularities vary, from the application of the opposite gender's plural suffix to stem changes within the word. For example:

Singular	Plural
אָב (father, a father)	אָבוֹת (fathers)
אִישׁ (man, a man)	אֲנָשִׁים (men)[4]

Irregular plurals will be noted in the vocabulary and must be memorized.

[3] "Geminate" comes from the Latin *geminus*, "twin" – thus the name of the constellation *Gemini.*
[4] אֲנָשִׁים is originally the plural of אֱנוֹשׁ, but in usage it is the plural of אִישׁ.

6.4 Prefixed Prepositions and the Rule of *Shewa*

English prepositions are freestanding. On the other hand, a Hebrew preposition can be separable (a separate word – e.g.: נֶ֫גֶד—vocabulary, ch. 2) or inseparable (**proclitic**, meaning that it is attached to the beginning of its object).

The three inseparable prepositions are:

בְּ	in, with, by
כְּ	like, as, according to
לְ	to, for

In most cases the proclitic preposition is attached to its object without any further change. For example:

בְּבַ֫יִת (in a house)

לְמֶ֫לֶךְ (for a king)

כְּאָח (like a brother)

Three special cases should be noted:

1. When the preposition's object has the definite article attached, the *heh* of the definite article is dropped, but its vowel and the *dagesh forte* are preserved. The proclitic preposition takes the place of the dropped *heh*. For example:

הַבַּ֫יִת	+	בְּ	=	בַּבַּ֫יִת
הַמֶּ֫לֶךְ	+	לְ	=	לַמֶּ֫לֶךְ
הָאָח	+	כְּ	=	כָּאָח

Compensatory lengthening due to the presence of the definite article is retained. Pay close attention to (1) the vowel under the proclitic preposition and (2) the presence or absence of the *dagesh*; these will be clues about whether a definite article is indicated even though it may be obscured by the proclitic preposition.

2. Before a consonant with a vocal *shewa*, the *shewa* of the proclitic preposition becomes a *ḥireq* and the latter *shewa* becomes silent. For example:

    מְלָכִים +　　לְ　　=　　לִמְלָכִים

    This is an application of the **rule of *shewa***. Except on rare occasions, Hebrew does not allow two vocal *shewas* to exist side by side. When such a situation would occur, as it would when prefixing a preposition to a word that already begins with a vocal *shewa*, the first *shewa* becomes a *ḥireq* and the latter becomes silent, closing the syllable.

    One exception should be noted: when the first letter of the word (before the addition of the proclitic preposition) is a *yod*, the silent *shewa* is not written:

    יְהוּדָה +　　לְ　　=　　לִיהוּדָה　　(not * לִיְהוּדָה)

3. Before a consonant with a compound *shewa*, the preposition takes the short vowel associated with that compound *shewa*. For example:

    עֲבָדִים +　　בְּ　　=　　בַּעֲבָדִים

    This is often known as the second rule of *shewa.* One exception should be noted in the combination of לְ and אֱלֹהִים:

    אֱלֹהִים +　　לְ　　=　　לֵאלֹהִים

    The *aleph* is quiescent (see 5.3), and the *lamed*'s vowel lengthens to a *ṣere*.

6.5 Vocabulary

אָב	(masc.) father (pl.: אָבוֹת)[5]
אָח	brother (pl.: אַחִים)
אִישׁ	man, husband; person (pl.: אֲנָשִׁים)
אִשָּׁה	woman, wife (pl.: נָשִׁים)
אֲשֶׁר	the relative pronoun (who, whom, which, that, where)[6]
בְּ	(prep.) in, with, by
בַּ֫יִת	(masc.) house (pl.: בָּתִּים)
בֵּן	son (pl.: בָּנִים)
בַּת	daughter (pl.: בָּנוֹת)
זֶ֫בַח	sacrifice
יוֹם	(previous vocabulary ch. 2) day (pl.: יָמִים)
יָם	(previous vocabulary – ch. 1) sea (pl.: יַמִּים)
כְּ	(prep.) like, as, according to
לְ	(prep.) to, for
לֶ֫חֶם	bread, food
מִצְרַ֫יִם	Egypt
נֶ֫גַע	plague, affliction
סֵ֫פֶר	something written, scroll, letter
קָבַץ	to gather together, collect, assemble
קָדוֹשׁ	holy
קָדַשׁ	to be holy
קֹ֫דֶשׁ	something holy, holiness, pl.: votive offerings
רֹאשׁ	(previous vocabulary – ch. 1) head, top, chief (pl.: רָאשִׁים)
רָדַף	to pursue, follow

---

[5] Even though the plural form appears feminine, the grammatical gender of the lexical form indicates that אָבוֹת is masculine.

[6] אֲשֶׁר is extremely flexible, encompassing the range of all the English relative pronouns. Learn "wh-" for אֲשֶׁר and then adjust the remainder of the English gloss to fit the context.

6.6 Language Exercises

A. Parse the following verbal forms.

תִּלְבַּשׁ

גָּאָ֫לְתָּ

יִלְכְּדוּ

נִכְבַּד

תִּכְרְתוּ

נָתָ֫תִּי

יִגָּשׁוּ

יִסְפּוֹר

לָקַחְתְּ

אֶעֱבֹר

B. Translate the following prepositional phrases.

בַּמָּקוֹם

לִדְבָרִים

בְּדָם

בַּיּוֹם

בַּשָּׁמַ֫יִם

לְעֹלָה

כַּנְּבִיאִים

בְּיוֹם

לְאִשָּׁה

בַּבַּ֫יִת

לָאִישׁ

C. Translate the following sentences and parse each verb. Use your lexicon to look up the glosses for any words you do not know from your vocabulary.

Ex. 12:25 — הָאָרֶץ אֲשֶׁר יִתֵּן יְהוָה

Gen. 36:31, altered — הַמְּלָכִים אֲשֶׁר מָלְכוּ בְּאָרֶץ

1 Sam. 4:18 — זָקֵן הָאִישׁ וְכָבֵד

Ex. 21:32, altered — כֶּסֶף יִתֵּן לַאדֹן

Jer. 27:8, altered — הַגּוֹי וְהַמַּמְלָכָה אֲשֶׁר לֹא־יַעַבְדוּ אֶת־
נְבוּכַדְנֶאצַּר

1 Sam. 26:16, altered — לֹא־טוֹב הַדָּבָר אֲשֶׁר לֹא־שְׁמַרְתֶּם

1 Kings 11:11, altered — וְלֹא שָׁמַרְתָּ אֶת־הַבְּרִית

Deut. 32:30 — אֵיכָה יִרְדֹּף אֶחָד אֶלֶף

Num. 4:15 — וְלֹא־יִגְּעוּ אֶל־הַקֹּדֶשׁ

Gen. 43:1 — וְהָרָעָב כָּבֵד בָּאָרֶץ

6.7 Exegetical Exercises—Meaning in Context

Establishing the semantic range of a word (see 5.7) does *not* establish its meaning in a particular verse. Instead, the semantic range establishes the set of all possible meanings that a word could have in a particular verse. While the method of 5.7 could be repeated word by word through a passage *ad nauseam*, the practicalities of reading do not permit the time required to do so.

A. In practice, a good lexicon provides the first stop in ascertaining a word's semantic range. When a word has particular importance to a passage, the word-study resources mentioned in 5.7 provide further detail. For each word, the authors and editors have worked through the process of 5.7, considered the historical development of the Hebrew language, consulted cognate languages (see 19.9), and summarized their results as a lexical entry. In consulting either the lexica or the word-study resources, you are consulting a summary of scholarship on a particular word. For any issue of significance, you should always consult multiple lexica or word-study resources. Much like a commentary, each one represents one person's (or group's) opinion, and the various resources do not always agree on the semantic range of a word.

   Using the lexicon assigned by your instructor, summarize the semantic range of the Hebrew noun בַּ֫עַל.

B. After establishing the semantic range of a word, you are not yet ready to translate it. In actual usage this entire semantic range is rarely intended by the speaker or author.[7] To continue the English example from 5.7, the speaker who states, "This tastes funny,"

[7] When someone claims a word means every possible element of its semantic range, he or she has committed an exegetical fallacy called "illegitimate totality transfer."

intends to communicate the portion of the word's semantic range related to unpleasantness, not the portion related to humor. Native speakers of a language usually process such distinctions so quickly that they are unaware of doing so. But when working in a foreign language, especially an ancient language, such processing often needs to be made explicit.

Well-meaning religious teachers, laypeople, and sometimes even scholars commit the exegetical error of attempting to read every possible piece of a word's semantic range into a particular usage, thereby abusing the available linguistic data. A native speaker is usually aware of such linguistic misuse, but when working in an ancient language without native speakers to check one's interpretation, caution is in order. Unless double entendre (a purposeful use of multiple meanings) is intended, a word should be assumed to have only one meaning in each use, with that meaning being a subset of the word's semantic range.[8] How can this specific meaning be ascertained? In short, context is king. Therefore, when considering the semantic range of a given word, one should note the contexts in which the subsets of its semantic range are used. To return to the English example of *funny*, the portion of its semantic range that refers to unpleasantness usually deals with the senses ("tastes funny," "smells funny," "looks funny," etc.), while the portion of the semantic range that relates to humor is often in the context of communication and utterance.

Return to the word בַּ֫עַל. Consider the passages that the lexica use as examples of each portion of its semantic range. What are the common contexts that activate each portion of the semantic range that you defined above?

[8] This is particularly true when reading prose texts. Poetic texts often permit a wider range of word usage and involve more relaxed syntactic constraints.

In Judges 9:3, Abimelech goes to the בַּעֲלֵי of Shechem. This is the construct plural form of the noun בַּ֫עַל (see 10.3). Consult the surrounding context of Judges 9 in an English translation. Which portion of the semantic range of בַּ֫עַל is intended in Judges 9:3? Which portions are not? How should this word be translated in Judges 9:3?

C. Now consider the כָּבוֹד of God in Exodus 33:22. Using the lexicon assigned by your instructor and checking all other lexica available to you, summarize the semantic range of the Hebrew noun כָּבוֹד.

Consider the passages that the lexica use as examples of each portion of this word's semantic range. What are the common contexts that activate each portion of the semantic range you defined above?

In Exodus 33:22, God states: בַּעֲבֹר כְּבֹדִי ("when my כָּבוֹד passes by"). Read verses 18–23 to consider the context of this statement. Which portion of the semantic range of כָּבוֹד that you outlined above is in view? Why?

How then should כָּבוֹד be translated in verse 22?

ז (7) Qal Volitives

7.1 Volitives

Volitives (from the Latin volus: "will") indicate an action that is somehow willed by a speaker or writer. In Hebrew a volitive can be expressed in the first, second, or third person of the verb. The first-person volitive is called a **cohortative**, the second-person volitive an **imperative**, and the third-person volitive a **jussive**. Volitives often appear formally similar or identical to imperfects, but they are a different verbal conjugation.

7.2 Cohortative

The **cohortative** verb form is the expression of will in either the first-person singular or plural, for the speaker alone or as part of a group. For example:

אֶעְבְּרָה בְאַרְצֶךָ ("*Let me pass* through your land."—Deut. 2:27)

נַעֲשֶׂה אָדָם בְּצַלְמֵנוּ ("*Let us make* man in our image."—Gen. 1:26)

נֵלְכָה דֹּתָיְנָה ("*Let us go* to Dothan."—Gen. 37:17)

Examination of the first two examples above shows that the cohortative can take two forms: one resembles the imperfect plus the addition of ָה (*-ah*), as in Deuteronomy 2:27; the other is formally identical to the imperfect, as in Genesis 1:26.

The cohortative form with the ָה ending is more common. When the ending is added to the verbal form, it usually causes a change in the word's accentual pattern, triggering vowel reduction:

ָה + אֶעֱבֹר > אֶעְבְּרָה ("Let me pass . . . ."—Deut. 2:27)

ָה + נִכְרֹת > נִכְרְתָה ("Let us cut . . . ."—Gen. 31:44)

In cases without the ָה suffix, the cohortative is formally indistinguishable from the imperfect and must be recognized by its context.

The cohortative should be translated to express its volitive sense, usually by the English helping verb *let* or *may*. Hence, Deuteronomy 2:27 and Genesis 1:26 are usually rendered "*let me* pass" and "*let us* make" for the singular and plural cohortatives, respectively. The translations of cohortatives with and without the ָה ending are the same.

7.3 Imperative

The **imperative** verb form is the direct expression of command to another. Accordingly, imperatives are second-person forms, whether singular or plural, indicating "*You* do this or that." The imperative paradigm therefore has four elements—the second-person singular and plural, masculine and feminine:

Qal Imperative Paradigm

	Verbal Form	Suffix	Gloss
2ms	קְטֹל	---	you (ms) kill
2fs	קִטְלִי	ִי ---	you (fs) kill
2mp	קִטְלוּ	וּ ---	you (mp) kill
2fp	קְטֹלְנָה	נָה ---	you (fp) kill

This paradigm must be memorized. This should be easily accomplished if the imperfect paradigm has been solidly learned, as the imperative form appears as if the prefix of the imperfect form has been removed:

	Imperfect	Suffix...Prefix	Prefix Removed		Imperative
2ms	תִּקְטֹל	--- תִּ	תִּקְטֹל	→	קְטֹל
2fs	תִּקְטְלִי	ִי --- תִּ	תִּקְטְלִי	→	קִטְלִי
2mp	תִּקְטְלוּ	וּ --- תִּ	תִּקְטְלוּ	→	קִטְלוּ
2fp	תִּקְטֹלְנָה	נָה --- תִּ	תִּקְטֹלְנָה	→	קְטֹלְנָה

Note that (1) the vowel under the first root letter in the 2fs and 2mp forms is *hireq*, since according to the rule of *shewa* two vocal *shewas* cannot stand side by side (see 6.4), and (2) other theme vowels (e.g.: *pataḥ* and *ṣere*) are possible, as the imperative's theme vowel matches that of the imperfect form.

The 2ms imperative can also occur with an *-āh* ending. If it does so, the vowel structure of the imperative changes:

קָטְלָה < קְטֹל + ָה

In this situation the vowel on the first syllable is *qameṣ ḥatup̄* because it is a closed, unstressed syllable. The meaning does not change when this form is used instead of the קְטֹל form. Also note the potential for confusion between this form and the Qal perfect 3fs (קָֽטְלָה). The distinction in vowels will enable you to avoid confusing the two.

7.4 Jussive

The **jussive** verb form is the expression of will regarding a third party. It usually requires the English helping verb *may*, as in the sentence "May he rest in peace." For example:

כֹּה יַעֲשֶׂה יְהוָה לִי ("Thus may the LORD do to me . . . ."—Ruth 1:17)

In most cases, the jussive is identical in form to the imperfect. This similarity obscures the fact that they are different verbal forms. (The explanation of the difference requires a discussion of other Semitic languages and proto-Semitic linguistics and is best not undertaken in an introductory grammar.)

Differences in form do occur in certain types of roots and stems, including III-*heh* verbs, middle-weak verbs, and Hiphil stems (these will be mentioned when those areas are addressed). For example, the 3ms jussive form of היה (see sections 3.6 and 5.1) is a "short form" in comparison to the imperfect:

יִהְיֶה Qal Imperfect 3ms of היה, "he will be"

יְהִי Qal Jussive 3ms of היה, "let him be"

When no formal difference exists, jussives and imperfects must be distinguished by context. For example:

שִׁלְחוּ מִכֶּם אֶחָד וְיִקַּח אֶת־אֲחִיכֶם ("Send one of you and let him bring your brother." —Gen. 42:16)

In some cases, even context will not distinguish the two forms, and the correct translation is therefore ambiguous:

כָּל־אֹיְבָי יָשֻׁבוּ יֵבֹשׁוּ ("Let all my enemies turn back and be ashamed" OR "All my enemies will turn back and be ashamed"—Ps. 6:11 [Engl. 6:10])

7.5 Negation

As you have learned from your vocabulary, לֹא is a negative particle glossed as "no, not." לֹא is used to negate verbal statements in both the perfect and imperfect. Volitives, however, are negated by a different Hebrew particle, אַל. For negative commands and wishes, this distinction enables one to easily discern whether the verb in question is an imperfect or a volitive in the first and third person forms.

There are two types of negative prohibitions for second person forms:

לֹא + 2nd person imperfect – signifying a categorical prohibition

אַל + 2nd person jussive (using terminology usually reserved for the third person forms) – signifying a one time prohibition

For further information, see section 7.8 below.

7.6 Vocabulary

אֶ֫בֶן	stone
אֹ֫הֶל	tent
גְּבוּל	boundary, territory
חֶ֫רֶב	sword
יָד	hand, forearm
כֶּ֫סֶף	silver, money
מִדְבָּר	desert, wilderness, steppe
מִקְדָּשׁ	holy place, sanctuary
מִשְׁפָּחָה	extended family, clan
נַ֫עַר	young man, servant
נַעֲרָה	young (unmarried) girl, female attendant
נֶ֫פֶשׁ	throat, neck, self, soul
עֵץ	tree, timber, wood (collective noun)
עַם	people, clan
פֶּה	mouth, opening
שַׂר	king's representative, prince, head, leader
שָׂ֫דֶה	field, pasture, arable land
שֵׁם	name, reputation
שַׁ֫עַר	gate
תָּ֫וֶךְ	midst

7.7 Language Exercises

A. Write out the Qal imperative paradigm for קטל from memory.

B. Apply the paradigm from (A) to write out the Qal imperative forms of the following verbs.

מלך　　　שׁמר　　　עבר　　　זכר　　　כרת

C. Parse the following verbal forms.

לְבַשׁ

יִגַּשׁ

חָשַׁבְתָּ

יִלְבְּשׁוּ

גַּשׁ

נָֽפְלָה

תִּפֹּלְנָה

סִפְרוּ

גַּע

כָּֽבְדָה

D. Translate the following sentences and parse each verb. Use your lexicon to look up the glosses for any words you do not know from your vocabulary. Note that names are no longer marked in gray.

Gen. 30:25 — כַּאֲשֶׁר יָלְדָה רָחֵל אֶת־יוֹסֵף

Gen. 15:5 — וּסְפֹר הַכּוֹכָבִים

Judg. 4:16, altered — וּבָרָק רָדַף הָרֶכֶב וְהַמַּחֲנֶה

Joel 2:16, altered — אִסְפוּ־הָעָם קָהָל קַבְּצוּ

Isa. 22:10, altered — וְאֶת־הַבָּתִּים בִּירוּשָׁלַיִם סְפַרְתֶּם

Josh. 10:42, altered	וְאֵת הַמְּלָכִים וְאֶת־הָאָרֶץ לָכַד יְהוֹשֻׁעַ
Gen. 30:31, altered	אָמַר יַעֲקֹב לֹא־תִתֵּן מְאוּמָה
1 Sam. 2:15, altered	אָמַר לָאִישׁ תְּנָה בָשָׂר לַכֹּהֵן
Ex. 8:21, altered [Engl. 8:25]	קָרָא פַּרְעֹה אֶל־מֹשֶׁה וְאָמַר לְכוּ זִבְחוּ לֵאלֹהִים בָּאָרֶץ׃
Gen. 33:12, altered	אָמַר עֵשָׂו נֵלֵכָה

7.8 Exegetical Exercises—Types of Negation

As discussed above, Hebrew has two main negative particles: לֹא (for ongoing negation) and אַל (for one-time negation). These particles not only negate different verbal tenses (imperfect versus volitive) but also carry different nuances. The negation אַל plus jussive is typically used for a one-time negative command, whereas the negation לֹא plus imperfect is typically used for a negative command that expects continued, ongoing obedience, a solemn prohibition.

A. Consider, for instance, the form of Exodus 20:13–15. Translate each commandment, parse the verb, and use your lexicon to provide a gloss.

Ex. 20:13	לֹא תִרְצָח
Ex. 20:14	לֹא תִנְאָף
Ex. 20:15	לֹא תִגְנֹב

All three forms are imperfects negated by לֹא, as befitting the Decalogue.

In contrast, translate each of the following, parse the verb, and use your lexicon to provide a gloss.

Gen. 18:3 אַל תַּעֲבֹר

Gen. 15:1 אַל תִּירָא[1]

Each form is a one-time request, which fits the context.

B. This type of observation helps in appreciating nuance. For example, in Genesis 42:38 Jacob refuses to allow Benjamin to travel to Egypt with his brothers. As the famine intensifies, Jacob instructs his sons in 43:2:

שִׁבְרוּ־לָנוּ מְעַט־אֹכֶל

1. Parse שִׁבְרוּ and translate Genesis 43:2. (Translate לָנוּ as "for us.")

2. Judah, speaking on behalf of his brothers, quotes Joseph's warning to them in verse 5:

   לֹא־תִרְאוּ פָנַי בִּלְתִּי אֲחִיכֶם אִתְּכֶם

   Parse תִרְאוּ. The root of the verb is ראה, and the *heh* has been assimilated (see ch. 24).

3. פָּנַי בִּלְתִּי אֲחִיכֶם אִתְּכֶם may be translated as "my face unless your brother is with you." Combined with your parsing of the verb, how would you translate this clause?

---

[1] The root of this verb begins with *yod*, and *yod* often loses a silent *shewa* (cf. לִיהוּדָה in section 6.4).

4. Given your translation, what type of prohibition had Joseph issued to his brothers? How does this help you understand the dynamics of the interaction between Jacob and his sons in Genesis 43?

C. Look up the following passages in your Hebrew Bible. What level of prohibition is given, ongoing or one-time? How does this help you understand the nature of each prohibition?

Lev. 3:17	"You shall not eat fat or blood"
2 Chron. 11:4	"You shall not go up against your relatives"
Ex. 16:29	"Let no one go out of his place"
Lev. 18:21	"You shall not give any of your children"
Joel 2:13	"Do not rend your garments"
Gen. 21:16	"May I not see"
Ps. 83:2[2]	"Do not keep silent, O God"

[2] This is verse 1 in English translations.

ח (8) Particles

8.1 Existence

Existence and nonexistence are expressed by two particles,[1] יֵשׁ and אֵין:

יֶשׁ־שֶׁבֶר בְּמִצְרָיִם ("There is grain in Egypt."—Gen. 42:2)

יֵשׁ גֹּאֵל קָרוֹב מִמֶּנִּי ("There is a redeemer nearer than me."—Ruth 3:12)

וְאִישׁ אֵין בָּאָרֶץ ("And there is not a man on the earth . . . ."—Gen. 19:31)

אֵין־אֶשְׁכּוֹל ("There is no stalk (of grapes) . . . ."—Micah 7:1)

8.2 Definite Direct Object Marking

את, the marker of the definite direct object, has already been introduced in your vocabulary (see section 2.9). It is used to mark a definite direct object in a sentence. As mentioned in 4.6, Hebrew words are considered definite for the sake of agreement if they have the definite article, are proper nouns, or are the object of a possessive suffix.[2]

This particle can be vocalized in two ways, as either אֵת or אֶת־. Note the danger of confusion between the definite direct object marker and the preposition אֵת/אֶת ("with"), which is spelled identically.

8.3 *Waw*

The *waw* (ו) is, in essence, a connector. While most often translated as "and," it can also be translated as "but," depending on the context.

בַּזָּהָב וּבַכֶּסֶף וּבַנְּחֹשֶׁת ("in gold and in silver and in bronze"—Ex. 35:32)

[1] A particle is a word that conveys a grammatical function, such as the relationship between various words in a sentence.

[2] This is a slight oversimplification, since not all nouns with a possessive suffix are truly identifiable, but it suffices for a rule of thumb while learning the language.

וְאֶל־קַיִן וְאֶל־מִנְחָתוֹ לֹא שָׁעָה ("But he did not have regard for Cain and his offering ."—Gen. 4:5)

Depending on the phonetic context, this *waw* can have a number of vocalizations:

- The common form before a consonant: וְ.
- Before the three consonants known as labials (made with the lips), ב, מ, and פ: וּ.[3]
- Before a consonant with a vocal *shewa*: וּ (*shureq*).
- Before a compound *shewa*, it takes the short vowel corresponding to the compound *shewa*'s vocalization: וַ, וֶ, or וָ.

8.4 הִנֵּה

The particle הִנֵּה was often translated "behold" in older Bible translations. While this serves in some contexts, the particle is meant to call one's attention to the following noun and indicate immediacy or presence, almost telling the reader, "Look!" The traditional translation of "behold" may be used at times, but often the particle הִנֵּה is best not translated at all, though the nuance should be noted.

וַיְהִי הַשֶּׁמֶשׁ בָּאָה וַעֲלָטָה הָיָה וְהִנֵּה תַנּוּר עָשָׁן וְלַפִּיד אֵשׁ ("And when the sun had gone down and it was dark, a smoking pot and a torch of fire were there . . . ."—Gen. 15:17)

וַיַּשְׁכִּמוּ בַבֹּקֶר מִמָּחֳרָת וְהִנֵּה דָגוֹן נֹפֵל לְפָנָיו אַרְצָה לִפְנֵי אֲרוֹן יְהוָה ("But when they arose the next morning, there was Dagan, fallen to the ground upon his face before the ark of the LORD."—1 Sam. 5:4a)

The choice of whether to include an English equivalent for הִנֵּה is largely a question related to the style that the translator wishes to use, because "behold" often feels archaic.

[3] This וּ represents one of the few cases in which a vowel can begin a syllable in Hebrew.

8.5 אֲשֶׁר

The particle אֲשֶׁר, already introduced in your vocabulary, is the relative pronoun. Relative pronouns connect independent and dependent clauses. Accordingly, אֲשֶׁר can be translated with a range of terms depending on the relationship of the two clauses in question:

הָאֲנָשִׁים אֲשֶׁר הָלְכוּ ("The men <u>who</u> went . . . ."—Gen. 14:24)

הָאִשָּׁה אֲשֶׁר נָתַתָּה ("The woman, <u>whom</u> you gave . . . ."—Gen. 3:12)

עֵינַיִם אֲשֶׁר עַל־דֶּרֶךְ ("Enaim, <u>which</u> is on the road . . . ."—Gen. 38:14)

הָעֵץ אֲשֶׁר בְּתוֹךְ־הַגָּן ("The tree <u>that</u> is in the middle of the garden . . . ."—Gen. 3:3)

הַמָּקוֹם אֲשֶׁר־עָמַד ("The place <u>where</u> he had stood . . . ."—Gen. 19:27)

Though less common in classical Biblical Hebrew, a relative clause may also be marked by a prefixed *shin* (שׁ), which plays the same role as אֲשֶׁר.[4]

יֵשׁ דָּבָר שֶׁיֹּאמַר רְאֵה־זֶה חָדָשׁ ("Is there a thing of which one says, 'See, this is new?"—Eccl. 1:10)

8.6 מִן

You have already learned the prefixed prepositions (6.4) and several independent prepositions from your vocabulary. The preposition מִן (vocabulary, ch. 2) should be noted because it ends in *nun*. Recall from 2.2 that *nun* tends to assimilate to a following consonant under many circumstances.

מִן can be connected to the following word by a *maqqēp̄*, as in Genesis 2:22:

מִן־הָאָדָם ("From the man")

מִן can also be prefixed to the following word—upon which the assimilation of *nun* occurs—causing the doubling of the following consonant, as indicated by the *dagesh forte*:

מִשָּׂפָה < מִן + שָׂפָה ("From a tongue")

[4] This use of שׁ is the dominant way to mark a relative clause in many other dialects of Hebrew.

When the word to which מִן is prefixed begins with a *begadkephat* letter, the *dagesh lene* in that letter becomes a *dagesh forte*:

בֵּן + מִן > מִבֵּן ("From a son")[5]

When the word to which מִן is prefixed begins with a guttural, the *ḥireq* usually changes to a *ṣere* via compensatory lengthening, though the *ḥireq* is occasionally preserved via virtual doubling:

אֶ֫רֶץ + מִן > מֵאֶ֫רֶץ ("From a land")

When מִן is prefixed to a word that has the definite article, the same rule of compensatory lengthening applies. Unlike the other prefixed prepositions, the *heh* of the definite article is retained:

הַגְּדוּד + מִן > מֵהַגְּדוּד ("From the raid")

8.7 Interrogatives

Hebrew can explicitly mark a question in two ways: (1) via one of several special interrogative particles and (2) via the interrogative *heh*.

Common interrogative particles include:

מִי—who/whom?

מַה—what?

אֵי / אַיֵּה—where?

אֵיךְ / אֵיכָה—how?

Note that מַה usually doubles the following consonant, resulting in a *dagesh forte*. Before gutturals and *resh*, the vowel can change to a *qameṣ* or *segol*.

מִ֤י יְהוָה֙ אֲשֶׁ֣ר אֶשְׁמַ֣ע בְּקֹל֔וֹ ("Who is the Lord, that I should obey his voice?"—Ex. 5:2)

מַה־מָּצָ֫אתָ ("What have you found?"—Gen. 31:37)

[5] Note that the *dagesh forte* therefore creates a closed first syllable: mib | bēn .

Hebrew also explicitly marks questions with a *heh* prefixed to the sentence, called the **interrogative *heh***. The vowel for this interrogative *heh* depends on the following consonant:

- The usual form is הֲ.
- Before a consonant with a *shewa* and before a guttural, it is הַ.
- Before a consonant with a *qameṣ*, it is הֶ.

הֲתַחַת אֱלֹהִים אָנִי ("Am I in the place of God?"—Gen. 50:19)

Be careful to distinguish the interrogative *heh* from the definite article, as both are attached to the beginning of a following word. Unlike the definite article, the interrogative *heh* does not double the following letter.

At other times Hebrew does not mark a question at all. Even though the sentence is interrogative, it appears identical to a declarative sentence:

גַּם אֶת־הַטּוֹב נְקַבֵּל מֵאֵת הָאֱלֹהִים וְאֶת־הָרָע לֹא נְקַבֵּל ("Shall we receive good from God and not receive evil?"—Job 2:10)

מִמָּוֶת אֶגְאָלֵם ("Shall I redeem them from death?"—Hos. 13:14)

In such situations, you must use the surrounding context to decide whether to translate the clause as a question or a statement.

8.8 נָא

נָא is a particle of address often used when directly addressing another. נָא used to be glossed as "please," and older translations will often translate it accordingly. But contextually, נָא often does not indicate "please," and translating it as such alters the nuance of meaning. Consider:

הִנֵּה־נָא יָדַעְתִּי כִּי אִשָּׁה יְפַת־מַרְאֶה אָתְּ ("See, I know that you are a woman of great beauty"—Gen. 12:11)

וַיהוָה אָמַר אֶל־אַבְרָם ... שָׂא נָא עֵינֶיךָ וּרְאֵה ("And the Lord said to Abram . . ., 'Lift up your eyes.'"—Gen. 13:14)

In the example from Genesis 12, an ancient Near Eastern patriarch would not have been using *please* in an interaction with his wife. In Genesis 13, God is not asking Abram to "please lift up your eyes," but is giving him a command. For this reason, נָא is usually best left untranslated into English, since there is no equivalent English word.

8.9 Directional *Heh*

When Hebrew indicates motion in a direction, that motion is often marked by the addition of a *heh* to the end of the noun in question. This **directional *heh*** is not accented.

לוּזָה אֲשֶׁר בְּאֶרֶץ כְּנַעַן ("Toward Luz, which is in the land of Canaan"—Gen. 35:6)

ָה+ לוּז > לוּזָה ("toward Luz")

Feminine nouns ending in ָה regularly change their final *heh* to a *taw* before the directional *heh*.

וַתָּבֹא תִּרְצָתָה ("And she came to Tirzah"—1 Kings 14:17)

ָה+ תִּרְצָה > תִּרְצָתָה ("to Tirzah")

The addition of a directional *heh* will often cause changes in the noun's normal vowel pattern:

קֵדְמָה אֶל־אֶרֶץ קֶדֶם ("eastward, to the country of the east"—Gen. 25:6)

ָה+ קֶדֶם > קֵדְמָה ("eastward/toward the east")

8.10 Vocabulary

אַחַר / אַחֲרֵי	(prep. or adv.) after, behind
אֵי / אַיֵּה	where?
אֵיךְ / אֵיכָה	how? (also as an exclamation: “How!”)
אֵין	there is not/are not (particle of nonexistence)
אֶל	(prep.) to, toward
אֵת / אֶת	definite direct object marker (see section 2.9)
אֵת / אֶת	(prep.) with
בֵּין	(prep.) between
בְּתוֹךְ	(prep.) in the middle of, in the midst of (see תָּ֫וֶךְ in section 7.6)
הִנֵּה	“behold” (particle of immediacy – often untranslated)
יֵשׁ	there is/are (particle of existence)
לְמַ֫עַן	(prep.) on account of, for the sake of
לִפְנֵי	(prep.) before, in front of
מָה	what?
מִי	who/whom?
מַ֫עַל	(prep.) above
נָא	particle of address (untranslated)
עַד	(prep.) until, as far as
עַל	(prep.) on, upon, on account of, over
עַל־דְּבַר	(prep.) because, on account of
עִם	(prep.) with
תַּ֫חַת	(prep.) under, in place of

8.11 Language Exercises

A. Parse the following verbal forms.

תִּכְבְּדִי

זִבְחוּ

קְחִי

תִּגְּעוּ

אֶפְקוֹד

בָּטָחְתָּ

עֲבֹד

לָבְשׁוּ

נִפְלוּ

יִסְפּוֹר

B. Translate the following sentences and parse each verb. Use your lexicon to look up the glosses for any words you do not know from your vocabulary.

Ex. 8:6 [Engl. 8:10] — אֵין כַּיהוָה

Gen. 44:4 — רְדֹף אַחֲרֵי הָאֲנָשִׁים

Gen. 14:24 — רַק אֲשֶׁר אָכְלוּ הַנְּעָרִים

Gen. 47:4 — אֵין מִרְעֶה לַצֹּאן

Gen. 2:22 — הַצֵּלָע אֲשֶׁר־לָקַח מִן־הָאָדָם

1 Sam. 7:5, altered	קִבְצוּ אֶת־יִשְׂרָאֵל הַמִּצְפָּתָה
Eccl. 7:20	כִּי אָדָם אֵין צַדִּיק בָּאָרֶץ אֲשֶׁר יַעֲשֶׂה־טּוֹב וְלֹא יֶחֱטָא׃
Gen. 14:21, altered	אָמַר הַמֶּלֶךְ אֶל־אַבְרָם תֶּן הַנֶּפֶשׁ וְהָרְכֻשׁ קַח׃
1 Chron. 21:2	לְכוּ[6] סִפְרוּ אֶת־יִשְׂרָאֵל מִבְּאֵר שֶׁבַע וְעַד־דָּן

8.12 Exegetical Exercises—*Ketiv/Qere*

A. Understanding the *Ketiv* and *Qere*. The Masoretes, who provided the vowel pointing used in the Hebrew text, were essentially conservators of a reading tradition—a way of speaking the consonantal Hebrew text aloud. The Masoretes did not invent the vocalization of the text that their markings preserve; instead, they were intent on preserving the tradition handed down to them, which included both the consonantal text (without consistent vowel markings, but including *matres*) and the reading tradition (the pronunciation of each word, or the vocalization of the consonantal text). The Masoretic copyists both preserved the consonantal text and indicated vowels by the supralinear and sublinear marking system of vowel points that you have learned.

At times, however, these two goals are slightly incompatible because the reading tradition requires the pronunciation of a word in a way that does not match the consonantal text. How could this be handled? The Masoretic approach was consistently conservative regarding the consonantal text that had been received, so the Masoretes would not venture to change any consonant in the text, even when their reading tradition was inconsistent with the letter or letters. Instead, the Masoretes would leave

[6] Qal Imperative mp of הלך, glossed as "go"

the consonantal text exactly as they had received it and place what they believed the actual consonantal text should be in the margin.

The written text, as received, is called the *Ketiv* (כְּתִיב – "what is written") and remains in place. The spoken reading, as read aloud, is called the *Qere* (קְרֵי – "what is read aloud") and is given in the margin of most modern critical editions above a ק to mark it as a *Qere* reading. For example, look up Joshua 24:3 in your Hebrew text. BHS graphically presents this section of the book of Joshua as:

24 1 וַיֶּאֱסֹף[a] יְהוֹשֻׁעַ אֶת־כָּל־שִׁבְטֵי יִשְׂרָאֵל שְׁכֶמָה וַיִּקְרָא לְזִקְנֵי 24
יִשְׂרָאֵל וּלְרָאשָׁיו וּלְשֹׁפְטָיו וּלְשֹׁטְרָיו וַיִּתְיַצְּבוּ לִפְנֵי הָאֱלֹהִים׃
2 וַיֹּאמֶר יְהוֹשֻׁעַ אֶל־כָּל־הָעָם כֹּה־אָמַר יְהוָה אֱלֹהֵי יִשְׂרָאֵל בְּעֵבֶר 2
הַנָּהָר יָשְׁבוּ אֲבוֹתֵיכֶם מֵעוֹלָם תֶּרַח אֲבִי אַבְרָהָם וַאֲבִי נָחוֹר וַיַּעַבְדוּ
אֱלֹהִים אֲחֵרִים׃ 3 וָאֶקַּח אֶת־אֲבִיכֶם אֶת־אַבְרָהָם מֵעֵבֶר 3
הַנָּהָר וָאוֹלֵךְ אוֹתוֹ בְּכָל־אֶרֶץ כְּנָעַן וָאַרְבֶּ[a] אֶת־זַרְעוֹ וָאֶתֶּן־לוֹ אֶת־ (וארבה ק)
יִצְחָק׃ 4 וָאֶתֵּן לְיִצְחָק אֶת־יַעֲקֹב וְאֶת־עֵשָׂו וָאֶתֵּן לְעֵשָׂו אֶת־הַר 4
שֵׂעִיר לָרֶשֶׁת אוֹתוֹ וְיַעֲקֹב וּבָנָיו יָרְדוּ מִצְרָיִם[a]׃ 5 וָאֶשְׁלַח אֶת־מֹשֶׁה 5
וְאֶת־אַהֲרֹן[a] וָאֶגֹּף אֶת־מִצְרַיִם כַּאֲשֶׁר[b] עָשִׂיתִי בְּקִרְבּוֹ וְאַחַר הוֹצֵאתִי
אֶתְכֶם׃[c] 6 וָאוֹצִיא[c] אֶת־אֲבוֹתֵיכֶם[d] מִמִּצְרַיִם וַתָּבֹאוּ הַיָּמָּה וַיִּרְדְּפוּ 6
מִצְרַיִם אַחֲרֵי אֲבוֹתֵיכֶם בְּרֶכֶב וּבְפָרָשִׁים יַם־סוּף׃ 7 וַיִּצְעֲקוּ אֶל־ 7
יְהוָה וַיָּשֶׂם מַאֲפֵל[a] בֵּינֵיכֶם ׀ וּבֵין הַמִּצְרִים וַיָּבֵא עָלָיו אֶת־הַיָּם
וַיְכַסֵּהוּ וַתִּרְאֶינָה עֵינֵיכֶם אֵת אֲשֶׁר־עָשִׂיתִי בְּמִצְרָיִם וַתֵּשְׁבוּ בַמִּדְבָּר
יָמִים רַבִּים׃ 8 וָאָבִאה[a] אֶתְכֶם אֶל־אֶרֶץ הָאֱמֹרִי הַיּוֹשֵׁב בְּעֵבֶר 8 (ואביא ק)
הַיַּרְדֵּן וַיִּלָּחֲמוּ אִתְּכֶם וָאֶתֵּן אוֹתָם בְּיֶדְכֶם וַתִּירְשׁוּ אֶת־אַרְצָם
וָאַשְׁמִידֵם מִפְּנֵיכֶם׃ 9 וַיָּקָם בָּלָק בֶּן־צִפּוֹר מֶלֶךְ מוֹאָב וַיִּלָּחֶם 9

[16]Mm 679. [17]Mm 915. Cp 24 [1]Mm 4234. [2]Mm 274. [3]Mm 1373. [4]Mm 4077 א. [5]Mp sub loco. [6]Mm 817. [7]Mm 1378. [8]Mm 247. [9]Mm 402. [10]Mm 639.

14 [a] prp בָּא cf ממנו || 16 [a–a] > 𝔊* || Cp 24,1 [a] sic L, mlt Mss Edd 'וַיֶּא || 3 [a] K וָאַרְב, mlt Mss ut Q || 4 [a] nonn Mss יָמָּה– || 5 [a–a] > 𝔊 || [b] 𝔊* ἐν σημείοις οἷς cf 𝔖𝔙, l frt בְּאֹתוֹת א' cf Nu 14,11; $𝔊^{BO}$ ἐν οἷς = בַּא' || 5/6 [c–c] > 𝔊 || [d–d] > $𝔊^{Mss}$ || 7 [a] prp אֹפֶל (מ dttg) || 8 [a] K אָה–, nonn Mss ut Q.

The small circle above וָאַרְבֶּ can be used to mark multiple marginal notations, so it does not always indicate a *Qere* reading. However, if the marginal notation does indicate a *Qere* reading, the relevant word in the main text will be marked by this small circle.

Note that the *Qere* reading has no vowel pointing. Where are the vowels for the *Qere*? They are found on the *Ketiv*, in the main text. To pronounce the *Qere*, the reader must take the vowel pointing from the *Ketiv* and apply it to the consonants of the *Qere*.[7] In Joshua 24:3 the situation is as follows:

Ketiv:	וארב
Ketiv with Masoretic Vowel Points:	וָאַרְבֶּ
Qere:	וארבה
Qere with Vowel Points Applied:	וָאַרְבֶּה

In Joshua 24:3 the Masoretes viewed this word as if it had a ה as the final letter, even though their text did not have that ה. Out of a reluctance to ever change the consonantal text, even though they were confident that ה should be present, they would not add it. Instead, they provided it in the *Qere* marginal note.[8]

For another example, look at Judges 9:8 in your BHS or BHQ. Following the same process in this case yields:

Ketiv:	מלוכה
Ketiv with Masoretic Vowel Points:	מָלְוכָה
Qere:	מלכה
Qere with Vowel Points Applied:	מָלְכָה

[7] To assist the reader, some reading editions put the two forms side by side, marking the *Ketiv* with K and the *Qere* with Q, and printing the vowel pointing on the *Qere* instead.

[8] This example also shows the oversimplification of this traditional *Ketiv/Qere* explanation. The basic concept of a division between an oral *Qere* and a written *Ketiv* works well enough as a model for the phenomenon of *Ketiv/Qere* readings, but not all *Ketiv* and *Qere* readings would have different sounds. (Read the vocalized *Ketiv* and *Qere* of Joshua 24:3 aloud—there is no difference.) The phenomenon of *Ketiv/Qere* is more complex than the simple explanation presented here, but this presentation is sufficient at early stages of study.

Here the Masoretic vocal tradition indicated that there should not be a ו present, but instead of removing it the Masoretes left their received consonantal text unchanged, indicating their reading tradition in the *Qere* notation.

Using your Hebrew text, write out the *Ketiv* consonants, the *Qere* consonants, and the vocalized *Qere* (the *Qere* consonants with the vowel points supplied) for the *Ketiv/Qere* in the following verses.

	Ketiv Consonants	*Qere* Consonants	Vocalized *Qere*
Judg. 9:8	מלוכה	מלכה	מָלְכָה
2 Sam. 5:2			
Gen. 9:21			
2 Kings 20:4			
1 Kings 22:49			
Micah 1:3			

B. Perpetual *Ketiv/Qere*. Several *Ketiv/Qere* variations are simply assumed when reading the text and therefore not noted. By far the most common of these is the Tetragrammaton, the divine name, which is given in the text as יְהוָה but without any indication of a marginal *Qere*. The reading tradition is to simply speak *"adonai."*

Other perpetual *Ketiv/Qere* readings will be noted as they occur in the exercises.

ט (9) Independent Personal Pronouns; Qal Participles

9.1 Independent Personal Pronouns

Pronouns are words that stand in place of nouns, as in these English examples:

- Jim hit Bill with the ball.
- *He* hit Bill with the ball.
- Jim hit *him* with the ball.
- Jim hit *him* with *it*.

The paradigm for the Hebrew independent personal pronoun is as follows:

Independent Personal Pronoun Paradigm

	Pronoun	Gloss
3ms	הוּא	he
3fs	הִיא	she
2ms	אַתָּ / אַתָּה	you (ms)
2fs	אַתְּ	you (fs)
1cs	אֲנִי / אָנֹכִי	I
3mp	הֵם / הֵ֫מָּה	they (mp)
3fp	הֵ֫נָּה	they (fp)
2mp	אַתֶּם	you (mp)
2fp	אַתֶּן / אַתֵּ֫נָּה	you (fp)
1cp	אֲנַ֫חְנוּ	we

This paradigm must be memorized.

Notes:

- The independent personal pronouns are only used as the subject of a clause, not as the object.
- In the second- and first-person forms, the independent personal pronouns show similarities to the endings of the perfect:

	Ending	Qal Perfect of קטל	Independent Personal Pronoun
2ms	־תָּ	קָטַ֫לְתָּ	אַתָּ / אַתָּה
2fs	־תְּ	קָטַלְתְּ	אַתְּ
1cs	־תִי	קָטַ֫לְתִּי	אֲנִי / אָנֹכִי
2mp	־תֶּם	קְטַלְתֶּם	אַתֶּם
2fp	־תֶּן	קְטַלְתֶּן	אַתֶּן / אַתֵּ֫נָה
1cp	־נוּ	קָטַ֫לְנוּ	אֲנַ֫חְנוּ

- The 3fs pronoun in the Pentateuch is written with a *waw*, as הִוא, but it is still pronounced as הִיא. This is a perpetual *Qere* (see 8.12.B).
- Less common variant forms of the 2fs and 1cp can also occur:

אַתִּי for אַתְּ[1]

אֲנוּ or נַ֫חְנוּ for אֲנַ֫חְנוּ

The independent personal pronouns typically serve as the subject of a clause:

וַאֲנִי הִנְנִי מֵקִים אֶת־בְּרִיתִי אִתְּכֶם ("And I am establishing my covenant with you."—Gen. 9:9)

אָנֹכִי מָגֵן לָךְ ("I am a shield for you."—Gen. 15:1)

The Hebrew verb already encodes its subject information within the verbal form (see 9.5), so when the independent personal pronoun is used in a seemingly duplicative way, it signals emphasis.

יְהוָה הוּא הָאֱלֹהִים אֵין עוֹד ("The LORD, **He** is God. There is none other."—1 Kings 8:60)

9.2 Qal Active Participle

A **participle** is a form that has elements of both a verb and a noun/adjective—the nominal/adjectival idea that corresponds to a verb's sense. In English, participles are usually marked by the ending *-ing* as in *running*, *walking*, *loving*, etc. The Hebrew participle is formed by applying typical noun/adjective endings to the verbal root:

[1] Note the similarity between this form and the example of Judges 5:7 in 3.10.

Qal Active Participle Paradigm

	Verbal Form	Suffix	Translation
ms	קֹטֵל	--	killing/one who kills
fs	קֹטֶ֫לֶת	ֶת	killing/one who kills
fs (alt. form)	קֹטְלָה	ָה	killing/one who kills
mp	קֹטְלִים	ִים	killing/ones who kill
fp	קֹטְלוֹת	וֹת	killing/ones who kill

This paradigm must be memorized.

Other than an alternative feminine singular form, this paradigm follows that of the noun, as is expected for a form that is a verbal noun/adjective. The feminine singular form קֹטֶ֫לֶת is more common than the form ending in ָה, but both occur. Note the use of the *holem* vowel in the first syllable, a strong indicator of the Qal active participle form.[2]

Recall that the use of *matres lectiones* is common in Hebrew; the forms קֹטֵל and קוֹטֵל are both Qal active participles with no difference in meaning or parsing.

9.3 Qal Passive Participle

The **passive** voice of a verb indicates that its subject receives the action of that verb, e.g., "Bill *was hit* by the ball." At one point in its history, Hebrew had a more fully developed Qal passive conjugation in its verbal system. In Biblical Hebrew, the Qal passive participle is a remnant of that more robust Qal passive.

Qal Passive Participle Paradigm

	Verbal Form	Suffix	Translation
ms	קָטוּל	--	one being killed
fs	קְטוּלָה	ָה	one being killed
mp	קְטוּלִים	ִים	ones being killed
fp	קְטוּלוֹת	וֹת	ones being killed

This paradigm must be memorized.

[2] Note that the names of two biblical books are participle forms: שֹׁפְטִים and קֹהֶלֶת (see section 1.9.B).

Note that the endings remain those of the typical noun/adjective paradigm. The theme vowel *shureq* is a strong indicator of the Qal passive participle. This form may be written instead with a *qibbuṣ* as קְטֻל. As expected, the *qameṣ* in the first syllable reduces to a vocal *shewa* because of propretonic reduction (see 3.5).

9.4 Parsing Participles

Because the participle combines elements of both a verb and a noun, it is parsed by indicating the verbal stem, voice (active or passive), conjugation (participle), gender, number, root, and gloss.[3] For example:

	Verbal Stem	Voice	Conjugation	Gender	Number	Root	Gloss
קֹטֶלֶת	Qal	Active	Participle	f	s	קטל	"killing/one who kills"
קְטוּלִים	Qal	Passive	Participle	m	p	קטל	"being killed/ ones being killed"

9.5 Uses of the Participle

The perfect, imperfect, and volitive conjugations represent the class of **finite verbs**. A finite verb has a clear subject (stated or implied) and forms the core of an independent clause. Hebrew finite verbs are marked for tense and/or aspect.[4] Participles represent the first of two **nonfinite** verb forms, which are not marked for tense and/or aspect.[5]

The participle can be used in three major nonfinite ways corresponding to the three uses of the adjective discussed in 4.6. In later Hebrew it can also be used in a fourth, more verbal way, as a replacement for a finite verb.

---

[3] Because the participle does not encode person (first, second, or third), person is not included in the parsing of a participle.
[4] The exact nuance of the Hebrew finite verbal system regarding tense and/or aspect is much debated.
[5] The other will be infinitives (see ch. 13).

1. Attributive Use. When used in an attributive sense, the participle acts as an adjective modifying a noun. Like an adjective, the attributive participle follows and agrees with its "head noun" in gender, number, and definiteness:

    הָאֲנָשִׁים הָעֹמְדִים ("the men who were standing"—1 Sam. 17:26)

    The English translation of an attributive participle most often uses the pronoun *who*, representing the Hebrew attributive participle with an English relative clause, though the *-ing* form alone is acceptable English style in many cases. The tense (past, present, or future) of the English relative clause must be inferred from the context in which the participle is used because the form itself does not convey a time value.[6]

2. Predicative Use. When used predicatively, the participle's verbal nature is more evident. As with a predicative adjective, the predicative participle agrees with its noun in gender and number. It does not agree with it in definiteness, since a predicate cannot take the definite article. The verbal sense of the predicative participle is that of either a continuous or an imminent action.

    The time sense of a predicative participle is not indicated by its form and must be inferred from the surrounding context. When this time sense is past or present, the continuous nature of the participle is more often in view:

    וְהוּא יֹשֵׁב בִּסְדֹם ("And he was dwelling in Sodom."—Gen. 14:12)
    עֹלֶה תִמְנָ֫תָה ("He is going to Timnah."—Gen. 38:13)[7]

    When this time sense is future, the predicate participle often indicates imminent action:

    אָנֹכִי הֹלֵךְ ("I am about to go . . . ."—1 Kings 2:2)
    אַתֶּם עֹבְרִים ("You are about to pass through . . . ."—Deut. 2:4)

[6] In the case of 1 Sam. 17:26, noted here, the "were" in the translation must be inferred from the context, because of the past tense narrative genre of the passage.
[7] The participle form is עֹלֶה because this comes from a III-ה verb. This type of verb is covered in chapter 24.

3. Substantive Use. When used substantively, the participle serves a nominal function like any substantivized adjective:

   הַנֹּגֵעַ ("the one who touches"—Lev. 11:39)
   הַיֹּשֵׁב ("the one who sits"—Lev. 15:6)

   Substantivized participles can become lexicalized (meaning they become treated as if they are simply nouns):

   שֹׁפֵט ("judge")
   כֹּהֵן ("priest")

4. In addition to these "standard" uses, the participle often functions as a substitute for a finite verb in later texts such as Ecclesiastes and Chronicles.

   דּ֤וֹר הֹלֵךְ֙ וְד֣וֹר בָּ֔א וְהָאָ֖רֶץ לְעוֹלָ֥ם עֹמָֽדֶת׃ ("A generation comes and a generation goes, but the earth remains forever."—Eccl. 1:4)

9.6 Uses of *min*

You have already learned the preposition מִן, glossed as "from, away from." Two further uses should be noted:

The **comparative *min*** uses the preposition to mark the lesser of two items in a comparison:

וַיֶּאֱהַב גַּם־אֶת־רָחֵל מִלֵּאָה ("And he loved Rachel more than Leah."—Gen. 29:30)

וְעַתָּה הֲטוֹב טוֹב אַתָּה מִבָּלָק ("And now are you better than Balak?"—Judg. 11:25)

מַה־מָּתוֹק מִדְּבַשׁ וּמֶה עַז מֵאֲרִי ("What is sweeter than honey, and what is stronger than a lion?"—Judg. 14:18)

The **partitive *min*** uses the preposition to indicate "some" of a thing or group:

מִן־הָאָדֹם ("some of the stew"—Gen. 25:30)

מִן־הָעָם ("some of the people"—Gen. 33:15)

There are other common uses of מִן. For further detail, consult an intermediate lexicon.

9.7 Vocabulary

אָחוֹת	sister
אָז	then, at that time
אַ֫יִל	ram; ruler, mighty one
אַךְ	(adv.) surely; only; however, but
אֵם	mother
אַף	(conj.) also, even
בְּהֵמָה	cattle, domestic animals; beasts
בָּמָה	hill, high place
בַּ֫עַד	behind; through, out of; round about; for the benefit of
בָּשָׂר	skin, flesh, meat
חוֹמָה	wall
חוּץ	outside
חָצֵר	court, enclosure (of a building); unwalled village
יַ֫יִן	wine
כִּי	that, since, because, for, although, surely
כִּי אִם־	but, surely; except, unless, only
לַ֫יְלָה	night
לָ֫מָּה / לָמָה	why?
נְאֻם	an oracle of
רִאשׁוֹן	first

9.8 Language Exercises

A. Parse and translate the following forms. Examples:

	Verbal Stem	Conjugation (incl. Participle Voice)	Person	Gender	Number	Root	Gloss
יִגְדַּל	Qal	Imperfect	3	m	s	גדל	He will be(come) great
קְטוּלִים	Qal	Passive Participle		m	p	קטל	Being killed/ones being killed

אָהֲבָה

הֹלְכוֹת

מֹלֶכֶת

לְכוּ[8]

זָכוּר

נוֹתֵן

אֹהֶבֶת

קַח

יִגְדְּלוּ

לֹקְחִים

אָהוּב

זִכְרוּ

הֹלְכָה

תִּשְׁלַחְנָה

הֲלַכְתֶּם

[8] See p. 98, note 6.

B. Translate the following sentences and parse each verb and participle. Use your lexicon to look up the glosses for any words you do not know from your vocabulary.

Gen. 42:6	וְיוֹסֵף הוּא הַשַּׁלִּיט עַל־הָאָרֶץ
Ps. 119:127, altered	עַל־כֵּן אָהַבְתִּי הַמִּצְוֹת מִזָּהָב
Lev. 26:36, altered	נָפְלוּ וְאֵין רֹדֵף
Jer. 26:15	כִּי־דָם נָקִי אַתֶּם נֹתְנִים
Num. 16:7	הָאִישׁ אֲשֶׁר־יִבְחַר יְהוָה הוּא הַקָּדוֹשׁ
Gen. 40:8	חֲלוֹם חָלַמְנוּ וּפֹתֵר אֵין
Ps. 52:5	אָהַבְתָּ רָע מִטּוֹב
Zech. 2:6	אָנָה אַתָּה הֹלֵךְ
Ps. 32:10	הַבּוֹטֵחַ בַּיהוָה
Deut. 16:18	שֹׁפְטִים וְשֹׁטְרִים תִּתֶּן

Judg. 4:22	וְהִנֵּה בָרָק רֹדֵף אֶת־סִיסְרָא
Deut. 4:24, altered	כִּי יְהוָה אֵשׁ אֹכְלָה הוּא אֵל קַנָּא
Gen. 40:3, altered	הַמְּקוֹם אֲשֶׁר יוֹסֵף אָסוּר שָׁם
Gen. 2:10	וְנָהָר יֹצֵא מֵעֵדֶן

9.9 Exegetical Exercises—Appreciating Nuance

The skills of word study (5.7 and 6.7) give you a better appreciation of certain passages, since the careful reader of the Hebrew text can understand nuances that would be missed while reading in translation. This is especially true when multiple words have overlapping ranges of meaning, what is called a **semantic field**.

A. Jephthah and the Leaders of Gilead. In Judges 10:18, under the threat of Ammonite invasion, the leaders of Gilead search for the man to lead their armies. They indicate that the man who leads the fight will be ראשׁ over all those who live in Gilead.

   Survey several English translations of ראשׁ. What sense does it have from these translations?

Study the word רֹאשׁ with the tools available to you. What is its semantic range? What does it mean in this passage?

When the leaders of Gilead approach Jephthah to lead their armies (Judg. 11:6), the text states: וַיֹּאמְרוּ לְיִפְתָּח לְכָה וְהָיִיתָה[9] לָּנוּ[10] לְקָצִין

Translate this and parse the verbs. What is the Hebrew word for the position they offer Jephthah?

Survey several English translations of this word. What sense does it have from these translations?

Study this word with the tools available to you. What is its semantic range? What does it mean in this passage?

---

[9] This is a Qal converted perfect 2ms of היה, glossed as "to be" (see ch. 24). Translate here as "and be."

[10] I.e., "for us" (see 11.2).

Look at verse 9. Jephthah is willing to lead them under only one of these two labels. Skim the verse in Hebrew to see which title he will accept. Based on the result of your word studies, why has Jephthah insisted on this title?

B. Ruth and Boaz. In Ruth 2:10, as Ruth responds to Boaz's first act of charity, she refers to herself by her ethnic identity:

מַדּוּעַ מָצָאתִי חֵן בְּעֵינֶיךָ לְהַכִּירֵנִי[11] וְאָנֹכִי נָכְרִיָּה[12]

Translate Ruth's statement, parsing the verbs. What term has Ruth used for herself? While this term is literally true, it also carries a huge weight of cultural baggage. Study the word with the resources available to you. What does it imply?

In verse 13, after Boaz's gracious response, Ruth uses a different term for herself: שִׁפְחָה. Check this term in both the NIV and ESV. How is it translated?

[11] Hiphil infinitive construct of נכר, glossed as "to recognize" + 1cs object suffix (see ch. 16). Translate as "to recognize me."

[12] Note the pronunciation of this word, with a *qameṣ ḥatup̄.*

Study the word שִׁפְחָה with the tools available to you. What is its semantic range? What does it mean when Ruth uses it in this verse?

In Ruth 3:9, when Ruth speaks to Boaz at night on the threshing floor, she uses a third term for herself: אָמָה. Check this term in both the NIV and ESV. How is it translated?

Study the word אָמָה with the tools available to you. (Do not simply use one resource, but consult the other tools at your disposal. Where do they differ in opinion from each other?) What is the semantic range of אָמָה? What does it mean when Ruth uses it in this verse?

Given the track of Ruth in the book from 2:10 (נָכְרִיָּה) to 2:13 (שִׁפְחָה) to 3:9 (אָמָה), what can you say about her change in status and relationship over this narrative's time period?

י (10) Construct Phrases

10.1 The Construct State

In addition to gender and number, Hebrew nouns also have **state**. Until now, the nouns you have seen have all been in the **absolute state**. Hebrew has no word that corresponds to the English *of*, which is typically called the **genitive function**.[1] Instead, when Hebrew indicates the genitive function, a word is put into the construct state:

Absolute State	Construct State
חוֹמָה (a wall)	חוֹמַת (a wall of)
סוּסָה (a mare)	סוּסַת (a mare of)

10.2 The Construct Phrase

A **construct phrase** is composed of one or more nouns in the construct state followed by a final noun in the absolute state:

Abs. ← Constr.

עֵץ־חַיִּים ("a tree of life"—Prov. 3:18)

Abs. ← Constr.

יוֹם יְשׁוּעָה ("a day of salvation"—Isa. 49:8)

Abs. ← Constr. ← Constr.

אֶרֶץ בְּנֵי־עַמּוֹן ("the land of the sons of Ammon"—Deut. 2:19)

[1] In contrast to languages such as Greek and Latin, Hebrew has retained few formal markers of nominal case. One can, however, still talk about the various *functions* of nominal cases, even though those functions are inferred from the syntax of the language instead of being explicitly marked by the morphology of the noun.

Several terminologies are commonly used for the two nouns involved in a construct phrase:

Absolute Noun	←	Construct Noun
Nomen Rectum[2]	←	Nomen Regens
Free Form	←	Bound Form
Genitive Noun	←	Head Noun

For clarity, the terms *absolute noun* and *construct noun* will be used in the explanations that follow, but when reading secondary literature or other works, you will likely encounter many of these terms.

10.3 Formation of the Construct State

The construct forms of the noun סוּס ("horse") are:

	Construct Noun			Endings		
	Singular	Dual	Plural	Singular	Dual	Plural
Masculine	סוּס	סוּסֵי	סוּסֵי	--	ֵי	ֵי
Feminine	סוּסַת	סוּסְתֵי	סוּסוֹת	ַת	ְתֵי	וֹת

For סוּס the masculine singular and feminine plural forms of the construct noun are identical to the absolute forms, but the feminine singular, dual, and masculine plural forms show changes to their endings.

When a noun is placed in the construct state, the ending changes are regular:

- The feminine singular ending changes to *-at:*

  תּוֹרָה (absolute), but תּוֹרַת (construct)

  תּוֹרַת הַנָּזִיר ("the law of the Nazirite"—Num. 6:21)

- The masculine plural ending changes to *-ê*:

  אֱלֹהִים (absolute), but אֱלֹהֵי (construct)

  אֱלֹהֵי הָאֱמֹרִי ("the gods of the Amorites"—Judg. 6:10)

---

[2] This is the Latin grammatical terminology. *Rectum* means "governed," with the sense that the Nomen Rectum is controlled by the preceding construct noun. *Regens* means "governing," with the sense that the construct noun is controlling the following absolute noun.

- The dual *-áyim* changes to *-ê*:

  שְׂפָתַ֫יִם (absolute), but שִׂפְתֵי (construct)

  שִׂפְתֵי זָרָה ("the lips of a prohibited woman"—Prov. 5:3)

When the absolute and construct forms of a noun are identical, you must use context to distinguish them.

Beyond these changes in endings, other changes occur during the formation of the construct state, primarily because nouns in construct tend to lose their accentual stress; a construct chain is read (for purposes of stress) as if it were a single word. The changes that this loss of stress creates include the following.

Vowels will tend to shorten:

- *Ṣere* often becomes *segol* in monosyllabic nouns:

  בֵּן (absolute), but בֶּן (construct)

  בֶּן־דָּוִד ("the son of David"—2 Sam. 13:1)

- Final *qameṣ* often becomes a *pataḥ*:

  יָד (absolute), but יַד (construct)

  יַד־יְהוָה ("the hand of the LORD"—Ex. 9:3)

Other noun endings will change:

- Final *segol heh* becomes *ṣere heh*:

  מַחֲנֶה (absolute), but מַחֲנֵה (construct)

  מַחֲנֵה רְאוּבֵן ("the camp of Reuben"—Num. 2:16)

Vowel reduction commonly occurs:

- *Qameṣ* and *ṣere* in unstressed open syllables reduce to a vocal *shewa*:

  שָׁלוֹם (absolute), but שְׁלוֹם (construct)

  שְׁלוֹם יְרוּשָׁלִָם ("the peace of Jerusalem"—Ps. 122:6)

- This vowel reduction commonly occurs alongside other changes:

  דָּבָר (absolute), but דְּבַר (construct)

  דְּבַר־יְהוָה ("the word of the LORD"—Gen. 15:1)

- Vowel reduction also can commonly trigger the rule of *shewa*:

  דְּבָרִים > * דְּבָרֵי > דִּבְרֵי

  דִּבְרֵי הַנְּבִאִים ("the words of the prophets"—2 Chron. 18:12)

Diphthongs contract (see section 4.2):

- *-awe* contracts to *-ô*:

  מָוֶת (absolute), but מוֹת (construct)

  מוֹת יְהוֹשֻׁעַ ("the death of Joshua"—Judg. 1:1)

- *-ayi* contracts to *-ê*:

  בַּיִת (absolute), but בֵּית (construct)

  בֵּית שָׁאוּל ("the house of Saul"—2 Sam. 3:1)

Segolate nouns (see section 6.1) show their original vowel patterns (*qaṭl/qiṭl/quṭl*) in the plural:

- *qaṭl* form:

  מְלָכִים (absolute), but מַלְכֵי (construct)[3]

  מַלְכֵי מִדְיָן ("the kings of Midian"—Num. 31:8)

- *qoṭl* form:

  אֳהָלִים (absolute), but אָהֳלֵי (construct)

  אָהֳלֵי־שֵׁם ("the tents of Shem"—Gen. 9:27)

---

[3] The *kaph* retains its spirantized form even though it now follows a silent *shewa*.

Participles, given their verbal and nominal/adjectival nature, can be placed in the construct state by following the same patterns:

שֹׁמְרֵי הַבַּיִת ("the keepers of the house"—Eccl. 12:3)

אֹהֵב כֶּסֶף ("a lover of money"—Eccl. 5:9)

10.4 Irregular Construct Forms

Most construct forms are accounted for by the patterns in 10.3, and irregular construct forms are usually noted in the lexicon. The following irregular construct forms are common and should be memorized:

Absolute	Construct	Example	
אִשָּׁה	אֵשֶׁת (wife of)	אֵשֶׁת־יְהוּדָה	("the wife of Judah"—Gen. 38.12)
אָב	אֲבִי (father of)	אֲבִי כְנָעַן	("the father of Canaan"—Gen. 9:22)
אָח	אֲחִי (brother of)	אֲחִי כָלֵב	("the brother of Caleb"—Josh. 15:17)
פֶּה	פִּי (mouth of)	פִּי הַמְּעָרָה	("the mouth of the cave"—Josh. 10:18)

10.5 The Definiteness of the Construct Phrase

A construct phrase as a whole will be definite or indefinite, but definiteness is only marked on the absolute noun. Recall that a Hebrew noun is considered definite if it (1) has the definite article attached, (2) is a proper noun, or (3) has a possessive pronoun (see ch. 11) attached:

Abs. ← Constr.

בְּתוֹךְ הַמָּיִם ("in the midst of the waters"—Gen. 1:6)

Abs. ← Constr.

חוֹמַת גַּת ("the wall of Gath"—2 Chron. 26:6)

Abs. ← Constr.

מֵאֶרֶץ מִצְרָיִם ("from the land of Egypt"—Gen. 21:21)

A prefixed preposition on the construct noun will not indicate the presence of a definite article in its vocalization because the definite article is attached only to the absolute noun.

וּלְחוֹמַ֣ת הָעִ֔יר ("and for the wall of the city"—Neh. 2:8)

In the rare case in which one wishes to say "a ____ of (Proper Noun)," the construct phrase is not used, because the definite absolute noun would mark the entire phrase as definite. Instead, the preposition לְ is used to mark this construction:

Abs. + Const.

בֶּן־יִשַׁי ("the son of Jesse"—1 Sam. 20:27)

Abs. + לְ + Abs.

בֵּן לְיִשַׁי ("a son of Jesse"—1 Sam. 16:18)

An adjective that modifies any member of the construct chain is placed after the absolute noun, *not* in the middle of the phrase. Such an adjective will agree in gender and number with the noun it modifies. If it agrees in gender and number with more than one noun in a construct phrase, context must be used to identify which noun it modifies.

אִ֥ישׁ אֱלֹהִ֖ים קָד֣וֹשׁ ("a holy man of God"—2 Kings 4:9)

Nouns in construct may, however, take the directional *heh*:

Abs. ← Constr. ← ה + Constr.

אַ֥רְצָה בְנֵי־קֶֽדֶם ("to the land of the people of the east"—Gen. 29:1)

10.6 *Kol*

The word כֹּל ("any, each, every, all") is almost always in the construct state. It may be written with or without a *mater*, and it may be linked to the following word by the *maqqēp̄* and spelled with a *qameṣ ḥatup̄*:

כֹּל שִׂיחַ הַשָּׂדֶה ("any bush of the field"—Gen. 2:5)

כָּל־חַיַּת הָאָרֶץ ("every beast of the earth"—Gen. 9:2)

10.7 Superlatives

While מִן typically indicates comparison (see section 9.6), Hebrew can indicate the superlative ("most" in English) either by a noun repeated in a construct phrase or by a substantivized adjective:

קֹ֫דֶשׁ קֳדָשִׁים ("most holy"—Lev. 7:1)

קֹ֫דֶשׁ הַקֳּדָשִׁים ("the holy of holies"—Ex. 26:34 = "the Most Holy Place")

שִׁיר הַשִּׁירִים ("the song of songs"—Song 1:1 = "the greatest of songs")

הַיָּפָה בַּנָּשִׁים ("the beautiful (one) among women"—Song 1:8 = "the most beautiful of women")

10.8 Vocabulary

בְּכוֹר	firstborn
בָּקָר	herd, cattle
בֹּ֫קֶר	morning, tomorrow
דֹּר	generation, lifetime
חֵמָה	heat, rage, wrath, poison
יָמִין	right side, right hand, south
כָּנָף	wing, skirt, edge
כַּף	palm, sole
לְבַד	except, apart from, beside
לָשׁוֹן	tongue, gulf
מָ֫וֶת	death, dying
נֶ֫גֶב	south, arid terrain
נָהָר	river
נַ֫חַל	wadi, stream
עָפָר	dust, soil
עֶ֫צֶם	bone
עֶ֫רֶב	sunset, evening
פַּ֫עַם	step, pace; time
רֵעַ	friend, companion
שֶׁ֫מֶן	oil, fat

10.9 Language Exercises

A. Identify whether the following nouns are in the absolute state, are in the construct state, or are ambiguous (potentially either absolute or construct).

סוּסָה

סוּס

סוּסַת

צוּר

אַמַּת

דִּבְרֵי

בֵּן

מְקוֹם

מִצְוָה

מֵי

עָרִים

כָּבוֹד

דְּבַר

לְבוֹת

B. Translate the following construct phrases. Use your lexicon to look up the glosses for any words you do not know from your vocabulary.

Gen. 47:27 בְּאֶ֫רֶץ מִצְרַ֫יִם

Gen. 47:26 אַדְמַת הַכֹּהֲנִים

Gen. 2:9	כָּל־עֵץ
Isa. 11:2	רוּחַ חָכְמָה
1 Chron. 29:22	בֶּן־דָּוִיד[4]
Prov. 14:19	שַׁעֲרֵי צַדִּיק
Isa. 1:19	טוּב הָאָרֶץ
Prov. 23:9	בְּאָזְנֵי כְסִיל
Ex. 3:8	מְקוֹם הַכְּנַעֲנִי
Ex. 24:10	אֱלֹהֵי יִשְׂרָאֵל

C. Translate the following and parse all verbs and participles. Use your lexicon to look up the glosses for any words you do not know from your vocabulary.

1 Chron. 23:13 בְּנֵי עַמְרָם אַהֲרֹן וּמֹשֶׁה

[4] Spelled דָּוִד (Dāwīd) in most other books but דָּוִיד (Dāwîd) in Chronicles. For the long *ḥireq* see section 1.3.

Gen. 13:14

וּרְאֵה[5] מִן־הַמָּקוֹם אֲשֶׁר־אַתָּה שָׁם צָפֹנָה וָנֶגְבָּה וָקֵדְמָה
וָיָמָּה

Gen. 1:30

וּֽלְכָל־חַיַּת הָאָרֶץ וּלְכָל־עוֹף הַשָּׁמַיִם וּלְכֹל ׀ רוֹמֵשׂ עַל־

הָאָרֶץ אֲשֶׁר־בּוֹ[6] נֶפֶשׁ חַיָּה

Ex. 3:11

מִי אָנֹכִי כִּי אֵלֵךְ אֶל־פַּרְעֹה

Neh. 4:4 [Engl. 4:10]

כָּשַׁל כֹּחַ הַסַּבָּל

Gen. 3:1

וְהַנָּחָשׁ הָיָה[7] עָרוּם מִכֹּל חַיַּת הַשָּׂדֶה אֲשֶׁר עָשָׂה[8] יְהוָה

אֱלֹהִים

---

[5] Qal Imperative ms of ראה, glossed as "to see" (see ch. 24).

[6] "In it" (see ch. 11).

[7] Qal Perf. 3ms of היה, glossed as "to be" (see ch. 24)

[8] Qal Perf. 3ms of עשה, glossed as "to make" (see ch. 24)

Ex. 4:10 לֹ֩א אִ֨ישׁ דְּבָרִ֜ים אָנֹ֗כִי

Prov. 2:20 לְ֭מַעַן תֵּלֵ֣ךְ בְּדֶ֣רֶךְ טוֹבִ֑ים וְאָרְח֖וֹת צַדִּיקִ֣ים תִּשְׁמֹֽר׃

Ex. 3:1 וּמֹשֶׁ֗ה הָיָ֥ה רֹעֶ֛ה אֶת־צֹ֛אן יִתְר֥וֹ

Ex. 3:18 וְעַתָּ֗ה נֵֽלֲכָה־נָּ֞א דֶּ֣רֶךְ שְׁלֹ֤שֶׁת יָמִים֙ בַּמִּדְבָּ֔ר

10.10 Exegetical Exercises—Sound Connections

A. Hebrew Poetry. One can quickly note the most common form of a line of Hebrew poetry by surveying almost any psalm at random. Consider Psalm 3:1–4 in the ESV translation:

1 O LORD, how many are my foes!
Many are rising against me;
2 many are saying of my soul,
there is no salvation for him in God. *Selah*

3 But you, O LORD, are a shield about me,
my glory, and the lifter of my head.
4 I cried aloud to the LORD,
and he answered me from his holy hill. *Selah*

There are four lines of poetry, each of which clearly divides into two pieces. This form of a poetic line is typically called a **bicolon**, and it is the most common (though not the only) form of a line of Hebrew poetry. A bicolon almost always contains a correspondence between the two cola (the first and second portions of the verse). This correspondence is called **parallelism**. Hebrew parallelism is most commonly a connection of meaning in some sense. In Psalm 3:1–4 there are different types of meaning correspondence between the two cola in each line of poetry, but the correspondences are clearly those of meaning.

Other forms of connection are possible, however. Consider the cases of Ecclesiastes 7:1a and Proverbs 11:2a, again in the ESV translation:

> A good name is better than precious ointment.—Eccl. 7:1a
>
> When pride comes, then comes disgrace.—Prov. 11:2a

Each of these is part of a larger line of poetry that is itself a bicolon, but each has an internal correspondence that cannot be seen in English translation. Read each aloud in Hebrew.

> ט֤וֹב שֵׁ֖ם מִשֶּׁ֣מֶן ט֑וֹב—Eccl. 7:1a
>
> בָּֽא־זָ֭דוֹן וַיָּבֹ֣א קָל֑וֹן—Prov. 11:2a

What is the correspondence? It is a correspondence of sound, the roll and echo of the words.

B. The Challenge of Translation. When translating from one language to another, there is always loss. As the Italian adage goes, *traduttore, traditore* ("translator, traitor"), a phrase made famous because it captures both meaning and sound play. Rarely is a translator so lucky as to represent both when translating a work into a different language.

In the case of Ecclesiastes 7:1a and Proverbs 11:2a, a translator faces the stark choice of accurately reflecting either the meaning of the Hebrew words or their rhythm and rhyme. In Hebrew the words שֵׁם ("name") and שֶׁמֶן ("oil/ointment") create a sound play. In English, *name* and *ointment* do not. Similarly, in Hebrew זָדוֹן ("pride") and קָלוֹן ("disgrace") rhyme, but in English they do not. To accurately reflect the meaning of the verses in English, the translator must lose the vocal connection of the sound play.

In these verses the translational loss does not significantly impede understanding, though the elegance of the poetry is of necessity compromised. In other cases, however, the use of an English text can leave the reader unaware of connections that the author would have intended.

C. Identifying Connections. Read Genesis 11:1-9 (the tower of Babel narrative) aloud in Hebrew. Reference an English Bible as necessary to help with the translation.

1. What is the stated goal of the builders in verse 4b? They wish to make a *name* for themselves. What is the Hebrew word for *name*? This word recurs in v.9 as שְׁמָהּ ("its name").

2. What word that is similar in sound occurs in verses 2, 7, 8, and 9?

3. Note verse 4's description of the tower and where its top will be. What sounds recur in the description?

4. How do the echoing sounds in these three conspicuous, repeated words help inform a reader about the exegetical point of the passage?

5. The placement of 11:1–9 in the book of Genesis is striking. Look at chapters 10–11 in an English Bible. What type of text surrounds this passage?

6. Why would one genealogy (11:10–26) be separated from the rest (10:1–32) and placed after the tower of Babel narrative in Genesis 11:1–9? Read verse 10 aloud. How does this genealogy connect to 11:1–9?[9]

7. Identify the significant descendant of the genealogy recounted in 11:10-26, who becomes the focus of the next chapters of Genesis. Look at verse 2 of Genesis 12. How does this connect to 11:1–9? Who is the actor in 12:2? How does this connection magnify the meaning of both Gen. 11:1-9 and 12:1-3?

D. Identifying Tensions. Reading a text in translation can cause a reader to miss intentional tensions that a native speaker would quickly catch.

One common rhetorical technique in wisdom literature is placing two proverbial sayings in proximity to challenge the reader to identify the senses in which each saying is true and how each statement applies. For example, consider Proverbs 26:4–5 (ESV):

> 4 Answer not a fool according to his folly, lest you be like him yourself.
>
> 5 Answer a fool according to his folly, lest he be wise in his own eyes.

Proverbs immediately challenges the reader to ask how these proverbs fit together. Should one answer a fool or not? When? How?

Here the ESV translation accurately reflects the tension in the Hebrew original. But consider the following cases.

---

[9] Note that the references to בָּבֶל and שִׁנְעָר in Gen. 10:10 may also have influenced the placement of these verses in their position in the narrative.

1. Read Ecclesiastes 2:2 and 8:15a in translation:

   "I said of laughter, 'It is mad,' and of pleasure, 'What use is it?'"—Eccl. 2:2 (ESV)

   "And I commend joy, for man has nothing better under the sun but to eat and drink and be joyful . . . ."—Eccl. 8:15a (ESV)

   Now read them in Hebrew:

   2 לִשְׂחֹ֥וק אָמַ֖רְתִּי מְהֹולָ֑ל וּלְשִׂמְחָ֖ה מַה־זֹּ֥ה עֹשָֽׂה׃

   15a וְשִׁבַּ֤חְתִּֽי אֲנִי֙ אֶת־הַשִּׂמְחָ֔ה אֲשֶׁ֨ר אֵֽין־טֹ֤וב לָֽאָדָם֙ תַּ֣חַת הַשֶּׁ֔מֶשׁ
   כִּ֛י אִם־לֶאֱכֹ֥ול וְלִשְׁתֹּ֖ות וְלִשְׂמֹ֑וחַ

   Which noun is common to the two verses? What then is the tension with which the author is wrestling?

   How could you change the ESV translation to repeat the gloss so the reader can see the tension in English?

2. Read Ecclesiastes 7:3, 9 in translation:

   "Sorrow is better than laughter, for by sadness of face the heart is made glad."—Eccl. 7:3 (ESV)

   "Be not quick in your spirit to become angry, for anger lodges in the heart of fools."—Eccl. 7:9 (ESV)

Now read them in Hebrew:

3 טֹ֥וב כַּ֖עַס מִשְּׂחֹ֑ק כִּֽי־בְרֹ֥עַ פָּנִ֖ים יִ֥יטַב לֵֽב׃

9 אַל־תְּבַהֵ֥ל בְּרֽוּחֲךָ֖ לִכְע֑וֹס כִּ֣י כַ֔עַס בְּחֵ֥יק כְּסִילִ֖ים יָנֽוּחַ׃

Which noun is common to the two verses? What then is the tension with which the author is wrestling?

How could you change the ESV translation to repeat the gloss so the reader can see the tension in English?

Knowledge of Hebrew helps you, via sound, notice connections and tensions in the text that cannot often be reflected in translation and will enrich your own study and interpretation.

יא (11) Suffixed Pronouns

11.1 Suffixed Pronouns

The independent personal pronouns (9.1) hardly exhaust the use of pronouns in Biblical Hebrew. In fact, Hebrew pronouns are regularly attached to other words as suffixes. These suffixed pronouns can be either objective (לוֹ = "to him") or possessive (דְּבָרוֹ = "his word").

There are three types of suffixed pronouns:

	Type 1	Type 2	Type 3
3ms ("him/his")	וֹ־	הוּ־	◌ָיו־
3fs ("she/her")	◌ָהּ־	הָ־	◌ֶ֫יהָ־
2ms ("you/your")	◌ְךָ־	ךָ־	◌ֶ֫יךָ־
2fs ("you/your")	◌ָךְ־	ךְ־	◌ַ֫יִךְ־
1cs ("me/my")	◌ִי־	נִי־	◌ַי־
3mp ("them/their")	הֶם־ / ◌ָם־	הֶם־	◌ֵיהֶם־
3fp ("them/their")	הֶן־ / ◌ָן־	הֶן־	◌ֵיהֶן־
2mp ("you/your")	כֶם־	כֶם־	◌ֵיכֶם־
2fp ("you/your")	כֶן־	כֶן־	◌ֵיכֶן־
1cp ("us/our")	נוּ־	נוּ־	◌ֵ֫ינוּ־

The historical development of the spelling of these suffixed forms is frequently debated because the forms appear in related, but varied, spellings in different dialects of Hebrew and other Semitic languages. The focus here is not explaining the development of the forms, but simply recognizing them as they occur in the biblical text.

11.2 Pronominal Suffixes on Prepositions and Particles

Each preposition (see section 6.4) or particle that accepts the suffixed pronouns will take one of these three types of suffixed pronouns.

לְ (Type 1)		כְּ (Type 2)		עַל (Type 3)	
לוֹ	to him	כָּמוֹהוּ	like him	עָלָיו	on him
לָהּ	to her	כָּמוֹהָ	like her	עָלֶיהָ	on her
לְךָ	to you (ms)	כָּמוֹךָ	like you (ms)	עָלֶיךָ	on you (ms)
לָךְ	to you (fs)	כָּמוֹךְ	like you (fs)	עָלַיִךְ	on you (fs)
לִי	to me	כָּמוֹנִי	like me	עָלַי	on me
לָהֶם	to them (m)	כָּהֶם	like them (m)	עֲלֵיהֶם	on them (m)
לָהֶן	to them (f)	כָּהֵן / כָּהֵנָּה	like them (f)	עֲלֵיהֶן	on them (f)
לָכֶם	to you (mp)	כָּכֶם	like you (mp)	עֲלֵיכֶם	on you (mp)
לָכֶן	to you (fp)	כָּכֶן	like you (fp)	עֲלֵיכֶן	on you (fp)
לָנוּ	to us	כָּמוֹנוּ	like us	עָלֵינוּ	on us
Also following this pattern: בְּ עִם אֵת בֵּין הִנֵּה יֵשׁ אַיִן		Also following this pattern: מִן עוֹד אַיִן		Also following this pattern: אֶל עַד תַּחַת אַחֲרֵי לִפְנֵי סָבִיב	

Each of these three paradigms must be memorized.

Notes:

Type 1 suffixes:

- Note in 11.1 the possibility of alternative forms of the Type 1 suffixes in the 3mp and 3fp forms.
- עָלָיו, the 3ms form of עַל (Type 3), is pronounced *ʿālâw*. The spelling, which would imply a pronunciation of *ʿālāyw*, is an historical spelling.[1]
- עִם and אֵת both take Type 1 suffixes. Each form is from a geminate base[2] (עמם and אתת), and the attested forms with suffixes therefore show a doubling, e.g.: עִמּוֹ ("with him") and אִתָּהּ ("with her").

[1] An historical spelling is a "holdover" spelling from a time when a word had a different pronunciation. Over time, the spoken form of a language will drift, but the spelling of written forms often changes more slowly, leading to cases where a word is written one way but spoken aloud in a way that does not seem to match the spelling.

[2] In a geminate noun (see 6.2) the second and third root letters are identical.

- The marker of the definite direct object (אֵת) is spelled identically to the preposition אֵת, but with suffixed pronouns they can be distinguished because the marker of the definite direct object takes the form ־אֹת or ־אֶת (each without doubling) instead of ־אִתּ (with doubling). Hence:
  - אֹתוֹ = "him" (direct object), but אִתּוֹ = "with him" (prepositional phrase)
  - אֶתְכֶם = "you (mp)" (direct object), but אִתְּכֶם = "with you (mp)" (prepositional phrase)
- עִמִּי (the 1cs form of עִם) also has an irregular (but quite common) alternative form as עִמָּדִי.
- The accent on the 1cp form is essential, since the same form accented on the ultima could look like the perfect form of a III-*heh* verb (see 23.2).
- The 1cs and 1cp forms of הִנֵּה do not show the expected *dagesh* in the *nun*, instead being הִנְנִי and הִנְנוּ.
- The 3ms suffix attached to יֵשׁ creates the form יֶשְׁנוֹ instead of the expected יֵשׁוֹ.
- אַיִן can take either a Type 1 or Type 2 suffix.

Type 2 suffixes:

- Both כְּ and מִן attach the singular suffixes to a longer form of the pronoun, ־כָּמוֹ and ־מִמֶּנ, respectively.
- For מִן:
  - The *nun* of this form assimilates in the 2ms and 2fs, producing מִמְּךָ and מִמֵּךְ.
  - In the 3ms and 3fs forms the *nun* remains, but the *heh* of the suffix assimilates, producing מִמֶּ֫נּוּ and מִמֶּ֫נָּה.
  - In addition to the expected 1cs form מִמֶּ֫נִּי, a shortened form (מִנִּי) is common.

Type 3 suffixes:

- The preposition לִפְנֵי takes the form ־לְפָנ for all singular forms and for the 1cp. Hence: לְפָנָיו and לְפָנֵ֫ינוּ, etc.

11.3 Pronominal Suffixes on Nouns

Pronominal suffixes are attached to the **construct form** of a noun. Singular nouns take Type 1 suffixes (with minor changes), while dual and plural nouns take Type 3 suffixes.

Because the suffixes themselves have both singular and plural forms and the noun can have singular and plural forms, the full paradigm is quite extensive.

Masculine Singular Noun (Type 1 Suffixes)	
סוּסוֹ	his horse
סוּסָהּ	her horse
סוּסְךָ	your (ms) horse
סוּסֵךְ	your (fs) horse
סוּסִי	my horse
סוּסָם	their (m) horse
סוּסָן	their (f) horse
סוּסְכֶם	your (mp) horse
סוּסְכֶן	your (fp) horse
סוּסֵ֫נוּ	our horse

Feminine Singular Noun (Type 1 Suffixes)	
סוּסָתוֹ	his mare
סוּסָתָהּ	her mare
סוּסָֽתְךָ	your (ms) mare
סוּסָתֵךְ	your (fs) mare
סוּסָתִי	my mare
סוּסָתָם	their (m) mare
סוּסָתָן	their (f) mare
סוּסַתְכֶם	your (mp) mare
סוּסַתְכֶן	your (fp) mare
סוּסָתֵ֫נוּ	our mare

Masculine Plural Noun (Type 3 Suffixes)	
סוּסָיו	his horses
סוּסֶ֫יהָ	her horses
סוּסֶ֫יךָ	your (ms) horses
סוּסַ֫יִךְ	your (fs) horses
סוּסַי	my horses
סוּסֵיהֶם	their (m) horses
סוּסֵיהֶן	their (f) horses
סוּסֵיכֶם	your (mp) horses
סוּסֵיכֶן	your (fp) horses
סוּסֵ֫ינוּ	our horses

Feminine Plural Noun (Type 3 Suffixes)	
סוּסוֹתָיו	his mares
סוּסוֹתֶ֫יהָ	her mares
סוּסוֹתֶ֫יךָ	your (ms) mares
סוּסוֹתַ֫יִךְ	your (fs) mares
סוּסוֹתַי	my mares
סוּסוֹתֵיהֶם	their (m) mares
סוּסוֹתֵיהֶן	their (f) mares
סוּסוֹתֵיכֶם	your (mp) mares
סוּסוֹתֵיכֶן	your (fp) mares
סוּסוֹתֵ֫ינוּ	our mares

These forms connect to the nouns based on the endings exhibited, not the actual gender of the noun.

These paradigms do not need to be memorized; they simply apply the patterns from 11.2 to the masculine and feminine forms of the noun. These paradigms should be studied, however, until you can easily identify both noun and suffix.

Adding pronominal suffixes to nouns lengthens the word, which can cause familiar changes. For example, propretonic reduction is common:

דָּבָר   דָּ | בָר

(but)   tonic | pretonic

דְּבָרוֹ   דְּ | בָ | רוֹ

tonic | pretonic | propretonic

In other cases, the addition of the suffix and vowel reduction would cause two vocal *shewas* in succession, triggering the rule of *shewa*:

צְדָקָה   צְ | דָ | קָה

(but)   tonic | pretonic | propretonic

צִדְקָתוֹ   צְ | דְ | קָ | תוֹ *

tonic | pretonic | propretonic | first

Notes:

- When suffixes are attached to segolate nouns (6.1), the original vowel pattern (qiṭl, qaṭl, qoṭl [quṭl]) is often seen, though it is not evident in some forms of the plural because of vowel reduction:

  מֶ֫לֶךְ = "a king," but "their king" = מַלְכָּם (from the original *מַלְךְ)
  עֲטֶרֶת־מַלְכָּם ("the crown of their king"—2 Sam. 12:30)

  מְלָכִים = "kings," but "our kings" = מְלָכֵ֫ינוּ (from the original *מַלְךְ)
  אֲנַחְנוּ מְלָכֵ֫ינוּ כֹהֲנֵ֫ינוּ ("we, our kings, our priests"—Ezra 9:7)

- When suffixes are attached to geminate nouns (6.2), the doubling of the second and third root letter will reappear:

עַם = "a people," but "his people" = עַמּוֹ
וַיֹּאמֶר אֶל־עַמּוֹ ("And he said to his people"—Ex. 1:9)

חֹק = "a statute," but "their statutes" = חֻקֵּם
וּבְחֻקֹּתֵיהֶם לֹא תֵלֵכוּ ("And in their statutes you shall not walk"—Lev. 18:3)

- When suffixes are attached to a nouns containing a diphthong (4.2), the contraction patterns occur:

מָוֶת = "death," but "her death" = מוֹתָהּ
וּכְעֵת מוּתָהּ ("and around the time of her death"—1 Sam. 4:20)

- Recall that some nouns have irregular construct forms (10.4), such as אָב. This impacts the addition of suffixed pronouns:

אָב = "father," but "her father" = אָבִיהָ
וַתֹּאמֶר אֶל־אָבִיהָ ("And she said to her father"—Gen. 31:35)

- The common nouns בֵּן (son) and שֵׁם (name) reduce their vowel with the addition of the suffix. This often causes the application of the rule of *shewa*, producing a *hireq*:

בֵּן = "son," but "my son" = בְּנִי
וְלֹא־יִמְשֹׁל בְּנִי בָּכֶם ("And my son will not rule over you."—Judg. 8:23)

בֵּן = "son," but "your son" = בִּנְךָ
שְׁלְחָה אֵלַי אֶת־דָּוִד בִּנְךָ ("Send David your son to me."—1 Sam. 16:19)

שֵׁם = "name," but "his name" = שְׁמוֹ
וַיִּקְרָא אֶת־שְׁמוֹ אֱנוֹשׁ ("And he called his name Enosh."—Gen. 4:26)

שֵׁם = "name," but "your name" = שִׁמְךָ
וְהָיָה שִׁמְךָ אַבְרָהָם ("But your name will be Abraham."—Gen. 17:5)

- The common nouns אִשָּׁה (woman, wife) and בַּת (daughter) revert to a more original form of the noun:

  אִשָּׁה = "woman, wife," but "my wife" = אִשְׁתִּי
  כִּי־הִיא לֹא אִשְׁתִּי ("for she is not my wife"—Hos. 2:4)

  בַּת = "daughter," but "his daughter" = בִּתּוֹ
  וּבִתּוֹ שֶׁאֱרָה ("And his daughter was Sheerah."—1 Chron. 7:24)

11.4 Resumptive Pronouns

In relative clauses (clauses usually introduced by אֲשֶׁר but also sometimes by שֶׁ), the clause is often concluded by a preposition with a suffixed pronoun. This **resumptive pronoun** helps clarify the referent of the clause, but it would be redundant in English and therefore is not translated.

בַּדֶּרֶךְ אֲשֶׁר תֵּלְכוּ־בָהּ (lit. "on the journey which you would go *on it*"—Gen. 42:38 → "on the journey on which you would go")

גּוֹי אֲשֶׁר לֹא־תִשְׁמַע לְשֹׁנוֹ (lit. "a nation which you will not understand *its* language"—Deut. 28:49 → "a nation whose language you will not understand")

11.5 Possession

Possession is often expressed by a simple suffixed pronoun, as above. Possession may also be expressed by the combination of יֵשׁ and לְ. Woodenly, this would be "There is to X . . . ," expressing possession.

יֶשׁ־לִי רָב ("I have plenty."—Gen. 33:9)

Nonpossession is most commonly expressed by the combination of אֵין and לְ:

אֵין לָהּ וָלָד ("She had no child."—Gen. 11:30)

11.6 Vocabulary

אֱמֶת[3]	truth, trustworthiness, faithfulness
גָּדוֹל	great
גֵּר	stranger, alien (protected citizen)
חַטָּאת	sin, sin offering
טָמֵא	unclean, ceremonially unclean
יְשׁוּעָה[4]	help, salvation, deliverance
יֶ֫תֶר	remainder, excess
מַחֲנֶה	camp, army
מַטֶּה	stick, staff; tribe
מִלְחָמָה	battle, war
מֶ֫לֶךְ	king, ruler
מַמְלָכָה	dominion, kingdom
מִשְׁפָּט	decision, judgment; law
מִשְׁתֶּה	banquet, feast
עֶ֫בֶד	servant, slave
עֲבוֹדָה	work, service; worship
עוֹד	again, still, as long as
פָּנִים	front, face
פֶּ֫תַח	opening, entrance, door
שָׁכַב	to lie down, to have sex

[3] אֱמֶת is not a segolate and is therefore stressed on the final syllable. It is from the root אמן, with a likely original form * אֱמֶנְתְ.

[4] This is the name of Jesus in Hebrew, a variant of the name יְהוֹשׁוּעָה ("Joshua.")

11.7 Language Exercises

A. Identify the noun and the possessive suffix; then translate the phrase.

Example: דְּבָרְךָ- דָּבָר + 2ms suffix = your word

בְּנִי

אֱלֹהֵיהֶם

אֲבִיהֶם

אֲחֵיכֶם

אֱלֹהֶיךָ

אָחִינוּ

עָרֵיהֶם

אֲדֹנִי

חֻקֹּתֶיךָ

שְׁמֶךָ

B. Identify the preposition or particle and the suffix; then translate the phrase.

Example: עִמָּכֶם – עִם + 2mp suffix = with you (mp)

אִתָּנוּ

אִתְּכֶם

לוֹ

אֵלֶיךָ

אֲלֵהֶם

הִנְנִי

לְךָ

אֵלֵינוּ

אֵלָיו

C. Translate the following sentences and parse each verb and participle. Use your lexicon to look up the glosses for any words you do not know from your vocabulary.

Ex. 4:5 יְהוָה אֱלֹהֵי אֲבֹתָם אֱלֹהֵי אַבְרָהָם אֱלֹהֵי יִצְחָק וֵאלֹהֵי יַעֲקֹב

Gen. 47:29 אִם־נָא מָצָאתִי חֵן בְּעֵינֶיךָ

Ex. 3:13 מַה־שְּׁמוֹ מָה אֹמַר[5] אֲלֵהֶם׃

Judg. 9:1 וְאֶל־כָּל־מִשְׁפַּחַת בֵּית־אֲבִי אִמּוֹ[6]

Gen. 43:8 שִׁלְחָה הַנַּעַר אִתִּי

Isa. 6:8, altered שָׁמַעְתִּי אֶת־הַקּוֹל אֹמֵר אֶת־מִי אֶשְׁלַח וּמִי יֵלֶךְ־לָנוּ

Num. 27:9a וְאִם־אֵין לוֹ בַּת

Ex. 4:4a, altered אָמַר יְהוָה אֶל־מֹשֶׁה שְׁלַח יָדְךָ וֶאֱחֹז בִּזְנָבוֹ

[5] Qal Imperf. 1cs of אמר, glossed as “to say” (see ch. 22)

[6] Note that there are four construct nouns before the absolute noun in this phrase. The awkward phrasing seems to be a patriarchal method of referring to maternal ancestry.

Ex. 3:5b כִּ֣י הַמָּק֗וֹם אֲשֶׁ֤ר אַתָּה֙ עוֹמֵ֣ד עָלָ֔יו אַדְמַת־קֹ֖דֶשׁ הֽוּא׃

1 Kings 1:11, altered אָמַר נָתָן אֶל־בַּת־שֶׁבַע אֵם־שְׁלֹמֹה֙ הֲל֣וֹא שָׁמַ֔עַתְּ כִּ֥י מָלַ֖ךְ אֲדֹנִיָּ֣הוּ

בֶן־חַגִּ֑ית וַאֲדֹנֵ֥ינוּ דָוִ֖ד לֹ֥א יָדָֽע׃

11.8 Exegetical Exercises—Using the Masoretic Accentual System

Until now you have used the Masoretic accents solely for noting where the stress is placed in a word. While a full explanation of the Masoretic accentuation system is beyond the scope of an introductory course, one basic feature—the major disjunctive accents—is particularly helpful to beginning readers. You will have noticed in the text that each word that is individually pronounced has an accent placed on it. These accents are of two types—conjunctive (connecting two words) and disjunctive (dividing two words)—and they are used in the cantillation (singing) of the text in the synagogue. The disjunctive accents are most helpful to the beginning reader because they provide conceptual divisions within a verse.

There are two different accentuation systems: one for the books of Psalms, Proverbs, and Job, and the one for the rest of the Old Testament. Only the latter is covered here. There are eighteen disjunctive accents in this part of the Masoretic accentuation system, with the first eight falling into three tiers:

1. Primary Division—the ***ṣillûq***. The text that the Masoretes received indicated verse divisions with the *soph pasûq*, the large colon that follows each verse. For example, Genesis 1:1:

   בְּרֵאשִׁ֖ית בָּרָ֣א אֱלֹהִ֑ים אֵ֥ת הַשָּׁמַ֖יִם וְאֵ֥ת הָאָֽרֶץ׃

   The *ṣillûq*, which is under the *aleph* on הָאָֽרֶץ, accompanies the *soph pasûq* on the last word of the verse.

2. Second Division—the ***athnach***. The verse is then divided into two portions (often termed the A and B portions) by the *athnach*, the caret-shaped accent. These divisions do not need to be equal in length (though they often are similar). The *athnach* instead marks the verse's conceptual midpoint, and it is placed on the last word of the first portion of the verse. In Genesis 1:1 above, the *athnach* is under the *heh* in אֱלֹהִ֑ים.

3. Third Division—Multiple Options. In a short verse such as Genesis 1:1, there is little need for more disjunctive accents; in a longer verse, more disjunctive accents come into play. The next tier of disjunctive accents is illustrated on the word אֶ֫רֶץ:

   אֶ֒רֶץ Segolta

   אֶ֓רֶץ Shalshelet

   אֶ֔רֶץ Zaqef qaton

   אֶ֕רֶץ Zaqef gadol

   אֶ֗רֶץ Revia

   אֶ֖רֶץ Tifcha

   Each of these disjunctive accents has approximately equal rank, subdividing either the A or the B portion of a verse.

These accents allow the beginning reader to subdivide a verse into more manageable portions, which can be considered somewhat independently. For students facing a long verse, these accents break the text into bite-size pieces for initial translation work. The accentuation is not to be considered inspired, and sometimes scholars rightly disagree with the current accentuation of certain verses. But the accentuation recorded in the Masoretic Text is a faithful record of the reading tradition of the text as the Masoretes received it. At a minimum the accents provide a record of how the Masoretes understood the conceptual division of each verse, and even if the advanced student may begin to find places where he or she disagrees with the priority of the Masoretic accents, the beginning student usually finds them to be a welcome help.

For the following passage, mark each of the three levels of division:

1. Note the *ṣillûq* and the *soph pasûq* dividing the text into verses.
2. For each verse, find the *athnach* and mark the division of the verse between the A and B portions.
3. Find the next-level accent and mark the division(s) *within* the A and B portions. (The text will contain many additional accents, which you may disregard at this juncture.)

Gen. 1:1-8

בְּרֵאשִׁ֖ית בָּרָ֣א אֱלֹהִ֑ים אֵ֥ת הַשָּׁמַ֖יִם וְאֵ֥ת הָאָֽרֶץ׃ וְהָאָ֗רֶץ הָיְתָ֥ה תֹ֙הוּ֙ וָבֹ֔הוּ וְחֹ֖שֶׁךְ
עַל־פְּנֵ֣י תְה֑וֹם וְר֣וּחַ אֱלֹהִ֔ים מְרַחֶ֖פֶת עַל־פְּנֵ֥י הַמָּֽיִם׃ וַיֹּ֥אמֶר אֱלֹהִ֖ים יְהִ֣י א֑וֹר וַֽיְהִי־
אֽוֹר׃ וַיַּ֧רְא אֱלֹהִ֛ים אֶת־הָא֖וֹר כִּי־ט֑וֹב וַיַּבְדֵּ֣ל אֱלֹהִ֔ים בֵּ֥ין הָא֖וֹר וּבֵ֥ין הַחֹֽשֶׁךְ׃
וַיִּקְרָ֨א אֱלֹהִ֤ים ׀ לָאוֹר֙ י֔וֹם וְלַחֹ֖שֶׁךְ קָ֣רָא לָ֑יְלָה וַֽיְהִי־עֶ֥רֶב וַֽיְהִי־בֹ֖קֶר י֥וֹם אֶחָֽד׃ פ
וַיֹּ֣אמֶר אֱלֹהִ֔ים יְהִ֥י רָקִ֖יעַ בְּת֣וֹךְ הַמָּ֑יִם וִיהִ֣י מַבְדִּ֔יל בֵּ֥ין מַ֖יִם לָמָֽיִם׃ וַיַּ֣עַשׂ אֱלֹהִים֮
אֶת־הָרָקִיעַ֒ וַיַּבְדֵּ֗ל בֵּ֤ין הַמַּ֙יִם֙ אֲשֶׁר֙ מִתַּ֣חַת לָרָקִ֔יעַ וּבֵ֣ין הַמַּ֔יִם אֲשֶׁ֖ר מֵעַ֣ל לָרָקִ֑יעַ
וַֽיְהִי־כֵֽן׃ וַיִּקְרָ֧א אֱלֹהִ֛ים לָֽרָקִ֖יעַ שָׁמָ֑יִם וַֽיְהִי־עֶ֥רֶב וַֽיְהִי־בֹ֖קֶר י֥וֹם שֵׁנִֽי׃

יב (12) Qal Narrative and Converted Perfect

12.1 The Preterite

The imperfect conjugation (5.1) is known as a **prefix conjugation** because it is dominated by the addition of prefixes to the verbal root. Older Semitic languages, from which Hebrew descended, had a second prefix conjugation known as the **preterite**, which indicated past time.[1] The imperfect conjugation originally involved a longer vowel ending at the end of the word, and the preterite had a shorter ending (or no vowel ending) at the end of the word. By the time of Biblical Hebrew, however, these final vowels had been dropped, making the imperfect appear identical to the preterite.

The preterite survives in Biblical Hebrew mainly in poetic passages and in a specific conjugation called the narrative tense (also often called the **waw-consecutive** or the ***wayyiqṭol***):

יָ֤שֶׁת חֹ֨שֶׁךְ סִתְר֗וֹ ("He made darkness his covering,"—Ps. 18:2)

וַיֹּ֣אמֶר יְהוָ֗ה ("And the LORD said . . ."—Gen. 6:7)

In prose the preterite also occasionally appears in a non-narrative tense form, often following the adverb אָז ("then"):

אָ֣ז יָשִֽׁיר־מֹשֶׁה֩ וּבְנֵ֨י יִשְׂרָאֵ֜ל אֶת־הַשִּׁירָ֤ה הַזֹּאת֙ לַֽיהוָ֔ה ("Then Moses and the people of Israel sang this song to the LORD,"—Ex. 15:1)

12.2 The Qal Narrative

The **narrative tense** is by far the most common use of the preterite in Biblical Hebrew. The narrative verb indicates *sequential action in past time*, making it a regular feature of most narrative passages in the Old Testament.

---

[1] See 3.7. Whereas debate continues regarding the exact nuances of elements in the Hebrew finite verbal system, the preterite is the one form in Biblical Hebrew that is clearly tensed, indicating past time action.

The form of the Qal narrative appears *as if* the imperfect received the addition of a *waw* and the doubling of its first letter:[2]

Imperfect	Narrative
יִקְטֹל	וַיִּקְטֹל
יִשְׁלַח	וַיִּשְׁלַח

Thus each of these forms would be parsed as a Qal narrative 3ms of קטל or שׁלח, respectively.

For the narrative 1cs form the *aleph* cannot double, resulting in compensatory lengthening of the *pataḥ* vowel associated with the *waw* to *qameṣ* (see 4.5):

Imperfect	Narrative
אֶעֱמֹד	וָאֶעֱמֹד

Remember that *this relationship between the narrative and the imperfect is only "as if,"* because the narrative is a remnant of the preterite, not an adaptation of the imperfect conjugation.

Also note the difference between the narrative form and the *waw* + imperfect:

Narrative	*Waw* + Imperfect
וַיִּקְטֹל	וְיִקְטֹל
וַיִּשְׁלַח	וְיִשְׁלַח

The narrative has a *pataḥ or qameṣ* and the doubling of the letter following the *waw*, whereas a *waw* + imperfect has a *shewa* and no doubling of the following letter.

The narrative tense has the most restricted use of any Hebrew conjugation, being used almost exclusively for the sequential telling of past-tense narration. Given the large amount of narrative text in Biblical Hebrew, however, it occurs frequently. Though I-*aleph* verbs will not be fully discussed until chapter 22, note that the common verb אָמַר shows a slightly

[2] Some grammars refer to the narrative tense as a "**converted imperfect**." This terminology, however, is historically inaccurate and often confusing to the student, so it will be avoided here.

different vowel pattern (a *ḥolem* in the first syllable) in both the imperfect and narrative forms because the first radical is an *aleph*:

Imperfect	Narrative
יֹאמַ֫ר	וַיֹּאמַ֫ר
יֹ֫אמֶר	וַיֹּ֫אמֶר

These forms and the other narrative forms have no difference in meaning—only a difference in vowel occasioned by *aleph* as the first root letter.[3] Both of these forms are 3ms, differing only in the character of the vowel on the *mem*. The *ḥolem* occurs through the entire imperfect and narrative conjugations (e.g.: not just 3ms, but also 3fs, 2ms, 2fs, etc.).

12.3 The Qal Converted Perfect

A "simple *waw*" (*waw* + *shewa*) can also be prefixed to a perfect conjugation verb, making a **converted perfect.**[4] Whereas the narrative form shows sequence in past-tense narration, the converted perfect shows sequence in other contexts. This sequence can be for future action, various modal senses, an imperative sense, or an ongoing/iterative past action:

וְלָקַחְתִּ֫י[5] אֶתְכֶם לִי לְעָם ("And I will take you for myself as a people"—Ex. 6:7)

וּשְׁמָרַ֫נִי בַּדֶּרֶךְ הַזֶּה אֲשֶׁר אָנֹכִי הוֹלֵךְ ("If he will guard me on this way which I am going . . . ."—Gen. 28:20)

וְאָהַבְתָּ֫ אֵת יְהוָה אֱלֹהֶיךָ ("And you shall love the LORD your God"—Deut. 6:5)

וְהִשְׁקָה אֶת־כָּל־פְּנֵי־הָאֲדָמָה ("It would water all the face of the ground"—Gen. 2:6b)

The converted perfect form is parsed as a converted perfect, but it takes its translational sense from the verb that leads off its sequence. For example, consider the larger context of two of the examples above:

---

[3] This is a phonological change that also occurs for other verbs whose first root letter is *aleph*; it is not a change that impacts the parsing or the meaning of the word.

[4] Whereas the narrative form *appears* to be (but is not) a converted imperfect, the converted perfect truly is a perfect form converted into a future or modal use. It most likely arose on analogy with the narrative tense.

[5] Note that the 1cs and 2ms forms of the converted perfect have the accent on the final syllable, a formal indicator of the converted perfect. The same is true for Deut. 6:5 that follows.

אִם־יִהְיֶה אֱלֹהִים עִמָּדִי וּשְׁמָרַנִי בַּדֶּרֶךְ הַזֶּה אֲשֶׁר אָנֹכִי הוֹלֵךְ	("If God will be with me, and if he will guard me on this way which I am going"—Gen. 28:20)

יִהְיֶה = Qal imperfect 3ms of היה—translated as conditional because of אִם: "if he will"

וּשְׁמָרַנִי = Qal converted perfect 3ms of שׁמר—translated also as conditional: "if he will guard"

וְאֵד יַעֲלֶה מִן־הָאָרֶץ וְהִשְׁקָה אֶת־כָּל־פְּנֵי־הָאֲדָמָה׃	("And a mist would go up from the earth and it would water all the face of the ground."—Gen. 2:6)

יַעֲלֶה = Qal imperfect 3ms of עלה—translated as past durative: "would go up"

וְהִשְׁקָה = Hiphil (see ch. 16) converted perfect 3ms of שׁקה—translated also as past durative: "would water"

12.4 Word Order and Hebrew Narrative Patterns

A. Past-Tense Narration. Hebrew narratives usually begin either with a perfect verbal form or with the verb וַיְהִי (the Qal narrative 3ms of היה—"and it was"),[6] followed by a sequence of narrative verbs.

Narr. Perf.

וּמִקְנֶה רַב הָיָה לִבְנֵי רְאוּבֵן וְלִבְנֵי־גָד עָצוּם מְאֹד וַיִּרְאוּ אֶת־אֶרֶץ יַעְזֵר וְאֶת־אֶרֶץ גִּלְעָד

Narr. Narr.

וְהִנֵּה הַמָּקוֹם מְקוֹם מִקְנֶה׃ וַיָּבֹאוּ בְנֵי־גָד וּבְנֵי רְאוּבֵן וַיֹּאמְרוּ אֶל־מֹשֶׁה וְאֶל־אֶלְעָזָר הַכֹּהֵן

("And the possessions of the children of Reuben and the children of Gad were great, exceedingly so, and they saw the land of Jazer and the land of Gilead, and the place

[6] For the lack of doubling of the *yod*, see 4.4. Compare this form with the jussive of היה (see section 7.4).

was a place of livestock. And the children of Reuben and the children of Gad came, and they said to Moses and to Eliezer the priest . . . ."—Num. 32:1-2)

Narr. וַיְהִי

וַיְהִי אַחֲרֵי מוֹת יְהוֹשֻׁעַ וַיִּשְׁאֲלוּ בְּנֵי יִשְׂרָאֵל בַּיהוָה

"And after[7] the death of Joshua, the children of Israel enquired of the LORD"—Judg. 1:1a

B. Future or Modal Narration. Similarly, a future or conditional narrative sequence begins with a verb that establishes the verbal sense of the passage. This form is then followed by a series of converted perfect forms:

Conv. Perf. Imperf.

עַל־כֵּן יַעֲזָב־אִישׁ אֶת־אָבִיו וְאֶת־אִמּוֹ וְדָבַק בְּאִשְׁתּוֹ וְהָיוּ לְבָשָׂר אֶחָד׃ ("Therefore a man shall leave his father and his mother and he shall cleave to his wife and they shall be one flesh."—Gen. 2:24)

[7] More woodenly "And it was, after . . . ." However, וַיְהִי marks the beginning of the narrative unit and is often best left untranslated.

12.5 Vocabulary

לָמַד	to learn
מִשְׁכָּן	abode, the tabernacle (cf: שָׁכַן below)
קָבַר	to bury
קֶ֫בֶר	grave
קֶ֫רֶב	entrails, inner parts
קָרַב	to draw near, approach
קָרוֹב	nearby, close
קָרְבָּן[8]	offering, gift
רֹעֶה	shepherd
שָׁפַךְ	to pour, shed blood; to pour out; to heap up
שָׂרַף	to burn
שָׁבַר	to break, break down
שֶׁ֫בֶר	breaking, break; collapse
שָׁכַן	to dwell, reside
שָׁכֵן	resident, neighbor
שָׁלוֹם	prosperity, success; welfare; peace
שָׁלֵם[9]	to be completed, ready; to be healthy, unharmed; to keep peace
שָׁלֵם	(adj.) whole, untouched, undivided
שֶׁ֫לֶם	salvation or peace offering

[8] See Mark 7:11 **κορβᾶν** ("Corban").

[9] The sense of the name שְׁלֹמֹה ("Solomon") should therefore be apparent.

12.6 Language Exercises

A. Parse and translate the following forms.

וַיֹּ֫אמֶר

תִּתֵּן

וְאֶתְּנָה

וַתִּצְחַק

הוֹלֵךְ

נֹפֶ֫לֶת

וַיִּפֹּל

סְפֹר

וַתִּקְרָא

וְנִשְׁבְּרָה

וַיִּקַּח

וַיִּתֵּן

וַיְהִי

נָפְלָה

וַיֹּ֫אמְרוּ

B. Translate the following sentences and parse each verb and participle. Use your lexicon to look up the glosses for any words you do not know from your vocabulary.

Ex. 18:17 וַיֹּ֛אמֶר חֹתֵ֥ן מֹשֶׁ֖ה אֵלָ֑יו לֹא־טוֹב֙ הַדָּבָ֔ר אֲשֶׁ֥ר אַתָּ֖ה עֹשֶֽׂה׃

Gen. 43:8a וַיֹּאמֶר֩ יְהוּדָ֨ה אֶל־יִשְׂרָאֵ֜ל אָבִ֗יו שִׁלְחָ֥ה הַנַּ֛עַר אִתִּ֖י

Ex. 1:9 וַיֹּ֖אמֶר אֶל־עַמּ֑וֹ הִנֵּ֗ה עַ֚ם בְּנֵ֣י יִשְׂרָאֵ֔ל רַ֥ב וְעָצ֖וּם מִמֶּֽנּוּ׃

Ex. 7:4a וְלֹֽא־יִשְׁמַ֤ע אֲלֵכֶם֙ פַּרְעֹ֔ה וְנָתַתִּ֥י אֶת־יָדִ֖י בְּמִצְרָ֑יִם

Gen. 43:1 וְהָרָעָ֖ב כָּבֵ֥ד בָּאָֽרֶץ׃

Ex. 6:30 וַיֹּ֥אמֶר מֹשֶׁ֖ה לִפְנֵ֣י יְהוָ֑ה הֵ֤ן אֲנִי֙ עֲרַ֣ל שְׂפָתַ֔יִם וְאֵ֕יךְ יִשְׁמַ֥ע אֵלַ֖י
פַּרְעֹֽה׃

Ex. 3:1a

וּמֹשֶׁ֗ה הָיָ֥ה רֹעֶ֛ה אֶת־צֹ֛אן יִתְר֥וֹ חֹתְנ֖וֹ כֹּהֵ֣ן מִדְיָ֑ן

Ex. 3:5

וַיֹּ֖אמֶר אַל־תִּקְרַ֣ב הֲלֹ֑ם שַׁל[10]־נְעָלֶ֙יךָ֙ מֵעַ֣ל רַגְלֶ֔יךָ כִּ֣י הַמָּק֗וֹם אֲשֶׁ֤ר אַתָּה֙

עוֹמֵ֣ד עָלָ֔יו אַדְמַת־קֹ֖דֶשׁ הֽוּא׃

Ex. 3:6a

וַיֹּ֗אמֶר אָנֹכִי֙ אֱלֹהֵ֣י אָבִ֔יךָ אֱלֹהֵ֧י אַבְרָהָ֛ם אֱלֹהֵ֥י יִצְחָ֖ק וֵאלֹהֵ֣י יַעֲקֹ֑ב

Num. 32:29, altered

וַיֹּ֨אמֶר מֹשֶׁ֜ה אֲלֵהֶ֗ם אִם־יַעַבְר֣וּ בְנֵי־גָ֣ד וּבְנֵי־רְאוּבֵ֣ן׀ אִ֠תְּכֶם אֶת־

הַיַּרְדֵּ֞ן כָּל־חָל֤וּץ לַמִּלְחָמָה֙ לִפְנֵ֣י יְהוָ֔ה וּנְתַתֶּ֥ם לָהֶ֛ם אֶת־אֶ֥רֶץ הַגִּלְעָ֖ד

לַאֲחֻזָּֽה׃

12.7 Exegetical Exercises—Irony

Names in Biblical Hebrew usually have significance, indicating something about the individual in question, the events or national situation at the time of his or her birth, etc. In translation, names are usually transliterated (rendered in the letters of the new language, but with the

[10] Qal Imperative ms of נשׁל, glossed as "to loosen."

original sounds), not translated.[11] Exceptions occur when the names can be easily understood in either language (e.g.: *Shoemaker* in English and *Schumacher* in German), but for the most part translation of names would create great confusion in the reader, leaving him or her unable to easily track proper nouns.

Unfortunately, the meaning of those names is lost in transliteration, which often causes readers to miss connections or ironies in the passage in question. For example, consider the beginning of the book of Ruth. Translate Ruth 1:1-3 with your lexicon and the notes provided. Names are in gray text.

וַיְהִ֗י בִּימֵי֙ שְׁפֹ֣ט הַשֹּׁפְטִ֔ים וַיְהִ֥י רָעָ֖ב בָּאָ֑רֶץ וַיֵּ֨לֶךְ אִ֜ישׁ מִבֵּ֧ית לֶ֣חֶם יְהוּדָ֗ה לָגוּר֙[12]
בִּשְׂדֵ֣י מוֹאָ֔ב ה֥וּא וְאִשְׁתּ֖וֹ וּשְׁנֵ֥י[13] בָנָֽיו׃ וְשֵׁ֣ם הָאִ֣ישׁ אֱלִימֶ֡לֶךְ וְשֵׁם֩ אִשְׁתּ֨וֹ נָעֳמִ֜י וְשֵׁ֥ם
שְׁנֵֽי־בָנָ֣יו ׀ מַחְל֤וֹן וְכִלְיוֹן֙ אֶפְרָתִ֔ים מִבֵּ֥ית לֶ֖חֶם יְהוּדָ֑ה וַיָּבֹ֥אוּ[14] שְׂדֵי־מוֹאָ֖ב וַיִּֽהְיוּ[15]־
שָֽׁם׃ וַיָּ֥מָת[16] אֱלִימֶ֖לֶךְ אִ֣ישׁ נָעֳמִ֑י וַתִּשָּׁאֵ֥ר[17] הִ֖יא וּשְׁנֵ֥י בָנֶֽיהָ׃

Instead of transliterating the following names, determine their meanings:

בֵּית לֶ֫חֶם —This name is a construct phrase.

אֱלִימֶ֫לֶךְ —This name is a verbless clause.

[11] The names were usually originally transliterated into German and came into English usage via the German forms. This is why many names in the English Old Testament begin with *J*. In German the letter *j* is used to transliterate the Hebrew *yod*, whereas English typically transliterates the Hebrew *yod* with *y*.

[12] Qal Inf. Const. of גור, glossed as "to sojourn" (see ch. 26).

[13] This is the construct form of the numeral *two*—translate as "two of" (see ch. 18).

[14] Qal Narr. 3mp of בוא, glossed as "to go" (see ch. 26).

[15] Qal Narr. 3mp of היה, glossed as "to be" (see ch. 24).

[16] Qal Narr. 3ms of מות, glossed as "to die" (see ch. 26).

[17] Niph. Narr. 3fs of נשׁא, glossed as "to be left"—translate as "she was left" (see ch. 19).

מַחְלוֹן —This name is from the root חלה. Look up that root in your lexicon. What is its gloss? What is the meaning of the name?

כִּלְיוֹן —This name is most likely from the root כלה. Look up that root in your lexicon. What is its gloss? What is the meaning of the name?

Now consider the ironies that begin the book of Ruth:

What is the agricultural situation in Bethlehem? What is the irony of its name?

What occurred to Elimelech, Naomi's husband, in verse 3? How does that set the book of Ruth off on an ironic note?

What is the meaning of the name נָעֳמִי? (Look it up in your lexicon. If the name is not in the lexicon, look up its root: נעם.) What is the irony of her name?

יג (13) Qal Infinitives; Demonstratives

13.1 Qal Infinitive Absolute

Hebrew has two forms of infinitives: the **infinitive absolute** and the **infinitive construct**. You can tell by the name *infinitive* that these forms are nonfinite (see 9.5) verbal forms, which are not marked for time/aspect. The infinitive forms also do not inflect for person, gender, or number.

The infinitive absolute has the vowel pattern *qameṣ—ḥolem*:

קָטוֹל

Remember that the presence or absence of a mater does not impact the parsing of a word. קָטֹל and קָטוֹל are both the Qal infinitive absolute of קטל.

The infinitive absolute is commonly used in several ways:

1. To add certainty to a finite verb. In this use the infinitive absolute precedes (except in rare cases) a finite verb of the same root to indicate certainty.

   Impf. Inf. Abs.

   כֹּל אֲשֶׁר־יְדַבֵּר בּוֹא יָבוֹא ("Everything that he says will certainly come to pass."—1 Sam. 9:6)

   Impf. Inf. Abs.

   הֲמָלֹךְ תִּמְלֹךְ עָלֵינוּ ("Will you truly reign over us?"—Gen. 37:8)

2. To indicate concurrent action. In this use two different infinitive absolutes are used to indicate action occurring at the same time.

   Inf. Abs. Inf. Abs.

   וַיֵּלֶךְ הָלוֹךְ וְאָכֹל ("And he went, going and eating"—Judg. 14:9)

3. As a command. Especially in older texts, a command can be indicated via the infinitive absolute.

Inf.
Abs.
זָכוֹר אֶת־יוֹם הַשַּׁבָּת ("Remember the Sabbath day"—Ex. 20:8)

4. As a simple verbal noun.

Inf.
Abs.
אָכֹל דְּבַשׁ הַרְבּוֹת לֹא־טוֹב ("Eating too much honey is not good."—Prov. 25:27)

For less common uses of the infinitive absolute, consult an intermediate grammar or syntax.

13.2 Qal Infinitive Construct

The second infinitive form, the infinitive construct, is also not inflected for person, gender, or number. It follows the vowel pattern *shewa—ḥolem*:

קְטֹל

This form is identical to the Qal imperative ms. Only context indicates whether it is an imperative or an infinitive construct.

I-*nun* verbs can show infinitive construct forms with or without the presence of the *nun*. If the *nun* is not present, the form adds a *taw*—as if to compensate for the loss of the *nun*. The infinitive construct without the *nun* is a **by-form**, a variant form which is unexpected based on the system of the language but interchangeable with the more expected form.[1]

Root	Inf. Const. with *nun*	Inf. Const. without *nun*
נגע	נְגֹעַ	גַּעַת
נתן	נְתֹן	תֵּת

[1] By forms can occur at either the morpheme (word) level or at the grammatical level (as here).

Note especially the form of the infinitive construct of נתן without the *nun* (תֵּת), because it preserves only one of the original three root letters, and it is difficult to identify. **This form should be memorized, because it is quite common.**

The infinitive construct is commonly used after the preposition לְ to express purpose or result:

וַיָּבֹאוּ מִכָּל־הָעַמִּים לִשְׁמֹעַ אֵת חָכְמַת שְׁלֹמֹה ("And they came from all the peoples to listen to the wisdom of Solomon."—1 Kings 5:14 [Engl. 4:34])

The infinitive construct is also commonly used after the prepositions בְּ and כְּ to express a temporal clause:

וְהָיָה בְּעָבְרְכֶם אֶת־הַיַּרְדֵּן ("And when[2] you pass over the Jordan"—Deut. 27:4)

The infinitive construct is typically negated by לְבִלְתִּי ("not"):

לְבִלְתִּי שְׁמֹעַ אֶל־הַכֹּהֵן ("not listening to the priest"—Deut. 17:12)

13.3 Pronominal Suffixes on Infinitive Constructs

The infinitive construct can take pronominal suffixes like those attached to nouns (see 11.3). When this occurs, the form of the infinitive construct changes in advance of the suffix to either קְטָל־ (with 2ms and 2mp suffixes) or קָטְל־ (with all other suffixes):

קָטְלִי "my killing" (The vowel is a *qameṣ ḥatup̄.*)

קָטְלְךָ "your killing" (The vowel is again a *qameṣ ḥatup̄.*)

The suffix attached to the infinitive construct may be subjective (the antecedent of the suffix doing the action of the infinitive construct) or objective (the antecedent of the suffix receiving the action of the infinitive construct):

[2] Woodenly "And it will be when you pass over . . . ." The converted perfect form of היה is setting the time frame for the infinitive construct.

Inf.
Const.

עָזְבֵךְ אֶת־יְהוָה אֱלֹהָיִךְ ("Your abandoning the LORD your God"—Jer. 2:17; subjective)

Inf. Const. — Impf. — Inf. Abs.

אִם־מָאֵן יְמָאֵן אָבִיהָ לְתִתָּהּ לוֹ ("If her father completely refuses to give her to him . . ."—Ex. 22:16; objective)

13.4 Demonstratives

Demonstratives are pointing words—words that indicate a specific item or set. In English the demonstratives are *this/that* and *these/those*. Beyond the indication of definiteness, the demonstratives indicate a specificity.

Demonstratives are typically classed as "near" (this/these) and "far" (that/those).

Near Demonstrative Paradigm

	Singular		Plural	
Masculine	זֶה	this	אֵלֶּה	these
Feminine	זֹאת	this	אֵלֶּה	these

This paradigm must be memorized.

Far Demonstrative Paradigm

	Singular		Plural	
Masculine	הוּא	that	הֵם / הֵמָּה	those
Feminine	הִיא	that	הֵן / הֵנָּה	those

This paradigm must be memorized.

Note that the third person personal pronouns (see section 9.1) are employed as the far demonstratives. Demonstratives either stand as independent nouns (see section 4.1) or serve as attributive adjectives, following the same agreement rules with the noun they modify (see section 4.6).

זֶה חַסְדֵּךְ אֲשֶׁר תַּעֲשִׂי עִמָּדִי ("This is the kindness you must do for me."—Gen. 20:13)

וְאָמְרוּ אִשְׁתּוֹ זֹאת ("And they will say, 'This is his wife.'"—Gen. 12:12)

הִוא הָעִיר הַגְּדֹלָה ("That is the great city."—Gen. 10:12)

בַּדּוֹר הַזֶּה ("in this generation"—Gen. 7:1)

לָתֶת לְךָ אֶת־הָאָרֶץ הַזֹּאת ("to give to you this land"—Gen. 15:7)

אַחֲרֵי הַדְּבָרִים הָאֵלֶּה ("after these things"—Gen. 22:20)

בַּיָּמִים הָהֵם ("in those days"—Gen. 6:4)

13.5 Pausal Forms

Recall the first- and second-level disjunctive accents from 11.8—the *ṣillûq* and the *athnach*. These two disjunctive accents create a brief pause in the reading of the text. (Technically all disjunctive accents mark some amount of a pause, but the pause is more substantial with these two accents.) The pause created by these two disjunctive accents can cause minor vowel changes in a word. When these vowel changes occur at the point of a major disjunctive accent, the word is said to be "in pause" or "a pausal form." Particularly common vowel changes are:

1. The lengthening of *pataḥ* to *qameṣ*.
2. The shift from *segol* to *qameṣ.*
3. *Shewa* becoming a full vowel.
4. The 2ms pronoun shifting from ךָ to ָךְ.

These changes do not need to be memorized. If a form seems anomalous, simply check whether it is in a position where it may be explained as a pausal form, e.g.: the vocalization of הָאָרֶץ in Genesis 1:1:

בְּרֵאשִׁית בָּרָא אֱלֹהִים אֵת הַשָּׁמַיִם וְאֵת הָאָרֶץ׃

13.6 Vocabulary

חֵן	grace, charm, favor
טָהוֹר	pure, clean
טוֹבָה	good things, goodness
לְבִלְתִּי	not
מָכַר	to sell, betray to others
מִקְנֶה	property, livestock; possessions
מָשַׁל	to rule
סָגַר	to shut
עָנִי	poor, wretched, needy, afflicted
עָזַר	to help, assist, aid
עֵ֫זֶר	help, assistance
עֵצָה	advice, plan
עָרַךְ	to lay out, set in rows; get ready; draw up a battle line
רָחַץ	to wash, bathe
רָכַב	to ride, mount
רֶ֫כֶב	chariot
רַע	evil, wickedness, misfortune
שָׂבַע	to eat or drink one's fill, satisfy oneself
שִׁיר	song
תְּפִלָּה	prayer

13.7 Language Exercises

A. Parse and gloss the following forms.

לֵאמֹר

לָתֵת

לִקְרָאתָם

וְאֶקְחָה

וַיִּתֵּן

עָשָׂה

עֹמֵד

וַיְהִי

נָתַתִּי

וַיִּסְגֹּר

B. Translate the following sentences and parse each verb and participle. Use your lexicon to look up the glosses for any words you do not know from your vocabulary.

Gen. 43:3 וַיֹּאמֶר אֵלָיו יְהוּדָה לֵאמֹר[3]

Num. 1:5 וְאֵלֶּה שְׁמוֹת הָאֲנָשִׁים אֲשֶׁר יַעַמְדוּ אִתְּכֶם

[3] This form of the Qal infinitive construct can simply introduce a quotation. It often can be left untranslated.

וַיֹּ֣אמֶר יְהוָ֔ה אֶל־מֹשֶׁ֥ה וְאֶֽל־אַהֲרֹ֖ן לֵאמֹֽר׃ Ex. 7:8

עֵ֤ת לַהֲרוֹג֙ וְעֵ֣ת לִרְפּ֔וֹא עֵ֥ת לִפְר֖וֹץ ... וְעֵ֣ת לִשְׂח֔וֹק עֵ֥ת סְפ֖וֹד וְעֵ֥ת Eccl. 3:3-4

רְקֽוֹד׃

וְעַתָּ֗ה אִם־שָׁמ֤וֹעַ תִּשְׁמְעוּ֙ בְּקֹלִ֔י[4] וּשְׁמַרְתֶּ֖ם אֶת בְּרִיתִ֑י Ex. 19:5a

וַיֵּ֤לֶךְ הָלוֹךְ֙ וְאָכֹ֔ל וַיֵּ֙לֶךְ֙ אֶל־אָבִ֣יו וְאֶל־אִמּ֔וֹ וַיִּתֵּ֥ן לָהֶ֖ם וַיֹּאכֵ֑לוּ Judg. 14:9

וַיֹּאמְר֡וּ שָׁא֣וֹל שָֽׁאַל־הָ֠אִישׁ לָ֣נוּ וּלְמֽוֹלַדְתֵּ֜נוּ לֵאמֹ֗ר הַע֨וֹד אֲבִיכֶ֥ם חַי֙ Gen. 43:7

הֲיֵ֥שׁ לָכֶ֖ם אָ֑ח

[4] The idiom שָׁמַע בְּקֹל is best glossed as “to obey.”

Ex. 3:19a וַאֲנִ֣י יָדַ֔עְתִּי כִּ֠י לֹֽא־יִתֵּ֥ן אֶתְכֶ֛ם מֶ֥לֶךְ מִצְרַ֖יִם לַהֲלֹ֑ךְ

Ex. 3:21 וְנָתַתִּ֛י אֶת־חֵ֥ן הָֽעָם־הַזֶּ֖ה בְּעֵינֵ֣י מִצְרָ֑יִם וְהָיָה֙ כִּ֣י תֵֽלֵכ֔וּן לֹ֥א

תֵלְכ֖וּ רֵיקָֽם׃

13.8 Exegetical Exercises—Frozen Forms

Since the meaning of a word is based on how it is used, its meaning can change over time. A commonly cited example is the English word *nice*, which originally meant *ignorant*. Today "she is a nice woman" does not mean "she is ignorant," though it once would have! Such developments also occur in theological terms. *Atonement* comes from "at one" + "-ment," but contemporary English speakers do not have the etymology in mind when using or hearing the word.[5] The interpreter of a text must avoid the **etymological fallacy**—the idea that a word's meaning is inherent and unchanging based on its origin. Because changes occur over time, you must be aware of **frozen forms**—uses of a word that may have once connected to its etymology but were no longer connected in the mind of a speaker or author.

A straightforward example is the preposition לִפְנֵי. It can easily be recognized as the combination of the preposition לְ and the construct form of פָּנִים, which originally meant "before the face of." While that original meaning still fits many contexts, it does not fit many others—except quite analogically. For example:

[5] The phenomenon of "dead metaphors" is similar. In such cases the once-literal meaning of a term has been lost to changes in technology or culture; the term still exists, but its literal meaning is often unknown to a current speaker. Consider the following: "the *glove box* of a car," "*dialing* a phone number," "*cranking* the car," etc.

מִ֣י יִתְיַצֵּ֔ב לִפְנֵ֖י בְּנֵ֥י עֲנָֽק ("Who can stand before the sons of Anak?"—Deut. 9:2)

וַיָּנֻ֕סוּ לִפְנֵ֖י אַנְשֵׁ֥י הָעָֽי ("And they fled before the men of Ai."—Josh. 7:4)

In each case it is clearly not the face of the adversary that intimidates or conquers, and while one could woodenly translate each text with "before the face of" (e.g.: "And they fled before the face of the men of Ai."), it is clear that the word לִפְנֵי no longer requires an obvious sense of "face."

Even more telling:

שְׁנָתַ֖יִם לִפְנֵ֥י הָרָֽעַשׁ ("two years before the earthquake"—Amos 1:1)

If לִפְנֵי is to be interpreted etymologically, Amos 1:1 stretches the etymology to the breaking point. Instead, לִפְנֵי has become a frozen form in which a speaker or author who uses the word no longer even considers its etymological meaning. In the majority of Biblical Hebrew, לִפְנֵי simply meant "before," with the text's author no longer conscious of its etymology.

A. Etymology versus use. Determine the etymology of each of the following phrases; then translate the verse in which it is used. Note the similarities and differences between the etymology of the word and its use in context.

עַל־פִּי

Etymology:

Gen. 43:7 וַיֹּאמְר֗וּ שָׁא֣וֹל שָֽׁאַל־הָ֠אִישׁ לָ֣נוּ וּלְמֽוֹלַדְתֵּ֜נוּ לֵאמֹ֗ר הַע֨וֹד אֲבִיכֶ֥ם חַי֙ הֲיֵ֣שׁ לָכֶ֣ם אָ֔ח וַנַּ֨גֶּד[6]־ל֔וֹ עַל־פִּ֖י הַדְּבָרִ֣ים הָאֵ֑לֶּה

[6] Hiph. Narr. 1cp of נגד, glossed as "to tell"

מִפְּנֵי

Etymology:

Gen. 6:13 כִּֽי־מָלְאָ֥ה הָאָ֛רֶץ חָמָ֖ס מִפְּנֵיהֶ֑ם

B. Ehud and the men of Benjamin. Ehud is described in Judges 3:15 as אִ֥ישׁ אִטֵּ֖ר יַד־יְמִינ֑וֹ. Translate this phrase. What options does the lexicon give to translate אִטֵּר? What would the phrase אִטֵּר יַד־יְמִינוֹ mean etymologically?

Is Ehud to be considered crippled in his right hand or just considered a left-handed man? Judges 3:12–30 could be consistent with either interpretation. This phrase is used again in Judges 20:16:

מִכֹּל֙ הָעָ֣ם הַזֶּ֔ה שְׁבַ֤ע מֵאוֹת֙ אִ֣ישׁ בָּח֔וּר אִטֵּ֖ר יַד־יְמִינ֑וֹ כָּל־זֶ֗ה קֹלֵ֧עַ בָּאֶ֛בֶן אֶל־הַֽשַּׂעֲרָ֖ה וְלֹ֥א יַחֲטִֽא[7]׃

Translate this verse; then review the surrounding context in an English Bible. Only one of the two possible meanings in Judges 3 makes sense contextually in Judges 20. Which one?

[7] Hiphil Imperf. 3ms of חטא, glossed as “to miss” (see ch. 16).

אִ֣ישׁ אִטֵּ֣ר יַד־יְמִינ֑וֹ, then, has most likely become a frozen phrase—most likely in Judges 3:15 and almost certainly in Judges 20:16.

C. An ambiguous case. Translate Leviticus 5:25 [Engl. 6:6].

וְאֶת־אֲשָׁמ֥וֹ יָבִ֖יא[8] לַֽיהוָ֑ה אַ֧יִל תָּמִ֛ים מִן־הַצֹּ֖אן בְּעֶרְכְּךָ֣ לְאָשָׁ֑ם אֶל־הַכֹּהֵֽן׃

Concentrate on the phrase בְּעֶרְכְּךָ. It is composed of the preposition בּ, the noun עֵרֶךְ, and a possessive suffix. Review עֵרֶךְ in a lexicon.

Compare your translation of this phrase to several major English translations:

HCSB: Then he must bring his restitution offering to the LORD: an unblemished ram from the flock according to your assessment of its value as a restitution offering to the priest.

ESV: And he shall bring to the priest as his compensation to the LORD a ram without blemish out of the flock, or its equivalent for a guilt offering.

NIV: And as a penalty they must bring to the priest, that is, to the LORD, their guilt offering, a ram from the flock, one without defect and of the proper value.

NJPS: Then he shall bring to the priest, as his penalty to the LORD, a ram without blemish from the flock, or the equivalent, as a guilt offering.

Which translations are treating בְּעֶרְכְּךָ as a frozen phrase and which are translating it piece-by-piece in line with its etymology? Which translation do you prefer? Why?

---

[8] Hiphil Imperf. 3ms of בוא, glossed as "to bring" (see chs. 16; 26).

יד (14) Piel

14.1 The Piel Stem

The Piel represents the second verbal stem (*binyan*—see 3.2) covered in this grammar. There will be five more: the Pual, the Hiphil, the Hophal, the Niphal, and the Hithpael. These six non-Qal stems are called the **derived stems**, since they may be thought of as deriving from the more basic Qal form. These seven stems (the Qal plus the six derived stems) constitute the vast majority of the Hebrew verbal system.

Each of these derived stems is named from the 3ms perfect conjugation of the verb, and the name therefore will help you remember the formation of the *binyan*. However, these names originated not with the root קטל, which we use for most of our paradigms, but with the root פעל.[1] If you write out the name of the stem with the root letters פעל and transfer that vowel pattern to קטל, you will have the 3ms form of the perfect:

פעל → * פִּעֵּל (hypothetical 3ms form, though note *ayin* cannot actually double)

קטל → קִטֵּל (Piel Perf. 3ms of קטל)

Each of these seven stems can be put into each verbal inflection already taught in the Qal. Just as there is a Qal perfect, a Qal imperfect, a Qal participle, etc., there is a Piel perfect, a Piel imperfect, a Piel participle, etc. The use and translational values of these inflections (simple future, modals, etc.) do not change because the verb is in another stem. Accordingly, a Piel perfect has the same range of translational values learned for the Qal perfect.

The exact difference between the Qal and the other six verbal stems is frequently debated, and the explanation of that debate would require a summary of many years of literature. Thus, that explanation is left for an advanced syntax class. One can note, however, the broad outlines of the relationship between the Piel and the Qal:

[1] In Arabic, the *ayin* can double, so פעל is a readily-usable word to present paradigms. Since *ayin*, as a guttural, cannot double in Hebrew, it is less often used to present paradigms.

- The Piel often represents the **resultative** counterpart to the Qal: while שָׁלַח translates as "he sent," שִׁלַּח translates as "he sent away."[2]
- The Piel often represents the **causative** counterpart to the Qal: while לָמַד translates as "he learned," לִמֵּד translates as "he taught."
- The Piel often makes an intransitive Qal verb transitive (i.e., taking a direct object), a use called the **factitive**: while קָדַשׁ translates as "he was holy," קִדֵּשׁ translates as "he consecrated."[3]
- The Piel is often the **declarative** counterpart to the Qal: while צָדַק translates as "to be right/righteous," צִדֵּק translates as "to declare right/righteous."
- The Piel is often the **denominative** form, the form used when a verb is derived from an associated noun: כֹּהֵן is the noun for *priest*, and כִּהֵן translates as "to act as a priest."[4]
- Other relationships—though less common—also exist, including verbs that occur only in the Piel stem.

This diversity of functions has led to the robust debate about the exact relationship of the Piel and the Qal. When verbs occur in both stems, the relationship can be examined. When a verb occurs only in the Piel, its relationship to a hypothetical Qal form cannot be determined.

The formation of the Piel is focused on the doubling of the second root letter. Thus, it is sometimes called the **D-Stem**, which stands for *Doppeltstamm* ("doubled stem" in German).

As 14.2–14.7 show, the endings for various inflections of the verb have already been learned. These paradigms will require study but not memorization, since they can be derived from what you already know. You should be able to parse any verbs in the Piel, but memorizing the paradigms is not required.

---

[2] This use of the Piel is commonly presented as **intensive**: while שָׁבַר translates as "he broke," שִׁבֵּר translates as "he smashed." This debate is largely because of the derivational (not inflectional) nature of the Hebrew verbal system (see 16.10).

[3] This use of the Piel is often a **state-causative**, with the subject causing another noun to enter a particular state.

[4] Consider the English verb *to text* that arose from the noun *text*, itself a shortened form of *text message*.

14.2 The Piel Perfect

The Piel perfect is formed by doubling the second root letter and adding the same endings learned for the Qal perfect.

Piel Perfect Paradigm

	Verbal Form	Suffix	Gloss*
3ms	קִטֵּל	--	he slaughtered
3fs	קִטְּלָה	ָה	she slaughtered
2ms	קִטַּלְתָּ	תָּ	you (ms) slaughtered
2fs	קִטַּלְתְּ	תְּ	you (fs) slaughtered
1cs	קִטַּלְתִּי	תִּי	I slaughtered
3cp	קִטְּלוּ	וּ	they slaughtered
2mp	קִטַּלְתֶּם	תֶּם	you (mp) slaughtered
2fp	קִטַּלְתֶּן	תֶּן	you (fp) slaughtered
1cp	קִטַּלְנוּ	נוּ	we slaughtered

*The root קטל does not actually occur in the Piel, so the glosses provided here (and on subsequent paradigms) are hypothetical.

Notes:

- The *ṣere* theme vowel is common to Piel forms but is evident only in the 3ms form of the perfect. A *pataḥ* or *segol* theme vowel is also possible.
- The presence of the *shewa* under the second root letter can cause an anomalous loss of the *dagesh*.

> Tip-Offs for the Piel Perfect
>
> - Doubled second root letter
> - First vowel *ḥireq*

14.3 The Piel Imperfect

The Piel imperfect is formed by doubling the second root letter and adding the same prefixes and suffixes learned for the Qal imperfect:

Piel Imperfect Paradigm

	Verbal Form	Prefix...Suffix	Gloss
3ms	יְקַטֵּל	--- י	he will slaughter
3fs	תְּקַטֵּל	--- תּ	she will slaughter
2ms	תְּקַטֵּל	--- תּ	you (ms) will slaughter
2fs	תְּקַטְּלִי	ִי --- תּ	you (fs) will slaughter
1cs	אֲקַטֵּל	--- א	I will slaughter
3mp	יְקַטְּלוּ	וּ --- י	they (mp) will slaughter
3fp	תְּקַטֵּלְנָה	נָה --- תּ	they (fp) will slaughter
2mp	תְּקַטְּלוּ	וּ --- תּ	you (mp) will slaughter
2fp	תְּקַטֵּלְנָה	נָה --- תּ	you (fp) will slaughter
1cp	נְקַטֵּל	--- נ	we will slaughter

Notes:

- The 1cs form takes a compound *shewa* instead of a simple vocal *shewa*, since *aleph* is a guttural.
- The presence of the *shewa* under the second root letter can cause an anomalous loss of the *dagesh*.

Tip-Offs for the Piel Imperfect

- Doubled second root letter
- *Shewa* under the prefix letter
- *Pataḥ* vowel under first root letter

14.4 The Piel Narrative

The Piel narrative is formed regularly by the addition of וַ־. The presence of the *shewa* commonly causes the loss of the *dagesh* in the prefix: וַיְדַבֵּר, not *וַיְּדַבֵּר (see 4.4).

14.5 The Piel Volitives

As with the Qal, the **Piel cohortative** can either be identical to the imperfect or have the form of the imperfect plus the addition of ָה (cf. Qal Cohortative in section 7.2).

The **Piel imperative** is formed in the same way as the Qal imperative: removing the prefix letter from the imperfect (cf. Qal Imperative in section 7.3).

Piel Imperative Paradigm

	Verbal Form	Suffix	Gloss
2ms	קַטֵּל	---	you (ms) slaughter
2fs	קַטְּלִי	ִי ---	you (fs) slaughter
2mp	קַטְּלוּ	וּ ---	you (mp) slaughter
2fp	קַטֵּלְנָה	נָה ---	you (fp) slaughter

Notes:

- The *dagesh* in the second root letter may be lost in certain phonetic environments.
- The ms imperative may take the final *-ah* ending, as in Qal imperatives (see 7.3).

Tip-Offs for the Piel Imperative

- Doubled second root letter
- *Pataḥ* vowel under first root letter

The **Piel jussive** is often, like the Qal, formally identical to the imperfect. Keep in mind the caution of 7.4—they are different verbal forms.

14.6 The Piel Participle

The participle forms in the derived stems begin with מְ־:

Piel Participle Paradigm

	Verbal Form	Suffix	Gloss*
ms	מְקַטֵּל	--	one who slaughters
fs	מְקַטֶּלֶת	ֶת	one who slaughters
fs (alt. form)	מְקַטְּלָה	ָה	one who slaughters
mp	מְקַטְּלִים	ִים	ones who slaughter
fp	מְקַטְּלוֹת	וֹת	ones who slaughter

> Tip-Offs for the Piel Participle:
>
> - Doubled second root letter
> - *Pataḥ* vowel under first root letter
> - *Shewa* under the *mem* (though Pual participles will share this characteristic)

Piel participles are always active, since the passive function is handled by the Pual (see ch. 15).

14.7 The Piel Infinitives

The **Piel infinitive absolute**[5] and **infinitive construct** are identical:

קַטֵּל

This form is also identical to the ms imperative; context is necessary to distinguish them.

[5] The Piel infinitive absolute can also be formed as קַטֹּל.

14.8 Vocabulary

בִּקֵּשׁ	(Piel) to seek, search for; discover, find
דִּבֵּר	(Piel) to say, speak
זָעַק	to cry, cry for help
כִּפֶּר	(Piel) to atone, appease, make amends
כַּפֹּרֶת	atonement cover (on the ark)[6]
לִמֵּד	(Piel) to teach
מָאַס	to refuse, reject
עֵבֶר	bank, edge; other side
עַל־כֵּן	Therefore (cf. לָכֵן, section 2.9)
פָּתַח	to open
פִּתַּח	(Piel) to untie, let loose, set free
קִטֵּר	(Piel) to make a sacrifice, make something go up in smoke
קְטֹרֶת	incense
שָׁכַח	to forget
שִׁלַּח	(Piel) to let go free; expel

[6] Via Luther (*Gnadestuhl*), this has traditionally been called "the mercy seat."

14.9 Language Exercises

A. Parse and gloss the following forms.

תְּפַתֵּחַ

קִטְּרוּ

וַנֹּאמֶר

וַתְּדַבֵּר

מְשַׁלֵּחַ

אֲבַקֵּשׁ

פִּתַּח

פַּתֵּחַ

דִּבֵּר

מְדַבֵּר

B. Translate the following and parse all verbs and participles. Use your lexicon to look up the glosses for any words you do not know from your vocabulary. Verbal forms that have not yet been introduced are marked with footnotes.

Ex. 5:1–2 וְאַחַר בָּאוּ[7] מֹשֶׁה וְאַהֲרֹן וַיֹּאמְרוּ אֶל־פַּרְעֹה כֹּה־אָמַר יְהוָה אֱלֹהֵי יִשְׂרָאֵל

שַׁלַּח אֶת־עַמִּי וְיָחֹגּוּ[8] לִי בַּמִּדְבָּר׃ וַיֹּאמֶר פַּרְעֹה מִי יְהוָה אֲשֶׁר אֶשְׁמַע

[7] Qal Perf. 3cp of בוא, glossed as “to come, go” (see ch. 26).

[8] Qal Juss. 3mp of חגג, glossed as “to celebrate a festival” (see ch. 28).

בְקֹלוֹ לְשַׁלַּח אֶת־יִשְׂרָאֵל לֹא יָדַעְתִּי אֶת־יְהוָה וְגַם אֶת־יִשְׂרָאֵל לֹא

אֲשַׁלֵּחַ׃

2 Sam. 3:17–18 וּדְבַר־אַבְנֵר הָיָה עִם־זִקְנֵי יִשְׂרָאֵל לֵאמֹר גַּם־תְּמוֹל גַּם־שִׁלְשֹׁם הֱיִיתֶם[9]

מְבַקְשִׁים אֶת־דָּוִד לְמֶלֶךְ עֲלֵיכֶם׃ וְעַתָּה עֲשׂוּ[10] כִּי יְהוָה אָמַר אֶל־דָּוִד

לֵאמֹר בְּיַד ׀ דָּוִד עַבְדִּי הוֹשִׁיעַ[11] אֶת־עַמִּי יִשְׂרָאֵל מִיַּד פְּלִשְׁתִּים וּמִיַּד

כָּל־אֹיְבֵיהֶם׃

Ex. 6:2–3a וַיְדַבֵּר אֱלֹהִים אֶל־מֹשֶׁה וַיֹּאמֶר אֵלָיו אֲנִי יְהוָה׃ וָאֵרָא[12] אֶל־אַבְרָהָם אֶל־

יִצְחָק וְאֶל־יַעֲקֹב בְּאֵל שַׁדָּי וּשְׁמִי יְהוָה לֹא נוֹדַעְתִּי[13] לָהֶם׃

---

[9] Qal Perf. 2mp of היה, glossed as "to be" (see ch. 24).

[10] Qal Imperative mp of עשה, glossed as "to do" (see ch. 24).

[11] Hiph. Inf. Const. of ישע, glossed as "to deliver"—translate as "I will deliver" (see ch. 27).

[12] Niph. Narr. 1cs of ראה, glossed as "to present oneself"—translate as "I revealed myself" (see chs. 19, 24).

[13] Niph. Perf. 1cs of ידע, glossed as "to make oneself known"—translate as "I did (not) make myself known" (see chs. 19, 27).

Gen. 42:30 דִּבֶּר הָאִישׁ אֲדֹנֵי הָאָרֶץ אִתָּנוּ קָשׁוֹת וַיִּתֵּן אֹתָנוּ כִּמְרַגְּלִים אֶת־הָאָרֶץ

Deut. 31:22, altered וַיִּכְתֹּב מֹשֶׁה אֶת־הַשִּׁירָה הַזֹּאת בַּיּוֹם הַהוּא וַיְלַמֵּד אֹתָהּ אֶת־בְּנֵי יִשְׂרָאֵל׃

2 Kings 23:8a וַיָּבֵא[14] אֶת־כָּל־הַכֹּהֲנִים מֵעָרֵי יְהוּדָה וַיְטַמֵּא אֶת־הַבָּמוֹת אֲשֶׁר קִטְּרוּ־

שָׁמָּה הַכֹּהֲנִים מִגֶּבַע עַד־בְּאֵר שָׁבַע

14.10 Exegetical Exercises—Uses of כִּי

The particle כִּי has a range of uses that often confuse the beginning student. At least four separate uses are common:

A. Causal. Most uses of כִּי are causal, for which it is glossed "because, for, since." A **causal** כִּי most commonly follows the main clause to which it connects.[15] The key to identifying this use of כִּי is its role connecting two clauses—and that the connection is one of causation.

וְעַתָּה הָשֵׁב אֵשֶׁת־הָאִישׁ כִּי־נָבִיא הוּא ("And now return the man's wife, for he is a prophet."—Gen. 20:7)

B. Complementary. כִּי also commonly provides the necessary information to complete another word or clause. A **complementary** כִּי usually follows the main clause to which it

---

[14] Hiph. Narr. 3ms of בוא, glossed as "to bring" (see ch. 26).

[15] This is a rule of thumb, since exceptions do exist (e.g., Gen. 3:14).

connects. When used to connect a complement, כִּי is glossed “that.” This use of כִּי is identified by the semantics of the clause; a previous word, phrase, or clause requires a complement to complete its sense.

וַיַּרְא יְהוָה כִּי רַבָּה רָעַת הָאָדָם בָּאָרֶץ (“The LORD saw that mankind’s wickedness was great upon the earth.”—Gen. 6:5)

C. Temporal/Conditional. כִּי is also used to mark the condition (glossed as “if, though”) or temporal situation (glossed as “when, as”) of a clause. A **temporal** or **conditional** כִּי precedes the main clause of an utterance.

כִּי־אֶרְאֶה שָׁמֶיךָ (“When I consider your heavens . . . .”—Ps. 8:4—temporal)

וְכִי־יִגַּח שׁוֹר אֶת־אִישׁ אוֹ אֶת־אִשָּׁה (“And if an ox gores a man or a woman . . . .”—Ex. 21:28—conditional)

D. Introduction of a Solemn Declaration. כִּי is also used to introduce a solemn declaration. This use of כִּי is not always easily translated into English but should be noted when considering the force of a statement.

כִּי־בָרֵךְ אֲבָרֶכְךָ (“Surely I will bless you.”—Gen. 22:17)

Translate the following clauses involving כִּי. Indicate which of the four uses of כִּי is evidenced and why. Check the surrounding context in an English translation if you have difficulty.

Gen. 8:9 וְלֹא־מָצְאָה הַיּוֹנָה מָנוֹחַ לְכַף־רַגְלָהּ וַתָּשָׁב[16] אֵלָיו אֶל־הַתֵּבָה

כִּי־מַיִם עַל־פְּנֵי כָל־הָאָרֶץ

[16] Qal Narr. 3fs of שׁוּב, glossed as “to return” (see ch. 26).

1 Sam. 15:26, altered

וַיֹּאמֶר שְׁמוּאֵל אֶל־שָׁאוּל לֹא אָשׁוּב[17] עִמָּךְ כִּי מָאַסְתָּ אֶת־דְּבַר יְהוָה

Gen. 20:6

גַּם אָנֹכִי יָדַעְתִּי כִּי בְתָם־לְבָבְךָ עָשִׂיתָ[18] זֹּאת

2 Kings 4:29

כִּי־תִמְצָא אִישׁ לֹא תְבָרֵכ

Lev. 25:20

וְכִי תֹאמְרוּ מַה־נֹּאכַל בַּשָּׁנָה הַשְּׁבִיעִת

Gen. 20:9

וַיִּקְרָא אֲבִימֶלֶךְ לְאַבְרָהָם וַיֹּאמֶר לוֹ מֶה־עָשִׂיתָ[19] לָּנוּ וּמֶה־

חָטָאתִי לָךְ כִּי־הֵבֵאתָ[20] עָלַי וְעַל־מַמְלַכְתִּי חֲטָאָה גְדֹלָה

Gen. 21:30

וַיֹּאמֶר כִּי אֶת־שֶׁבַע כְּבָשֹׂת תִּקַּח מִיָּדִי בַּעֲבוּר תִּהְיֶה־לִּי

לְעֵדָה כִּי חָפַרְתִּי אֶת־הַבְּאֵר הַזֹּאת׃

---

[17] Qal Perf. 1cs of שׁוב, glossed as “to return” (see ch. 26).

[18] Qal Perf. 2ms of עשׂה, glossed as “to do” (see ch. 24).

[19] Qal Perf. 2ms of עשׂה, glossed as “to do” (see ch. 24).

[20] Hiph. Perf. 2ms of בוא, glossed as “to bring” (see ch. 26).

טו (15) Pual

15.1 The Pual Stem

The Pual stem is the passive counterpart to the Piel. For example:

שִׁבֵּר "it smashed" (active)

שֻׁבַּר "it was smashed" (passive)

Given its relationship to the Piel, the Pual unsurprisingly shares its major characteristic of doubling the second root letter. Whatever nuance (intensive, factitive, etc.) is attributed to a verb in its Piel form is usually also attributed to the verb in its Pual form.

15.2 The Pual Perfect

The Pual perfect is formed by doubling the second root letter and adding the same endings learned for the Qal and Piel perfect:

Pual Perfect Paradigm

	Verbal Form	Suffix	Gloss*
3ms	קֻטַּל	--	he was slaughtered
3fs	קֻטְּלָה	ָה	she was slaughtered
2ms	קֻטַּ֫לְתָּ	תָּ	you (ms) were slaughtered
2fs	קֻטַּלְתְּ	תְּ	you (fs) were slaughtered
1cs	קֻטַּ֫לְתִּי	תִּי	I was slaughtered

3cp	קֻטְּלוּ	וּ	they were slaughtered
2mp	קֻטַּלְתֶּם	תֶּם	you (mp) were slaughtered
2fp	קֻטַּלְתֶּן	תֶּן	you (fp) were slaughtered
1cp	קֻטַּלְנוּ	נוּ	we were slaughtered

*Note that the root קטל does not actually occur in the Pual, so the glosses provided here and in the following paradigms are hypothetical.

Tip-Offs for the Pual Perfect:

- Doubled second root letter (though shared with Piel)
- First vowel *qibbuṣ*

15.3 The Pual Imperfect

The Pual imperfect is formed by doubling the second root letter and adding the same prefixes and suffixes learned for the Qal and Piel imperfect:

Pual Imperfect Paradigm

	Verbal Form	Prefix...Suffix	Gloss*
3ms	יְקֻטַּל	--- יְ	he will be slaughtered
3fs	תְּקֻטַּל	--- תְּ	she will be slaughtered
2ms	תְּקֻטַּל	--- תְּ	you (ms) will be slaughtered
2fs	תְּקֻטְּלִי	ִי --- תְּ	you (fs) will be slaughtered
1cs	אֲקֻטַּל	--- אֲ	I will be slaughtered

3mp	יְקֻטְּלוּ	י --- וּ	they (mp) will be slaughtered
3fp	תְּקֻטַּלְנָה	ת --- נָה	they (fp) will be slaughtered
2mp	תְּקֻטְּלוּ	ת --- וּ	you (mp) will be slaughtered
2fp	תְּקֻטַּלְנָה	ת --- נָה	you (fp) will be slaughtered
1cp	נְקֻטַּל	נ ---	we will be slaughtered

Tip-Offs for the Pual Imperfect:

- Doubled second root letter (though shared with Piel)
- Vocal *shewa* under the prefix (though shared with Piel)
- *Qibbuṣ* under first root letter

15.4 The Pual Narrative

Like the Piel narrative, the Pual narrative is formed regularly via the addition of ־וַ. The *shewa* under the prefix letter causes the loss of the *dagesh* in the prefix, as in the Piel (e.g., וַיְדֻבַּר, not * וַיְּדֻבַּר).

15.5 The Pual Participle

As with the Piel (and all derived stems), the Pual participle begins with a prefixed מְ־:

Pual Participle Paradigm

	Verbal Form	Suffix	Gloss*
ms	מְקֻטָּל	--	one who was slaughtered
fs	מְקֻטֶּלֶת	ֶת	one who was slaughtered
fs (alt. form)	מְקֻטָּלָה	ָה	one who was slaughtered
mp	מְקֻטָּלִים	ִים	ones who were slaughtered
fp	מְקֻטָּלוֹת	וֹת	ones who were slaughtered

Tip-Offs for the Pual Participle:

- Doubled second root letter (though shared with Piel participle)
- *Shewa* under the *mem* (though shared with Piel participle)
- *Qibbuṣ* vowel under first root letter

Pual participles are always passive; the active function is handled by the Piel (see ch. 14).

15.6 Vocabulary

אָחַז	to seize, grasp
אֲחֻזָּה	possession, property; landed property
בְּרִית	Covenant (cf. כָּרַת in section 3.8)
דָּרַךְ	to tread, trample
דֶּ֫רֶךְ	(fem.) way, road
זָרַע	to sow
זֶ֫רַע	seed, offspring, descendants
חָפֵץ	to enjoy; to feel inclined
חֵ֫פֶץ	joy, delight
חֹ֫שֶׁךְ	darkness
כָּשַׁל	to stumble, stagger
מִזְרָח	sunrise, east
מָשַׁח	to smear with liquid, anoint
מָשִׁיחַ	anointed one (cf. Greek Μεσσίας and English "messiah")
עָוֹן	misdeed, sin, iniquity; guilt
פָּרַשׂ	to spread out, stretch over; stretch out one's hands
שָׁבַת	to cease, stop
שַׁבָּת	Sabbath
שָׁחַט	to slaughter
שֶׁ֫קֶר	lie

15.7 Language Exercises

A. Parse and gloss the following forms.

אֻכַּלְתָּ

שֻׁלְּחָה

שֻׁלַּחְתִּי

פֻּתַּח

וַיְפַתַּח

מְפַתֵּחַ

תֻּנִּי

וָאֵלֵךְ

אָמוֹר

נֵלֵךְ

B. Translate the following and parse all verbs and participles. Use your lexicon to look up the glosses for any words you do not know from your vocabulary. Verbal forms that have not yet been introduced are marked with footnotes.

Song 8:8b — מַה־נַּעֲשֶׂה֙[1] לַאֲחֹתֵ֔נוּ בַּיּ֖וֹם שֶׁיְּדֻבַּר[2]־בָּֽהּ׃

[1] Qal Imperf. 1cp of עשׂה, glossed as “to do” (see ch. 24).

[2] For the שֶׁ, see 8.5.

Dan. 10:11 וַיֹּ֣אמֶר אֵלַ֗י דָּנִיֵּאל֙ אִֽישׁ־חֲמֻד֔וֹת הָבֵ֗ן[3] בַּדְּבָרִ֡ים אֲשֶׁר֩ אָנֹכִ֨י דֹבֵ֤ר אֵלֶ֙יךָ֙

וַעֲמֹ֣ד עַל־עָמְדֶ֔ךָ כִּ֛י עַתָּ֖ה שֻׁלַּ֣חְתִּי אֵלֶ֑יךָ וּבְדַבְּרוֹ֙ עִמִּ֔י אֶת־הַדָּבָ֥ר הַזֶּ֖ה

עָמַ֥דְתִּי מַרְעִֽיד[4]׃

Jer. 50:20 בַּיָּמִ֨ים הָהֵ֜ם וּבָעֵ֣ת הַהִ֗יא נְאֻם־יְהוָ֡ה יְבֻקַּ֞שׁ אֶת־עֲוֺ֤ן יִשְׂרָאֵל֙ וְאֵינֶ֔נּוּ

וְאֶת־חַטֹּ֥את יְהוּדָ֖ה וְלֹ֣א תִמָּצֶ֑אינָה[5] כִּ֥י אֶסְלַ֖ח לַאֲשֶׁ֥ר אַשְׁאִֽיר[6]׃

Gen. 1:27 וַיִּבְרָ֨א אֱלֹהִ֤ים ׀ אֶת־הָֽאָדָם֙ בְּצַלְמ֔וֹ בְּצֶ֥לֶם אֱלֹהִ֖ים בָּרָ֣א אֹת֑וֹ זָכָ֥ר

וּנְקֵבָ֖ה בָּרָ֥א אֹתָֽם׃

---

[3] Hiph. Imperative ms of בין, glossed as “to understand” (see chs. 16, 26).

[4] Hiph. Part. ms of רעד, glossed as “to tremble”—translate as “trembling” (see ch. 16).

[5] Niph. Imperf. 3fp of מצא, glossed as “to be found” (see chs. 19, 25).

[6] Hiph. Imperf. 1cs of שׁאר, glossed as “to leave” (see ch. 16).

Judg. 1:1–2

וַיְהִי אַחֲרֵי מוֹת יְהוֹשֻׁעַ וַיִּשְׁאֲלוּ בְּנֵי יִשְׂרָאֵל בַּיהוָה לֵאמֹר מִי יַעֲלֶה[7]־

לָּנוּ אֶל־הַכְּנַעֲנִי בַּתְּחִלָּה לְהִלָּחֶם[8] בּוֹ׃ וַיֹּאמֶר יְהוָה יְהוּדָה יַעֲלֶה הִנֵּה

נָתַתִּי אֶת־הָאָרֶץ בְּיָדוֹ׃

1 Kings 21:27–28

וַיְהִי כִשְׁמֹעַ אַחְאָב אֶת־הַדְּבָרִים הָאֵלֶּה וַיִּקְרַע בְּגָדָיו וַיָּשֶׂם[9]־שַׂק עַל־

בְּשָׂרוֹ וַיָּצוֹם[10] וַיִּשְׁכַּב בַּשָּׂק וַיְהַלֵּךְ אַט׃ וַיְהִי דְּבַר־יְהוָה אֶל־אֵלִיָּהוּ

הַתִּשְׁבִּי לֵאמֹר׃

---

[7] Qal Imperf. 3ms of עלה, glossed as "to go up" (see ch. 24).

[8] Niph. Inf. Const. of לחם, glossed as "to fight" (see ch. 19).

[9] Qal Narr. 3ms of שׂים, glossed as "to put" (see ch. 26).

[10] Qal Narr. 3ms of צום, glossed as "to fast" (see ch. 26).

Ps. 87:2–3 אֹהֵב יְהוָה שַׁעֲרֵי צִיּוֹן מִכֹּל מִשְׁכְּנוֹת יַעֲקֹב׃ נִכְבָּדוֹת[11] מְדֻבָּר בָּךְ עִיר

הָאֱלֹהִים סֶלָה׃

Judg. 1:12–13 וַיֹּאמֶר כָּלֵב אֲשֶׁר־יַכֶּה[12] אֶת־קִרְיַת־סֵפֶר וּלְכָדָהּ[13] וְנָתַתִּי לוֹ אֶת־

עַכְסָה בִתִּי לְאִשָּׁה׃ וַיִּלְכְּדָהּ[14] עָתְנִיאֵל בֶּן־קְנַז אֲחִי כָלֵב הַקָּטֹן מִמֶּנּוּ

וַיִּתֶּן־לוֹ אֶת־עַכְסָה בִתּוֹ לְאִשָּׁה׃

15.8 Exegetical Exercises—Word Order

When using language, speakers and writers communicate not only through the meaning of the words but also through the order in which the words are spoken or written. For instance, word order is especially significant in English: "Jim hit Sally," versus "Sally hit Jim." Because the Hebrew verbal forms encode more information than English verbal forms, word order is not as important in Hebrew as it is in English, but it remains significant for communication.

A. Word Order in Verbless Clauses. The two pieces (called "constituents") of a verbless clause are the **subject** and **predicate**. Verbless clauses introduced by a *waw* are most

[11] Niph. Part. fp of כבד, glossed as "to be glorious"—translate "glorious things" (see ch. 19).
[12] Hiph. Imperf. 3ms of נכה, glossed as "to strike, smite" (see chs. 16, 24).
[13] Qal Conv. Perf. 3ms of לכד, glossed as "to capture" + 3fs object suffix—translate "and captures it" (see ch. 21).
[14] This form also has a 3fs object suffix.

often **circumstantial clauses**, which give background information defining the conditions (circumstances) of the action or event in the sentence's main clause, e.g.:

וְעֵ֤ץ הַֽחַיִּים֙ בְּת֣וֹךְ הַגָּ֔ן ("and the tree of life was in the middle of the garden"—Gen. 2:9)

Noncircumstantial verbless clauses can be loosely classified into two types: **descriptive clauses** and **identifying clauses**.[15]

Descriptive clauses have an indefinite predicate preceding the subject, as in:

מְרַגְּלִ֣ים אַתֶּ֔ם ("You are spies."—literally, "Spies you are."—Gen. 42:9)

Identifying clauses have a definite predicate following the subject, as in:

אֲנִ֣י יוֹסֵ֔ף ("I am Joseph."—Gen. 45:3)

As the names indicate, the function of a descriptive clause is to characterize the subject by the predicate, while the function of an identifying clause is to create a one-to-one correspondence between the subject and predicate.[16]

Translate the following verbless clauses and classify them as circumstantial, descriptive, or identifying.

Ex. 6:2 אֲנִ֥י יְהוָֽה

Gen. 24:65 ה֣וּא אֲדֹנִ֑י

Gen. 13:2 וְאַבְרָ֖ם כָּבֵ֣ד מְאֹ֑ד

---

[15] This explanation is of necessity brief and oversimplifies a vast literature on the Hebrew verbless clause, but it suffices to introduce the variation in verbless clause word order.

[16] This general rule of word order in verbless clauses can be overcome by other linguistic factors. For example, Genesis 18:27 is a descriptive clause, but the word order is *Subject–Predicate* to contrast with the preceding clause.

Gen. 9:25 אָר֣וּר כְּנָ֑עַן

Ex. 2:6 מִיַּלְדֵ֥י הָֽעִבְרִ֖ים זֶֽה

Judg. 3:17 וְעֶגְל֕וֹן אִ֖ישׁ בָּרִ֥יא מְאֹֽד

B. Word Order in Narrative Prose Verbal Clauses.[17] Word order in verbal clauses typically focuses on the three major constituents of a clause: the subject, verb, and object. (Modifiers such as prepositional phrases and adverbs are considered minor constituents and may be interspersed in the clause.) The word order of a given clause can therefore be summarized with the letters SVO (Subject–Verb–Object), VSO (Verb–Subject–Object), etc.

Standard Prose Narrative Word Order. The standard word order for the major constituents of a clause in Hebrew prose is **Verb–(Subject)–Object.**[18] This is commonly abbreviated as V–(S)–O, V(S)O, or VSO.

As mentioned in 3.2, the Hebrew verb does not require an explicit subject. An explicit subject is typically given at the start of a unit of discourse—often what English speakers would call a paragraph—and does not need to be repeated (e.g.: English—"James went to dinner. He decided to eat fish. He chose a flounder . . ."). The subject is explicitly mentioned again only in (1) a long narrative, which creates the need to "remind" the reader of the subject's identity, or (2) switching to another subject.

[17] These word-order patterns focus on Hebrew narrative prose. Spoken Hebrew prose (i.e.: reported dialogue) shares some of these characteristics, such as being verb-initial, but it is more flexible in its patterns and syntax. The importance of word order in Hebrew poetry is a subject of debate, since poetry generally observes a much more loose set of syntactic requirements.

[18] The eminent Hebrew grammarian Paul Joüon held that the basic word order of a Hebrew verbal clause was *Subject–Verb*, and he is still followed by a few grammarians. Most, however, follow the work of Muraoka (e.g.: *Emphatic Words and Structures in Biblical Hebrew* [Leiden: Brill, 1985]) and others, who note that the descriptive evidence is highly tilted toward a *Verb–Subject* word order for Biblical Hebrew narrative.

V(S)O is therefore the standard word order (called "unmarked") in prose narrative. When this word order is interrupted in narrative prose, the clause with the differing word order should be specially considered, because it breaks the pattern. This clause is termed "marked" in its word order, as the differing word order communicates meaning.

Circumstantial Clauses. As noted above, if the marked clause has the word order *waw* + verbless clause, it is typically a circumstantial clause. *A circumstantial clause is not sequential to the narrative but instead serves a different function, most commonly to give background information.*

For example, Genesis 1:1–3:

1 בְּרֵאשִׁית בָּרָא אֱלֹהִים אֵת הַשָּׁמַיִם וְאֵת הָאָרֶץ׃

2 וְהָאָרֶץ הָיְתָה תֹהוּ וָבֹהוּ וְחֹשֶׁךְ עַל־פְּנֵי תְהוֹם וְרוּחַ אֱלֹהִים מְרַחֶפֶת עַל־פְּנֵי
הַמָּיִם׃

3 וַיֹּאמֶר אֱלֹהִים יְהִי אוֹר וַיְהִי־אוֹר׃

1—"In the beginning, God created the heavens and the earth." (VSO; perfect verb)

2—"Now the earth was formless and void, and darkness was upon the face of the deep," (SVP; perfect verb)

"And the spirit of God was hovering over the face of the waters." (SVP; participle)

3—"And God said, 'Let there be light.'" (VSO; narrative verb)

The word order indicates that verse 2 is not a second sequential step in the narrative, but instead provides background information to the reader about the situation in which the narrative sequence takes place. This is a *circumstantial clause*, with the break in word order emphasizing the background situation before the action of verse 3.

Exodus 2:25–3:1 has been divided into clauses below. Verse numbers are in bold italics, while footnotes are not. Translate and mark the word order for each clause. Note which clauses have marked word orders and what those marked word orders show.

25 וַיַּ֥רְא[19] אֱלֹהִ֖ים אֶת־בְּנֵ֣י יִשְׂרָאֵ֑ל

וַיֵּ֖דַע[20] אֱלֹהִֽים׃

1 וּמֹשֶׁ֗ה הָיָ֥ה רֹעֶ֛ה אֶת־צֹ֛אן יִתְר֥וֹ חֹתְנ֖וֹ כֹּהֵ֣ן מִדְיָ֑ן

וַיִּנְהַ֤ג אֶת־הַצֹּאן֙ אַחַ֣ר הַמִּדְבָּ֔ר

וַיָּבֹ֛א[21] אֶל־הַ֥ר הָאֱלֹהִ֖ים חֹרֵֽבָה׃

Emphatic Clauses. In other cases the sequential nature of the narrative continues, but either the subject or the object is *fronted* in the clause, creating a different word order.[22] Moving either the subject or object into the first position of the clause breaks the typical pattern and creates attention. This is commonly considered a position of emphasis.

For example, Genesis 22:1:

1 וַיְהִ֗י אַחַר֙ הַדְּבָרִ֣ים הָאֵ֔לֶּה

וְהָ֣אֱלֹהִ֔ים נִסָּ֖ה אֶת־אַבְרָהָ֑ם

וַיֹּ֣אמֶר אֵלָ֔יו אַבְרָהָ֖ם

וַיֹּ֥אמֶר הִנֵּֽנִי׃

---

[19] Qal Narr. 3ms of ראה, glossed as "to see" (see ch. 24).

[20] Qal Narr. 3ms of ידע, glossed as "to know" (see ch. 27).

[21] Qal Narr. 3ms of בוא, glossed as "to come" (see ch. 26).

[22] The marked word-order combinations SVO, OVS, VOS, SOV, and OSV are all possible.

1a—And (it was) after these things (V; narrative verb, discourse begins)

1b—God tested Abraham (SVO; perfect verb)

1c—And he said to him, “Abraham” (VO; narrative verb)

1d—And he said, “Here I am.” (VO; narrative verb)

The word order in the second clause (וְהָֽאֱלֹהִ֔ים נִסָּ֖ה אֶת־אַבְרָהָ֑ם) is SVO and is therefore marked, putting the subject into the presumed position of emphasis.

As various authors point out, simply noting that a subject or object is in an emphatic position is insufficient.[23] Instead, you should ask what that emphasis indicates. In the case of Genesis 22 the emphasis is clear in the context of the narrative: this testing was divine, with God as the initiator.

Judges 1:17–21 has been divided into clauses below. Translate and mark the word order for each clause. Note which clauses have marked word orders and what each marked word order shows.

17 וַיֵּ֣לֶךְ יְהוּדָה֙ אֶת־שִׁמְע֣וֹן אָחִ֔יו

וַיַּכּ֕וּ[24] אֶת־הַֽכְּנַעֲנִ֖י יוֹשֵׁ֣ב צְפַ֑ת

וַיַּחֲרִ֖ימוּ[25] אוֹתָ֑הּ

וַיִּקְרָ֥א אֶת־שֵׁם־הָעִ֖יר חָרְמָֽה׃

[23] E.g.: Barry Bandstra, “Word Order and Emphasis in Biblical Hebrew Narrative,” in *Linguistics and Biblical Hebrew*, ed. Walter R. Bodine (Winona Lake, IN: Eisenbrauns, 1992), 109–123.

[24] Hiph. Narr. 3mp of נכה, glossed as “to strike” (see ch. 24).

[25] Hiph. Narr. 3mp of הרם, glossed as “to completely destroy, devote to God” (see ch. 16).

*18*וַיִּלְכֹּ֤ד יְהוּדָה֙ אֶת־עַזָּ֣ה וְאֶת־גְּבוּלָ֔הּ וְֽאֶת־אַשְׁקְל֖וֹן וְאֶת־גְּבוּלָ֑הּ וְאֶת־עֶקְר֖וֹן וְאֶת־גְּבוּלָֽהּ׃

*19*וַיְהִ֤י יְהוָה֙ אֶת־יְהוּדָ֔ה

וַיֹּ֖רֶשׁ[26] אֶת־הָהָ֑ר

כִּ֣י לֹ֤א לְהוֹרִישׁ֙[27] אֶת־יֹשְׁבֵ֣י הָעֵ֔מֶק כִּי־רֶ֥כֶב בַּרְזֶ֖ל לָהֶֽם׃

*20*וַיִּתְּנ֤וּ לְכָלֵב֙ אֶת־חֶבְר֔וֹן

כַּאֲשֶׁ֖ר דִּבֶּ֣ר מֹשֶׁ֑ה

וַיּ֣וֹרֶשׁ[28] מִשָּׁ֔ם אֶת־שְׁלֹשָׁ֖ה בְּנֵ֥י הָעֲנָֽק׃

*21*וְאֶת־הַיְבוּסִי֙ יֹשֵׁ֣ב יְרוּשָׁלִַ֔ם לֹ֥א הוֹרִ֖ישׁוּ[29] בְּנֵ֣י בִנְיָמִ֑ן

וַיֵּ֨שֶׁב[30] הַיְבוּסִ֜י אֶת־בְּנֵ֤י בִנְיָמִן֙ בִּיר֣וּשָׁלִַ֔ם עַ֖ד הַיּ֥וֹם הַזֶּֽה׃

---

[26] Hiph. Narr. 3ms of ירשׁ, glossed as "to possess" (see chs. 16, 27).

[27] Hiph. Inf. Const. of ירשׁ, glossed as "to dispossess" (see chs. 16, 27).

[28] Hiph. Narr. 3ms of ירשׁ, glossed as "to dispossess" (see chs. 16, 27).

[29] Hiph. Perf. 3mp of ירשׁ, glossed as "to dispossess" (see chs. 16, 27).

[30] Qal Narr. 3ms of ישׁב, glossed as "to dwell" (see ch. 27).

Consult Judges 19:10–16. Which two cities are involved? Which Israelite tribe inhabits Gibeah?

Review Judges 19:17–20:48. Note how the tribe of Benjamin is repeatedly cast in a negative light. Now review chapter 1. How has the anti-Benjamite slant of the book been previewed as early as chapter 1? (Which tribes are successful and which are not? Where is Benjamin's failure particularly noted?)

Given Judges 1:21, what is the irony in the comparison of Jebusite Jerusalem and Benjamite Gibeah in 19:10–16?

טז (16) Hiphil

16.1 The Hiphil Stem

The Hiphil is the fourth verbal stem (*binyan*) covered in this grammar. The major relationship of the Hiphil to the Qal is causation: in the Hiphil, a subject causes the action of the Qal to occur:

קָטַל he killed (Qal)

הִקְטִיל he caused (someone) to kill (Hiphil)

As with the Piel, however, a single generalization does not explain every instance of the Hiphil. Some verbs occur only in the Hiphil or follow other patterns. The main uses of the Hiphil include:

- **Causation:**
  - Of **action**—when the Hiphil verb causes the action indicated by the Qal to occur, as in:

    וַיַּעֲבֵר אֱלֹהִים רוּחַ עַל־הָאָרֶץ ("And God caused a wind to pass over the earth"—Gen. 8:1)

    וַיַּפְשִׁיטוּ אֶת־יוֹסֵף אֶת־כֻּתָּנְתּוֹ ("And they caused Joseph to strip off his coat"—Gen. 37:23)

  - Of **state** (factitive)—when the Hiphil verb causes a state to become a fact, as in:

    וְהִרְחַבְתִּי אֶת־גְּבוּלֶךָ ("And I will widen your borders"—Ex. 34:24)

- **Internal Causation:** when the Hiphil verb indicates a subject causing itself to enter a state, but with no separate object, as in:

  וְכֹל אֲשֶׁר־יַעֲשֶׂה יַצְלִיחַ ("And everything he does, he prospers"—Ps. 1:3)

  הֵן עַד־יָרֵחַ וְלֹא יַאֲהִיל ("Look as far as the moon, and it is not bright"—Job 25:5)

- **Denominative:**[1] when the Hiphil verb is formed from a noun, as in:

  כִּי לֹא הִמְטִיר יְהוָה אֱלֹהִים עַל־הָאָרֶץ ("For the LORD God had not yet made it rain upon the earth"—Gen. 2:5)

A comparison of the functions of the Piel (14.1) and the Hiphil shows that the two stems can overlap in function. Accordingly, though you can generalize the Piel as factitive/intensive and the Hiphil as causative, you must always remember that such descriptions are only generalizations, not ironclad rules.

16.2 The Hiphil Perfect

The Hiphil perfect is formed by the addition of a *heh* before the verbal root. The *ḥireq yod* theme vowel implied by the name *Hiphil* is apparent only in the 3ms, 3fs, and 3cp forms.

Hiphil Perfect Paradigm

	Verbal Form	Suffix	Gloss
3ms	הִקְטִיל	--	he caused to kill
3fs	הִקְטִ֫ילָה	ָה	she caused to kill
2ms	הִקְטַ֫לְתָּ	תָּ	you (ms) caused to kill
2fs	הִקְטַלְתְּ	תְּ	you (fs) caused to kill
1cs	הִקְטַ֫לְתִּי	תִּי	I caused to kill
3cp	הִקְטִ֫ילוּ	וּ	they caused to kill
2mp	הִקְטַלְתֶּם	תֶּם	you (mp) caused to kill
2fp	הִקְטַלְתֶּן	תֶּן	you (fp) caused to kill
1cp	הִקְטַ֫לְנוּ	נוּ	we caused to kill

[1] Denominatives also occur in the Piel (see 14.1).

> Tip-Offs for the Hiphil Perfect:
>
> - Prefixed הִ־ (though this will also occur in certain Niphal forms—see 19.4, 19.6)
> - *ḥireq yod* in third-person forms

16.3 The Hiphil Imperfect

The Hiphil imperfect does not show the ה prefix that is evident in the perfect; it has dropped out because of the presence of the verbal prefix.

יַקְטִיל < יְהַקְטִיל*

The *ḥireq yod* theme vowel occurs in all forms except the 3fp and 2fp.

Hiphil Imperfect Paradigm

	Verbal Form	Prefix...Suffix	Gloss
3ms	יַקְטִיל	--- י	he will cause to kill
3fs	תַּקְטִיל	--- תּ	she will cause to kill
2ms	תַּקְטִיל	--- תּ	you (ms) will cause to kill
2fs	תַּקְטִ֫ילִי	ִי --- תּ	you (fs) will cause to kill
1cs	אַקְטִיל	--- א	I will cause to kill
3mp	יַקְטִ֫ילוּ	וּ --- י	they (mp) will cause to kill
3fp	תַּקְטֵ֫לְנָה	נָה --- תּ	they (fp) will cause to kill
2mp	תַּקְטִ֫ילוּ	וּ --- תּ	you (mp) will cause to kill
2fp	תַּקְטֵ֫לְנָה	נָה --- תּ	you (fp) will cause to kill
1cp	נַקְטִיל	--- נ	we will cause to kill

> Tip-Offs for the Hiphil Imperfect:
>
> - Prefix vowel of *pataḥ* (though an I-guttural Qal imperfect may also have this vowel—see 22.4)
> - *ḥireq yod* in all forms except 3fp and 2fp

16.4 The Hiphil Narrative

With the addition of the וַ־ to make a narrative form, the *ḥireq yod* of the imperfect usually becomes a *ṣere*:

יַקְטִיל (imperfect), but וַיַּקְטֵל (narrative)

16.5 The Hiphil Volitives

Hiphil imperatives show the *heh* prefix (no longer hidden by the verbal prefix) and either a *ḥireq yod* or *ṣere* theme vowel.

Hiphil Imperative Paradigm

	Verbal Form	Suffix	Gloss
2ms	הַקְטֵל	---	you (ms) cause to kill
2fs	הַקְטִ֫ילִי	ִי ---	you (fs) cause to kill
2mp	הַקְטִ֫ילוּ	וּ ---	you (mp) cause to kill
2fp	הַקְטֵ֫לְנָה	נָה ---	you (fp) cause to kill

Hiphil jussives (the third-person volitive form) typically show the same shift from *ḥireq yod* to *ṣere* as the narrative form.

Hiphil Jussive Paradigm

	Verbal Form	Suffix	Gloss
3ms	יַקְטֵל	---	may he cause to kill
3fs	תַּקְטֵל	ִי ---	may she cause to kill
3mp	יַקְטֵ֫לוּ	וּ ---	may they (mp) cause to kill
3fp	תַּקְטֵ֫לְנָה	נָה ---	may they (fp) cause to kill

The Hiphil cohortative shows the expected forms: אַקְטִ֫ילָה and נַקְטִ֫ילָה.

16.6 The Hiphil Participle

As with all derived stems, the Hiphil participle shows a prefixed *mem*. The *ḥireq yod* theme vowel is visible in all except the fs form.

Hiphil Participle Paradigm

	Verbal Form	Suffix	Gloss
ms	מַקְטִיל	--	one who causes to kill
fs	מַקְטֶ֫לֶת	ֶת	one who causes to kill
mp	מַקְטִילִים	ִים	ones who cause to kill
fp	מַקְטִילוֹת	וֹת	ones who cause to kill

Tip-Offs for the Hiphil Participle:

- Prefix of מַ־
- *ḥireq yod* in all forms except fs

16.7 The Hiphil Infinitives

The Hiphil infinitive construct shows a prefixed *heh* and the *ḥireq yod* vowel:

הַקְטִיל

The Hiphil infinitive absolute shows the prefixed *heh* but with a *ṣere* vowel:

הַקְטֵל

16.8 Vocabulary

אִבַּד	(Piel) to destroy
הֶאֱבִיד	(Hiph.) to exterminate, wipe out
אֲדָמָה	earth, ground; land, arable land
אָסַר	to bind, capture, confine
אַף	nose, nostrils; anger (forms the dual אַפַּיִם instead of plural)
בַּ֫עַל	lord, master, owner; husband; Baal
הִגִּיד	(Hiph.) to tell, announce, inform
הִזְכִּיר	(Hiph.) to make known, mention; to profess, praise
חֲצִי	half, half the height, middle
הִשְׁכִּים	(Hiph.) to get up early, do something early
הִשְׁלִיךְ	(HIph.) to throw, to cast
לִקְרַאת	opposite, contrary to (prep. + inf. const.)
עֹז	might, strength
צָבָא	military service, campaign; military men, troops; heavenly warriors[2]
רוּחַ	breeze, wind, breath; spirit
רָעָב	hunger, famine
שָׂמַח	to rejoice, be glad
שִׂמַּח	(Piel) to gladden, make merry
שִׂמְחָה	Joy
שָׁאַל	to ask

[2] The plural form, צְבָאוֹת, is the origin of the English "Sabaoth," as in Martin' Luther's *A Mighty Fortress is Our God*: "Lord Sabaoth his name," meaning "Lord of hosts."

16.9 Language Exercises

A. Parse and gloss the following forms.

אַזְכִּיר

יַשְׁלִיךְ

יַשְׁלֵךְ

אֱסֹר

שְׁלֹחַ

הִשְׁלִ֫יכָה

הִגַּ֫דְתָּ

יְשַׁלַּח

תַּגִּיד

הַגֵּד

הֶאֱבַדְתָּ

הַזְכִּיר

הַשְׁלֵךְ

מַאֲבִיד

שָׁלַ֫חְתִּי

B. Translate the following and parse each verb and participle. Use your lexicon to look up the glosses for any words you do not know from your vocabulary.

Ex. 14:10–12

וּפַרְעֹה הִקְרִיב וַיִשְׂאוּ[3] בְנֵי־יִשְׂרָאֵל אֶת־עֵינֵיהֶם וְהִנֵּה מִצְרַיִם ׀ נֹסֵעַ

אַחֲרֵיהֶם וַיִּירְאוּ[4] מְאֹד וַיִּצְעֲקוּ בְנֵי־יִשְׂרָאֵל אֶל־יְהוָה׃ וַיֹּאמְרוּ אֶל־מֹשֶׁה

הֲמִבְּלִי אֵין־קְבָרִים בְּמִצְרַיִם לְקַחְתָּנוּ[5] לָמוּת[6] בַּמִּדְבָּר ...׃ הֲלֹא־זֶה

הַדָּבָר אֲשֶׁר דִּבַּרְנוּ אֵלֶיךָ בְמִצְרַיִם לֵאמֹר חֲדַל מִמֶּנּוּ וְנַעַבְדָה אֶת־

מִצְרָיִם כִּי טוֹב לָנוּ עֲבֹד אֶת־מִצְרַיִם מִמֻּתֵנוּ[7] בַּמִּדְבָּר׃

---

[3] The expected *dagesh* in the *sin* has dropped out because of the *shewa* under the letter. See 4.4.

[4] Qal Narr. 3mp of ירא, glossed as "to fear" (see chs. 25, 27).

[5] Qal Perf. 2ms of לקח plus a 1cp object suffix (see ch. 21).

[6] Qal Inf. Const. of מות, glossed as "to die" (see ch. 26).

[7] מִן + Qal Inf. Const. of מות, glossed as "to die" + 1cs suffix (see ch. 26).

Ex. 3:20

וְשָׁלַחְתִּ֤י[8] אֶת־יָדִי֙ וְהִכֵּיתִ֣י[9] אֶת־מִצְרַ֔יִם בְּכֹל֙ נִפְלְאֹתַ֔י[10] אֲשֶׁ֥ר אֶעֱשֶׂ֖ה

בְּקִרְבּ֑וֹ וְאַחֲרֵי־כֵ֖ן יְשַׁלַּ֥ח אֶתְכֶֽם׃

Ex. 7:10–13

וַיָּבֹ֨א[11] מֹשֶׁ֤ה וְאַהֲרֹן֙ אֶל־פַּרְעֹ֔ה וַיַּ֣עֲשׂוּ[12] כֵ֔ן כַּאֲשֶׁ֖ר צִוָּ֣ה יְהוָ֑ה וַיַּשְׁלֵ֨ךְ

אַהֲרֹ֜ן אֶת־מַטֵּ֗הוּ לִפְנֵ֥י פַּרְעֹ֛ה וְלִפְנֵ֥י עֲבָדָ֖יו וַיְהִ֥י לְתַנִּֽין׃ וַיִּקְרָא֙ גַּם־פַּרְעֹ֔ה

לַחֲכָמִ֖ים וְלַֽמְכַשְּׁפִ֑ים וַיַּעֲשׂ֨וּ[13] גַם־הֵ֜ם חַרְטֻמֵּ֥י מִצְרַ֛יִם בְּלַהֲטֵיהֶ֖ם כֵּֽן׃

וַיַּשְׁלִ֙יכוּ֙ אִ֣ישׁ מַטֵּ֔הוּ וַיִּהְי֖וּ[14] לְתַנִּינִ֑ם וַיִּבְלַ֥ע מַטֵּֽה־אַהֲרֹ֖ן אֶת־מַטֹּתָֽם׃

וַיֶּחֱזַק֙ לֵ֣ב פַּרְעֹ֔ה וְלֹ֥א שָׁמַ֖ע אֲלֵהֶ֑ם כַּאֲשֶׁ֖ר דִּבֶּ֥ר יְהוָֽה׃

[8] You will need to consult section 13.7, where you translated Ex. 3:19, in order to determine the translational value of this verbal form.

[9] Hiph. Conv. Perf. 1cs of נכה, glossed as “to strike” (see ch. 24).

[10] Niph. Part. fp of פלא, glossed as “to be wonderful”—note the possessive suffix on this form (see ch. 19).

[11] Qal Narr. 3ms of בוא, glossed as “to go” (see ch. 26).

[12] Qal Narr. 3mp of עשה, glossed as “to do” (see ch. 24).

[13] Qal Narr. 3mp of עשה, glossed as “to do” (see ch. 24).

[14] Qal Narr. 3mp of היה, glossed as “to be” (see ch. 24).

Ex. 14:15 וַיֹּ֤אמֶר יְהוָה֙ אֶל־מֹשֶׁ֔ה מַה־תִּצְעַ֖ק אֵלָ֑י דַּבֵּ֥ר אֶל־בְּנֵֽי־יִשְׂרָאֵ֖ל וְיִסָּֽעוּ׃

Josh. 6:12–13 (*Qere*) וַיַּשְׁכֵּ֥ם יְהוֹשֻׁ֖עַ בַּבֹּ֑קֶר וַיִּשְׂא֥וּ[15] הַכֹּהֲנִ֖ים אֶת־אֲר֥וֹן יְהוָֽה׃ וְשִׁבְעָ֨ה הַכֹּהֲנִ֜ים

נֹשְׂאִ֗ים שִׁבְעָ֞ה שׁוֹפְר֣וֹת הַיֹּבְלִ֘ים לִפְנֵ֣י אֲר֣וֹן יְהוָה֒ הֹלְכִ֣ים הָל֔וֹךְ וְתָקְע֖וּ

בַּשּׁוֹפָר֑וֹת וְהֶחָלוּץ֙ הֹלֵ֣ךְ לִפְנֵיהֶ֔ם וְהַמְאַסֵּ֗ף הֹלֵךְ֙ אַחֲרֵי֙ אֲר֣וֹן יְהוָ֔ה הָל֖וֹךְ

וְתָק֥וֹעַ בַּשּׁוֹפָרֽוֹת׃

16.10 Exegetical Exercises—Revocalization

As mentioned in 8.12, the Masoretes—who provided the vowel pointing used in the Hebrew text—were conservators of a reading tradition handed down to them. The Masoretes enshrined this reading tradition in their system of vowel pointing near the end of the first millennium A.D.—more than one thousand years after these texts were authored.

Every language changes over time as patterns of speech change. In English, for instance, compare the language of *Beowulf* with modern American English or even modern British English. Such language change creates a situation in which a reading tradition can misinterpret words or phrases. Until the Masoretes set down their reading tradition in vowel

[15] See footnote 3.

pointing, the reader of the Hebrew text supplied vowels from memory to the consonantal written text.

At times the consonantal text can be interpreted in multiple ways, depending on which vowels are supplied. For example, consider Amos 9. Verse 11 begins the final section of the book, a description of בַּיּ֣וֹם הַה֔וּא, a day of eschatological restoration for Israel. Among the various descriptions of "that day" is the purpose statement beginning verse 12:

לְמַ֨עַן יִֽירְשׁ֜וּ אֶת־שְׁאֵרִ֤ית אֱדוֹם֙.

Translate this phrase. The verb is a Qal Imperfect 3ms from the root ירשׁ.

Now consult Acts 15:17, where the followers of Jesus in Jerusalem meet with Paul and Barnabas to discuss whether Gentiles who converted to Christianity must be circumcised according to the Law of Moses. James seems to chair the meeting as he offers the final word, stating that the prophet Amos agrees with his judgment. It is especially important for James's purposes that the Gentiles be part of this vision in Amos, alongside all Israel's restoration. As is true for many New Testament writers, Luke has James quoting from a Greek text of Amos, not from the Hebrew reading tradition.[16] How does the Greek text in Acts 15:17 end up with the translation "remnant of men" rather than "remnant of Edom" from the Hebrew reading tradition? How could an original consonantal text את שארת אדם be vocalized to result in that reading?

The idea of a revocalization suggests that over the centuries the Masoretic reading tradition somehow applied the wrong vowels to the consonantal text.[17] While caution is still in order, suggesting a *revocalization* of the text—a reading of the text with different vowels—is a less severe proposal than suggesting an *emendation* of the text—a change to the consonantal

[16] This Greek text is not identical to Amos 9:11–12 in the Septuagint as it exists today.
[17] The purpose of quoting Acts 15:17 here is not to argue for a revocalization of Amos 9:12, just to simply acknowledge that different reading traditions exist.

text available to us.[18] When a commentator proposes a revocalization, the proposal is not technically a change to the text of the Scriptures but instead an appeal to read that text in a different way. Consider Genesis 49:24b from the midst of the blessing on Joseph.

Translate the Masoretic text: מִשָּׁם רֹעֶה אֶבֶן יִשְׂרָאֵל

Note that the ESV translation of this verse has a textual note.

ESV translation: "from there is the Shepherd, the Stone of Israel."

ESV textual note: "or 'by the name of the Shepherd, the Stone of Israel.'"

What word explains the difference between the ESV translation and the textual note? Write the Hebrew text without any vowel pointing.

What vocalization would create the reading "by the name of the Shepherd"?

Modern translations usually accept some revocalizations, possibly indicating them in textual notes but sometimes not marking them. Using your lexicon as necessary, analyze the following revocalizations.

[18] This is not meant to imply that emendations are always wrong, just to point out that a revocalization is a much smaller proposed change.

A. Ps. 58:2 [Engl. 58:1] הַאֻמְנָם אֵלֶם צֶדֶק תְּדַבֵּרוּן

Your Translation:

ESV Translation: “Do you indeed decree what is right, you gods?”

Hebrew Word Requiring Revocalization (Consonants Only)	Vocalization That Would Produce ESV Text

B. Prov. 6:24a לִשְׁמָרְךָ מֵאֵשֶׁת רָע

Your Translation:

NIV Translation: “Keeping you from your[19] neighbor’s wife”

Hebrew Word Requiring Revocalization (Consonants Only)	Vocalization That Would Produce NIV Text

C. Ps. 109:17b וְלֹא־חָפֵץ בִּבְרָכָה וַתִּרְחַק מִמֶּנּוּ

Your Translation:

HCSB Translation: “He took no delight in blessing—let it be far from him.”

Hebrew Word Requiring Revocalization (Consonants Only)	Vocalization That Would Produce HCSB Text

[19] Do not concern yourself about the origin of the pronoun “your,” which the NIV translation infers. The revocalization lies elsewhere in the verse.

יז (17) Hophal

17.1 The Hophal Stem

Just as the Pual is the passive counterpart to the Piel stem, so the Hophal is the passive counterpart to the Hiphil stem. Whatever nuance the Hiphil of a verb indicates is made passive in the Hophal:

הִקְטִיל he caused to kill (Hiphil)

הָקְטַל he was caused to kill (Hophal)

The Hophal is a relatively infrequent pattern. As a beginning student, you should concentrate only on the perfect, imperfect, participle, and infinitive absolute forms, since the other forms are rare.

17.2 The Hophal Perfect

The Hophal perfect shares the prefixed *heh* of the Hiphil but has either a *qibbuṣ* or a *qameṣ ḥatup* as its initial vowel. (Recall from 1.3 that these vowels are related, both being *u*-class vowels.)

Hophal Perfect Paradigm

	u-type Verbal Form	*o*-type Verbal Form	Suffix	Gloss
3ms	הֻקְטַל	הָקְטַל	--	he was caused to kill
3fs	הֻקְטְלָה	הָקְטְלָה	ָה	she was caused to kill
2ms	הֻקְטַלְתָּ	הָקְטַלְתָּ	תָּ	you (ms) were caused to kill
2fs	הֻקְטַלְתְּ	הָקְטַלְתְּ	תְּ	you (fs) were caused to kill
1cs	הֻקְטַלְתִּי	הָקְטַלְתִּי	תִּי	I was caused to kill

3cp	הֻקְטְלוּ	הָקְטְלוּ	וּ	they were caused to kill
2mp	הֻקְטַלְתֶּם	הָקְטַלְתֶּם	תֶּם	you (mp) were caused to kill
2fp	הֻקְטַלְתֶּן	הָקְטַלְתֶּן	תֶּן	you (fp) were caused to kill
1cp	הֻקְטַ֫לְנוּ	הָקְטַ֫לְנוּ	נוּ	we were caused to kill

In the paradigm above, the vowel is a *qameṣ ḥatup̄*, not a *qameṣ* (see 2.5).

Tip-Offs for the Hophal Perfect:

- Prefixed הָ/הֻ with either a *qibbuṣ* or a *qameṣ ḥatup*
- *pataḥ* theme vowel (when it does not reduce)

17.3 The Hophal Imperfect

The Hophal imperfect takes a prefix with either a *qibbuṣ* or a *qameṣ ḥatup*. The theme vowel is *pataḥ* when it does not reduce to *shewa*.

Hophal Imperfect Paradigm

	u-type Verbal Form	*o*-type Verbal Form	Prefix Suffix	Gloss
3ms	יֻקְטַל	יָקְטַל	י ---	he will be caused to kill
3fs	תֻּקְטַל	תָּקְטַל	תּ ---	she will be caused to kill
2ms	תֻּקְטַל	תָּקְטַל	תּ ---	you (ms) will be caused to kill
2fs	תֻּקְטְלִי	תָּקְטְלִי	תּ --- ִי	you (fs) will be caused to kill
1cs	אֻקְטַל	אָקְטַל	א ---	I will be caused to kill

3mp	יֻקְטְלוּ	יָקְטְלוּ	י --- וּ	they (mp) will be caused to kill
3fp	תֻּקְטַלְנָה	תָּקְטַלְנָה	ת --- נָה	they will be caused to kill
2mp	תֻּקְטְלוּ	תָּקְטְלוּ	ת --- וּ	you (mp) will be caused to kill
2fp	תֻּקְטַלְנָה	תָּקְטַלְנָה	ת --- נָה	you (fp) will be caused to kill
1cp	נֻקְטַל	נָקְטַל	נ ---	we will be caused to kill

Tip-Offs for the Hophal Imperfect:

- Prefix takes either a *qibbuṣ* or a *qameṣ ḥatup*
- *pataḥ* theme vowel (when it does not reduce)

17.4 The Hophal Participle

Just like the other derived stems, the Hophal participle has a prefixed מ. The vowel, as with the Hophal perfect and imperfect, can be either *qibbuṣ* or a *qameṣ ḥatup*:

Hophal Participle Paradigm

	u-type Verbal Form	*o*-type Verbal Form	Suffix	Gloss
Ms	מֻקְטָל	מָקְטָל	--	one who is caused to kill
Fs	מֻקְטֶלֶת	מָקְטֶלֶת	ֶת	one who is caused to kill
Mp	מֻקְטָלִים	מָקְטָלִים	ִים	ones who are caused to kill
Fp	מֻקְטָלוֹת	מָקְטָלוֹת	וֹת	ones who are caused to kill

Tip-Offs for the Hophal Participle:

- Prefix of מְ־ with *qibbuṣ* or a *qameṣ ḥatup*
- *qameṣ* in all forms except fs

17.5 The Hophal Infinitive Absolute

The Hophal infinitive absolute has a prefixed *heh* with a *qameṣ ḥatup* and a *ṣere* theme vowel:

הָקְטֵל

17.6 Vocabulary

בֶּ֫גֶד	garment, cloak, covering
דָּבַק	to stick to
הִדְבִּיק	(Hiph.) to overtake; cause to stick
דָּרַשׁ	to seek, turn to; inquire, consult
הִבִּיט	(Hiph.) to look; consider; accept
הֶ֫בֶל	breath, vanity, idols
הִשִּׂיג	(Hiph.) to overtake, reach; to be sufficient
הִשְׂכִּיל	(Hiph.) to make wise, give insight; understand, be prudent
חֹ֫דֶשׁ	new moon, month
חֶ֫סֶד	loyalty, faithfulness, goodness, graciousness
כֶּ֫בֶשׂ	young ram
כֹּחַ	power, strength, property
כָּעַס	to be irritated, vexed
הִכְעִיס	(Hiph.) to irritate; provoke to anger
נִכַּר	(Piel) to deface
הִכִּיר	(Hiph.) to investigate; to recognize; to know, acknowledge
נָכְרִי[1]	a foreigner (*nokrî*)
רָחַק	to be distant
הִרְחִיק	(Hiph.) to remove (make distant)
רָחוֹק	far

[1] נָכְרִיָּה (fs) = "foreign woman" in Proverbs.

17.7 Language Exercises

A. Parse and gloss the following forms.

הִשְׁכִּים

שֻׁלְּחָה

אָמוֹר

מֻשְׁלֶ֫כֶת

וַיַּשְׁכֵּם

תֹּאמַ֫רְנָה

וְהִשְׁלַחְתִּי

הָשְׁלְכוּ

וַתֻּשְׁלְכִי

הַשְׁכֵּם

B. Translate the following and parse all verbs and participles. Use your lexicon to look up the glosses for any words you do not know from your vocabulary.

1 Kings 13:24b–25

וַתְּהִ֤י[2] נִבְלָתוֹ֙ מֻשְׁלֶ֣כֶת בַּדֶּ֔רֶךְ וְהַחֲמוֹר֙ עֹמֵ֣ד אֶצְלָ֔הּ וְהָֽאַרְיֵ֔ה עֹמֵ֖ד אֵ֥צֶל

הַנְּבֵלָֽה׃ וְהִנֵּ֨ה אֲנָשִׁ֜ים עֹבְרִ֗ים וַיִּרְא֤וּ[3] אֶת־הַנְּבֵלָה֙ מֻשְׁלֶ֣כֶת בַּדֶּ֔רֶךְ וְאֶת־

[2] Qal Narr. 3fs of היה, glossed as “to be” (see ch. 24).

[3] Qal Narr. 3mp of ראה, glossed as “to see” (see ch. 24).

הָאַרְיֵה עֹמֵד אֵצֶל הַנְּבֵלָה וַיָּבֹאוּ[4] וַיְדַבְּרוּ בָעִיר אֲשֶׁר הַנָּבִיא הַזָּקֵן יֹשֵׁב

בָּהּ׃

Ex. 14:1–4a

וַיְדַבֵּר יְהוָה אֶל־מֹשֶׁה לֵּאמֹר׃ דַּבֵּר אֶל־בְּנֵי יִשְׂרָאֵל וְיָשֻׁבוּ[5] וְיַחֲנוּ[6] ...

עַל־הַיָּם׃ וְאָמַר פַּרְעֹה לִבְנֵי יִשְׂרָאֵל נְבֻכִים[7] הֵם בָּאָרֶץ סָגַר עֲלֵיהֶם

הַמִּדְבָּר׃ וְחִזַּקְתִּי אֶת־לֵב־פַּרְעֹה וְרָדַף אַחֲרֵיהֶם

Ps. 22:11–12

עָלֶיךָ הָשְׁלַכְתִּי מֵרָחֶם מִבֶּטֶן אִמִּי אֵלִי אָתָּה׃ אַל־תִּרְחַק מִמֶּנִּי כִּי־צָרָה

קְרוֹבָה כִּי־אֵין עוֹזֵר׃

---

[4] Qal Narr. 3mp of בוא, glossed as "to go" (see ch. 26).

[5] Qal Juss. 3mp of שׁוב, glossed as "they shall turn" (see ch. 26).

[6] Qal Juss. 3mp of חנה, glossed as "they shall camp" (see ch. 24).

[7] Niph. Part. mp of בוך, glossed as "to wander around in confusion" (see ch. 26).

Num. 21:2–3

וַיִּדַּר יִשְׂרָאֵל נֶדֶר לַיהוָה וַיֹּאמַר אִם־נָתֹן תִּתֵּן אֶת־הָעָם הַזֶּה בְּיָדִי

וְהַחֲרַמְתִּי אֶת־עָרֵיהֶם׃ וַיִּשְׁמַע יְהוָה בְּקוֹל יִשְׂרָאֵל וַיִּתֵּן אֶת־הַכְּנַעֲנִי

וַיַּחֲרֵם אֶתְהֶם וְאֶת־עָרֵיהֶם וַיִּקְרָא שֵׁם־הַמָּקוֹם חָרְמָה׃

Gen. 19:27–28

וַיַּשְׁכֵּם אַבְרָהָם בַּבֹּקֶר אֶל־הַמָּקוֹם אֲשֶׁר־עָמַד שָׁם אֶת־פְּנֵי יְהוָה׃ וַיַּשְׁקֵף

עַל־פְּנֵי סְדֹם וַעֲמֹרָה וְעַל־כָּל־פְּנֵי אֶרֶץ הַכִּכָּר וַיַּרְא[8] וְהִנֵּה עָלָה קִיטֹר

הָאָרֶץ כְּקִיטֹר הַכִּבְשָׁן׃

Ex. 22:16 [Engl. 22:17]

אִם־מָאֵן יְמָאֵן אָבִיהָ לְתִתָּהּ לוֹ כֶּסֶף יִשְׁקֹל כְּמֹהַר הַבְּתוּלֹת׃

---

[8] Qal Narr. 3ms of ראה, glossed as “to see” (see ch. 24).

17.8 Exegetical Exercises—Identifying Mispointed Qal Passives

Earlier in the history of the language, well before the Masoretes did their work, Hebrew had a fully functional **Qal passive *binyan***. This Qal passive *binyan* would have had all of the major conjugations previously discussed: perfect (ch. 3), imperfect (ch. 5), volitives (ch. 7), etc. As its name indicates, this would have been the passive counterpart to the Qal, just as the Pual is the passive counterpart to the Piel and the Hophal is the passive counterpart to the Hiphil.

Over time the role of the Qal passive was taken over more and more by the Niphal (see ch. 19); the only place it remained in use was the Qal passive participle covered in chapter 9. By the time the Masoretic reading tradition became fixed, the existence of these older forms was no longer recognized, so the vowel pointing in the Masoretic Text preserves a reading tradition that included Qal passive participles but no longer knew of other Qal passive forms. The Masoretes did, however, understand the meaning of the verses they read. They could tell that various forms were passive, and those forms had to be vocalized in some way. Commonly, then, truly Qal passive forms were vocalized by the Masoretes as Pual or Hophal forms.

For example, translate Genesis 12:15.

וַיִּרְא֤וּ[9] אֹתָהּ֙ שָׂרֵ֣י פַרְעֹ֔ה וַיְהַלְל֥וּ[10] אֹתָ֖הּ אֶל־פַּרְעֹ֑ה וַתֻּקַּ֥ח הָאִשָּׁ֖ה בֵּ֥ית פַּרְעֹֽה׃

Based on the Masoretic pointing, how would you parse וַתֻּקַּח?

[9] Qal Narr. 3mp of ראה, glossed as "to see" (see ch. 24).

[10] Piel Narr. 3mp of הלל, glossed as "to praise" (see ch. 28).

Check your lexicon. Does the root לקח ever occur in the Piel or Hiphil?

This indicates that וַתֻּקַּח is actually a Qal passive form that the Masoretes mispointed as a Pual. If a root shows its active form only in the Qal yet shows passive forms in the Pual or Hophal, there is a realistic chance that this form is a Qal passive that the Masoretic reading tradition treated as a Pual or a Hophal.

Translate the following clauses. Parse each verb according to the Masoretic vocalization. Consult your lexicon to determine whether the verb in question has corresponding Piel or Hiphil forms. Based on whether there are such forms, determine whether it is (1) a true Pual or Hophal form or (2) likely to be an original Qal passive form that was mispointed by the Masoretes.

Gen. 18:4	יֻקַּח־נָא מְעַט־מַיִם
Translation:	
Parsing:	
Originally a Qal Passive? (Yes/No)	

Isa. 1:20 חֶ֣רֶב תְּאֻכְּל֔וּ

Translation:

Parsing:

Originally a Qal Passive? (Yes/No)

Ps. 87:3 [Engl. Ps. 87:2) מְ֭דֻבָּ֣ר בָּ֑ךְ

Translation:

Parsing:

Originally a Qal Passive? (Yes/No)

Obad. 1 וְצִ֙יר בַּגּוֹיִ֣ם שֻׁלָּ֔ח

Translation:

Parsing:

Originally a Qal Passive? (Yes/No)

Gen. 4:15 שִׁבְעָתַ֖יִם יֻקָּ֑ם

Translation:

Parsing:

Originally a Qal Passive? (Yes/No)

Hophal

Dan. 9:1	אֲשֶׁר הָמְלַךְ עַל מַלְכוּת כַּשְׂדִּים
Translation:	
Parsing:	
Originally a Qal Passive? (Yes/No)	
Gen. 35:26	אֵלֶּה בְּנֵי יַעֲקֹב אֲשֶׁר יֻלַּד־לוֹ בְּפַדַּן אֲרָם
Translation:	
Parsing:	
Originally a Qal Passive? (Yes/No)	

יח (18) Numbers and Counting

18.1 Cardinal Numbers 1–10

Cardinal numbers are the typical counting numbers (i.e., one, two, three, etc.). They have both masculine and feminine forms:

	Masculine		Feminine	
	Absolute	Construct	Absolute	Construct
One	אֶחָד	אַחַד	אַחַת	אַחַת
Two	שְׁנַיִם	שְׁנֵי	שְׁתַּיִם	שְׁתֵּי
Three	שָׁלֹשׁ	שְׁלֹשׁ	שְׁלֹשָׁה	שְׁלֹשֶׁת
Four	אַרְבַּע	אַרְבַּע	אַרְבָּעָה	אַרְבַּעַת
Five	חָמֵשׁ	חֲמֵשׁ	חֲמִשָּׁה	חֲמֵשֶׁת
Six	שֵׁשׁ	שֵׁשׁ	שִׁשָּׁה	שֵׁשֶׁת
Seven	שֶׁבַע	שְׁבַע	שִׁבְעָה	שִׁבְעַת
Eight	שְׁמֹנֶה	שְׁמֹנֶה	שְׁמֹנָה	שְׁמֹנַת
Nine	תֵּשַׁע	תְּשַׁע	תִּשְׁעָה	תִּשְׁעַת
Ten	עֶשֶׂר	עֶשֶׂר	עֲשָׂרָה	עֲשֶׂרֶת

The masculine and feminine absolute forms should be memorized.

Notes:

- The numeral **one** is most commonly used as an attributive adjective: (1) it follows the noun it modifies and (2) it agrees with the noun in gender and definiteness.

  הָאַיִל הָאֶחָד ("one ram"—Ex. 29:15)

  הַצִּפּוֹר הָאֶחָת ("one bird"—Lev. 14:5)

  The numeral *one* can also be used in construct with a noun: it agrees in gender, but it cannot (as a construct form) take the definite article:

  אַחַד הָעָם ("one of the people"—Gen. 26:10)

- The numeral **two** is a dual form in both the absolute and construct. In the absolute form, it may be used as a substantive, agreeing in gender with the noun to which it connects appositionally, or it may be used as an attributive adjective.

  שְׁנַ֛יִם מִכָּל־הַבָּשָׂר ("two from all flesh"—Gen. 7:15)—Absolute
  אֵילִם שְׁנָ֑יִם ("two rams"—Ex. 29:1)—Absolute
  שְׁתֵּי נָשִׁים ("two wives"—Gen. 4:19)—Construct
  שְׁנֵי־בְנֵי־יַעֲקֹב ("two of the sons of Jacob"—Gen. 34:25)—Construct

- The numerals **three** through **ten** are also treated as substantives. They are used with plural nouns unless the noun in question is a collective.

  שְׁלֹשָׁה בָנִים ("three sons"—Gen. 6:10)
  חֲמִשָּׁה אֲנָשִׁים ("five men"—Gen. 47:2)
  חָמֵשׁ אַמּוֹת ("five cubits"—Ex. 27:18)
  שֶׁבַע כִּבְשֹׂת הַצֹּאן ("seven ewe lambs of the flock"—Gen. 21:28)

  Note the relationship between the gender of the noun and the gender of the number. Masculine nouns (e.g.: אֲנָשִׁים ,בָנִים) take numbers that are feminine in form, and feminine nouns (e.g.: אַמּוֹת ,כִּבְשֹׂת) take numbers that are masculine in form.

  This is called **gender discord**, and it is true for the numbers three through nine and all numbers ending in three through nine (i.e.: 13–19, 23–29, 33–39, etc.).[1] This agreement corresponds to a noun's actual gender; if a feminine noun irregularly takes the ־ִים ending to form its plural, the number attached to it will still exhibit gender discord, as in:

  שְׁלֹשׁ הֶעָרִים ("three cities"—Num. 35:14)—עָרִים is a feminine plural

- Pronominal suffixes can be attached to numerals, as in:

  שְׁנֵיהֶם ("the two of them"—Gen. 21:27)
  שְׁלָשְׁתָּם ("the three of them"—Num. 12:4)

[1] This tendency is also commonly called **chiastic concord**.

18.2 Larger Cardinal Numbers

The **teens** are formed by combining the numeral ten with the numbers one through nine:

		for Masculine Nouns		for Feminine Nouns
Eleven[2]		אַחַד עָשָׂר		אַחַת עֶשְׂרֵה
	or	עַשְׁתֵּי עָשָׂר	or	עַשְׁתֵּי עֶשְׂרֵה
Twelve		שְׁנֵים עָשָׂר		שְׁתֵּים עֶשְׂרֵה
	or	שְׁנֵי עָשָׂר	or	שְׁתֵּי עֶשְׂרֵה
Thirteen*		שְׁלֹשָׁה עָשָׂר		שְׁלֹשׁ עֶשְׂרֵה
Fourteen*		אַרְבָּעָה עָשָׂר		אַרְבַּע עֶשְׂרֵה
Fifteen*		חֲמִשָּׁה עָשָׂר		חֲמֵשׁ עֶשְׂרֵה
etc.				

*Note the change in the gender of the numeral per gender discord (see 18.1 above).

Other than **twenty**, which is the plural of עֶשֶׂר ("ten"), the **tens** are the masculine plural forms of the numbers three through nine:

Twenty	עֶשְׂרִים	(plural of "ten")
Thirty	שְׁלֹשִׁים	(plural of "three")
Forty	אַרְבָּעִים	(plural of "four")
Fifty	חֲמִשִּׁים	(plural of "five")
etc.		

These tens may be combined with the numbers one through nine as necessary, linked by וְ.[3]

אַרְבַּע וּשְׁלֹשִׁים שָׁנָה ("thirty-four years"—Gen. 11:16)

תֵּשַׁע וְעֶשְׂרִים שָׁנָה ("twenty-nine years"—Gen. 11:24)

---

[2] The two options for *eleven* are not simply two different constructions; they employ two different words.

[3] This can also be done in English, as when Abraham Lincoln began the Gettysburg Address with the famous phrase "Four score and seven years ago."

The hundreds and thousands are formed from מֵאָה ("hundred"), אֶלֶף ("thousand"), and רִבּוֹת ("ten thousand/myriad") with the numbers one through nine:

One hundred	מֵאָה (const. מְאַת)	
Two hundred	מָאתַיִם	(dual form of "one hundred")
Three hundred	שְׁלֹשׁ מֵאוֹת	
etc.		

One thousand	אֶלֶף	
Two thousand	אַלְפַּיִם	(dual form of "one thousand")
Three thousand	שְׁלֹשֶׁת אֲלָפִים	
etc.		

Ten thousand	רְבָבָה / רִבּוֹת	
Twenty thousand	רִבּוֹתַיִם	(dual form of "ten thousand")
Thirty thousand	שְׁלֹשׁ רִבּוֹת	
etc.		

The masculine form of the number is used with the plurals מֵאוֹת ("hundreds") and רִבּוֹת ("ten thousands" or "myriads"), while the feminine form of the number is used with the plural אֲלָפִים ("thousands").

וְנֹחַ בֶּן־שֵׁשׁ מֵאוֹת שָׁנָה	("Now Noah was 600 years old . . ."—Gen. 7:6)
וְכֶסֶף פְּקוּדֵי הָעֵדָה מְאַת כִּכָּר וְאֶלֶף וּשְׁבַע מֵאוֹת וַחֲמִשָּׁה וְשִׁבְעִים שֶׁקֶל בְּשֶׁקֶל הַקֹּדֶשׁ׃	("And the silver of all the ones of the congregation who were counted was 100 talents and 1,775 shekels, according to the shekel of the sanctuary."—Ex. 38:25)
וְרָדְפוּ מִכֶּם חֲמִשָּׁה מֵאָה וּמֵאָה מִכֶּם רְבָבָה יִרְדֹּפוּ	("Five of you will pursue a hundred, and a hundred of you will pursue ten thousand."—Lev. 26:8a)

וַיִּהְיוּ פְקֻדֵיהֶם
לְמִשְׁפְּחֹתָם אַלְפַּיִם שְׁבַע מֵאוֹת
וַחֲמִשִּׁים׃

("And the ones who were counted by their clans were 2,750."—Num. 4:36)

וַתְּהִי מֶחֱצַת הָעֵדָה מִן־הַצֹּאן
שְׁלֹשׁ־מֵאוֹת אֶלֶף וּשְׁלֹשִׁים אֶלֶף
שִׁבְעַת אֲלָפִים וַחֲמֵשׁ מֵאוֹת׃
וּבָקָר שִׁשָּׁה וּשְׁלֹשִׁים אָלֶף׃
וַחֲמֹרִים שְׁלֹשִׁים אֶלֶף וַחֲמֵשׁ
מֵאוֹת׃ וְנֶפֶשׁ אָדָם שִׁשָּׁה עָשָׂר
אָלֶף׃

("And the congregation's half was 337,500 of the sheep, and 36,000 cattle, and 30,500 donkeys, and 16,000 people."—Num. 31:43–46)

18.3 Ordinal Numbers

Ordinal numbers express position—first, second, etc. The Hebrew ordinals have masculine and feminine forms.

	Masculine	Feminine
First	רִאשׁוֹן	רִאשׁוֹנָה
Second	שֵׁנִי	שֵׁנִית
Third	שְׁלִישִׁי	שְׁלִישִׁית
Fourth	רְבִיעִי	רְבִיעִית
Fifth	חֲמִישִׁי	חֲמִישִׁית
Sixth	שִׁשִּׁי	שִׁשִּׁית
Seventh	שְׁבִיעִי	שְׁבִיעִית
Eighth	שְׁמִינִי	שְׁמִינִית
Ninth	תְּשִׁיעִי	תְּשִׁיעִית
Tenth	עֲשִׂירִי	עֲשִׂירִית

Notes:

- The ordinal **first** is related to the Hebrew word **ראשׁ** ("head, top, chief"). The remaining masculine ordinals end in *yod*, while the remaining feminine ordinals end in *taw*.
- The Hebrew ordinals normally function as attributive adjectives, following the noun and agreeing in gender and definiteness. While agreement in definiteness is common, exceptions occur.
- The ordinals above **tenth** are identical to the cardinal numbers.

וְשֵׁם הַנָּהָר הַשְּׁלִישִׁי חִדֶּקֶל	("And the name of the third river is the Tigris."—Gen. 2:14)
וּבַיּוֹם הַשְּׁמִינִי יִקַּח שְׁנֵי־כְבָשִׂים תְּמִימִם	("And on the eighth day he shall take two perfect male lambs."—Lev. 14:10)
וְהָיָה אִם־לֹא יַאֲמִינוּ לָךְ וְלֹא יִשְׁמְעוּ לְקֹל הָאֹת הָרִאשׁוֹן	("And if they will not believe you or listen to the first sign . . ."—Ex. 4:8)
וְהָיָה לָכֶם לְמִשְׁמֶרֶת עַד אַרְבָּעָה עָשָׂר יוֹם לַחֹדֶשׁ הַזֶּה	("And it will be a requirement for you until the fourteenth day of this month."—Ex. 12:6)

18.4 Vocabulary

אוֹר	daylight, dawn; light
אֶלֶף	thousand
הִקְרִיב	(Hiph.) to bring near; to offer a sacrifice
כִּסֵּא	seat, throne, chair
כָּתַב	to write
מֵאָה	hundred
מִגְדָּל	tower, watchtower
מִגְרָשׁ	pastureland belonging to a city
מְלָאכָה	business, work; handiwork, craftsmanship
מְלוּכָה	kingdom
מַלְכוּת	royal dominion, kingship
נַחֲלָה	Inheritance; inalienable, hereditary property
נְחֹשֶׁת	bronze, copper
סִפֵּר	(Piel) to count; to make known; to report, tell
עֵד[4]	testimony, witness
פַּר	bull, steer
צָרָה	need, distress, anxiety
קִדֵּשׁ	(Piel) to make something holy; to dedicate or consecrate
הִקְדִּישׁ	(Hiph.) to mark as holy or consecrated
רִבּוֹת / רְבָבָה	ten thousand, myriad
רַק	only
רִאשׁוֹן	first
שִׁלֵּם	(Piel) to make complete; to make restitution; to reward; to finish
תּוֹרָה	law; direction, instruction, rule

[4] See the raised *ayin* and *dalet* of the MT of Deut. 6:4, which functions as a testimony (an עֵד).

18.5 Language Exercises

Translate the following and parse each verb and participle. Use your lexicon to look up the glosses for any words you do not know from your vocabulary.

Gen. 5:3–5

וַיְחִי[5] אָדָם שְׁלֹשִׁים וּמְאַת שָׁנָה וַיּוֹלֶד[6] בִּדְמוּתוֹ כְּצַלְמוֹ וַיִּקְרָא אֶת־שְׁמוֹ

שֵׁת׃ וַיִּהְיוּ[7] יְמֵי־אָדָם אַחֲרֵי הוֹלִידוֹ[8] אֶת־שֵׁת שְׁמֹנֶה מֵאֹת שָׁנָה וַיּוֹלֶד בָּנִים

וּבָנוֹת׃ וַיִּהְיוּ כָּל־יְמֵי אָדָם אֲשֶׁר־חַי[9] תְּשַׁע מֵאוֹת שָׁנָה וּשְׁלֹשִׁים שָׁנָה

וַיָּמֹת[10]׃

Ex. 29:15–16

וְאֶת־הָאַיִל הָאֶחָד תִּקָּח וְסָמְכוּ אַהֲרֹן וּבָנָיו אֶת־יְדֵיהֶם עַל־רֹאשׁ הָאָיִל׃

וְשָׁחַטְתָּ אֶת־הָאָיִל וְלָקַחְתָּ אֶת־דָּמוֹ וְזָרַקְתָּ עַל־הַמִּזְבֵּחַ סָבִיב׃

---

[5] Qal Narr. 3ms of חיה, glossed as "to live" (see ch. 24).

[6] Hiph. Narr. 3ms of ילד, glossed as "to bear, to beget" (see ch. 27). Note: repeated in following exercises.

[7] Qal Narr. 3mp of היה, glossed as "to be" (see ch. 24).

[8] Hiph. Inf. Const. of ילד, glossed as "to bear, to beget" + 3ms object suffix (see chs. 21, 27). Note: repeated in following exercises.

[9] Qal Perf. 3ms of חיה, glossed as "to live" (see ch. 24).

[10] Qal Narr. 3ms of מות, glossed as "to die" (see ch. 26).

Gen. 5:6–8

וַיְחִי־שֵׁת חָמֵשׁ שָׁנִים וּמְאַת שָׁנָה וַיּוֹלֶד אֶת־אֱנוֹשׁ׃ וַיְחִי־שֵׁת אַחֲרֵי הוֹלִידוֹ

אֶת־אֱנוֹשׁ שֶׁבַע שָׁנִים וּשְׁמֹנֶה מֵאוֹת שָׁנָה וַיּוֹלֶד בָּנִים וּבָנוֹת׃ וַיִּהְיוּ כָּל־

יְמֵי־שֵׁת שְׁתֵּים עֶשְׂרֵה שָׁנָה וּתְשַׁע מֵאוֹת שָׁנָה וַיָּמֹת׃

Gen. 5:9–11

וַיְחִי אֱנוֹשׁ תִּשְׁעִים שָׁנָה וַיּוֹלֶד אֶת־קֵינָן׃ וַיְחִי אֱנוֹשׁ אַחֲרֵי הוֹלִידוֹ אֶת־קֵינָן

חֲמֵשׁ עֶשְׂרֵה שָׁנָה וּשְׁמֹנֶה מֵאוֹת שָׁנָה וַיּוֹלֶד בָּנִים וּבָנוֹת׃ וַיִּהְיוּ כָּל־יְמֵי

אֱנוֹשׁ חָמֵשׁ שָׁנִים וּתְשַׁע מֵאוֹת שָׁנָה וַיָּמֹת׃

Gen. 5:12–14

וַיְחִי קֵינָן שִׁבְעִים שָׁנָה וַיּוֹלֶד אֶת־מַהֲלַלְאֵל׃ וַיְחִי קֵינָן אַחֲרֵי הוֹלִידוֹ אֶת־

מַהֲלַלְאֵל אַרְבָּעִים שָׁנָה וּשְׁמֹנֶה מֵאוֹת שָׁנָה וַיּוֹלֶד בָּנִים וּבָנוֹת׃ וַיִּהְיוּ כָּל־

יְמֵי קֵינָן עֶשֶׂר שָׁנִים וּתְשַׁע מֵאוֹת שָׁנָה וַיָּמֹת׃

Gen. 5:15–17 וַֽיְחִ֣י מַֽהֲלַלְאֵ֔ל חָמֵ֥שׁ שָׁנִ֖ים וְשִׁשִּׁ֣ים שָׁנָ֑ה וַיּ֖וֹלֶד אֶת־יָֽרֶד׃ וַיְחִ֣י מַֽהֲלַלְאֵ֗ל

אַֽחֲרֵי֙ הוֹלִיד֣וֹ אֶת־יֶ֔רֶד שְׁלֹשִׁ֣ים שָׁנָ֔ה וּשְׁמֹנֶ֥ה מֵא֖וֹת שָׁנָ֑ה וַיּ֥וֹלֶד בָּנִ֖ים

וּבָנֽוֹת׃ וַיִּהְיוּ֙ כָּל־יְמֵ֣י מַֽהֲלַלְאֵ֔ל חָמֵ֤שׁ וְתִשְׁעִים֙ שָׁנָ֔ה וּשְׁמֹנֶ֥ה מֵא֖וֹת שָׁנָ֑ה

וַיָּמֹֽת׃

Gen. 5:18–20 וַֽיְחִי־יֶ֕רֶד שְׁתַּ֛יִם וְשִׁשִּׁ֥ים שָׁנָ֖ה וּמְאַ֣ת שָׁנָ֑ה וַיּ֖וֹלֶד אֶת־חֲנֽוֹךְ׃ וַֽיְחִי־יֶ֗רֶד אַֽחֲרֵי֙

הוֹלִיד֣וֹ אֶת־חֲנ֔וֹךְ שְׁמֹנֶ֥ה מֵא֖וֹת שָׁנָ֑ה וַיּ֥וֹלֶד בָּנִ֖ים וּבָנֽוֹת׃ וַיִּהְיוּ֙ כָּל־יְמֵי־

יֶ֔רֶד שְׁתַּ֤יִם וְשִׁשִּׁים֙ שָׁנָ֔ה וּתְשַׁ֥ע מֵא֖וֹת שָׁנָ֑ה וַיָּמֹֽת׃

Gen. 5:21–24 וַֽיְחִ֣י חֲנ֔וֹךְ חָמֵ֥שׁ וְשִׁשִּׁ֖ים שָׁנָ֑ה וַיּ֖וֹלֶד אֶת־מְתוּשָֽׁלַח׃ וַיִּתְהַלֵּ֨ךְ[11] חֲנ֜וֹךְ אֶת־

הָֽאֱלֹהִ֗ים אַֽחֲרֵי֙ הוֹלִיד֣וֹ אֶת־מְתוּשֶׁ֔לַח שְׁלֹ֥שׁ מֵא֖וֹת שָׁנָ֑ה וַיּ֥וֹלֶד בָּנִ֖ים

[11] Hithp. Narr. 3ms of הלך, glossed as “to walk” (see ch. 20).

וּבָנוֹת׃ וַיְהִי כָּל־יְמֵי חֲנוֹךְ חָמֵשׁ וְשִׁשִּׁים שָׁנָה וּשְׁלֹשׁ מֵאוֹת שָׁנָה׃ וַיִּתְהַלֵּךְ

חֲנוֹךְ אֶת־הָאֱלֹהִים וְאֵינֶנּוּ כִּי־לָקַח אֹתוֹ אֱלֹהִים׃

Gen. 7:2–3 מִכֹּל הַבְּהֵמָה הַטְּהוֹרָה תִּקַּח־לְךָ שִׁבְעָה שִׁבְעָה אִישׁ וְאִשְׁתּוֹ וּמִן־הַבְּהֵמָה

אֲשֶׁר לֹא טְהֹרָה הִוא שְׁנַיִם אִישׁ וְאִשְׁתּוֹ׃ גַּם מֵעוֹף הַשָּׁמַיִם שִׁבְעָה שִׁבְעָה

זָכָר וּנְקֵבָה לְחַיּוֹת[12] זֶרַע עַל־פְּנֵי כָל־הָאָרֶץ׃

Gen. 22:3–4 וַיַּשְׁכֵּם אַבְרָהָם בַּבֹּקֶר וַיַּחֲבֹשׁ אֶת־חֲמֹרוֹ וַיִּקַּח אֶת־שְׁנֵי נְעָרָיו אִתּוֹ וְאֵת

יִצְחָק בְּנוֹ וַיְבַקַּע עֲצֵי עֹלָה וַיָּקָם[13] וַיֵּלֶךְ אֶל־הַמָּקוֹם אֲשֶׁר־אָמַר־לוֹ

---

[12] Piel Inf. Const. of חיה, glossed as “to preserve alive” (see ch. 24).

[13] Qal Narr. 3ms of קום, glossed as “to arise, rise” (see ch. 26).

הָאֱלֹהִֽים׃ בַּיּ֣וֹם הַשְּׁלִישִׁ֔י וַיִּשָּׂ֨א אַבְרָהָ֧ם אֶת־עֵינָ֛יו וַיַּ֥רְא[14] אֶת־הַמָּק֖וֹם

מֵרָחֹֽק׃

18.6 Exegetical Exercises—Letters for Numbers

You will notice that this book's preface employs Roman numerals for page numbers, while the main body of the book is marked with Arabic numerals. Roman numerals use letters to represent numbers, which was relatively common in ancient writing systems.

Hebrew writing systems also commonly use the letters of the alphabet to indicate numbers—*aleph* = 1, *beth* = 2, *gimel* = 3, etc. This practice occurs in non-Biblical Hebrew texts and can also be used in formatting published editions of the Hebrew OT text (for instance, מלכים א = 1 Kings; מלכים ב = 2 Kings). Chapter numbers may also be marked by letters.

The letters א through ט mark the numbers 1–10, the letters י through צ mark the tens (20, 30, 40, etc.), and the letter ק marks 100.

1	א	10	י	20	כ
2	ב	11	יא	30	ל
3	ג	12	יב	40	מ
4	ד	13	יג	50	נ
5	ה	14	יד	60	ס
6	ו	15	טו	70	ע
7	ז	16	טז	80	פ
8	ח	17	יז	90	צ
9	ט	18	יח	100	ק
		19	יט		

[14] Qal Narr. 3ms of ראה, glossed as "to see" (see ch. 24).

For numbers above 10, letters are used as digits, working right to left to create a number (כח is therefore 28; נד is therefore 54; etc.). Note that 15 and 16 are not written as you might expect—יה and יו—but as טו and טז, to avoid seeming to write an abbreviation for יהוה, the divine name.

Determine the number indicated by each of the following:

ח	יד	מד	מ
נה	לט	ד	כ
כו	מז	טו	לא
נ	יא	צט	קנב

Until now, the only way you've used the **Masorah Parva (Mp)**—the information next to the Hebrew text in BHS or BHQ—has been to analyze the *Ketiv/Qere*. On any page of BHS or BHQ, however, you will see many notes that are not indicative of a *Qere* reading. The Mp contains several other types of notes, the most common being frequency notes, which count the frequency of certain forms or words in the Hebrew text.

Looking at the portion of Joshua 24:3 discussed in section 8.12, you can see a note in the Mp concerning the word וָאוֹלֵךְ. This is a frequency note marked by ד with a supralinear dot indicating that the ד is being used as a number.

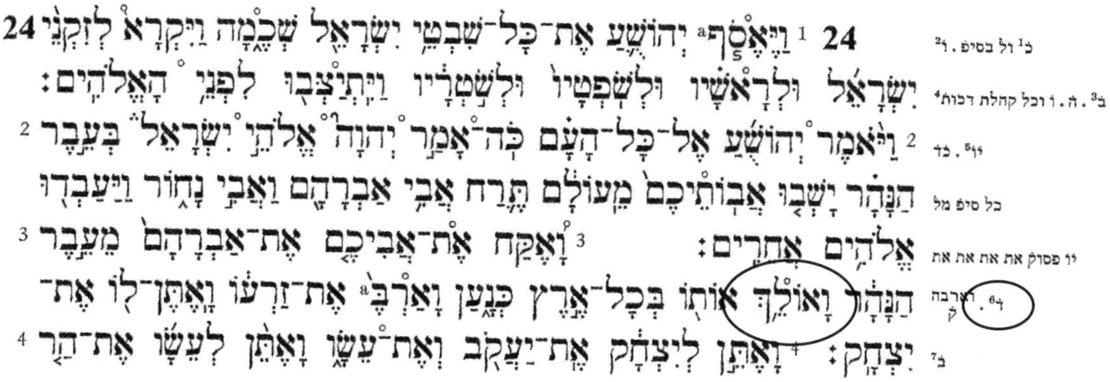

This ד therefore indicates that this particular spelling of the word occurs four times in the Hebrew text of the OT.[15] Of particular note is ל indicating a *hapax legomenon*—a form written only once. (This will be discussed in 22.9 and 23.6.)[16]

Using your BHS or BHQ, find the Mp notes for the following words and insert them in the chart below. Use your knowledge of Hebrew letters for numbers to indicate how many times the specific form occurs in the Hebrew text of the OT. If there is more than one Mp note on a single line, the marginal notes are ordered from right to left to correspond with the marks in the text.

Text	Word	Masorah Parva Frequency Note (Hebrew Letter)	Number of Occurrences of This Form in the Hebrew Text
Gen. 19:1	סְדֹמָה		
Isa. 34:16	נֶעְדָּרָה		
Gen. 6:14	גֹּפֶר		
Ps. 95:10	תֹּעֵי		
Gen. 19:2	אֲדֹנַי		
Gen. 1:12	לְמִינֵהוּ		
Gen. 1:8	יוֹם שֵׁנִי		

[15] These counts can be qualified by following information of many types. If additional wording follows the numerical count in the note, you should not assume that the count applies to the entire Hebrew text. It may be a count of only a specific spelling of a word, of the times a word is spelled defectively, or of the times a word occurs at the beginning of a verse; or it may be one of many other qualifications. For further information, consult a reference work on the Masorah.

[16] Not all *hapax legomena* are so marked. The function of the Mp's frequency notes was not to catalogue every *hapax legomenon* but to mark infrequent or unusual forms so that copyists would not harmonize them with more common forms.

Look up סְדֹם in a lexicon or a concordance. How many times does it occur?

The Mp note on Gen. 19:1 applies not to the noun סְדֹם, but only to the spelling with the additional ה. What is the grammatical function of this ה?

Translate אֲדֹנַי in Gen. 19:2, paying careful attention to the possessive suffix. What very common word in the Hebrew text is almost identical to אֲדֹנַי?

What copying mistake is the Mp note likely warning the scribe to avoid?

יט (19) Niphal

19.1 The Niphal Stem

The Niphal largely provides the passive counterpart to the Qal (similar to the Piel/Pual and Hiphil/Hophal relationships). But as with the other stems, the Niphal encompasses a range of meanings:

- **Passive**, when the subject receives the action:

  וּבְנָבִיא נִשְׁמָר ("and it was guarded by a prophet"—Hos. 12:14)

  וַיִּפָּתַח פִּי ("and my mouth was opened"—Ezek. 33:22)

- **Reflexive**, when the subject impacts itself with the verbal action:

  וַעֲמָשָׂא לֹא־נִשְׁמַר בַּחֶרֶב ("but Amasa did not guard himself against the sword"—2 Sam. 20:10)

  יִסָּמֵךְ אִישׁ עָלָיו ("a man supports himself upon it"—Isa. 36:6)

- **Resultative**, when the verb indicates a state of being resulting from the activity implied in the verbal root:

  וַתִּמָּלֵא הָאָרֶץ אֶת־הַמָּיִם ("and the land was filled with water"—2 Kings 3:20)

  כִּי נִבְהֲלוּ ("for they became horrified"—Gen. 45:3)

- **Active**, when the passive or reflexive sense of the verb has largely been forgotten in everyday use, even though it can sometimes be discerned with thought:[1]

  וַיִּלָּחֶם עִם־יִשְׂרָאֵל בִּרְפִידִם ("and he fought with Israel at Rephidim."—Ex. 17:8)

  לֹא־נִשְׁאַר בָּהֶם עַד־אֶחָד ("not one among them remained."—Ex. 14:28)

The Niphal stem is indicated by the addition of a *nun* before the verbal root. In some forms (perfect, participle, some infinitive absolutes) this *nun* is visible because of its position at the beginning of the word. In other forms, however (imperfect, imperative, infinitive construct, and some infinitive absolutes), this *nun* is assimilated into the following consonant and is no longer visible except as the *dagesh forte*.

[1] This is similar to the discussion of frozen forms (see 13.8).

19.2 The Niphal Perfect

The Niphal perfect is formed with a *nun* prefix and the same endings learned for the Qal perfect. The *nun* is visible because of the *ḥireq* vowel, making identification straightforward.

Niphal Perfect Paradigm

	Verbal Form	Suffix	Gloss
3ms	נִקְטַל	--	he was killed
3fs	נִקְטְלָה	ָה	she was killed
2ms	נִקְטַ֫לְתָּ	תָּ	you (ms) were killed
2fs	נִקְטַלְתְּ	תְּ	you (fs) were killed
1cs	נִקְטַ֫לְתִּי	תִּי	I was killed
3cp	נִקְטְלוּ	וּ	they were killed
2mp	נִקְטַלְתֶּם	תֶּם	you (mp) were killed
2fp	נִקְטַלְתֶּן	תֶּן	you (fp) were killed
1cp	נִקְטַ֫לְנוּ	נוּ	we were killed

Tip-Offs for the Niphal Perfect:

- Prefixed *nun* with *ḥireq* vowel
- *pataḥ* theme vowel (when it does not reduce to a *shewa*)

19.3 The Niphal Imperfect

The Niphal imperfect is formed with a *nun* prefix and the same prefixes and suffixes learned for the Qal imperfect. The *nun* of the Niphal is not visible in the imperfect forms because the imperfect's verbal prefixes precede it, causing it to close a syllable. The *nun* is then assimilated into the following consonant, with a *dagesh forte* marking the assimilation.

יִקָּטֵל < *יִנְקָטֵל

The Niphal imperfect forms therefore show a characteristic doubling of the first root letter.

Niphal Imperfect Paradigm

	Verbal Form	Prefix...Suffix	Gloss
3ms	יִקָּטֵל	--- יִ	he will be killed
3fs	תִּקָּטֵל	--- תִּ	she will be killed
2ms	תִּקָּטֵל	--- תִּ	you (ms) will be killed
2fs	תִּקָּטְלִי	ִי --- תִּ	you (fs) will be killed
1cs	אֶקָּטֵל	--- אֶ	I will be killed
3mp	יִקָּטְלוּ	וּ --- יִ	they (mp) will be killed
3fp	תִּקָּטַלְנָה	נָה --- תִּ	they (fp) will be killed
2mp	תִּקָּטְלוּ	וּ --- תִּ	you (mp) will be killed
2fp	תִּקָּטַלְנָה	נָה --- תִּ	you (fp) will be killed
1cp	נִקָּטֵל	--- נִ	we will be killed

The *nun* visible in the 1cp form is the prefixed *nun* of the imperfect, not the *nun* of the Niphal. The hypothetical original form would be נִנְקָטֵל*.

Tip-Offs for the Niphal Imperfect:

- Prefix vowel is a *ḥireq*
- First root letter takes a *qameṣ* vowel
- First root letter contains a *dagesh forte*

19.4 The Niphal Imperative

Like imperatives in the other stems, the Niphal imperative can be considered the imperfect without the prefix. But in the Niphal imperative a הִ־ prefix is added, and the *nun* remains assimilated into the first root letter:

Niphal Imperative Paradigm

	Verbal Form	Suffix	Gloss
2ms	הִקָּטֵל	---	you (ms) be killed
2fs	הִקָּטְלִי	ִי ---	you (fs) be killed
2mp	הִקָּטְלוּ	וּ ---	you (mp) be killed
2fp	הִקָּטַלְנָה	נָה ---	you (fp) be killed

Tip-Offs for the Niphal Imperative:

- Prefixed *heh* with a *ḥireq* (though beware of confusion with the Hiphil)
- First root letter takes a *qameṣ* vowel
- First root letter contains a *dagesh forte*

19.5 The Niphal Participle

The Niphal participle shows the prefixed נִ־ without assimilation, making identification straightforward.

Niphal Participle Paradigm

	Verbal Form	Suffix	Gloss
ms	נִקְטָל	--	one (ms) being killed
fs	נִקְטֶלֶת	ֶת	one (fs) being killed
fs (alt. form)	נִקְטָלָה	ָה	one (fs) being killed
mp	נִקְטָלִים	ִים	ones (mp) being killed
fp	נִקְטָלוֹת	וֹת	ones (fp) being killed

Tip-Offs for the Niphal Participle:

- Prefixed *nun* with *ḥireq* vowel
- Theme vowel is *qameṣ* (excepting fs form)

Note the potential confusion of a 3ms Niphal perfect (נִקְטַל) and the ms Niphal participle (נִקְטָל). They can be distinguished by the length of the *a*-class vowel (*pataḥ* versus *qameṣ*).

19.6 The Niphal Infinitives

The Niphal infinitive absolute can take two forms: in one the *nun* is visible, and in the other it is assimilated because of the הִ־ prefix (similar to the Niphal imperative).

נִקְטֹל Niph. Inf. Abs. of קטל

הִקָּטֹל Niph. Inf. Abs. of קטל

The Niphal infinitive construct is likewise formed with the הִ־ prefix:

הִקָּטֵל Niph. Inf. Const. of קטל

19.7 Vocabulary

אֹ֫זֶן	ear
אַחֵר	other, later, following
זִמֵּר	(Piel) to sing
הִכְרִית	(Hiph.) to exterminate; cut off
נִכְרַת	(Niph.) to be cut off, exterminated; to disappear
מִזְמוֹר	psalm, song
נִבָּא	(Niph.) to be in a prophetic trance, behave like a prophet
נִלְחַם	(Niph.) to fight
נִצַּל	(Piel) to rob; to deliver, save
הִצִּיל	(Hiph.) to tear out, remove, take away; to rescue, snatch, deliver
נִצַּל	(Niph.) to be saved
נִרְדָּף	(Niph.) to vanish, disappear
קָהָל	contingent, assembly
שָׂפָה	lip, edge, language
הִשְׁאִיר	(Hiph.) to leave over, spare, allow to survive
נִשְׁאַר	(Niph.) to remain, be left
שְׁאֵרִית	remnant, remainder
שֵׁ֫בֶט	stick, rod, staff; tribe
שֶׁ֫מֶשׁ	sun
תָּמִיד	lasting, continually

19.8 Language Exercises

A. Parse and gloss the following forms.

נִשְׁאָר

יִשָּׁאֵר

וָאֶשָּׁאֵר

יִנָּצֵל

נִצַּלְתֶּם

הִצַּ֫לְתָּ

יַצִּיל

הִנָּצֵל

כָּֽרְתוּ

יִכָּרֵת

הִכָּרֵת

הִכְרִית

B. Translate the following and parse each verb and participle. Use your lexicon to look up the glosses for any words you do not know from your vocabulary.

Ex. 14:14 יְהוָ֕ה יִלָּחֵ֣ם לָכֶ֑ם וְאַתֶּ֖ם תַּחֲרִישֽׁוּן׃

Gen. 5:1–2

זֶה סֵפֶר תּוֹלְדֹת אָדָם בְּיוֹם בְּרֹא אֱלֹהִים אָדָם בִּדְמוּת אֱלֹהִים עָשָׂה[2] אֹתוֹ׃

זָכָר וּנְקֵבָה בְּרָאָם[3] וַיְבָרֶךְ[4] אֹתָם וַיִּקְרָא אֶת־שְׁמָם אָדָם בְּיוֹם הִבָּרְאָם׃

Ex. 14:6–8

וַיֶּאְסֹר[5] אֶת־רִכְבּוֹ וְאֶת־עַמּוֹ לָקַח עִמּוֹ׃ וַיִּקַּח שֵׁשׁ־מֵאוֹת רֶכֶב בָּחוּר וְכֹל רֶכֶב

מִצְרָיִם וְשָׁלִשִׁם[6] עַל־כֻּלּוֹ׃ וַיְחַזֵּק יְהוָה אֶת־לֵב פַּרְעֹה מֶלֶךְ מִצְרַיִם וַיִּרְדֹּף

אַחֲרֵי בְּנֵי יִשְׂרָאֵל וּבְנֵי יִשְׂרָאֵל יֹצְאִים בְּיָד רָמָה[7]׃

Ex. 3:15–16

וַיֹּאמֶר עוֹד אֱלֹהִים אֶל־מֹשֶׁה כֹּה־תֹאמַר אֶל־בְּנֵי יִשְׂרָאֵל יְהוָה אֱלֹהֵי

אֲבֹתֵיכֶם אֱלֹהֵי אַבְרָהָם אֱלֹהֵי יִצְחָק וֵאלֹהֵי יַעֲקֹב שְׁלָחַנִי[8] אֲלֵיכֶם זֶה־שְּׁמִי

---

[2] Qal Perf. 3ms of עשׂה, glossed as “to make” (see ch. 24)

[3] Qal Perf. 3ms of ברא, glossed as “to create” + 3mp object suffix → “he created them” (see ch. 21).

[4] Piel Narr. 3ms of ברך, glossed as “to bless” (see ch. 22).

[5] Qal Narr. 3ms of אסר, glossed as “to make ready” (see ch. 22).

[6] This is a noun, not a number. Look in your lexicon under שָׁלִישׁ.

[7] Qal Part. fs of רום, glossed as “to be high” (see ch. 26).

[8] Qal Perf. 3ms of שׁלח, glossed as “to send” + 1cs object suffix → “he sent me” (see ch. 21).

לְעֹלָ֔ם וְזֶ֥ה זִכְרִ֖י לְדֹ֥ר דֹּֽר׃ לֵ֣ךְ וְאָסַפְתָּ֞ אֶת־זִקְנֵ֣י יִשְׂרָאֵ֗ל וְאָמַרְתָּ֤ אֲלֵהֶם֙ יְהוָ֞ה

אֱלֹהֵ֤י אֲבֹתֵיכֶם֙ נִרְאָ֣ה אֵלַ֔י אֱלֹהֵ֛י אַבְרָהָ֥ם יִצְחָ֖ק וְיַעֲקֹ֣ב לֵאמֹ֑ר פָּקֹ֤ד פָּקַ֙דְתִּי֙

אֶתְכֶ֔ם וְאֶת־הֶעָשׂ֥וּי[9] לָכֶ֖ם בְּמִצְרָֽיִם׃

לְמַ֗עַן תִּהְיֶ֥ה[10] זֹ֛את א֖וֹת בְּקִרְבְּכֶ֑ם כִּֽי־יִשְׁאָל֨וּן בְּנֵיכֶ֤ם מָחָר֙ לֵאמֹ֔ר מָ֛ה Josh. 4:6–7

הָאֲבָנִ֥ים הָאֵ֖לֶּה לָכֶֽם׃ וַאֲמַרְתֶּ֣ם לָהֶ֗ם אֲשֶׁ֨ר נִכְרְת֜וּ מֵימֵ֤י הַיַּרְדֵּן֙ מִפְּנֵי֙ אֲר֣וֹן

בְּרִית־יְהוָ֔ה בְּעָבְרוֹ֙ בַּיַּרְדֵּ֔ן נִכְרְת֖וּ מֵ֣י הַיַּרְדֵּ֑ן וְהָי֨וּ[11] הָאֲבָנִ֥ים הָאֵ֛לֶּה לְזִכָּר֖וֹן

לִבְנֵ֥י יִשְׂרָאֵ֖ל עַד־עוֹלָֽם׃

---

[9] Qal Pass. Part. ms of עשׂה, glossed as “to do” → “what has been done” (see ch. 24).

[10] Qal Imperf. 3fs of היה, glossed as “to be” (see ch. 24).

[11] Qal Conv. Perf. 3cp of היה, glossed as “to be” (see ch. 24).

Gen. 6:10–12

וַיּ֥וֹלֶד[12] נֹ֖חַ שְׁלֹשָׁ֣ה בָנִ֑ים אֶת־שֵׁ֖ם אֶת־חָ֥ם וְאֶת־יָֽפֶת׃ וַתִּשָּׁחֵ֥ת הָאָ֖רֶץ לִפְנֵ֣י

הָֽאֱלֹהִ֑ים וַתִּמָּלֵ֥א הָאָ֖רֶץ חָמָֽס׃ וַיַּ֧רְא[13] אֱלֹהִ֛ים אֶת־הָאָ֖רֶץ וְהִנֵּ֣ה נִשְׁחָ֑תָה כִּֽי־

הִשְׁחִ֧ית כָּל־בָּשָׂ֛ר אֶת־דַּרְכּ֖וֹ עַל־הָאָֽרֶץ׃

Lev. 26:3–8

אִם־בְּחֻקֹּתַ֖י תֵּלֵ֑כוּ וְאֶת־מִצְוֺתַ֣י תִּשְׁמְר֔וּ וַעֲשִׂיתֶ֖ם[14] אֹתָֽם׃ וְנָתַתִּ֥י[15] גִשְׁמֵיכֶ֖ם

בְּעִתָּ֑ם וְנָתְנָ֤ה הָאָ֙רֶץ֙ יְבוּלָ֔הּ וְעֵ֥ץ הַשָּׂדֶ֖ה יִתֵּ֥ן פִּרְיֽוֹ׃ ... וּרְדַפְתֶּ֖ם אֶת־אֹיְבֵיכֶ֑ם

וְנָפְל֥וּ לִפְנֵיכֶ֖ם לֶחָֽרֶב׃ וְרָדְפ֨וּ מִכֶּ֤ם חֲמִשָּׁה֙ מֵאָ֔ה וּמֵאָ֥ה מִכֶּ֖ם רְבָבָ֣ה יִרְדֹּ֑פוּ

וְנָפְל֧וּ אֹיְבֵיכֶ֛ם לִפְנֵיכֶ֖ם לֶחָֽרֶב׃

[12] Hiph. Narr. 3ms of ילד, glossed as "to bear, to beget" (see ch. 27).

[13] Qal Narr. 3ms of ראה, glossed as "to see" (see ch. 24).

[14] Qal Conv. Perf. 2mp of עשׂה, glossed as "to do" (see ch. 24).

[15] Translate the *waw* on this converted perfect as "then."

לֹא־תַסְגִּיר עֶבֶד אֶל־אֲדֹנָיו אֲשֶׁר־יִנָּצֵל אֵלֶיךָ מֵעִם אֲדֹנָיו׃ Deut. 23:16

וַיָּמָת[16] אֱלִימֶלֶךְ אִישׁ נָעֳמִי וַתִּשָּׁאֵר הִיא וּשְׁנֵי בָנֶיהָ׃ וַיִּשְׂאוּ[17] לָהֶם נָשִׁים Ruth 1:3–4

מֹאֲבִיּוֹת שֵׁם הָאַחַת עָרְפָּה וְשֵׁם הַשֵּׁנִית רוּת וַיֵּשְׁבוּ[18] שָׁם כְּעֶשֶׂר שָׁנִים׃

וַיַּעַל[19] יְהוּדָה וַיִּתֵּן יְהוָה אֶת־הַכְּנַעֲנִי וְהַפְּרִזִּי בְּיָדָם וַיַּכּוּם[20] בְּבֶזֶק עֲשֶׂרֶת Judg. 1:4–5

אֲלָפִים אִישׁ׃ וַיִּמְצְאוּ אֶת־אֲדֹנִי בֶזֶק בְּבֶזֶק וַיִּלָּחֲמוּ בוֹ וַיַּכּוּ[21] אֶת־הַכְּנַעֲנִי

וְאֶת־הַפְּרִזִּי׃

[16] Qal Narr. 3ms of מות, glossed as "to die" (see ch. 26).

[17] Qal Narr. 3mp of נשׂא, glossed as "to take" (see ch. 25).

[18] Qal Narr. 3mp of ישׁב, glossed as "to dwell" (see ch. 27).

[19] Qal Narr. 3ms of עלה, glossed as "to go up" (see ch. 24).

[20] Hiph. Narr. 3mp of נכה, glossed as "to strike" + 3mp object suffix → "and they struck them" (see chs. 21, 24).

[21] Hiph. Narr. 3mp of נכה, glossed as "to strike" (see ch. 24).

19.9 Exegetical Exercises—Oaths

Oaths occur relatively often in the OT, and their forms can confuse the beginning Hebrew student.

Introductions. An oath can be introduced by one of two main formulae:

- A Niphal form of שׁבע, "to swear":

  וַיִּשָּׁבַע מֹשֶׁה בַּיּוֹם הַהוּא לֵאמֹר אִם־לֹא הָאָרֶץ אֲשֶׁר דָּרְכָה רַגְלְךָ בָּהּ לְךָ תִהְיֶה לְנַחֲלָה

  ("And Moses swore on that day, saying, 'The land on which your foot has walked will be yours for an inheritance.'"—Josh. 14:9)

- X חַי ("by the life of X"):

  חַי־יְהוָה כִּי אֶת־אֲשֶׁר יֹאמַר יְהוָה אֵלַי אֹתוֹ אֲדַבֵּר

  ("As the Lord lives, whatever the Lord will say to me I will speak."—1 Kings 22:14)

Oaths with Asseverative כִּי ("Surely"). Positively phrased oaths most often follow the introductory formula with a כִּי clause.[22]

כַּאֲשֶׁר נִשְׁבַּעְתִּי לָךְ בַּיהוָה אֱלֹהֵי יִשְׂרָאֵל לֵאמֹר כִּי־שְׁלֹמֹה בְנֵךְ יִמְלֹךְ אַחֲרַי

("Just as I swore to you by the Lord, the God of Israel, saying, 'Surely Solomon your son will reign after me.'"—1 Kings 1:30)

Oaths with a Suppressed Apodosis. Negatively phrased oaths most often follow the introductory formula with אִם. This אִם introduces the first half of a conditional statement (the "if" condition, called the *protasis*), but the second half of the conditional statement (the "then" result, called the *apodosis*) is most often unstated. These are often best translated into English with "not."

[22] Other forms such as כִּי אִם and אִם לֹא occur, so this is not a rigid taxonomy.

חַי־יְהוָה וְחֵי־נַפְשְׁךָ אִם־אֶעֶזְבֶךָּ ("As the LORD lives and as you live, I will not abandon you."—2 Kings 4:30—lit. "As the LORD lives and as you live, if I abandon you . . . .")

נִשְׁבַּעְתִּי בְאַפִּי אִם־יְבֹאוּן אֶל־מְנוּחָתִי ("I swore in my wrath, 'They shall not enter my rest.'"—Ps. 95:11—lit. "I swore in my wrath, if they enter my rest . . . .")

Curses. Curses are often introduced by the maledictory statement כֹּה יַעֲשֶׂה יְהוָה וְכֹה יוֹסִיף ("Thus may the LORD do and thus may he add").

וַיִּשָּׁבַע הַמֶּלֶךְ שְׁלֹמֹה בַּיהוָה לֵאמֹר כֹּה יַעֲשֶׂה־לִּי אֱלֹהִים וְכֹה יוֹסִיף כִּי בְנַפְשׁוֹ דִּבֶּר אֲדֹנִיָּהוּ אֶת־הַדָּבָר הַזֶּה׃ ("And King Solomon swore by the LORD, saying, 'Thus may God do to me and thus may he add if Adonijah does not speak for this thing with his life.'"—1 Kings 2:23)

Translate the following oaths:

1 Sam. 19:6 וַיִּשְׁמַע שָׁאוּל בְּקוֹל יְהוֹנָתָן וַיִּשָּׁבַע שָׁאוּל חַי־יְהוָה אִם־יוּמָת[23]׃

2 Sam. 3:35b וַיִּשָּׁבַע דָּוִד לֵאמֹר כֹּה יַעֲשֶׂה־לִּי אֱלֹהִים וְכֹה יֹסִיף כִּי אִם־לִפְנֵי בוֹא[24]־

הַשֶּׁמֶשׁ אֶטְעַם־לֶחֶם אוֹ כָל־מְאוּמָה׃

---

[23] Hoph. Imperf. 3ms of מות, glossed as "to die" (see ch. 26).

[24] Qal Inf. Const. of בוא, glossed as "to come, go" (see ch. 26).

חַי־יְהוָ֗ה אִם־יִפֹּ֞ל מִשַּׂעֲרַ֤ת רֹאשׁוֹ֙ אַ֔רְצָה — 1 Sam. 14:45

וַיֹּ֕אמֶר כֹּֽה־יַעֲשֶׂה־לִּ֥י אֱלֹהִ֖ים וְכֹ֣ה יוֹסִ֑ף אִם־יַעֲמֹ֞ד רֹ֣אשׁ אֱלִישָׁ֧ע בֶּן־ — 2 Kings 6:31

שָׁפָ֛ט עָלָ֖יו הַיּֽוֹם׃

וַיִּשְׁמַ֥ע יְהוָ֖ה אֶת־ק֣וֹל דִּבְרֵיכֶ֑ם וַיִּקְצֹ֖ף וַיִּשָּׁבַ֥ע לֵאמֹֽר׃ אִם־יִרְאֶ֥ה[25] אִישׁ֙ — Deut. 1:34–35

בָּאֲנָשִׁ֣ים הָאֵ֔לֶּה הַדּ֥וֹר הָרָ֖ע הַזֶּ֑ה אֵ֚ת הָאָ֣רֶץ הַטּוֹבָ֔ה אֲשֶׁ֣ר נִשְׁבַּ֔עְתִּי לָתֵ֖ת

לַאֲבֹתֵיכֶֽם׃

[25] Qal. Imperf. 3ms of ראה, glossed as “to see” (see ch. 24).

כ (20) Hithpael

20.1 The Hithpael Stem

Just as the Niphal provides the reflexive counterpart to the Qal, the Hithpael provides the reflexive counterpart to the Piel and Pual stems. As with the other stems, no single generalization covers every use of the Hithpael, but its basic function is action referencing the subject himself, herself, or itself.

- **Reflexive**—when the subject impacts itself with the verbal action:

  הִתְחַזֵּק ("He strengthened himself."—2 Chron. 15:8)

  הִתְקַדָּשׁוּ ("They had consecrated themselves."—2 Chron. 5:11)

- **Reciprocal**—when the components of a plural subject impact each other:

  וַיִּתְקַשֵּׁר ("They conspired together."—2 Kings 9:14)

  יִתְלַכְּדוּ ("They clasp one another."—Job 41:9 [Engl. 41:17])

- **Iterative**—when the action is repeated:[1]

  בַּחֲשֵׁכָה יִתְהַלָּכוּ ("They walk about in darkness."—Ps. 82:5)

- **Active**—seeming much like a typical Qal verbal form:

  וְאִם לַיהוָה יֶחֱטָא־אִישׁ מִי יִתְפַּלֶּל־לוֹ ("but if someone sins against the Lord, who can intercede for him?"—1 Sam. 2:25)

  Sometimes the self-interest of the Hithpael may be apparent behind the active translation:

  וְיִתְפַּלֵּל אֵלָיו ("And he prays to it."—Isa. 44:17)

  At other times this reflexive sense may barely be evident, as in:

  וְיִתְפַּלֵּל בַּעַדְךָ ("And he will pray for you."—Gen. 20:7)

[1] This use of the Hithpael may be considered either (1) an independent use of the stem or (2) potentially a subset of the reflexive meaning, with the sense that the subject is still somewhat involved in the action.

- Though less common, Hithpael verbs can also be **denominative**, as in:

  אֶלְדָּד וּמֵידָד מִתְנַבְּאִים בַּמַּחֲנֶה ("Eldad and Medad are prophesying in the camp."—Num. 11:27)

20.2 The Hithpael Perfect

The Hithpael perfect is formed by a characteristic הִתְ־ prefix, the doubling of the second root letter, and the typical perfect suffixes.

Hithpael Perfect Paradigm

	Verbal Form	Suffix	Gloss
3ms	הִתְקַטֵּל	--	he killed himself
3fs	הִתְקַטְּלָה	ָה	she killed herself
2ms	הִתְקַטַּלְתָּ	תָּ	you (ms) killed yourself
2fs	הִתְקַטַּלְתְּ	תְּ	you (fs) killed yourself
1cs	הִתְקַטַּלְתִּי	תִּי	I killed myself
3cp	הִתְקַטְּלוּ	וּ	they killed themselves
2mp	הִתְקַטַּלְתֶּם	תֶּם	you (mp) killed yourselves
2fp	הִתְקַטַּלְתֶּן	תֶּן	you (fp) killed yourselves
1cp	הִתְקַטַּלְנוּ	נוּ	we killed ourselves

Tip-Offs for the Hithpael Perfect:

- Prefixed הִתְ־
- Doubled second root letter
- *pataḥ* vowel under first root letter

20.3 The Hithpael Imperfect

In the Hithpael imperfect the ־הִתְ prefix is present, but the ה is replaced with the consonant from the prefix. The Hithpael imperfect would have conceptually had both the imperfect prefix letter and the ־הִתְ prefix from the *binyan*, with the ה later being assimilated:

*יְהִתְקַטֵּל > יִתְקַטֵּל

Hithpael Imperfect Paradigm

	Verbal Form	Prefix…Suffix	Gloss
3ms	יִתְקַטֵּל	--- י	he will kill himself
3fs	תִּתְקַטֵּל	--- תּ	she will kill herself
2ms	תִּתְקַטֵּל	--- תּ	you (ms) will kill yourself
2fs	תִּתְקַטְּלִי	ִי --- תּ	you (fs) will kill yourself
1cs	אֶתְקַטֵּל	--- א	I will kill myself
3mp	יִתְקַטְּלוּ	וּ --- י	they (mp) will kill themselves
3fp	תִּתְקַטֵּלְנָה	נָה --- תּ	they (fp) will kill themselves
2mp	תִּתְקַטְּלוּ	וּ --- תּ	you (mp) will kill yourselves
2fp	תִּתְקַטֵּלְנָה	נָה --- תּ	you (fp) will kill yourselves
1cp	נִתְקַטֵּל	--- נ	we will kill ourselves

Tip-Offs for the Hithpael Imperfect:

- Infixed *taw* preceded by *ḥireq*
- Doubled second root letter
- *pataḥ* vowel under first root letter

20.4 The Hithpael Imperative

With the removal of the imperfect's prefix, the characteristic הִתְ־ prefix is fully visible in the Hithpael imperative.

Hithpael Imperative Paradigm

	Verbal Form	Suffix	Gloss
2ms	הִתְקַטֵּל	---	you (ms) kill yourself
2fs	הִתְקַטְּלִי	ִי ---	you (fs) kill yourself
2mp	הִתְקַטְּלוּ	וּ ---	you (mp) kill yourselves
2fp	הִתְקַטֵּלְנָה	נָה ---	you (fp) kill yourselves

Tip-Offs for the Hithpael Imperative:

- Prefixed הִתְ־
- Doubled second root letter
- *pataḥ* vowel under first root letter

20.5 The Hithpael Participle

The Hithpael participle contains the הִתְ־ prefix with the ה replaced by מ.

Hithpael Participle Paradigm

	Verbal Form	Suffix	Gloss
ms	מִתְקַטֵּל	--	one who kills himself
fs	מִתְקַטֶּלֶת	ֶת	one who kills herself
fs (alt. form)	מִתְקַטְּלָה	ָה	one who kills herself
mp	מִתְקַטְּלִים	ִים	ones who kill themselves
fp	מִתְקַטְּלוֹת	וֹת	ones who kill themselves

Tip-Offs for the Hithpael Participle:

- Prefixed מִתְ־
- Doubled second root letter
- *pataḥ* vowel under first root letter

20.6 The Hithpael Infinitives

The Hithpael infinitive absolute and infinitive construct are identical: הִתְקַטֵּל. This form is also identical to the 3ms perfect and the 2ms imperative.

20.7 Metathesis and Assimilation of *taw*

The chief challenges in recognizing Hithpael forms in the text come when one (or both) of two phenomena are evident: **metathesis** and **assimilation** of the *taw*. Metathesis is the transposition (switching places) of two consonants in a word, usually occurring because the changed order of the sounds creates easier pronunciation.[2] The assimilation of *taw* occurs when the *taw* assimilates into a following letter, doubling that letter.

Metathesis. In the Hithpael, whenever the *taw* of the הִתְ־ prefix (or יִתְ־, מִתְ־, etc.) precedes one of the letters known as **sibilants** (ס, צ, שׂ, and שׁ), metathesis occurs.

מִסְתַּתֵּר < מִתְסַתֵּר* one who hides himself (root = סתר)

מִשְׂתַּכֵּר < מִתְשַׂכֵּר* one who hires himself out (root = שׂכר)

יִשְׁתַּמֵּר < יִתְשַׁמֵּר* he will keep watch over himself (root = שׁמר)

The *ṣade* is not only a sibilant but also an emphatic consonant; it causes not only metathesis but also the *taw* to change to *ṭet*:[3]

נִצְטַדֵּק < נִצְתַּדֵּק* < נִתְצַדֵּק* we will prove ourselves innocent (root = צדק)

To correctly identify the root letters of a word, it is essential to recognize metathesis. For example, in the form וָאֶשְׁתַּמֵּר (Ps. 18:24), the root letters are שׁמר, *not* תמר.

Assimilation of *taw*. If a verbal root begins with a consonant known as a **dental** (ד, ט, and ת), the *taw* of the הִתְ־ (or יִתְ־, מִתְ־, etc.) prefix will assimilate, doubling the following consonant and marking that doubling with a *dagesh forte*.

יִטַּמְּאוּ < יִתְטַמְּאוּ* they will defile themselves (root = טמא)

מִדַּבֵּר < מִתְדַּבֵּר* one who converses (root = דבר)

---

[2] For the important verb הִשְׁתַּחֲוָה, see chapter 24.

[3] This is the change from a nonemphatic /t/ to an emphatic /ṭ/.

20.8 Vocabulary

אָ֫וֶן	wickedness, sin, injustice; disaster
אוֹת	sign, standard; (miraculous) event; mark (of seasons)
אֲרִי / אַרְיֵה	lion
אֶ֫רֶז	cedar
אֹ֫רֶךְ	length
בֶּ֫טֶן	belly, internal organs; womb
הִתְקַדֵּשׁ	(Hithp.) to keep oneself consecrated; to be sanctified
חִזֵּק	(Piel) to make firm or strong; strengthen
הִתְחַזֵּק	(Hithp.) to show courage; prove oneself strong
הֶחֱזִיק	(Hiph.) to seize, grasp, hold on to
מוֹעֵד	meeting, assembly; meeting place, time; festival
עֵדָה	assembly; throng, gang; community
עֵת	point in time, occasion, time
עַתָּה	now
פְּרִי	fruit
צְדָקָה	honesty, justice, entitlement, just cause
צֶ֫דֶק	equity, what is right, loyalty, salvation, well-being
צַדִּיק	innocent, righteous, just, upright
צָפוֹן	north
רָשָׁע	guilty

20.9 Language Exercises

A. Parse and translate the following forms.

הִתְפַּלֵּל

טָהֵר

אֶתְפַּלֵּל

וָאֶתְפַּלֵּל

מִתְפַּלְלִים

חִזַּ֫קְתִּי

יִתְחַזֵּק

נִתְחַזַּק

חָזַּ֫קְתָּ

הִקְדִּישׁוּ

מִתְקַדֶּ֫שֶׁת

הִתְקַדַּ֫שְׁתִּי

מְקֻדָּשׁ

יִתְקַדָּ֫שׁוּ

יִטְמְאוּ

יִטַמָּא

טִמֵּא

וָאֶשְׁתַּמֵּר

וַיִּשְׂכֹּר

B. Translate the following and parse each verb and participle. Use your lexicon to look up the glosses for any words you do not know from your vocabulary.

2 Chron. 15:8–10

וְכִשְׁמֹ֨עַ אָסָ֜א הַדְּבָרִ֣ים הָאֵ֗לֶּה וְהַנְּבוּאָה֮ עֹדֵ֣ד הַנָּבִיא֒ הִתְחַזַּ֗ק וַיַּעֲבֵ֤ר הַשִּׁקּוּצִים֙

מִכָּל־אֶ֣רֶץ יְהוּדָה֙ וּבִנְיָמִ֔ן וּמִן־הֶ֣עָרִ֔ים אֲשֶׁ֥ר לָכַ֖ד מֵהַ֣ר אֶפְרָ֑יִם וַיְחַדֵּשׁ֙ אֶת־

מִזְבַּ֣ח יְהוָ֔ה אֲשֶׁ֕ר לִפְנֵ֖י אוּלָ֥ם[4] יְהוָֽה׃ וַיִּקְבֹּ֗ץ אֶֽת־כָּל־יְהוּדָה֮ וּבִנְיָמִן֒ וְהַגָּרִים֙[5]

עִמָּהֶ֔ם מֵאֶפְרַ֥יִם וּמְנַשֶּׁ֖ה וּמִשִּׁמְע֑וֹן כִּֽי־נָפְל֨וּ עָלָ֤יו מִיִּשְׂרָאֵל֙ לָרֹ֔ב בִּרְאֹתָ֕ם[6] כִּֽי־

יְהוָ֥ה אֱלֹהָ֖יו עִמּֽוֹ׃ וַיִּקָּבְצ֥וּ יְרֽוּשָׁלִַ֖ם בַּחֹ֣דֶשׁ הַשְּׁלִישִׁ֑י לִשְׁנַ֛ת חֲמֵשׁ־עֶשְׂרֵ֖ה

לְמַלְכ֥וּת אָסָֽא׃

Num. 11:16–18

וַיֹּ֨אמֶר יְהוָ֜ה אֶל־מֹשֶׁ֗ה אֶסְפָה־לִּ֞י שִׁבְעִ֣ים אִישׁ֮ מִזִּקְנֵ֣י יִשְׂרָאֵל֒ אֲשֶׁ֣ר יָדַ֔עְתָּ כִּי־

הֵ֛ם זִקְנֵ֥י הָעָ֖ם וְשֹׁטְרָ֑יו וְלָקַחְתָּ֤ אֹתָם֙ אֶל־אֹ֣הֶל מוֹעֵ֔ד וְהִֽתְיַצְּב֥וּ שָׁ֖ם עִמָּֽךְ׃

[4] This is often found in the lexicon under the alternative spelling אֵילָם.

[5] Qal Part. mp of גור, glossed as "to sojourn" (see ch. 26).

[6] Qal Inf. Const. of ראה, glossed as "to see" + 3mp suffix (see ch. 24).

וְיָרַדְתִּ֗י וְדִבַּרְתִּ֣י עִמְּךָ֮ שָׁם֒ וְאָצַלְתִּ֗י מִן־הָר֛וּחַ אֲשֶׁ֥ר עָלֶ֖יךָ וְשַׂמְתִּ֣י[7] עֲלֵיהֶ֑ם

וְנָשְׂא֤וּ אִתְּךָ֙ בְּמַשָּׂ֣א הָעָ֔ם וְלֹא־תִשָּׂ֥א אַתָּ֖ה לְבַדֶּֽךָ׃ וְאֶל־הָעָ֨ם תֹּאמַ֜ר הִתְקַדְּשׁ֣וּ

לְמָחָר֮ וַאֲכַלְתֶּ֣ם בָּשָׂר֒ כִּ֡י בְּכִיתֶם֩[8] בְּאָזְנֵ֨י יְהוָ֜ה לֵאמֹ֗ר מִ֤י יַאֲכִלֵ֙נוּ֙[9] בָּשָׂ֔ר כִּי־

ט֥וֹב לָ֖נוּ בְּמִצְרָ֑יִם וְנָתַ֨ן יְהוָ֥ה לָכֶ֛ם בָּשָׂ֖ר וַאֲכַלְתֶּֽם׃

Gen. 20:17–18

וַיִּתְפַּלֵּ֥ל אַבְרָהָ֖ם אֶל־הָאֱלֹהִ֑ים וַיִּרְפָּ֨א אֱלֹהִ֜ים אֶת־אֲבִימֶ֧לֶךְ וְאֶת־אִשְׁתּ֛וֹ

וְאַמְהֹתָ֖יו וַיֵּלֵֽדוּ[10]׃ כִּֽי־עָצֹ֤ר עָצַר֙ יְהוָ֔ה בְּעַ֥ד כָּל־רֶ֖חֶם לְבֵ֣ית אֲבִימֶ֑לֶךְ עַל־

דְּבַ֥ר שָׂרָ֖ה אֵ֥שֶׁת אַבְרָהָֽם׃

[7] Qal Conv. Perf. 1cs of שׂים, glossed as "to set" (see ch. 26).
[8] Qal Perf. 2mp of בכה, glossed as "to weep" (see ch. 24).
[9] Hiph. Imperf. 3ms of אכל, glossed as "to feed" (see ch. 22).
[10] Qal Narr. 3mp of ילד, glossed as "to bear/beget children" (see ch. 27).

1 Sam. 26:1–2 וַיָּבֹ֤אוּ[11] הַזִּפִים֙ אֶל־שָׁא֔וּל הַגִּבְעָ֖תָה לֵאמֹ֑ר הֲל֨וֹא דָוִ֜ד מִסְתַּתֵּ֗ר בְּגִבְעַת֙

הַֽחֲכִילָ֔ה עַ֖ל פְּנֵ֥י הַיְשִׁימֹֽן׃ וַיָּ֣קָם[12] שָׁא֗וּל וַיֵּ֙רֶד֙[13] אֶל־מִדְבַּר־זִ֔יף וְאִתּ֛וֹ שְׁלֹֽשֶׁת־

אֲלָפִ֥ים אִ֖ישׁ בְּחוּרֵ֣י יִשְׂרָאֵ֑ל לְבַקֵּ֥שׁ אֶת־דָּוִ֖ד בְּמִדְבַּר־זִֽיף׃

Num. 7:88–89 וְכֹ֨ל בְּקַ֣ר זֶ֣בַח הַשְּׁלָמִ֗ים עֶשְׂרִ֣ים וְאַרְבָּעָה֮ פָּרִים֒ אֵילִ֤ם שִׁשִּׁים֙ עַתֻּדִ֣ים שִׁשִּׁ֔ים

כְּבָשִׂ֥ים בְּנֵֽי־שָׁנָ֖ה שִׁשִּׁ֑ים זֹ֚את חֲנֻכַּ֣ת הַמִּזְבֵּ֔חַ אַחֲרֵ֖י הִמָּשַׁ֥ח אֹתֽוֹ׃ וּבְבֹ֨א[14] מֹשֶׁ֜ה

אֶל־אֹ֣הֶל מוֹעֵד֮ לְדַבֵּ֣ר אִתּוֹ֒ וַיִּשְׁמַ֨ע אֶת־הַקּ֜וֹל מִדַּבֵּ֣ר אֵלָ֗יו מֵעַ֤ל הַכַּפֹּ֙רֶת֙ אֲשֶׁר֙

עַל־אֲרֹ֣ן הָעֵדֻ֔ת מִבֵּ֖ין שְׁנֵ֣י הַכְּרֻבִ֑ים וַיְדַבֵּ֖ר אֵלָֽיו׃

---

[11] Qal Narr. 3mp of בוא, glossed as “to come, go” (see ch. 26).

[12] Qal Narr. 3ms of קום, glossed as “to arise” (see ch. 26).

[13] Qal Narr. 3ms of ירד, glossed as “to go down, come down” (see ch. 27).

[14] Qal Inf. Const. of בוא, glossed as “to come, go” (see ch. 26).

Ex. 19:20–22 וַיֵּ֧רֶד[15] יְהוָ֛ה עַל־הַ֥ר סִינַ֖י אֶל־רֹ֣אשׁ הָהָ֑ר וַיִּקְרָ֨א יְהוָ֧ה לְמֹשֶׁ֛ה אֶל־רֹ֥אשׁ הָהָ֖ר

וַיַּ֥עַל[16] מֹשֶֽׁה׃ וַיֹּ֤אמֶר יְהוָה֙ אֶל־מֹשֶׁ֔ה רֵ֖ד[17] הָעֵ֣ד[18] בָּעָ֑ם פֶּן־יֶהֶרְס֤וּ[19] אֶל־יְהוָה֙

לִרְא֔וֹת[20] וְנָפַ֥ל מִמֶּ֖נּוּ רָֽב׃ וְגַ֧ם הַכֹּהֲנִ֛ים הַנִּגָּשִׁ֥ים אֶל־יְהוָ֖ה יִתְקַדָּ֑שׁוּ פֶּן־יִפְרֹ֥ץ

בָּהֶ֖ם יְהוָֽה׃

2 Sam. 10:11–13 וַיֹּ֗אמֶר אִם־תֶּחֱזַ֤ק[21] אֲרָם֙ מִמֶּ֔נִּי וְהָיִ֥תָה[22] לִּ֖י לִֽישׁוּעָ֑ה וְאִם־בְּנֵ֤י עַמּוֹן֙ יֶחֶזְק֣וּ[23]

מִמְּךָ֔ וְהָלַכְתִּ֖י לְהוֹשִׁ֥יעַ[24] לָֽךְ׃ חֲזַ֤ק וְנִתְחַזַּק֙ בְּעַד־עַמֵּ֔נוּ וּבְעַ֖ד עָרֵ֣י אֱלֹהֵ֑ינוּ

---

[15] Qal Narr. 3ms of ירד, glossed as "to go down, come down" (see ch. 27).

[16] Qal Narr. 3ms of עלה, glossed as "to go up" (see ch. 24).

[17] Qal Imperative ms of ירד, glossed as "to go down, come down" (see ch. 27).

[18] Hiph. Imperative ms of עוד, glossed as "to warn" (see ch. 26).

[19] Qal Imperf. 3mp of הרס, glossed as "to break through" (see ch. 22).

[20] Qal Inf. Const. of ראה, glossed as "to see" (see ch. 24).

[21] Qal Imperf. 3fs of חזק, glossed as "to be strong" (see ch. 22).

[22] Qal Conv. Perf. 2ms of היה, glossed as "to be" (see ch. 24).

[23] Qal Imperf. 3mp of חזק, glossed as "to be strong" (see ch. 22).

[24] Hiph. Inf. Const. of ישע, glossed as "to save, to deliver" (see ch. 27).

וַיהוָ֕ה יַעֲשֶׂ֥ה[25] הַטּ֖וֹב בְּעֵינָֽיו׃ וַיִּגַּ֣שׁ יוֹאָ֗ב וְהָעָם֙ אֲשֶׁ֣ר עִמּ֔וֹ לַמִּלְחָמָ֖ה בַּאֲרָ֑ם

וַיָּנֻ֖סוּ[26] מִפָּנָֽיו׃

Judg. 20:20–22

וַיֵּצֵא֙[27] אִ֣ישׁ יִשְׂרָאֵ֔ל לַמִּלְחָמָ֖ה עִם־בִּנְיָמִ֑ן וַיַּעַרְכ֨וּ אִתָּ֧ם אִֽישׁ־יִשְׂרָאֵ֛ל מִלְחָמָ֖ה

אֶל־הַגִּבְעָֽה׃ וַיֵּצְא֥וּ[28] בְנֵֽי־בִנְיָמִ֖ן מִן־הַגִּבְעָ֑ה וַיַּשְׁחִ֨יתוּ בְיִשְׂרָאֵ֜ל בַּיּ֣וֹם הַה֗וּא

שְׁנַ֨יִם וְעֶשְׂרִ֥ים אֶ֛לֶף אִ֖ישׁ אָֽרְצָה׃ וַיִּתְחַזֵּ֥ק הָעָ֖ם אִ֣ישׁ יִשְׂרָאֵ֑ל וַיֹּסִ֨פוּ[29] לַעֲרֹ֤ךְ

מִלְחָמָה֙ בַּמָּק֔וֹם אֲשֶׁר־עָ֥רְכוּ שָׁ֖ם בַּיּ֥וֹם הָרִאשֽׁוֹן׃

[25] Qal Juss. 3ms of עשׂה, glossed as "to do" (see ch. 24).

[26] Qal Narr. 3mp of נוס, glossed as "to flee" (see ch. 26).

[27] Qal Narr. 3ms of יצא, glossed as "to go out" (see ch. 27).

[28] Qal Narr. 3mp of יצא, glossed as "to go out" (see ch. 27).

[29] Hiph. Narr. 3mp of יסף, glossed as "to do again" (see ch. 27).

2 Kings 20:2–3

וַיַּסֵּב[30] אֶת־פָּנָיו אֶל־הַקִּיר וַיִּתְפַּלֵּל אֶל־יְהוָה לֵאמֹר׃ אָנָּה יְהוָה זְכָר־נָא אֵת

אֲשֶׁר הִתְהַלַּכְתִּי לְפָנֶיךָ בֶּאֱמֶת וּבְלֵבָב שָׁלֵם וְהַטּוֹב בְּעֵינֶיךָ עָשִׂיתִי[31] וַיֵּבְךְּ[32]

חִזְקִיָּהוּ בְּכִי גָדוֹל׃

2 Chron. 30:17–20

כִּי־רַבַּת בַּקָּהָל אֲשֶׁר לֹא־הִתְקַדָּשׁוּ וְהַלְוִיִּם עַל־שְׁחִיטַת הַפְּסָחִים לְכֹל לֹא

טָהוֹר לְהַקְדִּישׁ לַיהוָה׃ כִּי מַרְבִּית הָעָם רַבַּת מֵאֶפְרַיִם וּמְנַשֶּׁה יִשָּׂשכָר

וּזְבֻלוּן לֹא הִטֶּהָרוּ[33] כִּי־אָכְלוּ אֶת־הַפֶּסַח בְּלֹא כַכָּתוּב כִּי הִתְפַּלֵּל יְחִזְקִיָּהוּ

עֲלֵיהֶם לֵאמֹר יְהוָה הַטּוֹב יְכַפֵּר בְּעַד׃ כָּל־לְבָבוֹ הֵכִין[34] לִדְרוֹשׁ הָאֱלֹהִים

[30] Hiph. Narr. 3ms of סבב, glossed as "to turn" (see ch. 28).

[31] Qal Perf. 1cs of עשׂה, glossed as "to do" (see ch. 24).

[32] Qal Narr. 3ms of בכה, glossed as "to weep" (see ch. 24).

[33] Hithp. Perf. 3cp of טהר, glossed as "to cleanse oneself" (see ch. 23).

[34] Hiph. Perf. 3ms of כון, glossed as "to fix, make firm" (see ch. 26).

יְהוָ֖ה אֱלֹהֵ֣י אֲבוֹתָ֑יו וְלֹ֖א כְּטָהֳרַ֥ת הַקֹּֽדֶשׁ׃ וַיִּשְׁמַ֤ע יְהוָה֙ אֶל־יְחִזְקִיָּ֔הוּ וַיִּרְפָּ֖א

אֶת־הָעָֽם׃

20.10 Exegetical Exercises—Roots and Conjugations

With the addition of the Hithpael, all seven major stems have now been introduced. The relationships of these stems to each other was addressed as each individual stem was introduced, but they can now be summarized as follows:

<table>
<tr><th></th><th>Basic</th><th>Factitive</th><th>Causative</th></tr>
<tr><td>Active</td><td>Qal
קָטַל</td><td>Piel
קִטֵּל</td><td>Hiphil
הִקְטִיל</td></tr>
<tr><td>Passive</td><td rowspan="2">Niphal
נִקְטַל</td><td>Pual
קֻטַּל</td><td>Hophal
הָקְטַל</td></tr>
<tr><td>Reflexive</td><td>Hithpael
הִתְקַטֵּל</td><td></td></tr>
</table>

For instance, consider the root גנב. Using your lexicon, determine in which of the seven stems it occurs and its approximate meaning in each stem.

	Basic	Factitive	Causative
Active	Qal	Piel	Hiphil
Passive	Niphal	Pual	Hophal
Reflexive		Hithpael	

Similarly, consider the root שׁלח. Using your lexicon, determine in which of the seven stems it occurs and its approximate meaning in each stem.

	Basic	Factitive	Causative
Active	Qal	Piel	Hiphil
Passive	Niphal	Pual	Hophal
Reflexive		Hithpael	

I must emphasize that this chart *badly* oversimplifies the Hebrew verbal system, giving the impression that (1) any root can be freely used in any stem and (2) the relationships between the stems are always the same. In reality, few Hebrew roots occur in all seven stems, and as emphasized with the introduction of each stem, there are multiple uses of each derived stem.[35]

At issue is the linguistic distinction between an **inflectional system** and a **derivational system**. An inflectional system is closed and semantically regular with no gaps—a system that requires strict adherence. On the other hand, a derivational system is open, is more irregular, and has many gaps—a system that requires only a loose connection. Few roots occur in all seven stems, indicating that the Hebrew verbal system is derivational. Further, Hebrew is a member of the Semitic language family, and evidence from living Semitic languages shows the same lack of strict adherence to the pattern.

Because the Hebrew verbal system is derivational, the tendencies seen in the verbal system are just that—tendencies, not truly regular. There will be a frustrating number of exceptions to the relationships implied in the chart above, but that is expected in a derivational system.

The takeaway: a certain root being used in one stem instead of another *may* matter, but you cannot immediately *assume* that it matters. If a verbal root is attested in only one column of the chart, no conclusions can be made about the author's choice to use it in that stem. Verbs that do not occur in contrasting stems are termed **unclassified** and have only the nuance that can be discerned from their usage. For example, the root דבר ("to speak") occurs almost exclusively in the Piel. No particular nuance should be drawn because an author uses the Piel of דבר instead of the Qal.[36] Similarly, the root כתב ("to write") occurs—with a single exception—exclusively in the Qal and Niphal. No weight should be given to an author's choosing to use a Qal or Niphal form of כתב, because that was the only form available for use in the language.

---

[35] For example, the D-stem (Piel, Pual, Hithpael) is listed as factitive, but chapter 14 noted that the Piel can also be causative, declarative, denominative, etc.

[36] A few occurrences are parsed in the lexica as Qal forms, but they are almost all participles and proportionally so few (40 out of approximately 1,250 occurrences) as to be incidental.

Use your lexicon to check the stems in which the following roots occur. For which roots would it be potentially valuable to consider why the author chose to use a certain stem (Piel instead of Hiphil, Hophal instead of Niphal, etc.), and for which roots would such a discussion be irrelevant? Check the appropriate box:

Root	Choice of Stems Possibly Relevant (Well Attested in 2 or 3 Columns)	Choice of Stems Not Relevant (Occurs in Only 1 Column)
גאל I		
למד		
אבד I		
מות		
בוא		
דרשׁ		
אבה		
הלל II		
גלה		

כא (21) Pronominal Suffixes on Verbs

21.1 Object Suffixes on Verbs

We have previously introduced pronominal suffixes as they are attached to prepositions (see 11.2) and nouns (see 11.3). Pronominal suffixes can also be attached to verbs to indicate the object of the verb, as in:

לֹא כִבַּדְתָּנִי ("You have not honored me."—Isa. 43:23)
Piel Perf. 2ms of כבד, glossed as "to honor" + 1cs object suffix

הַשְׁלִיכֵהוּ ("Throw it down."—Ex. 4:3)
Hiph. Imperative ms of שׁלך, glossed as "to throw" + 3ms object suffix

The exact forms of the object pronouns when they are attached to verbs can initially seem bewildering because of the large variety of possible endings. If the goal is Hebrew composition (writing or speaking statements correctly in Biblical Hebrew), the correct attachment of the object suffixes to the verbs is an endeavor. Recognition of the object suffixes, however, is much less difficult. Essential at this stage is the correct recognition of both the object suffix and the verbal ending that precedes it.

The basic forms of the verbal suffixes are similar to those already covered in chapter 11:

Pronominal Suffixes (Chapter 11)		
	Type 1	Type 2
3ms	־וֹ	־הוּ
3fs	־◌ָהּ	־הָ
2ms	־◌ְךָ	־ךָ
2fs	־◌ֵךְ	־ךְ
1cs	־◌ִי	־נִי
3mp	־הֶם / ־◌ָם	־הֶם
3fp	־הֶן / ־◌ָן	־הֶן
2mp	־כֶם	־כֶם
2fp	־כֶן	־כֶן
1cp	־נוּ	־נוּ

Verbal Suffixes	
3ms	־הוּ / ־וֹ
3fs	הָ / ־ָהּ
2ms	־ךָ
2fs	־ךְ
1cs	־נִי / ־ִי
3mp	־הֶם / ־ם
3fp	־הֶן / ־ן
2mp	־כֶם
2fp	־כֶן
1cp	־נוּ

The difficulty in attaching suffixes to verbal forms is *connecting the suffix* to the various verbal endings—consonantal or vocalic—which can change the vowel preceding the suffix. Further, predictable changes occur in the verb when adding a new final syllable, which creates a new stress pattern in the word (see 3.5).

21.2 The Perfect with Object Suffixes

The verbal endings of the perfect undergo certain regular changes with the addition of object suffixes.

- The 3fs ending changes from ־ָה to either ־ָת or ־ַת:[1]

  קָטְלָה she killed → קְטָלַתְךָ she killed you (ms)

- The 2ms ending changes from ־תָּ to ־תּ:

  קָטַלְתָּ you (ms) killed → קְטַלְתּוֹ you (ms) killed him

- The 2fs ending changes from ־תְּ to ־תִּי:[2]

  קָטַלְתְּ you (fs) killed → קְטַלְתִּיו you (fs) killed him

- The 2mp ending changes from ־תֶּם to ־תּוּ (often spelled defectively as ־תֻּ):

  קְטַלְתֶּם you (mp) killed → קְטַלְתּוּהוּ you (mp) killed him

Be aware:

- The perfect suffixes ־וּ and ־ִי before an object suffix are often spelled defectively with a *qibbuṣ* or a *ḥireq*, respectively.
- Because of the change in the 2fs perfect's ending, the perfect forms of the 2fs and 1cs are identical once an object suffix is added. The 1cs with an object suffix is far more prevalent in Biblical Hebrew, so that form is more likely, though context is the final arbiter to distinguish the two forms.

---

[1] ־ָת and ־ַת represent a return to the original 3fs ending of ת.

[2] ־תִּי represents a return to the ancient 2fs ending (see 3.10).

Besides the changes in the perfect's verbal endings, the addition of a suffixed pronoun causes other changes in the vocalization of the verbal form. These often occur because of the **resyllabification** of the verb. Many of the perfect verbal forms end in an open syllable (see 3.2). The addition of the suffix will often form a new closed syllable at the end of the word. In such a situation, the following changes are common. The Qal shows more change than the other stems.

- A long vowel in an open syllable will often reduce to *shewa* according to the pattern of propretonic vowel reduction learned in 3.5:

קָטַל	he killed	→	קְטָלוֹ	he killed him
נָתַתִּי	I gave	→	נְתַתִּיךָ	I gave you (ms)
קִטֵּל	he slaughtered	→	קִטְּלוֹ	he slaughtered him

  This vowel reduction does not occur if the long vowel is a *mater* or the result of compensatory lengthening.

- A short vowel in an open syllable often lengthens:

קָטַל	he killed	→	קְטָלוֹ	he killed him
יָדַע	he knew	→	יְדָעָהּ	he knew her

  Note, however, that the short vowel *pataḥ* in Piel forms reduces (instead of lengthening) with the addition of the suffix:

קִדַּשׁ	he dedicated	→	קִדְּשׁוֹ	he dedicated him

- Corresponding to this change, a long vowel in what becomes a closed syllable must shorten. This feature is seen most often in the Piel forms of II-guttural verbs (see 23.3):

בֵּרֵךְ	he blessed	→	בֵּרַכְךָ	he blessed you (ms)

- A reduced vowel will often be restored to its original full vowel:

קָטְלוּ	they killed	→	קְטָלוּהוּ	they killed him

Finally, the object suffixes themselves show changes depending on the verbal form to which they are added. These changes involve the use (or nonuse) of connecting vowels when the suffix follows a consonant, though they may also involve slight spelling changes in the suffix.

Suffix	Added to 3ms or 2ms perfect forms (forms ending in a stressed consonant)	Added to 3fs perfect forms (forms ending in an unstressed consonant)	Added to all other perfect forms (forms ending in a vowel)
3ms	־וֹ / ־ָ֫הוּ	־וֹ / ־הוּ	־ו / ־הוּ
3fs	־ָהּ	־ָהּ	־ָהּ
2ms	־ְךָ	־ךָ	־ךָ
2fs	־ֵךְ	־ֶךְ	־ךְ
1cs	־ַ֫נִי	־נִי	־נִי
3mp	־ָם	־ַם	־ם
3fp	־ָן	־ַן	־ן
2mp	Not attested	Not attested	־כֶם
2fp	Not attested	Not attested	Not attested
1cp	־ָ֫נוּ	־נוּ	־נוּ

The Qal perfect of קטל with object suffixes is:

Suffix	Qal Perf. 3ms + object suffixes	Qal Perf. 3fs + object suffixes	Qal Perf. 1cs + object suffixes
3ms	קְטָלוֹ	קְטָלַ֫תְהוּ	קְטַלְתִּ֫יהוּ
3fs	קְטָלָהּ	קְטָלַ֫תָה	קְטַלְתִּ֫יהָ
2ms	קְטָלְךָ	קְטָלַ֫תְךָ	קְטַלְתִּ֫יךָ
2fs	קְטָלֵךְ	קְטָלַ֫תֶךְ	קְטַלְתִּיךְ
1cs	קְטָלַ֫נִי	קְטָלַ֫תְנִי	קְטַלְתִּ֫ינִי
3mp	קְטָלָם	קְטָלַ֫תַם	קְטַלְתִּים
3fp	קְטָלָן	קְטָלַ֫תַן	קְטַלְתִּין
2mp	Not attested	Not attested	קְטַלְתִּ֫יכֶם
2fp	Not attested	Not attested	Not attested
1cp	קְטָלָ֫נוּ	קְטָלַ֫תְנוּ	קְטַלְתִּ֫ינוּ

You should **not** focus on trying to reproduce these charts and paradigms. Focus instead on *recognizing* the object suffixes and verbal forms to which they are attached.

21.3 The Imperfect with Object Suffixes

Compared to the perfect, the imperfect forms of the verb show mercifully fewer changes with the addition of object suffixes, but several changes do occur.

- The *ḥolem* and *ṣere* theme vowels will reduce to *shewa* if they have not already done so (e.g.: 2fs forms):

  יִקְטֹל he will kill → יִקְטְלֶ֫נּוּ he will kill him

- Before the 2ms and 2mp suffixes, however, the vowels shorten instead of reducing:

  יִקְטֹל he will kill → יִקְטָלֶ֫ךָּ[3] he will kill you (ms)

- The *pataḥ* theme vowel lengthens instead of reducing:

  יִשְׁלַח he will send → יִשְׁלָחֶ֫נּוּ he will send him

The object suffixes are also preceded by an *-en-* infixed element. The *nun* is assimilated in some forms of the object suffixes:

3ms	־ֶ֫נּוּ *
3fs	־ֶ֫נָּה
2ms	־ֶךָּ
2fs	Not attested
1cs	־ֶנִּי
3mp	Not attested
3fp	Not attested
2mp	Not attested
2fp	Not attested
1cp	־ֶ֫נּוּ *

*These forms appear identical, though historically they are not. The 3ms form comes from **en+hu*

[3] The vowel in the second syllable is a *qameṣ ḥatup̄*, preserving the *o*-class vowel—though shortened.

(ֶ‾נְהוּ*), with the *heh* assimilating to the *nun.* The 1cp form comes from **en+nu* (ֶ‾נְנוּ*).

If the imperfect verbal form ends in a vowel, the connecting vowel is not present, as in יִקְטְלוּנוּ ("they will kill him").

21.4 The Volitive with Object Suffixes

Jussive and cohortative forms show the same changes as the imperfect forms discussed in the previous section. The object suffixes listed in 21.3 can also be applied to these volitive forms; a form such as יִשְׁלָחֶ֫נּוּ is formally ambiguous between the jussive and the imperfect, requiring a contextual judgment.

A second set of object suffixes lacking the *-en-* infix can also be used for volitive forms. This set of object suffix forms is a strong marker that the verbal form in question is a volitive, not an imperfect.

3ms	‾ֵ֫הוּ
3fs	‾ֶ֫הָ
2ms	‾ךָ
2fs	‾ֵךְ
1cs	‾ֵנִי
3mp	‾ֵם
3fp	‾ֵן
2mp	‾כֶם
2fp	Not attested
1cp	‾ֵ֫נוּ

Thus, יִשְׁלָחֶ֫נּוּ could be either imperfect ("he will send him") or jussive ("let him send him"), whereas יִשְׁלָחֵ֫הוּ is almost certainly jussive.

Imperative forms show similar behavior, though the details change because of their shorter length.

- In ***o*-class** imperatives the masculine singular form undergoes resyllabification, with the initial *shewa* becoming a *qameṣ ḥatup̄*. Note the preservation of the *o*-class vowel:

  קְטֹל (you) kill → קָטְלֵם (you) kill them (mp)

  The feminine singular and masculine plural forms are unchanged before an object suffix. The feminine plural form does not exist with object suffixes, being replaced by the corresponding masculine plural imperative form.

- In ***e*-class** imperatives the *ṣere* normally reduces to *shewa*:

  תֵּן (you) give → תְּנֶ֫הָ (you) give it (fs)

- In ***a*-class** imperatives the *pataḥ* lengthens to *qameṣ*, as in the imperfect:

  שְׁלַח (you) send → שְׁלָחֵ֫נִי (you) send me

As in the examples above, these imperatives take the same form of the object pronouns as other volitives.

21.5 Vocabulary

בַּרְזֶל	iron
גִּבּוֹר	hero, champion, warrior
גּוֹרָל	lot
דֶּ֫לֶת	door
הֵיכָל	palace, temple
זָכָר	man, male; male animal
זְרוֹעַ	arm, forearm; power, force, help
חָכְמָה	wisdom, skill, shrewdness
חָכָם	skillful, shrewd, wise
חֲלוֹם	dream
יָשָׁר	straight, level, smooth; proper, right, just
כֹּהֵן	priest
מְעַט	a little, a trifle
עוֹף	flying creature; bird
צַר	enemy
רֶ֫גֶל	foot, leg
רַב	numerous, many; much; great
רֹב	quantity, fullness; wealth; plenty
רֹחַב	breadth, width, expanse
תּוֹעֵבָה	abomination, abhorrence

21.6 Language Exercises

A. Parse and gloss the following forms. Include the identification of the object suffix where appropriate.

עֲמָדְךָ

וַיַּעֲמִידֵנִי

וַתְּדַבֵּר

דַּבְּרוֹ

מְקַדִּשְׁכֶם

מְקֻדָּשָׁי

וַיִּתְקַדְּשׁוּ

וַיִּלָּחֲמוּנִי

הַרְחִיקֻהוּ

הַכִּירֵנִי

B. Translate the following and parse each verb and participle. Use your lexicon to look up the glosses for any words you do not know from your vocabulary.

2 Chron. 24:25–26

וּבְלֶכְתָּם מִמֶּנּוּ כִּי־עָזְבוּ אֹתוֹ בְּמַחֲלֻיִים רַבִּים הִתְקַשְּׁרוּ עָלָיו עֲבָדָיו

בִּדְמֵי בְּנֵי יְהוֹיָדָע הַכֹּהֵן וַיַּהַרְגֻהוּ עַל־מִטָּתוֹ וַיָּמֹת[4] וַיִּקְבְּרֻהוּ בְּעִיר דָּוִיד

[4] Qal Narr. 3ms of מוּת, glossed as "to die" (see ch. 26).

וְלֹא קְבָרֻהוּ בְּקִבְרוֹת הַמְּלָכִים׃ וְאֵלֶּה הַמִּתְקַשְּׁרִים עָלָיו זָבָד בֶּן־שִׁמְעָת֙

הָֽעַמּוֹנִית וִיהוֹזָבָד בֶּן־שִׁמְרִית הַמּוֹאָבִית׃

Deut. 24:1–4 כִּֽי־יִקַּח אִישׁ אִשָּׁה וּבְעָלָהּ וְהָיָה[5] אִם־לֹא תִמְצָא־חֵן בְּעֵינָיו כִּי־מָצָא בָהּ֙

עֶרְוַת דָּבָר וְכָתַב לָהּ סֵפֶר כְּרִיתֻת֙ וְנָתַן בְּיָדָהּ וְשִׁלְּחָהּ מִבֵּיתוֹ׃ וְיָצְאָה[6]

מִבֵּיתוֹ וְהָלְכָה וְהָיְתָה[7] לְאִישׁ־אַחֵר׃ וּשְׂנֵאָהּ֙ הָאִישׁ הָאַחֲרוֹן וְכָתַב לָהּ

סֵפֶר כְּרִיתֻת֙ וְנָתַן בְּיָדָהּ וְשִׁלְּחָהּ מִבֵּיתוֹ אוֹ כִי יָמוּת[8] הָאִישׁ הָאַחֲרוֹן

אֲשֶׁר־לְקָחָהּ לוֹ לְאִשָּׁה׃ לֹא־יוּכַל[9] בַּעְלָהּ הָרִאשׁוֹן אֲשֶׁר־שִׁלְּחָהּ לָשׁוּב[10]

---

[5] Qal Conv. Perf. 3ms of היה, glossed as “to be” (see ch. 24).

[6] Qal Conv. Perf. 3fs of יצא, glossed as “to go out” (see ch. 27).

[7] Qal Conv. Perf. 3fs of היה, glossed as “to be” (see ch. 24).

[8] Qal Imperf. 3ms of מות, glossed as “to die” (see ch. 26).

[9] Qal Imperf. 3ms of יכל, glossed as “to be able, permitted” (see ch. 27).

[10] Qal Inf. Const. of שׁוב, glossed as “to return, do again” (see ch. 26).

לְקַחְתָּהּ לִהְיוֹת[11] לוֹ לְאִשָּׁה אַחֲרֵי אֲשֶׁר הֻטַּמָּאָה[12] כִּי־תוֹעֵבָה הִוא לִפְנֵי

יְהוָה וְלֹא תַחֲטִיא[13] אֶת־הָאָרֶץ אֲשֶׁר יְהוָה אֱלֹהֶיךָ נֹתֵן לְךָ נַחֲלָה׃

1 Kings 1:2–4 וַיֹּאמְרוּ לוֹ עֲבָדָיו יְבַקְשׁוּ לַאדֹנִי הַמֶּלֶךְ נַעֲרָה בְתוּלָה וְעָמְדָה לִפְנֵי

הַמֶּלֶךְ וּתְהִי[14]־לוֹ סֹכֶנֶת וְשָׁכְבָה בְחֵיקֶךָ וְחַם[15] לַאדֹנִי הַמֶּלֶךְ׃ וַיְבַקְשׁוּ

נַעֲרָה יָפָה בְּכֹל גְּבוּל יִשְׂרָאֵל וַיִּמְצְאוּ אֶת־אֲבִישַׁג הַשּׁוּנַמִּית וַיָּבִאוּ[16] אֹתָהּ

לַמֶּלֶךְ׃ וְהַנַּעֲרָה יָפָה עַד־מְאֹד וַתְּהִי[17] לַמֶּלֶךְ סֹכֶנֶת וַתְּשָׁרְתֵהוּ[18] וְהַמֶּלֶךְ

לֹא יְדָעָהּ׃

---

[11] Qal Inf. Const. of היה, glossed as "to be" (see ch. 24).

[12] Hothpaal Perf. 3fs of טמא, glossed as "to be defiled" (see ch. 28).

[13] Hiph. Imperf. 2ms of חטא, glossed as "to bring sin upon, make sinful" (see ch. 22).

[14] Qal Imperf. 3fs of היה, glossed as "to be" (see ch. 24).

[15] Qal Conv. Perf. 3ms of חמם, glossed as "to be warm" (see ch. 28).

[16] Hiph. Narr. 3mp of בוא, glossed as "to bring" (see ch. 26).

[17] Qal Narr. 3fs of היה, glossed as "to be" (see ch. 24).

[18] Piel Narr. 3fs of שׁרת, glossed as "to serve, minister" + 3ms suffix (see ch. 23).

Gen. 13:7–8

וַֽיְהִי[19]־רִ֗יב בֵּ֚ין רֹעֵ֣י מִקְנֵֽה־אַבְרָ֔ם וּבֵ֖ין רֹעֵ֣י מִקְנֵה־ל֑וֹט וְהַֽכְּנַעֲנִי֙ וְהַפְּרִזִּ֔י

אָ֖ז יֹשֵׁ֥ב בָּאָֽרֶץ׃ וַיֹּ֨אמֶר אַבְרָ֜ם אֶל־ל֗וֹט אַל־נָ֨א תְהִ֤י[20] מְרִיבָה֙ בֵּינִ֣י וּבֵינֶ֔ךָ

וּבֵ֥ין רֹעַ֖י וּבֵ֣ין רֹעֶ֑יךָ כִּֽי־אֲנָשִׁ֥ים אַחִ֖ים אֲנָֽחְנוּ׃

Josh. 1:1–3

וַיְהִ֕י אַחֲרֵ֛י מ֥וֹת מֹשֶׁ֖ה עֶ֣בֶד יְהוָ֑ה וַיֹּ֤אמֶר יְהוָה֙ אֶל־יְהוֹשֻׁ֣עַ בִּן־נ֔וּן מְשָׁרֵ֥ת[21]

מֹשֶׁ֖ה לֵאמֹֽר׃ מֹשֶׁ֥ה עַבְדִּ֖י מֵ֑ת[22] וְעַתָּה֩ ק֨וּם[23] עֲבֹ֜ר אֶת־הַיַּרְדֵּ֣ן הַזֶּ֗ה אַתָּה֙

וְכָל־הָעָ֣ם הַזֶּ֔ה אֶל־הָאָ֕רֶץ אֲשֶׁ֧ר אָנֹכִ֛י נֹתֵ֥ן לָהֶ֖ם לִבְנֵ֥י יִשְׂרָאֵֽל׃ כָּל־מָק֗וֹם

אֲשֶׁ֨ר תִּדְרֹ֧ךְ כַּף־רַגְלְכֶ֛ם בּ֖וֹ לָכֶ֣ם נְתַתִּ֑יו כַּאֲשֶׁ֥ר דִּבַּ֖רְתִּי אֶל־מֹשֶֽׁה׃

---

[19] Qal Narr. 3ms of היה, glossed as "to be" (see ch. 24).

[20] Qal Juss. 2ms of היה, glossed as "to be" (see ch. 24).

[21] Piel Part. ms שׁרת, glossed as "to serve" (see ch. 23).

[22] Qal Perf. 3ms of מות, glossed as "to die" (see ch. 26).

[23] Qal Imperative 3ms of קום, glossed as "to arise" (see ch. 26).

21.7 Exegetical Exercises—Dynamic and Formal Translation Philosophies

Hebrew professors (and students!) are often asked by friends, "Now that you know Hebrew, what is the best translation of the Old Testament/Hebrew Bible?" In response, you must ask, "For what purpose?" Because translations always make trade-offs (see 10.10.B), different translations will have different strengths and weaknesses. Usually these strengths and weaknesses will be the two sides of a necessary trade-off that the translators were forced to make.

A. Most broadly, the two poles of translation philosophy are called **formal equivalence** and **dynamic equivalence**.[24] A formal equivalence philosophy of translation attempts, as much as possible, to represent each Hebrew word with the most closely corresponding English word. A dynamic equivalence philosophy of translation attempts, as much as possible, to represent each Hebrew expression with the most closely corresponding English expression. For example, consider again the description of Ehud in Judges 3:15: אִֽישׁ אִטֵּ֖ר יַד־יְמִינ֑וֹ

- Review 13.8b and translate, with the help of your lexicon, word-for-word through the phrase. How would you render it in English?

- Check the NIV, ESV, and RSV. How do these three major translations render the phrase? Are these translations formal or dynamic in their approach to this specific phrase? How does this relate to their judgment regarding whether it is a frozen form (see 13.8)?

- To understand the rationale behind the translators' choice for these versions, consult the other two occurrences of this phrase in the Hebrew text: Judges 20:16 and

[24] These philosophies are not restricted to Hebrew/English translation; they apply conceptually to any source and target language when translating. Nor are such questions restricted to modern translations; they are also evident in ancient translations such as the various recensions of the Septuagint.

1 Chronicles 12:2. How do these citations support the translators' judgment in all of these translations?

B. Consider the example of 2 Chronicles 25:17:

וַיִּוָּעַץ[25] אֲמַצְיָהוּ מֶלֶךְ יְהוּדָה וַיִּשְׁלַח אֶל־יוֹאָשׁ בֶּן־יְהוֹאָחָז בֶּן־יֵהוּא מֶלֶךְ יִשְׂרָאֵל
לֵאמֹר לְךָ[26] נִתְרָאֶה[27] פָּנִים׃

- Translate the verse, using your lexicon as necessary and parsing the verbs. Note the *Ketiv/Qere* reading. Check your Hebrew Bible to determine the differing readings.

- Consider the last phrase, נִתְרָאֶה פָּנִים. How would you translate it under a formal-equivalence philosophy of translation?

- Compare your translation of this phrase to that of the NIV and ESV, and then read the passage's surrounding context. Considering the NIV and ESV, which is dynamic and which is formal in its translation of this phrase?

---

[25] Niph. Narr. 3ms of יעץ, glossed as "to take counsel" (see ch. 27).

[26] This is an imperative form, and the ה of the *Qere* reading is a **paragogic *heh***. This has caused a different vowel pattern than in the imperative paradigm. What is the remainder of the parsing?

[27] Hithpael Cohortative 1cs of ראה. Use your lexicon to determine the options to gloss this root in the Hithpael.

- What are the benefits of a formal-equivalence translation philosophy? What are its drawbacks?

- What are the benefits of a dynamic-equivalence translation philosophy? What are its drawbacks?

C. As presented above, the contrast between formal and dynamic equivalence can make the two philosophies of translation seem in binary opposition. In practice they represent the two ends of a spectrum, and any actual translation is always between the two poles. Further, no translation is perfectly consistent in the application of its chosen translational philosophy; the verse in question may have characteristics that override a translation committee's more general preference.

For these reasons it is better to talk about translations not as "formal versus dynamic" but as "more formal" or "more dynamic" in translation philosophy.

- Translate the following phrases using your lexicon:

  אִישׁ אִטֵּר יַד־יְמִינוֹ (Judg. 3:15—above)

  וְלָמָּה נָפְלוּ פָנֶיךָ (Gen. 4:6)

  וְלֹא יִמַּס[28] אֶת־לְבַב אֶחָיו כִּלְבָבוֹ (Deut. 20:8)

  כִּי־הוּא רֵאשִׁית אֹנוֹ (Deut. 21:17)

  נִתְרָאֶה פָנִים (2 Chron. 25:17—above)

- Check the following major translations to see how they render each phrase in English: NIV, ESV, HCSB, KJV, NLT. Categorize each translation's rendering of the phrase as "formal" or "dynamic" equivalence.

Phrase	NIV	ESV	HCSB	KJV	NLT
אִישׁ אִטֵּר יַד־יְמִינוֹ (Judg. 3:15)					
וְלָמָּה נָפְלוּ פָנֶיךָ (Gen. 4:6)					
וְלֹא יִמַּס אֶת־לְבַב אֶחָיו כִּלְבָבוֹ (Deut. 20:8)					
כִּי־הוּא רֵאשִׁית אֹנוֹ (Deut. 21:17)					
נִתְרָאֶה פָנִים (2 Chron. 25:17)					

[28] Niph. Imperf. 3ms of מסס, glossed as "to melt" (see ch. 28).

- Tabulate the number of times that each translation took a formal approach and the number of times that each took a dynamic approach. Based on only these five data points, how would you arrange these translations on a spectrum from most formally equivalent to most dynamically equivalent? Place each translation on the following spectrum:

Most Formally Equivalent	⟵——————————⟶	Most Dynamically Equivalent

Every translation has some formal and some dynamic equivalence. Translators do not choose between being purely formally equivalent and being purely dynamically equivalent (e.g.: all five translations treated אִישׁ אִטֵּר יַד־יְמִינוֹ in Judges 3:15 as “a left-handed man”). Instead, they choose where on the spectrum between formal and dynamic equivalence they wish to land, but the context of a particular passage may force its translation to be more or less dynamic.

כב (22) I-Guttural Verbs

22.1 Weak Letters in Verbs

Until now the Hebrew verbal system has been introduced with **strong** letters—those that exhibit few, if any, changes depending on their phonological environment. Several Hebrew letters, however, show various **weaknesses**; they behave differently from the typical strong letters. These weaknesses change the formation of verbal forms. The changes are usually predictable, but they can cause a verbal form to be more difficult to recognize or make the identification of the three-letter verbal root more difficult. The next six chapters concentrate on these weak letters and their impact on verbal forms. These verbs are typically named after the weak letter and the place in the verbal root (first, second, or third letter) that the weak form occupies.

- Chapter 22—I-Guttural verbs
- Chapter 23—II-Guttural verbs, III-*ḥet* and III-*ayin* verbs
- Chapter 24—III-*heh* verbs
- Chapter 25—II-*waw* and II-*yod* verbs (called **middle weak** verbs)
- Chapter 26—III-*aleph* verbs
- Chapter 27—I-*yod* verbs

22.2 Characteristics of Guttural Letters

The **gutturals** are the largest category of weak letters.[1] As covered in 2.4, the letters *aleph* (א), *heh* (ה), *ḥet* (ח), and *ayin* (ע) are gutturals and have several distinct characteristics. Three such characteristics have already been learned:

- They resist doubling, refusing to take a *dagesh forte* (4.5).
- They tend toward *a*-class vowels (5.1).
- They rarely take a simple vocal *shewa*, preferring a *compound shewa* (2.4).

[1] Another school of thought considers gutturals to be the strongest of root letters and therefore argues they show their characteristic behavior because of their strength. The important point, whether one wishes to consider the behavior of gutturals as a weakness or a strength, is simply that they behave differently from other Hebrew consonants.

To these three characteristics we add a fourth observation:

- The presence of a compound *shewa* often influences the preceding vowel, causing it to match the vowel sound of the compound *shewa.*

These four characteristics of gutturals come into play in various verbal forms, depending on whether the guttural is the first, second, or third root letter. Recall as well that *resh* (ר) often behaves in the same way as guttural letters (see 4.5).

22.3 I-Guttural Verbs in Qal

I-Guttural verbs follow the regular verbal pattern when there is no verbal prefix (e.g.: the Qal perfect), but their characteristics come into play more clearly in verbal forms with a prefix. The previously learned forms of the strong verb are given alongside the I-Guttural verb to promote comparison.

	Qal Perfect קטל	Qal Perfect עמד
3ms	קָטַל	עָמַד
3fs	קָֽטְלָה	עָֽמְדָה
2ms	קָטַלְתָּ	עָמַדְתָּ
2fs	קָטַלְתְּ	עָמַדְתְּ
1cs	קָטַלְתִּי	עָמַדְתִּי
3cp	קָֽטְלוּ	עָֽמְדוּ
2mp	קְטַלְתֶּם	עֲמַדְתֶּם
2fp	קְטַלְתֶּן	עֲמַדְתֶּן
1cp	קָטַלְנוּ	עָמַדְנוּ

	Qal Imperfect קטל	Qal Imperfect עמד
3ms	יִקְטֹל	יַעֲמֹד
3fs	תִּקְטֹל	תַּעֲמֹד
2ms	תִּקְטֹל	תַּעֲמֹד
2fs	תִּקְטְלִי	תַּעַמְדִי
1cs	אֶקְטֹל	אֶעֱמֹד
3mp	יִקְטְלוּ	יַעַמְדוּ
3fp	תִּקְטֹלְנָה	תַּעֲמֹדְנָה
2mp	תִּקְטְלוּ	תַּעַמְדוּ
2fp	תִּקְטֹלְנָה	תַּעֲמֹדְנָה
1cp	נִקְטֹל	נַעֲמֹד

*The full vowel under the guttural in the 2fs, 3mp, and 2mp imperfect forms is because of the rule of *shewa* (see 6.4).

The presence of the prefix in the Qal imperfect places the guttural consonant into a position where it would normally take a simple *shewa*. This simple *shewa* is replaced by a compound *shewa.* The resulting compound *shewa* colors the prefix letter's vowel so that the prefix letter takes the corresponding short vowel for the compound *shewa*. This tendency also occurs in the narrative forms.

כֹּל חֹבְלֵי הַיָּם אֶל־הָאָרֶץ יַעֲמֹדוּ ("All the sailors of the sea will stand upon the land."—Ezek. 27:29)

וַיַּעֲמֹד הַמֶּלֶךְ עַל־הָעַמּוּד ("And the king stood by the pillar."—1 Kings 23:3)

Note:

- As seen above, the gutturals' tendency to attract *a*-class vowels commonly causes this vowel sequence to be *pataḥ* followed by *ḥatep̄-patah*, as in:

  יַעֲמֹד He will stand

  Other combinations (e.g.: *segol* followed by *ḥatep̄-segol*) are possible:

  יֶחֱזַק He will be strong

  In general, if the stem vowel is *ḥolem*, the prefix vowel will be *pataḥ* (as in יַעֲמֹד). If the stem vowel is *pataḥ*, the prefix vowel will be *segol* (as in יֶחֱזַק).

  וּבַחֻרֵיהֶם בַּחֶרֶב תַּהֲרֹג ("And you will kill their young men with the sword."—2 Kings 8:12)

  לְמַעַן תֶּחֶזְקוּ ("so that you may be strong" —Deut. 11:8)

  Note that this is a general tendency, not a rule, as exceptions occur:

  אָמַר יְהוָה לְמֹשֶׁה אֱסֹף אֶת־הָעָם ("The Lord said to Moses, 'Gather the people.'"—Num. 21:16)

- I-*aleph* verbs will commonly have a *ḥolem* prefix vowel, as in:

  יֹאכְלוּ They will eat

  This pattern should already be familiar from the common form וַיֹּאמֶר.

כִּֽי־יוֹדֵ֣עַ יְ֭הוָה דֶּ֣רֶךְ צַדִּיקִ֑ים
וְדֶ֖רֶךְ רְשָׁעִ֣ים תֹּאבֵֽד׃ ("For the LORD knows the way of the righteous, but the way of the wicked will perish."—Ps. 1:6)

וַיֹּ֨אמֶר מֹשֶׁ֜ה אֶֽל־אַהֲרֹ֗ן
קַ֚ח צִנְצֶ֣נֶת אַחַ֔ת ("And Moses said to Aaron, 'Take a vessel.'"—Ex. 16:33)

- Forms that are regular, because the guttural is the first letter of the verbal form, include the Qal perfect, active participle, passive participle, converted perfect, and infinitive absolute. Forms that show the compound *shewa* include the Qal imperfect, volitives, narrative, and infinitive construct.

וְהָיָ֗ה כִּֽי־יִרְא֤וּ אֹתָךְ֙ הַמִּצְרִ֔ים
וְאָמְר֖וּ אִשְׁתּ֣וֹ זֹ֑את וְהָרְג֥וּ אֹתִ֖י ("And when the Egyptians see you, they will say, 'She is his wife,' and they will kill me."—Gen. 12:12)

וּבֵ֖ית צַדִּיקִ֣ים יַעֲמֹֽד ("but the house of the righteous will stand"—Prov. 12:17b)

The identification of I-Guttural Qal forms is usually straightforward if you remember that gutturals prefer a compound *shewa.*

22.4 I-Guttural Verbs in Piel/Pual/Hithpael

Because the Piel, Pual, and Hithpael stems do not typically create situations in which a *shewa* would be under the I-Guttural letter, their forms are regular.

יְהַלֶּלְךָ֣ זָ֣ר וְלֹא־פִ֑יךָ ("Let another praise you, and not your own mouth."—Prov. 27:2)

וְאֻסַּף֩ חֵ֨יל כָּל־הַגּוֹיִ֜ם סָבִ֗יב ("And the wealth of all the surrounding nations will be gathered."—Zech. 14:14)

22.5 I-Guttural Verbs in Hiphil/Hophal

Because the Hiphil and Hophal stems have a prefix in both the perfect and imperfect, I-Guttural verbs exhibit the compound *shewa* that one would expect:

	Hiph. Perfect קטל	Hiph. Perfect עמד	Hoph. Perfect קטל	Hoph. Perfect עמד
3ms	הִקְטִיל	הֶעֱמִיד	הָקְטַל	הָעֳמַד
3fs	הִקְטִילָה	הֶעֱמִידָה	הָקְטְלָה	הָעָמְדָה
2ms	הִקְטַלְתָּ	הֶעֱמַדְתָּ	הָקְטַלְתָּ	הָעֳמַדְתָּ
2fs	הִקְטַלְתְּ	הֶעֱמַדְתְּ	הָקְטַלְתְּ	הָעֳמַדְתְּ
1cs	הִקְטַלְתִּי	הֶעֱמַדְתִּי	הָקְטַלְתִּי	הָעֳמַדְתִּי
3cp	הִקְטִילוּ	הֶעֱמִידוּ	הָקְטְלוּ	הָעָמְדוּ
2mp	הִקְטַלְתֶּם	הֶעֱמַדְתֶּם	הָקְטַלְתֶּם	הָעֳמַדְתֶּם
2fp	הִקְטַלְתֶּן	הֶעֱמַדְתֶּן	הָקְטַלְתֶּן	הָעֳמַדְתֶּן
1cp	הִקְטַלְנוּ	הֶעֱמַדְנוּ	הָקְטַלְנוּ	הָעֳמַדְנוּ

	Hiph. Imperf. קטל	Hiph. Imperf. עמד	Hoph. Imperf. קטל	Hoph. Imperf. עמד
3ms	יַקְטִיל	יַעֲמִיד	יָקְטַל	יָעֳמַד
3fs	תַּקְטִיל	תַּעֲמִיד	תָּקְטַל	תָּעֳמַד
2ms	תַּקְטִיל	תַּעֲמִיד	תָּקְטַל	תָּעֳמַד
2fs	תַּקְטִילִי	תַּעֲמִידִי	תָּקְטְלִי	תָּעָמְדִי
1cs	אַקְטִיל	אַעֲמִיד	אָקְטַל	אָעֳמַד
3mp	יַקְטִילוּ	יַעֲמִידוּ	יָקְטְלוּ	יָעָמְדוּ
3fp	תַּקְטֵלְנָה	תַּעֲמֵדְנָה	תָּקְטַלְנָה	תָּעֳמַדְנָה
2mp	תַּקְטִילוּ	תַּעֲמִידוּ	תָּקְטְלוּ	תָּעָמְדוּ
2fp	תַּקְטֵלְנָה	תַּעֲמֵדְנָה	תָּקְטַלְנָה	תָּעֳמַדְנָה
1cp	נַקְטִיל	נַעֲמִיד	נָקְטַל	נָעֳמַד

As seen in these paradigms, the compound *shewa* used for a I-Guttural verb in the Hiphil or Hophal is typically:[2]

	Vowel Class	Compound *Shewa*
Hiphil Perfect	*e*-class	*ḥatep̄-segol*
Hiphil Imperfect	*a*-class	*ḥatep̄-pataḥ*
Hophal Perfect and Imperfect	*o*-class	*ḥatep̄-qameṣ*

Hiphil and Hophal imperatives, infinitives, and participles all behave similarly.

וְהֶעֱמִיד֙ בְּבֵ֣ית אֵ֔ל אֶת־כֹּהֲנֵ֥י הַבָּמ֖וֹת אֲשֶׁ֥ר עָשָֽׂה ("And he stationed in Bethel the priests for the high places which he had made."—1 Kings 12:32)

וַיַּעֲמִידֵ֣ם לָעַ֣ד לְעוֹלָ֑ם חָק־נָ֝תַ֗ן וְלֹ֣א יַעֲבֽוֹר׃ ("And he placed them forever; he gave a statute and it will not pass away."—Ps. 148:6)

וְהַמֶּ֨לֶךְ הָיָ֧ה מָעֳמָ֛ד בַּמֶּרְכָּבָ֖ה ("And the king was propped up in his chariot."—1 Kings 22:35)

Identification of these forms requires remembering only the preference of guttural consonants for a compound *shewa.*

22.6 I-Guttural Verbs in Niphal

Whereas in the other stems the main characteristic driving the behavior of I-Guttural verbs is the preference for a compound *shewa*, in the Niphal the gutturals' refusal to take a *dagesh forte* comes into play. Niphal perfects of I-Guttural verbs show the compound *shewa* and otherwise behave normally, but Niphal imperfects reflect either compensatory lengthening or virtual doubling (see 4.5).

[2] These are tendencies but by no means hard-and-fast rules, e.g.: the converted perfect form וְהַעֲמַדְתָּ in Numbers 3:6.

	Niph. Perfect קטל	Niph. Perfect עמד		Niph. Imperf. קטל	Niph. Imperf. עמד
3ms	נִקְטַל	נֶעֱמַד	3ms	יִקָטֵל	יֵעָמֵד
3fs	נִקְטְלָה	נֶעֶמְדָה	3fs	תִּקָטֵל	תֵּעָמֵד
2ms	נִקְטַ֫לְתָּ	נֶעֱמַ֫דְתָּ	2ms	תִּקָטֵל	תֵּעָמֵד
2fs	נִקְטַלְתְּ	נֶעֱמַדְתְּ	2fs	תִּקָטְלִי	תֵּעָמְדִי
1cs	נִקְטַ֫לְתִּי	נֶעֱמַ֫דְתִּי	1cs	אֶקָטֵל	אֵעָמֵד
3cp	נִקְטְלוּ	נֶעֶמְדוּ	3mp	יִקָטְלוּ	יֵעָמְדוּ
			3fp	תִּקָטַ֫לְנָה	תֵּעָמַ֫דְנָה
2mp	נִקְטַלְתֶּם	נֶעֱמַדְתֶּם	2mp	תִּקָטְלוּ	תֵּעָמְדוּ
2fp	נִקְטַלְתֶּן	נֶעֱמַדְתֶּן	2fp	תִּקָטַ֫לְנָה	תֵּעָמַ֫דְנָה
1cp	נִקְטַ֫לְנוּ	נֶעֱמַ֫דְנוּ	1cp	נִקָטֵל	נֵעָמֵד

*Note: This is an illustrative paradigm, because עמד does not occur in the Niphal.

In the imperfect the *nun* (נ) of the Niphal assimilates normally, but that assimilation cannot be marked by the *dagesh forte*. Compensatory lengthening occurs if the guttural is *aleph* (א), *ayin* (ע), or *resh* (ר), and virtual doubling occurs if the guttural is *heh* (ה) or *ḥet* (ח).

The Niphal imperative, infinitive construct, and one of the forms of the infinitive absolute all show similar behavior.

וּבְצַלְעִי֮ שָׂמְח֢וּ וְֽנֶאֱסָ֥פוּ	("And when I stumbled they rejoiced and gathered."—Ps. 35:15)
וַ֠יֵּאָסְפוּ כָּל־בַּעֲלֵ֨י שְׁכֶ֜ם וְכָל־בֵּ֣ית מִלּ֔וֹא	("And all the leaders of Shechem and all Beth-millo gathered together."—Judg. 9:6)

22.7 Vocabulary

הֶאֱמִין	(Hiph.) to believe, have trust in
נֶאֱמַן	(Niph.) to be reliable, faithful, trustworthy; to be permanent
אָסַף	to gather, bring in
נֶאֱסַף	(Niph.) to assemble, gather together
בָּחַר	to choose
בָּחוּר	young man
בָּעַר	to burn, blaze; to consume, burn up
בִּעֵר	(Piel) to kindle, to light
בֵּרֵךְ	(Piel) to bless
בָּרוּךְ	(Qal Pass. Part.) blessed
בְּרָכָה	blessing
הֶחֱרִים	(Hiph.) to put under the ban, devote to destruction
הִלֵּל	(Piel) to praise; eulogize
הִתְהַלֵּל	(Hithp.) to boast
הָרַג	to kill, slay
נִחַם	(Piel) to comfort, console
נִחַם	(Niph.) to regret, be sorry, repent; to console oneself
נֶעֱזַב	(Niph.) to be abandoned
שֵׁרֵת	(Piel) to serve, minister
תְּהִלָּה	praise, song of praise (Psalms = סֵפֶר תְּהִלִּים)

22.8 Language Exercises

A. Parse and gloss the following forms. Include the identification of the object suffix where appropriate.

עָמַ֫דְנוּ

אֶאֱסֹף

הֶאֱמִ֫ינוּ

בָּרוּךְ

תַּאַסְפִּי

וַתַּעֲמֹד

תַּעַזְבֶהָ

יֵאָמֵן

אֹסְפָם

עֲמֹ֫דוּ

עָזָ֫בָה

יִתְהַלֵּל

וַיֵּאָסֵף

נֶאֱמָנוֹת

יֵעָזְבוּ

B. Translate the following and parse each verb and participle. Use your lexicon to look up the glosses for any words you do not know from your vocabulary.

Josh. 24:1–4 (*Qere*)

וַיֶּאֱסֹף יְהוֹשֻׁעַ אֶת־כָּל־שִׁבְטֵי יִשְׂרָאֵל שְׁכֶמָה וַיִּקְרָא לְזִקְנֵי יִשְׂרָאֵל

וּלְרָאשָׁיו וּלְשֹׁפְטָיו וּלְשֹׁטְרָיו וַיִּתְיַצְּבוּ לִפְנֵי הָאֱלֹהִים׃ וַיֹּאמֶר יְהוֹשֻׁעַ אֶל־

כָּל־הָעָם כֹּה־אָמַר יְהוָה אֱלֹהֵי יִשְׂרָאֵל בְּעֵבֶר הַנָּהָר יָשְׁבוּ אֲבוֹתֵיכֶם

מֵעוֹלָם תֶּרַח אֲבִי אַבְרָהָם וַאֲבִי נָחוֹר וַיַּעַבְדוּ אֱלֹהִים אֲחֵרִים׃ וָאֶקַּח

אֶת־אֲבִיכֶם אֶת־אַבְרָהָם מֵעֵבֶר הַנָּהָר וָאוֹלֵךְ[3] אוֹתוֹ בְּכָל־אֶרֶץ כְּנָעַן

וָאַרְבֶּה[4] אֶת־זַרְעוֹ וָאֶתֶּן־לוֹ אֶת־יִצְחָק׃ וָאֶתֵּן לְיִצְחָק אֶת־יַעֲקֹב וְאֶת־עֵשָׂו

וָאֶתֵּן לְעֵשָׂו אֶת־הַר שֵׂעִיר לָרֶשֶׁת[5] אוֹתוֹ וְיַעֲקֹב וּבָנָיו יָרְדוּ מִצְרָיִם׃

[3] Hiph. Narr. 1cs of הלך, glossed as “to bring/made go” (see ch. 27).

[4] Hiph. Narr. 1cs of רבה, glossed as “to multiply” (see ch. 24).

[5] Qal Inf. Const. of ירשׁ, glossed as “to possess” (see ch. 27).

Judg. 9:1–5

וַיֵּ֨לֶךְ אֲבִימֶ֤לֶךְ בֶּן־יְרֻבַּ֙עַל֙ שְׁכֶ֔מָה אֶל־אֲחֵ֖י אִמּ֑וֹ וַיְדַבֵּ֣ר אֲלֵיהֶ֗ם וְאֶל־כָּל־
מִשְׁפַּ֛חַת בֵּית־אֲבִ֥י אִמּ֖וֹ לֵאמֹֽר׃ דַּבְּרוּ־נָ֞א בְּאָזְנֵ֣י כָל־בַּעֲלֵ֣י שְׁכֶם֮ מַה־טּ֣וֹב
לָכֶם֒ הַמְשֹׁ֨ל בָּכֶ֜ם שִׁבְעִ֣ים אִ֗ישׁ כֹּ֚ל בְּנֵ֣י יְרֻבַּ֔עַל אִם־מְשֹׁ֥ל בָּכֶ֖ם אִ֣ישׁ אֶחָ֑ד
וּזְכַרְתֶּ֕ם כִּֽי־עַצְמְכֶ֥ם וּבְשַׂרְכֶ֖ם אָֽנִי׃ וַיְדַבְּר֨וּ אֲחֵי־אִמּ֜וֹ עָלָ֗יו בְּאָזְנֵי֙ כָּל־
בַּעֲלֵ֣י שְׁכֶ֔ם אֵ֖ת כָּל־הַדְּבָרִ֣ים הָאֵ֑לֶּה וַיֵּ֤ט[6] לִבָּם֙ אַחֲרֵ֣י אֲבִימֶ֔לֶךְ כִּ֥י אָמְר֖וּ
אָחִ֥ינוּ הֽוּא׃ וַיִּתְּנוּ־לוֹ֙ שִׁבְעִ֣ים כֶּ֔סֶף מִבֵּ֖ית בַּ֣עַל בְּרִ֑ית וַיִּשְׂכֹּ֨ר בָּהֶ֜ם
אֲבִימֶ֗לֶךְ אֲנָשִׁ֤ים רֵיקִים֙ וּפֹ֣חֲזִ֔ים וַיֵּלְכ֖וּ אַחֲרָֽיו׃ וַיָּבֹ֤א[7] בֵית־אָבִיו֙ עָפְרָ֔תָה

[6] Qal Narr. 3ms of נטה, glossed as "to incline" (see ch. 24).

[7] Qal Narr. 3ms of בוא, glossed as "to go" (see ch. 26).

וַֽיַּהֲרֹ֞ג אֶת־אֶחָ֧יו בְּנֵֽי־יְרֻבַּ֛עַל שִׁבְעִ֥ים אִ֖ישׁ עַל־אֶ֣בֶן אֶחָ֑ת וַיִּוָּתֵ֞ר[8] יוֹתָ֧ם בֶּן־

יְרֻבַּ֛עַל הַקָּטֹ֖ן כִּ֥י נֶחְבָּֽא׃

Judg. 9:6–9 (*Qere*)

וַיֵּֽאָסְפ֜וּ כָּל־בַּעֲלֵ֣י שְׁכֶ֗ם וְכָל־בֵּ֣ית מִלּ֔וֹא וַיֵּ֣לְכ֔וּ וַיַּמְלִ֥יכוּ אֶת־אֲבִימֶ֖לֶךְ

לְמֶ֑לֶךְ עִם־אֵל֥וֹן מֻצָּ֖ב אֲשֶׁ֥ר בִּשְׁכֶֽם׃ וַיַּגִּ֣דוּ לְיוֹתָ֗ם וַיֵּ֜לֶךְ וַיַּעֲמֹד֙ בְּרֹ֣אשׁ

הַר־גְּרִזִּ֔ים וַיִּשָּׂ֥א קוֹל֖וֹ וַיִּקְרָ֑א וַיֹּ֣אמֶר לָהֶ֗ם שִׁמְע֤וּ אֵלַי֙ בַּעֲלֵ֣י שְׁכֶ֔ם וְיִשְׁמַ֥ע

אֲלֵיכֶ֖ם אֱלֹהִֽים׃ הָל֤וֹךְ הָֽלְכוּ֙ הָעֵצִ֔ים לִמְשֹׁ֥חַ עֲלֵיהֶ֖ם מֶ֑לֶךְ וַיֹּאמְר֥וּ לַזַּ֖יִת

מָלְכָ֥ה עָלֵֽינוּ׃ וַיֹּ֨אמֶר לָהֶ֜ם הַזַּ֗יִת הֶחֳדַ֙לְתִּי֙ אֶת־דִּשְׁנִ֔י אֲשֶׁר־בִּ֛י יְכַבְּד֥וּ

אֱלֹהִ֖ים וַאֲנָשִׁ֑ים וְהָ֣לַכְתִּ֔י לָנ֖וּעַ[9] עַל־הָעֵצִֽים׃

---

[8] Niph. Narr. 3ms of יתר, glossed as "to remain, be left" (see ch. 27).

[9] Qal Inf. Const. of נוע, glossed as "to hold sway" (see ch. 25).

Judg. 9:10–15 (*Qere*)

וַיֹּאמְרוּ הָעֵצִים לַתְּאֵנָה לְכִי־אַתְּ מָלְכִי עָלֵינוּ׃ וַתֹּאמֶר לָהֶם הַתְּאֵנָה

הֶחֳדַלְתִּי אֶת־מָתְקִי וְאֶת־תְּנוּבָתִי הַטּוֹבָה וְהָלַכְתִּי לָנוּעַ עַל־הָעֵצִים׃

וַיֹּאמְרוּ הָעֵצִים לַגֶּפֶן לְכִי־אַתְּ מָלְכִי עָלֵינוּ׃ וַתֹּאמֶר לָהֶם הַגֶּפֶן הֶחֳדַלְתִּי

אֶת־תִּירוֹשִׁי הַמְשַׂמֵּחַ אֱלֹהִים וַאֲנָשִׁים וְהָלַכְתִּי לָנוּעַ עַל־הָעֵצִים׃ וַיֹּאמְרוּ

כָל־הָעֵצִים אֶל־הָאָטָד לֵךְ אַתָּה מְלָךְ־עָלֵינוּ׃ וַיֹּאמֶר הָאָטָד אֶל־הָעֵצִים

אִם בֶּאֱמֶת אַתֶּם מֹשְׁחִים אֹתִי לְמֶלֶךְ עֲלֵיכֶם בֹּאוּ[10] חֲסוּ[11] בְצִלִּי וְאִם־אַיִן

תֵּצֵא[12] אֵשׁ מִן־הָאָטָד וְתֹאכַל אֶת־אַרְזֵי הַלְּבָנוֹן׃

---

[10] Qal Imperative mp of בוא, glossed as "come" (see ch. 26).

[11] Qal Imperative mp of חסה, glossed as "take refuge" (see ch. 24).

[12] Qal Juss. 3fs of יצא, glossed as "to come out/go out" (see ch. 27).

Judg. 9:16–21 וְעַתָּ֗ה אִם־בֶּאֱמֶ֤ת וּבְתָמִים֙ עֲשִׂיתֶ֔ם[13] וַתַּמְלִ֖יכוּ אֶת־אֲבִימֶ֑לֶךְ וְאִם־טוֹבָ֤ה
עֲשִׂיתֶם֙ עִם־יְרֻבַּ֣עַל וְעִם־בֵּית֔וֹ וְאִם־כִּגְמ֥וּל יָדָ֖יו עֲשִׂ֥יתֶם לֽוֹ׃ אֲשֶׁר־נִלְחַ֥ם
אָבִ֖י עֲלֵיכֶ֑ם וַיַּשְׁלֵ֤ךְ אֶת־נַפְשׁוֹ֙ מִנֶּ֔גֶד וַיַּצֵּ֥ל אֶתְכֶ֖ם מִיַּ֥ד מִדְיָֽן׃ וְ֠אַתֶּם
קַמְתֶּ֨ם[14] עַל־בֵּ֤ית אָבִי֙ הַיּ֔וֹם וַתַּהַרְג֧וּ אֶת־בָּנָ֛יו שִׁבְעִ֥ים אִ֖ישׁ עַל־אֶ֣בֶן אֶחָ֑ת
וַתַּמְלִ֜יכוּ אֶת־אֲבִימֶ֤לֶךְ בֶּן־אֲמָתוֹ֙ עַל־בַּעֲלֵ֣י שְׁכֶ֔ם כִּ֥י אֲחִיכֶ֖ם הֽוּא׃ וְאִם־
בֶּאֱמֶ֨ת וּבְתָמִ֧ים עֲשִׂיתֶ֛ם עִם־יְרֻבַּ֥עַל וְעִם־בֵּית֖וֹ הַיּ֣וֹם הַזֶּ֑ה שִׂמְחוּ֙
בַּאֲבִימֶ֔לֶךְ וְיִשְׂמַ֥ח גַּם־ה֖וּא בָּכֶֽם׃ וְאִם־אַ֕יִן תֵּ֤צֵא[15] אֵשׁ֙ מֵאֲבִימֶ֔לֶךְ וְתֹאכַ֛ל
אֶת־בַּעֲלֵ֥י שְׁכֶ֖ם וְאֶת־בֵּ֣ית מִלּ֑וֹא וְתֵצֵ֨א אֵ֜שׁ מִבַּעֲלֵ֥י שְׁכֶ֛ם וּמִבֵּ֥ית מִלּ֖וֹא

[13] Qal Perf. 2mp of עשׂה, glossed as "to do" (see ch. 24).

[14] Qal Perf. 2mp of קום, glossed as "to arise" (see ch. 26).

[15] Qal Juss. 3fs of יצא, glossed as "to come out/go out" (see ch. 27).

וְתֹאכַל אֶת־אֲבִימֶלֶךְ׃ וַיָּנָס[16] יוֹתָם וַיִּבְרַח וַיֵּלֶךְ בְּאֵרָה וַיֵּשֶׁב[17] שָׁם מִפְּנֵי

אֲבִימֶלֶךְ אָחִיו׃

22.9 Exegetical Exercises—*Hapax Legomena* and the Use of Other Semitic Languages, Part 1

A. The Challenge of *Hapax Legomena*. A ***hapax legomenon*** (plural: *hapax legomena*) is a term written only once within a specific context.[18] In biblical studies, a *hapax legomenon* is a word written only once in the Hebrew text of the Old Testament or once in the Greek text of the New Testament. This rarity creates a challenge in identifying the lexical meaning of the word. Usually you can triangulate a word's meaning by surveying all its uses in their contexts and looking for commonality (see 5.7). For example, consider the Hebrew word שְׁפֵלָה. The word occurs twenty times in nineteen verses: Deuteronomy 1:7; Joshua 9:1; 10:40; 11:2, 16; 12:8; 15:33; Judges 1:9; 1 Kings 10:27; 1 Chronicles 27:28; 2 Chronicles 1:15; 9:27; 26:10; 28:18; Jeremiah 17:26; 32:44; 33:13; Obadiah 19; Zechariah 7:7.

Survey these verses with your Hebrew Bible and an English translation side by side. Note which translation is given for שְׁפֵלָה in each case. What is the usual gloss for שְׁפֵלָה?

How have translators arrived at this gloss? Many of the verses have a list of three areas: the hill country, the Negev, and the שְׁפֵלָה. You can immediately note that שְׁפֵלָה is parallel to the hill country and the Negev in some sense (most likely by being a geographic region), but it is also distinct from them. Of the basic regions in Israel's geography, once the hill country and Negev are removed, the best options are the Jordan

---

[16] Qal Narr. 3ms of נוס, glossed as "to flee" (see ch. 26).

[17] Qal Narr. 3ms of ישׁב, glossed as "to dwell" (see ch. 27).

[18] The term comes from the Greek ἅπαξ λεγόμενον, meaning "said once." As a shorthand, many scholars will refer to a *hapax legomenon* as a "hapax."

Valley—which the OT indicates by the proper name הַיַּרְדֵּן—and the coastal plain. Process of elimination alone favors a translation of the lowland or coastal plain.

This idea is strengthened by the reference from Obadiah 19. In what way?

This idea is further strengthened by the meaning of the verb שָׁפֵל. Look it up in your lexicon. What is its lexical range of meaning?

The multiple uses of שְׁפֵלָה in the OT make identifying its meaning relatively straightforward.

On the other hand, when dealing with a *hapax legomenon* no such process is available. When considering the word, you have no other uses to compare. This raises the challenge: how can we know that we are translating the word correctly? We can consider the context and try to choose a translation fitting the verse in which it is included, but this process is fraught with danger because we are, in essence, making the word mean what we think it must mean.

But what if it doesn't? To use an extreme example, what if the word were actually a little-known negative particle, and we should negate the clause or phrase in which it was included? Of course, the odds of this extreme example are tiny, since negative particles are so common in a language that it would be exceptional for one to be used only once in the OT and become a *hapax legomenon*. Nonetheless, the methodological point must be admitted: if we are making a contextual guess at the meaning of a *hapax legomenon*, we could be very, very wrong. What better methodology is available?

When you encounter a *hapax legomenon* in the Greek of the New Testament, you can profitably search extrabiblical Greek for other uses, often discerning its meaning. In Old Testament study there is little such recourse, because almost all the relevant Hebrew is already in the biblical text. There are inscriptions to consult, but the sum of all such inscriptions provides relatively little new data for understanding the lexical meanings of rare words. Likewise, you can consult later Hebrew dialects such as Qumran Hebrew and Rabbinic Hebrew, but in doing so there is always the danger of anachronism.

B. The Contribution of Other Semitic Languages. Students of OT lexicography are helped by Hebrew being part of a broader family of languages called the Semitic language family. This includes Aramaic, Arabic, Akkadian, Ugaritic, and others. The exact family relationships among the Semitic languages are debated, but there is no question that all belong—at least at the high level—to the same language group. The concept of three letter roots—basic to Hebrew—is also basic to most of these languages, and they have significant shared vocabulary at the level of roots. Such corresponding roots are called **cognates**.

Consider the Hebrew word מֶלֶךְ, which you know well. This root is attested in most major Semitic languages:

Amorite: *mlk* → to rule

Aramaic: *mlk* → to rule

Akkadian: *mlk* → to discuss, advise

Phoenician: *mlk* → to rule

Ugaritic: *mlk* → to rule

You can see a strong (though not perfect—note the exception of Akkadian[19]) correspondence across the Semitic languages: the root *mlk* relates to the concept of ruling. (The Semitic languages have changed over time, so a cognate may not have exactly the same letters. Hebrew *shalôm* and Arabic *salām* are cognate even though they share only two of the three root letters in their current forms.)

If you are dealing with a *hapax legomenon* in Hebrew, the other Semitic languages may provide significant assistance. You can search for the corresponding root in other languages from the language family, understand the meaning of that root in those languages, and see whether that meaning would work for the Hebrew word in question.

[19] There remains a sense of authority in being an adviser (especially in a royal context), so the notion of authority is not completely absent from the Akkadian usage.

Consider the Hebrew *hapax legomena* כַּשִּׁיל and כֵּילַפֹּת from Psalm 74:6. In each case the word does not occur elsewhere in the Hebrew text of the OT. כַּשִּׁיל, though, occurs in Aramaic (glossed as "axe") and כֵּילָף in Akkadian and Aramaic (glossed as "pickaxe"). In this case it is a strong possibility that these words are not cognates but **loanwords** (words borrowed from one language by another) from Aramaic and Akkadian, respectively. Given that the context of the verse is the destruction of the temple, these meanings fit well, and we can be relatively comfortable in each word's translation.[20]

C. Song of Songs 1:10. Read Song of Songs 1:10:

נָאו֤וּ לְחָיַ֙יִךְ֙ בַּתֹּרִ֔ים צַוָּארֵ֖ךְ בַּחֲרוּזִֽים׃

Your cheeks are lovely with strings of jewels (earrings?), your neck with ________.

חֲרוּזִים is a *hapax legomenon* in the OT, but it is attested as a root in several other Semitic languages.[21]

Arabic: *ḫaraz* → a string of shells or beads

Aramaic: חרוזא → a stringer of pearls

Punic: חרז → chain

Given these three cognates, what is the likely translation of the Hebrew *hapax legomenon* חֲרוּזִים in Song of Songs 1:10?

---

[20] For more information on *hapax legomena* in Biblical Hebrew, consult Frederick Greenspahn, *Hapax Legomena in Biblical Hebrew*, SBLDS 74 (Chico, CA: Scholars Press, 1984); Paul Mankowski, *Akkadian Loanwords in Biblical Hebrew*, HSS 47 (Winona Lake, IN: Eisenbrauns, 2000).

[21] HALOT, 351. See also Roland Murphy, *The Song of Songs: A Commentary on the Book of Canticles or the Song of Songs*, Hermeneia (Minneapolis: Fortress Press, 1990), 131.

כג (23) II-Guttural and III-ח/ע Verbs

23.1 II-Guttural Verbs in the Qal, Niphal, Hiphil, and Hophal

The characteristics of gutturals discussed in 22.2 are again relevant if the guttural letter is in the second or third position in the root. Once these tendencies are accounted for, the Qal perfect and imperfect of II-Guttural verbs provide no surprises, with the guttural requiring a compound *shewa* in place of the strong paradigm's vocal *shewa*. The previously learned forms of the strong verb are again given to promote comparison.

	Qal Perfect קטל	Qal Perfect בער		Qal Imperfect קטל	Qal Imperfect בער
3ms	קָטַל	בָּעַר	3ms	יִקְטֹל	יִבְעַר
3fs	קָֽטְלָה	בָּֽעֲרָה	3fs	תִּקְטֹל	תִּבְעַר
2ms	קָטַ֫לְתָּ	בָּעַ֫רְתָּ	2ms	תִּקְטֹל	תִּבְעַר
2fs	קָטַלְתְּ	בָּעַרְתְּ	2fs	תִּקְטְלִי	תִּבְעֲרִי
1cs	קָטַ֫לְתִּי	בָּעַ֫רְתִּי	1cs	אֶקְטֹל	אֶבְעַר
3cp	קָֽטְלוּ	בָּֽעֲרוּ	3mp	יִקְטְלוּ	יִבְעֲרוּ
			3fp	תִּקְטֹ֫לְנָה	תִּבְעַ֫רְנָה
2mp	קְטַלְתֶּם	בְּעַרְתֶּם	2mp	תִּקְטְלוּ	תִּבְעֲרוּ
2fp	קְטַלְתֶּן	בְּעַרְתֶּן	2fp	תִּקְטֹ֫לְנָה	תִּבְעַ֫רְנָה
1cp	קָטַ֫לְנוּ	בָּעַ֫רְנוּ	1cp	נִקְטֹל	נִבְעַר

As expected, a similar change happens in the Qal fs and mp imperative forms and the Qal mp and fp active participle.

כַּפִּשְׁתִּים אֲשֶׁר בָּעֲרוּ בָאֵשׁ ("Like flax which has burned with fire"—Judg. 15:14)

מַרְאֵיהֶם כְּגַחֲלֵי־אֵשׁ בֹּעֲרוֹת ("Their appearance was like burning coals of fire."—Ezek. 1:13)

The Niphal, Hiphil, and Hophal forms of II-Guttural verbs show the same replacement of the simple *shewa* with a compound *shewa* when necessary, which at this point should occasion no difficulty in your recognizing and parsing these verbal forms.

23.2 II-Guttural Verbs in the Piel, Pual, and Hithpael

In the Piel, Pual, and Hithpael stems, the main effect of the guttural comes from its refusal to double via the *dagesh forte*. As expected, these stems respond to the inability to double the guttural with either compensatory lengthening (if the guttural is א, ע, or ר) or virtual doubling (if the guttural is ה or ח). In compensatory lengthening the *ḥireq* of the Piel lengthens to *ṣere*, the *qibbuṣ* of the Pual lengthens to *ḥolem*, and the *pataḥ* of the Hithpael lengthens to *qameṣ* (see 1.3).

	Piel Perfect קטל	Piel Perfect ברך	Piel Perfect מהר	Pual Perfect ברך	Pual Perfect מהר	Hithpael Perfect ברך	Hithpael Perfect מהר
3ms	קִטֵּל	בֵּרֵךְ	מִהֵר	בֹּרַךְ	מֻהַר	הִתְבָּרֵךְ	הִתְמַהֵר
3fs	קִטְּלָה	בֵּרְכָה	מִהֲרָה	בֹּרְכָה	מֻהֲרָה	הִתְבָּֽרְכָה	הִתְמַהֲרָה
2ms	קִטַּלְתָּ	בֵּרַכְתָּ	מִהַרְתָּ	בֹּרַכְתָּ	מֻהַרְתָּ	הִתְבָּרַכְתָּ	הִתְמַהַרְתָּ
2fs	קִטַּלְתְּ	בֵּרַכְתְּ	מִהַרְתְּ	בֹּרַכְתְּ	מֻהַרְתְּ	הִתְבָּרַכְתְּ	הִתְמַהַרְתְּ
1cs	קִטַּלְתִּי	בֵּרַכְתִּי	מִהַרְתִּי	בֹּרַכְתִּי	מֻהַרְתִּי	הִתְבָּרַכְתִּי	הִתְמַהַרְתִּי
3cp	קִטְּלוּ	בֵּרְכוּ	מִהֲרוּ	בֹּרְכוּ	מֻהֲרוּ	הִתְבָּֽרְכוּ	הִתְמַהֲרוּ
2mp	קִטַּלְתֶּם	בֵּרַכְתֶּם	מִהַרְתֶּם	בֹּרַכְתֶּם	מֻהַרְתֶּם	הִתְבָּרַכְתֶּם	הִתְמַהַרְתֶּם
2fp	קִטַּלְתֶּן	בֵּרַכְתֶּן	מִהַרְתֶּן	בֹּרַכְתֶּן	מֻהַרְתֶּן	הִתְבָּרַכְתֶּן	הִתְמַהַרְתֶּן
1cp	קִטַּלְנוּ	בֵּרַכְנוּ	מִהַרְנוּ	בֹּרַכְנוּ	מֻהַרְנוּ	הִתְבָּרַכְנוּ	הִתְמַהַרְנוּ

	Piel Imperfect קטל	Piel Imperfect ברך	Piel Imperfect מהר	Pual Imperfect ברך	Pual Imperfect מהר	Hithpael Imperfect ברך	Hithpael Imperfect מהר
3ms	יְקַטֵּל	יְבָרֵךְ	יְמַהֵר	יְבֹרַךְ	יְמֻהַר	יִתְבָּרֵךְ	יִתְמַהֵר
3fs	תְּקַטֵּל	תְּבָרֵךְ	תְּמַהֵר	תְּבֹרַךְ	תְּמֻהַר	תִּתְבָּרֵךְ	תִּתְמַהֵר
2ms	תְּקַטֵּל	תְּבָרֵךְ	תְּמַהֵר	תְּבֹרַךְ	תְּמֻהַר	תִּתְבָּרֵךְ	תִּתְמַהֵר
2fs	תְּקַטְּלִי	תְּבָרֲכִי	תְּמַהֲרִי	תְּבֹרְכִי	תְּמֻהֲרִי	תִּתְבָּרֲכִי	תִּתְמַהֲרִי
1cs	אֲקַטֵּל	אֲבָרֵךְ	אֲמַהֵר	אֲבֹרַךְ	אֲמֻהַר	אֶתְבָּרֵךְ	אֶתְמַהֵר
3mp	יְקַטְּלוּ	יְבָרֲכוּ	יְמַהֲרוּ	יְבֹרְכוּ	יְמֻהֲרוּ	יִתְבָּרֲכוּ	יִתְמַהֲרוּ
3fp	תְּקַטֵּלְנָה	תְּבָרֵכְנָה	תְּמַהֵרְנָה	תְּבֹרַכְנָה	תְּמֻהַרְנָה	תִּתְבָּרֵכְנָה	תִּתְמַהֵרְנָה
2mp	תְּקַטְּלוּ	תְּבָרֲכוּ	תְּמַהֲרוּ	תְּבֹרְכוּ	תְּמֻהֲרוּ	תִּתְבָּרֲכוּ	תִּתְמַהֲרוּ
2fp	תְּקַטֵּלְנָה	תְּבָרֵכְנָה	תְּמַהֵרְנָה	תְּבֹרַכְנָה	תְּמֻהַרְנָה	תִּתְבָּרֵכְנָה	תִּתְמַהֵרְנָה
1cp	נְקַטֵּל	נְבָרֵךְ	נְמַהֵר	נְבֹרַךְ	נְמֻהַר	נִתְבָּרֵךְ	נִתְמַהֵר

וַיהוָה בֵּרַךְ אֶת־אֲדֹנִי מְאֹד ("And the LORD has greatly blessed my master."—Gen. 24:35)

אֶת־הַמַּבּוּל מַיִם עַל־הָאָרֶץ לְשַׁחֵת כָּל־בָּשָׂר אֲשֶׁר־בּוֹ רוּחַ חַיִּים ("a flood of water upon the earth to destroy all flesh which has the breath of life in it"—Gen. 6:17)

וַיֹּאמֶר יַעֲקֹב לְבָנָיו לָמָּה תִּתְרָאוּ ("And Jacob said to his sons, 'Why do you look at each other?'"—Gen. 42:1)

If you pay attention to the rules of compensatory lengthening and virtual doubling, these forms should be relatively easy to identify and parse.

23.3 III-ח/ע Verbs

A ח or ע as the third root letter occasions few changes to the strong paradigms because the letter is rarely in a position that allows changes to its vowel. The main behavior of gutturals is a preference for an *a*-class vowel. The following should be noted:

- When the ח or ע is the final letter of the word *and* is preceded by a long vowel, it will often take a furtive *pataḥ* (see 5.4), as in:

  שְׁלֹחַ Qal Inf. Const.

  שָׁלוֹחַ Qal Inf. Abs.

  שֹׁלֵחַ Qal Active Part. ms

  The furtive *pataḥ* will occur similarly in the infinitive absolute of the derived stems, the Hiphil infinitive construct, ms active participles, and the ms Qal passive participle. It will also occur in some forms of the Hiphil perfect and imperfect.

כִּשְׁמֹעַ עֵשָׂו אֶת־דִּבְרֵי אָבִיו וַיִּצְעַק צְעָקָה גְּדֹלָה וּמָרָה עַד־מְאֹד	("When Esau heard the words of his father, he cried out a great and exceptionally bitter cry."—Gen. 27:34)
אֲנִי שֹׁלֵחַ אֶת־כָּל־מַגֵּפֹתַי אֶל־לִבְּךָ וּבַעֲבָדֶיךָ וּבְעַמֶּךָ	("I am about to send all my plagues on you and on your servants and on your people."—Ex. 9:14)

- Imperfect forms often show the guttural's preference for an *a*-class vowel, as in:

  יִשְׁלַח Qal Imperf. 3ms

  יְשַׁלַּח Piel Imperf. 3ms

  This preference for an *a*-class vowel holds true in the forms of the Qal and Piel imperfect in which the theme vowel does not reduce to *shewa*.

וַיְשַׁלַּח אֶת־הָעֹרֵב	("And he sent out a raven."—Gen. 8:7)
כֹּה אָמַר אֲדֹנָי יְהוִה הַשֹּׁמֵעַ ׀ יִשְׁמָע	("Thus says the LORD, 'He who hears, let him hear.'"—Ezek. 3:27)
לֹא־אֲדֹנִי שְׁמָעֵנִי הַשָּׂדֶה נָתַתִּי לָךְ	("No, my lord, listen to me. I hereby give you the field."—Gen. 23:11)

- The 2fs forms end in the vowel sequence *pataḥ-shewa* instead of two successive *shewas*:

  שָׁלַ֫חַתְּ Qal Perf. 2fs
  נִשְׁלַ֫חַתְּ Niph. Perf. 2fs
  שִׁלַּ֫חַתְּ Piel Perf. 2fs

This change to the vocalization of the 2fs form of the perfect holds true for all stems. Note that it creates a shift in the accent to the penultimate syllable of the word.

הֲל֣וֹא שָׁמַ֔עַתְּ כִּ֥י מָלַ֖ךְ אֲדֹנִיָּ֣הוּ בֶן־חַגִּ֑ית ("Have you not heard that Adonijah the son of Haggith has crowned himself king?"—1 Kings 1:11)

- The Piel perfect 3ms form will show a *pataḥ* instead of *ṣere*:

  שִׁלַּח Piel Perf. 3ms

וְשִׁלַּ֛ח אֶת־הַצִּפֹּ֥ר הַחַיָּ֖ה עַל־פְּנֵ֥י הַשָּׂדֶֽה ("And he shall let the living bird go into the field."—Lev. 14:7)

23.4 Vocabulary

גָּלָה	to uncover, reveal; to go into exile
גִּלָּה	(Piel) to uncover, disclose, reveal, expose
הֶגְלָה	(Hiph.) to deport, take into exile
נִגְלָה	(Niph.) to expose oneself, reveal oneself; be exposed
יָטַב	to go well; be pleasing
הֵיטִיב	(Hiph.) to do well with (someone); treat well
הוֹדוּ	(Hiph.) to praise God, give thanks, confess one's sin
חָנָה	to encamp
חֹק	prescription, rule, law, regulation
חֻקָּה	statute
נָטָה	to reach out, hold out, stretch out; to bow down
רָבָה	to be(come) numerous
הִרְבָּה	(Hiph.) to make numerous
רָעָה	to feed, graze, pasture
הִשְׁבִּיעַ	(Hiph.) to make someone swear
נִשְׁבַּע	(Niph.) to swear
שִׁחֵת	(Piel) to ruin, destroy
הִשְׁחִית	(Hiph.) to ruin, destroy, annihilate, wipe out

23.5 Language Exercises

A. Parse and translate the following forms. Include the identification of the object suffix where appropriate.

יִבְחֲרוּ

בָּרוּךְ

נִחָ֫מְתִּי

מְנַחֵם

הֶחֱזִ֫יקָה

בַּחֲרוּ

בֵּרְכוּ

וַיְּבְרַךְ

בָּחוּר

נִבְחַר

נִבְחָר

אֶנָּחֵם

מְבָֽרְכֶ֫יךְ

הִתְחַזֵּק

בְּחוּרֵי

B. Translate the following and parse each verb and participle. Use your lexicon to look up the glosses for any words you do not know from your vocabulary.

Gen. 27:41–43

וַיִּשְׂטֹם עֵשָׂו אֶת־יַעֲקֹב עַל־הַבְּרָכָה אֲשֶׁר בֵּרֲכוֹ אָבִיו וַיֹּאמֶר עֵשָׂו בְּלִבּוֹ

יִקְרְבוּ יְמֵי אֵבֶל אָבִי וְאַהַרְגָה אֶת־יַעֲקֹב אָחִי׃ וַיֻּגַּד לְרִבְקָה אֶת־דִּבְרֵי

עֵשָׂו בְּנָהּ הַגָּדֹל וַתִּשְׁלַח וַתִּקְרָא לְיַעֲקֹב בְּנָהּ הַקָּטָן וַתֹּאמֶר אֵלָיו הִנֵּה

עֵשָׂו אָחִיךָ מִתְנַחֵם לְךָ לְהָרְגֶךָ׃ וְעַתָּה בְנִי שְׁמַע בְּקֹלִי וְקוּם[1] בְּרַח־לְךָ

אֶל־לָבָן אָחִי חָרָנָה׃

Num. 22:37–40

וַיֹּאמֶר בָּלָק אֶל־בִּלְעָם הֲלֹא שָׁלֹחַ שָׁלַחְתִּי אֵלֶיךָ לִקְרֹא־לָךְ לָמָּה לֹא־

הָלַכְתָּ אֵלָי הַאֻמְנָם לֹא אוּכַל[2] כַּבְּדֶךָ׃ וַיֹּאמֶר בִּלְעָם אֶל־בָּלָק הִנֵּה־

[1] Qal Imperative ms of קום, glossed as "arise" (see ch. 26).

[2] Qal Imperf. 1cs of יכל, glossed as "to be able" (see ch. 27).

בָ֫אתִי[3] אֵלֶ֔יךָ עַתָּ֕ה הֲיָכֹ֥ול[4] אוּכַ֖ל דַּבֵּ֣ר מְא֑וּמָה הַדָּבָ֗ר אֲשֶׁ֨ר יָשִׂ֧ים[5]

אֱלֹהִ֛ים בְּפִ֖י אֹת֥וֹ אֲדַבֵּֽר׃ וַיֵּ֥לֶךְ בִּלְעָ֖ם עִם־בָּלָ֑ק וַיָּבֹ֖אוּ[6] קִרְיַ֥ת חֻצֽוֹת׃

וַיִּזְבַּ֥ח בָּלָ֖ק בָּקָ֣ר וָצֹ֑אן וַיְשַׁלַּ֣ח לְבִלְעָ֔ם וְלַשָּׂרִ֖ים אֲשֶׁ֥ר אִתּֽוֹ׃

Gen. 48:18–20

וַיֹּ֧אמֶר יוֹסֵ֛ף אֶל־אָבִ֖יו לֹא־כֵ֣ן אָבִ֑י כִּי־זֶ֣ה הַבְּכֹ֔ר שִׂ֥ים[7] יְמִינְךָ֖ עַל־רֹאשֽׁוֹ׃

וַיְמָאֵ֣ן אָבִ֗יו וַיֹּ֨אמֶר֙ יָדַ֤עְתִּֽי בְנִי֙ יָדַ֔עְתִּי גַּם־ה֥וּא יִהְיֶה[8]־לְּעָ֖ם וְגַם־ה֣וּא יִגְדָּ֑ל

וְאוּלָ֗ם אָחִ֤יו הַקָּטֹן֙ יִגְדַּ֣ל מִמֶּ֔נּוּ וְזַרְע֖וֹ יִהְיֶ֥ה מְלֹֽא־הַגּוֹיִֽם׃ וַיְבָרְכֵ֞ם בַּיּ֣וֹם

---

[3] Qal Perf. 1cs of בוא, glossed as "to come, enter" (see ch. 26).

[4] Qal Inf. Abs. of יכל, glossed as "to be able" (see ch. 27).

[5] Qal Imperf. 3ms of שׂים, glossed as "to set, place" (see ch. 26).

[6] Qal Narr. 3mp of בוא, glossed as "to come, enter" (see ch. 26).

[7] Qal Imperative ms of שׂים, glossed as "to set, place" (see ch. 26).

[8] Qal Imperf. 3ms of היה, glossed as "to be" (see ch. 24).

הַהוּא֮ לֵאמוֹר֒ בְּךָ֞ יְבָרֵ֤ךְ יִשְׂרָאֵל֙ לֵאמֹ֔ר יְשִֽׂמְךָ֣[9] אֱלֹהִ֔ים כְּאֶפְרַ֖יִם וְכִמְנַשֶּׁ֑ה

וַיָּ֥שֶׂם[10] אֶת־אֶפְרַ֖יִם לִפְנֵ֥י מְנַשֶּֽׁה׃

Deut. 16:13–15

חַ֧ג הַסֻּכֹּ֛ת תַּעֲשֶׂ֥ה[11] לְךָ֖ שִׁבְעַ֣ת יָמִ֑ים בְּאָ֨סְפְּךָ֔ מִֽגָּרְנְךָ֖ וּמִיִּקְבֶֽךָ׃ וְשָׂמַחְתָּ֖

בְּחַגֶּ֑ךָ אַתָּ֨ה וּבִנְךָ֤ וּבִתֶּ֙ךָ֙ וְעַבְדְּךָ֣ וַאֲמָתֶ֔ךָ וְהַלֵּוִ֗י וְהַגֵּ֛ר וְהַיָּת֥וֹם וְהָאַלְמָנָ֖ה

אֲשֶׁ֥ר בִּשְׁעָרֶֽיךָ׃ שִׁבְעַ֣ת יָמִ֗ים תָּחֹג֙[12] לַיהוָ֣ה אֱלֹהֶ֔יךָ בַּמָּק֖וֹם אֲשֶׁר־יִבְחַ֣ר

יְהוָ֑ה כִּ֣י יְבָרֶכְךָ֞ יְהוָ֣ה אֱלֹהֶ֗יךָ בְּכֹ֤ל תְּבוּאָֽתְךָ֙ וּבְכֹל֙ מַעֲשֵׂ֣ה יָדֶ֔יךָ וְהָיִ֖יתָ[13]

אַ֥ךְ שָׂמֵֽחַ׃

---

[9] Qal Juss. 3ms of שׂים, glossed as “to set, place” + 2ms suffix (see ch. 26).

[10] Qal Narr. 3ms of שׂים, glossed as “to set, place” (see ch. 26).

[11] Qal Imperf. 2ms of עשׂה, glossed as “to do” (see ch. 24).

[12] Qal Imperf. 2ms of חגג, glossed as “to keep a festival” (see ch. 28).

[13] Qal Conv. Perf. 2ms of היה, glossed as “to be” (see ch. 24).

23.6 Exegetical Exercises—*Hapax Legomena* and the Use of Other Semitic Languages, Part 2

A. Reading a Lexical Entry. When approaching the interpretation of a *hapax legomenon*, beginning students or pastors preparing to preach are rarely able to do primary research on cognate Semitic terms. Both training and time prevent it! But when reading robust commentaries or articles, you often find claimed parallels to words in other Semitic languages (with interpretations built on those claims), whether those words are *hapax legomena* or more commonly attested words. If the suggestion seems spurious or forced, or if it does not accord with standard Bible translations, it ought to be carefully assessed before being accepted.

How would a student or pastor accurately assess a commentator's claims? After all, comparative Semitic language study is quite technical and often intimidating. Nonetheless, claims require critical evaluation, since not all will hold up to scrutiny. In this regard the full entry (not just the gloss) in a lexicon can be helpful.

As an example, consider the HALOT entry for שְׁפִיפֹן:

> שְׁפִיפֹן: hapax legomenon Gn 49[17] . . . in Akk. *šibbu* is used to designate a mythological serpent (Landsberger *Fauna* 58f; AHw. 1226b; CAD Š/2, 375a: *šibbu* A); . . . Landsberger . . . looks for etymological support for Heb. שְׁפִיפוֹן by making a connection with the frequently supposed Arb. words . . . *saff, siff, suff*, a particularly dangerous type of snake with distinguishing white markings and black spots . . . : **horned viper**, ...†[14]

Note the beginning information in this lexical entry (the portion before the gloss is given in bold type). The first indication is that this word is a *hapax legomenon*. Much of what follows is a catalogue of scholarly citations, but scan either for abbreviations that may indicate other languages or for transliterations of words (usually given in italics) from other languages. What related words, according the lexical entry above, may help in understanding the meaning of שְׁפִיפֹן?

[14] HALOT, 1628b–29a.

Consider the comment of Gordon Wenham in his commentary on Genesis:

> The idea that Dan is small but potent is certainly conveyed by the image of him as a deadly snake. "A horned viper." The traditional identification is *Pseudocerestes fieldi*, a poisonous yellow snake (up to three feet long) with protuberances above its eyes that look like horns. It hides in crevices or burrows in the sand and bites animals that come within range (*EM* 8:249-50). "H.B. Tristram (*The Natural History of the Bible* [1868], 274) states that once whilst he was riding in the Sahara his horse suddenly started and reared, in the utmost terror; he could not discover the cause, until he noticed a Cerastes coiled up two or three paces in front, with its eyes intently fixed upon the horse, and ready to spring as the animal passed by" (Driver, 389).
>
> But what is the point of comparing Dan to a horned viper? In that the other tribal sayings nearly all appear to relate to the experiences of the tribes between the settlement and the rise of the monarchy, it is natural to look for the fulfillment of Jacob's prediction within the Book of Judges. . . . Through his own strength and various tricks, Samson defeated the Philistines on various occasions (Judg 13–16). Later the small tribe of Dan migrated northwards and sacked the unsuspecting town of Laish (Judg 17–18). Yet despite the prominence of the Danites in the Book of Judges, modern commentators are strangely reluctant to link these sayings about Dan here with the exploits of Samson or his tribe. Only Delitzsch, Dillmann, Driver, and König do so cautiously. Though it is unfashionable, I agree with this linkage.[15]

Evaluate this comment. Is Wenham's claimed translation of the word שְׁפִיפֹן as "a horned viper" defensible? How does this cause you to evaluate his claim of the fulfillment of this blessing/prophecy in the book of Judges?

[15] Gordon Wenham, *Genesis 16–50*, WBC (Waco, TX: Word Books, 1987), 481.

B. Psalm 15:3. Unfortunately, not every proposed parallel (whether to a *hapax legomenon* or a more common Hebrew word) in another Semitic language holds upon further examination. As illustrated above, the analysis of Semitic cognates has exceptional value and has provided insight after insight aiding the translation, understanding, and even exegesis of OT texts. But for all their value, we must recognize that proposed parallels require significant scholarly scrutiny. A proposed parallel may be debated and eventually rejected—especially if it is newly inventive. Let the reader of commentaries beware.

For example, the proposed rereading of the Hebrew text based on Semitic parallels was particularly in fashion in the 1960s—especially the work of Mitchell Dahood. The challenge with Dahood's scholarship was *not* that he was always wrong; he produced many remarkable insights. But an overzealousness on his part for finding parallels—especially between Hebrew and Ugaritic—could result in placing an excessive value on novelty. Consider Psalm 15:3 [Engl. 15:2]:

לֹא־רָגַ֬ל ׀ עַל־לְשֹׁנ֗וֹ לֹא־עָשָׂ֣ה לְרֵעֵ֣הוּ רָעָ֑ה וְ֝חֶרְפָּ֗ה לֹא־נָשָׂ֥א עַל־קְרֹבֽוֹ׃

Translate the verse, referencing your lexicon as necessary:

Dahood[16] translates 15:3 as follows: "He who does not trip over his tongue, who does no wrong to his fellowman, and casts no slur on his neighbor." What major difference do you note between your translation and Dahood's?

Dahood justifies his translation as follows:

3. *trip over his tongue.* This problematic version of *rāgal 'al l^{e}šōnō* considers the following elements. There is a pronounced penchant in Ugaritic and Hebrew to form

[16] Mitchell Dahood, *Psalms 1*, A B (Garden City, NY: Doubleday, 1966), 83.

denominative verbs from the names of parts of the body; in Ugaritic, at least nine examples have been recognized. See Dahood, *Biblica* 43 (1962), 364, to which *tqtnṣn*, "to crouch," from *qnṣ*, "shin," should be added; and *Biblica* 44 (1963), 204 f.[17]

Dahood argues that "trip" is the correct translation for a verb made from the noun רֶגֶל. To evaluate this claim, look at the lexical entry in HALOT for רָגַל:

רגל: denominative from רֶגֶל; MHeb. pt. passive רָגוּל hobbled (by tying together the lower leg and the thigh), hif. to accustom, see further Dalman *Wb.* 398a; DSS (Kuhn *Konkordanz* 199) pt. pu. fem. מרוגלת (1QM 5:13): on the meaning "in a belt" (with reference to a scabbard) see Maier *Texte* 1:130; 2:121, so also Lohse *Texte* 193; JArm. af.: 1. to accustom, lead astray; 2. to bend down: SamP. qal Nu 21^{32} *lirgål* to give information; MHeb. רָגִיל = JArm. רְגִילָא usual, practised; Sam. pa. pt. מרגל sprightly, fast (esp. of a messenger, Ben-H. *Lit.* Or. 3/2:88).

A. qal: pf. רָגַל to **slander**: with עַל־לְשֹׁנוֹ with his tongue Ps 15^{3}, cf. Sir 4^{28} רגל אל־לְשׁוֹן and 5^{14} בלשון; on 4^{28} see Smend p. 4 note, and see further Gunkel *Psalmen* 49 :: Dahood *Psalms* 1:83, 84.

B. Some etymological connection between the meaning to slander (qal und piel) and to spy out must exist (see Jenni *Piʿel* 220) but it cannot be determined with certainty; suggestions include: —a. to walk around as a slanderer (2S 19^{28}), a spy, a scout, so e.g. Gunkel loc. cit.; Kraus BK 15^{5}:252; Gesenius-B.; —b. taking the basic meaning of רגל as "to tumble" (→ עֵין רֹגֵל place name) > to pierce, to slander, so KBL.

pi. (Jenni *Piʿel* 220, 273): impf. וַיְרַגֵּל, וַיְרַגְּלוּ; impv. רַגְּלוּ; inf. cs. רַגֵּל, sf. רַגְּלָהּ; pt. pl. מְרַגְּלִים.

—1. to **move away from** a city, a country > to **spy out** Nu 21^{32} Dt 1^{24} Jos 6^{25} 7^{2} 14^{7} Ju 18$^{2.14.17}$ 2S 10^{3} 1C 19^{3}; pt. (as sbst.) **scout**, KBL spy Gn 42$^{9-34}$ (7 times), Jos 2^{1} 6^{22f} 1S 26^{4} 2S 15^{10} Sir 11^{30} (Smend *Sir.* = Vattioni *Ecclesiastico* 11^{28}).

—2. with בְּ and אֶל: to slander someone 2S 19^{28}; Sir 8^{4} text uncertain, תרגיל עם to joke with, have friendly relations with (Smend *Sir.*); cf. JArm. af. †[18]

[17] Ibid., 84.

[18] HALOT, 1183b–84a.

Note that Dahood is apparently correct to see a connection between the noun רֶגֶל and this verb, which is unsurprising given the root letters.

1. Scan the first portion of the entry—the portion before the gloss begins in section A. This word also occurs in Jewish Aramaic (JArm). What meaning does it have in Jewish Aramaic?

2. Scan the (A) portion of the entry where the word occurs in the Qal. This is not a true *hapax legomenon* because the root also occurs in the Piel, though there is only one biblical occurrence in the Qal. What meaning is suggested by the lexicon, in contrast to Dahood?

3. Scan the (B) portion of the entry. What connection does the lexicon suggest between רֶגֶל and רָגַל?

4. Given these observations, would you accept and teach Dahood's suggestion? Why or why not?

C. Rules of Thumb. It is rarely as simple as we wish to assess the evidence from other Semitic languages, and it is an art as much as a science. Several rules of thumb can be kept in mind:

- Is there cognate evidence from multiple Semitic languages or just one? If there is cognate evidence from a plethora of related languages, the odds of being able to use Semitic cognates to accurately define the Hebrew word improve.
- Are the other Semitic witnesses to the word or root unified or diverse? If the various languages contain proposed cognates that are unified in their meaning, the likelihood that the Hebrew term has the same meaning is bolstered. If so, this would be a case in which the word in question is likely common to all Semitic languages. On the other hand, if the various Semitic languages have cognates with a range of unrelated meanings, then unless some other argument is made you should be cautious about ascribing any of those meanings to Hebrew.
- Does the proposal fit with the context in Biblical Hebrew? While we must be careful to avoid "trying to make a word mean what we think it means" (see above), we must also avoid nonsensical readings. Not every possible cognate is an actual cognate—just ask the college student who walked into a drugstore in Spain to buy soap and asked for *sopa*. (The latter is soup, and yes, that college student was me!)
- Finally, does the proposed reading overturn tradition? The great Reformation doctrine *semper reformanda* reminds us that tradition is not valuable in and of itself, but only so far as it accurately reflects the Scriptures as correctly interpreted. Sometimes a traditional reading could be wrong, and there is room for advance in the study of Hebrew. Nonetheless, if a reading has been agreed on and unquestioned by both Jews and Christians for centuries, it ought not to be discarded too quickly for the newest fashion. The burden of proof should be on the author suggesting the change from the traditional reading. Sometimes that burden of proof is met, but other times it is not.

When reading commentaries and articles, the minister or student must assess their claims. Many are excellent and will spur insights into the passage in question, but others ought to be discarded. When reading secondary literature, *caveat emptor* ("let the buyer beware")—read critically.

כד (24) III-ה Verbs

24.1 The Consonant ה

The consonant ה is so weak that it often disappears in pronunciation, particularly when it ends a word or immediately precedes a suffix. In fact, the ה of III-ה verbs disappears in every inflected form.

This tendency of many III-ה forms is explained by the fact that, at an earlier historical stage of the language, III-ה verbs were actually III-י. This *yod* will appear in many paradigm forms where the *heh* of the root might be expected.

root: בנה < root: בני *

root: גלה < root: גלי * [1]

24.2 III-ה Perfects

The perfect forms of III-ה verbs use the same suffix endings as all other perfect forms, endings that you know from learning the Qal perfect paradigm (see 3.2). The loss of the ה from the root, however, creates certain changes in the vocalization of the form.

	Qal Perfect קטל	Qal Perfect בנה
3ms	קָטַל	בָּנָה
3fs	קָֽטְלָה	בָּֽנְתָה
2ms	קָטַ֫לְתָּ	בָּנִ֫יתָ
2fs	קָטַלְתְּ	בָּנִית
1cs	קָטַ֫לְתִּי	בָּנִ֫יתִי
3cp	קָֽטְלוּ	בָּנוּ
2mp	קְטַלְתֶּם	בְּנִיתֶם
2fp	קְטַלְתֶּן	בְּנִיתֶן
1cp	קָטַ֫לְנוּ	בָּנִ֫ינוּ

[1] The cognate (see 22.9) for Hebrew גלה in Aramaic is גלי.

This paradigm shows considerable change from the Qal perfect paradigm of the strong verb. **It must be memorized.**

Notes:

- The 3ms and 3fs forms show the consonant ה, but it is a *mater* that marks the long vowel *qameṣ*, not the third root letter, which has disappeared. In the 3fs form, the ה of the root changes to ת before the addition of the *qameṣ heh mater*.
- The ה of the 3cp form also disappears completely, with the verbal form showing only the first two root letters and the suffix.
- In all other forms the theme vowel becomes a *ḥireq yod*, and the ה is lost.
- The *ḥireq yod* in the second person and 1cs forms causes the spirantization of the ת because it is a *begadkephat* letter (see 1.2).

אֲשֶׁר־בָּנָה שְׁלֹמֹה אֶת־שְׁנֵי הַבָּתִּים	("When Solomon had built the two houses"—1 Kings 9:10)
וּבְנֵי רְאוּבֵן בָּנוּ אֶת־חֶשְׁבּוֹן וְאֶת־אֶלְעָלֵא וְאֵת קִרְיָתָיִם׃	("And the tribe of Reuben built Heshbon, Elealeh, and Kiriathaim."—Num. 32:37)
וּבָנִיתִי לוֹ בַּיִת נֶאֱמָן	("And I will build a solid house for him."—1 Sam. 2:34)

The derived stems show the same changes as the Qal, so the student who has memorized the Qal perfect III-ה paradigm and who pays attention to the tip-offs for the derived stems should be able to determine the parsing of each form. Forms of the derived stems are given with the verb גלה, since בנה occurs only in the Qal and Niphal:

	Qal Perfect בנה	Niphal Perfect בנה	Piel Perfect גלה	Pual Perfect גלה	Hithpael Perfect גלה	Hiphil Perfect גלה	Hophal Perfect גלה
3ms	בָּנָה	נִבְנָה	גִּלָּה	גֻּלָּה	הִתְגַּלָּה	הִגְלָה	הָגְלָה
3fs	בָּֽנְתָה	נִבְנְתָה	גִּלְּתָה	גֻּלְּתָה	הִתְגַּלְּתָה	הִגְלְתָה	הָגְלְתָה
2ms	בָּנִ֫יתָ	נִבְנֵ֫יתָ	גִּלִּ֫יתָ	גֻּלֵּ֫יתָ	הִתְגַּלִּ֫יתָ	הִגְלִ֫יתָ	הָגְלֵ֫יתָ
2fs	בָּנִית	נִבְנֵית	גִּלִּית	גֻּלֵּית	הִתְגַּלִּית	הִגְלִית	הָגְלֵית
1cs	בָּנִ֫יתִי	נִבְנֵ֫יתִי	גִּלִּ֫יתִי	גֻּלֵּ֫יתִי	הִתְגַּלִּ֫יתִי	הִגְלִ֫יתִי	הָגְלֵ֫יתִי
3cp	בָּנוּ	נִבְנוּ	גִּלּוּ	גֻּלּוּ	הִתְגַּלּוּ	הִגְלוּ	הָגְלוּ
2mp	בְּנִיתֶם	נִבְנֵיתֶם	גִּלִּיתֶם	גֻּלֵּיתֶם	הִתְגַּלִּיתֶם	הִגְלִיתֶם	הָגְלֵיתֶם
2fp	בְּנִיתֶן	נִבְנֵיתֶן	גִּלִּיתֶן	גֻּלֵּיתֶן	הִתְגַּלִּיתֶן	הִגְלִיתֶן	הָגְלֵיתֶן
1cp	בָּנִ֫ינוּ	נִבְנֵ֫ינוּ	גִּלִּ֫ינוּ	גֻּלֵּ֫ינוּ	הִתְגַּלִּ֫ינוּ	הִגְלִ֫ינוּ	הָגְלֵ֫ינוּ

Notes:

- The derived stems show a pattern similar to the Qal perfect, with the 3ms and 3fs forms containing a *qameṣ heh mater* and the other forms containing a *mater* with *yod*.
- Passive stems (Niphal, Pual, and Hophal) tend to have a *ṣere yod mater*, while active stems (Qal, Piel, and Hiphil) tend to have a *ḥireq yod mater*. The Hithpael also takes the *ḥireq yod mater*.

לְעֵינֵ֥י הַ֝גּוֹיִ֗ם גִּלָּ֥ה צִדְקָתֽוֹ ("He has revealed his righteousness in the sight of the nations."—Ps. 98:2)

וְהִגְלָ֣ה אֶֽת־כָּל־יְ֠רוּשָׁלַ͏ִם ("And he carried away all Jerusalem."—2 Kings 24:14)

וְנַעֲלָ֤ה הֶֽעָנָן֙ בַּבֹּ֔קֶר וְנָסָ֑עוּ ("And when the cloud lifted itself in the morning, they set out."—Num. 9:21)

Doubly weak verbs are also possible, especially I-Guttural and III-ה. Such forms show the weaknesses of each consonant—those detailed in chapter 22 and those detailed here.

	Qal Perfect קטל	Qal Perfect היה
3ms	קָטַל	הָיָה
3fs	קָטְלָה	הָיְתָה
2ms	קָטַלְתָּ	הָיִיתָ
2fs	קָטַלְתְּ	הָיִית
1cs	קָטַלְתִּי	הָיִיתִי
3cp	קָטְלוּ	הָיוּ
2mp	קְטַלְתֶּם	הֱיִיתֶם
2fp	קְטַלְתֶּן	הֱיִיתֶן
1cp	קָטַלְנוּ	הָיִינוּ

וְדָבַק בְּאִשְׁתּוֹ וְהָיוּ לְבָשָׂר אֶחָד	("And he will cleave to his wife and they shall be one flesh."—Gen. 2:24)
בְּרִיתִי אִתָּךְ וְהָיִיתָ לְאַב הֲמוֹן גּוֹיִם	("My covenant is with you, and you will be the father of many nations."—Gen. 17:4)
וְהָיְתָה צְעָקָה גְדֹלָה בְּכָל־אֶרֶץ מִצְרָיִם	("And there will be a great cry in all the land of Egypt."—Ex. 11:6)

24.3 III-ה Imperfects

The imperfect forms of III-ה verbs use the same prefix and suffix endings as all other imperfect forms, endings learned with the Qal imperfect paradigm (see 5.1). The loss of the ה from the root, however, creates changes in the vocalization of the form.

	Qal Imperfect קטל	Qal Imperfect בנה
3ms	יִקְטֹל	יִבְנֶה
3fs	תִּקְטֹל	תִּבְנֶה
2ms	תִּקְטֹל	תִּבְנֶה
2fs	תִּקְטְלִי	תִּבְנִי
1cs	אֶקְטֹל	אֶבְנֶה
3mp	יִקְטְלוּ	יִבְנוּ
3fp	תִּקְטֹלְנָה	תִּבְנֶינָה
2mp	תִּקְטְלוּ	תִּבְנוּ
2fp	תִּקְטֹלְנָה	תִּבְנֶינָה
1cp	נִקְטֹל	נִבְנֶה

This paradigm must be memorized.

Notes:

- The ה in the forms without a suffix is again a *mater*, not the ה from the root.
- The 3fp and 2fp forms take a *segol yod mater*.

כֹּ֚ה אָמַ֣ר יְהוָ֔ה לֹ֥א אַתָּ֛ה תִּבְנֶה־לִּ֥י הַבַּ֖יִת לָשָֽׁבֶת ("Thus says the LORD, 'You will not build the house for me to dwell.'"—1 Chron. 17:4)

ה֥וּא יִבְנֶה־בַּ֖יִת לִשְׁמִ֑י ("He will build a house for my name."—2 Sam. 7:13)

לֹ֣א יִהְיֶ֥ה־לְךָ֛ אֱלֹהִ֥ים אֲחֵרִ֖ים עַל־פָּנָֽיַ׃ ("You shall have no other gods before me."—Deut. 5:7)

The derived stems again show the same changes as the Qal, so if you memorize the Qal imperfect III-ה paradigm and pay attention to the tip-offs for the derived stems, you should be able to determine the parsing of each form. Forms of the derived stems are given once more with the verb גלה, since בנה occurs only in the Qal and Niphal.

	Qal Imperfect בנה	Niphal Imperfect בנה	Piel Imperfect גלה	Pual Imperfect גלה	Hithpael Imperfect גלה	Hiphil Imperfect גלה	Hophal Imperfect גלה
3ms	יִבְנֶה	יִבָּנֶה	יְגַלֶּה	יְגֻלֶּה	יִתְגַּלֶּה	יַגְלֶה	יָגְלֶה
3fs	תִּבְנֶה	תִּבָּנֶה	תְּגַלֶּה	תְּגֻלֶּה	תִּתְגַּלֶּה	תַּגְלֶה	תָּגְלֶה
2ms	תִּבְנֶה	תִּבָּנֶה	תְּגַלֶּה	תְּגֻלֶּה	תִּתְגַּלֶּה	תַּגְלֶה	תָּגְלֶה
2fs	תִּבְנִי	תִּבָּנִי	תְּגַלִּי	תְּגֻלִּי	תִּתְגַּלִּי	תַּגְלִי	תָּגְלִי
1cs	אֶבְנֶה	אֶבָּנֶה	אֲגַלֶּה	אֲגֻלֶּה	אֶתְגַּלֶּה	אַגְלֶה	אָגְלֶה
3mp	יִבְנוּ	יִבָּנוּ	יְגַלּוּ	יְגֻלּוּ	יִתְגַּלּוּ	יַגְלוּ	יָגְלוּ
3fp	תִּבְנֶינָה	תִּבָּנֶינָה	תְּגַלֶּינָה	תְּגֻלֶּינָה	תִּתְגַּלֶּינָה	תַּגְלֶינָה	תָּגְלֶינָה
2mp	תִּבְנוּ	תִּבָּנוּ	תְּגַלּוּ	תְּגֻלּוּ	תִּתְגַּלּוּ	תַּגְלוּ	תָּגְלוּ
2fp	תִּבְנֶינָה	תִּבָּנֶינָה	תְּגַלֶּינָה	תְּגֻלֶּינָה	תִּתְגַּלֶּינָה	תַּגְלֶינָה	תָּגְלֶינָה
1cp	נִבְנֶה	נִבָּנֶה	נְגַלֶּה	נְגֻלֶּה	נִתְגַּלֶּה	נַגְלֶה	נָגְלֶה

בְּיוֹם גְּאוֹנָיִךְ׃ בְּטֶרֶם תִּגָּלֶה רָעָתֵךְ ("in the day of your pride, before your wickedness was uncovered"—Ezek. 16:57)

שָׁם תַּעֲלֶה עֹלֹתֶיךָ וְשָׁם תַּעֲשֶׂה כֹּל אֲשֶׁר אָנֹכִי מְצַוֶּךָּ ("There you shall offer up your burnt offerings and there you shall do all which I am commanding you."—Deut. 12:14)

וִיהוּדָה הָגְלוּ לְבָבֶל בְּמַעֲלָם ("And Judah was exiled to Babylon because of their disloyalty."—1 Chron. 9:1)

24.4 Other III-ה Forms

A. Imperatives. The imperative of III-ה verbs is formed normally by removing the prefix from the imperfect. In the ms form, however, the vowel changes to a *ṣere heh mater*:

תִּבְנֶה (Qal Imperf. 2ms of בנה) → בְּנֵה (Qal Imperative ms of בנה)

The *heh* once again is a *mater*, not the *heh* from the verbal root. The other imperative forms show no change in vowel pattern from the corresponding imperfects.

וַיֹּאמֶר פַּרְעֹה עֲלֵה וּקְבֹר אֶת־אָבִיךָ כַּאֲשֶׁר הִשְׁבִּיעֶךָ׃	("And Pharaoh said, 'Go up and bury your father just as you have sworn.'"—Gen. 50:6)
בְּנוּ־לָכֶם עָרִים לְטַפְּכֶם	("Build for yourselves cities for your little children."—Num. 32:24)

B. Jussives and Narratives. Both **jussive** and **narrative** forms of III-ה verbs use a short form that does not include the final ֶה ending.

יִבְנֶה (Qal Imperf. 3ms of בנה) → יִ֫בֶן (Qal Juss. 3ms of בנה)

→ וַיִּ֫בֶן (Qal Narr. 3ms of בנה)

יְהִי אֱלֹהָיו עִמּוֹ וְיַעַל לִירוּשָׁלַםִ אֲשֶׁר בִּיהוּדָה וְיִבֶן אֶת־בֵּית יְהוָה אֱלֹהֵי יִשְׂרָאֵל	("May his God be with him, and let him go up to Jerusalem which is in Judah, and let him build the house of the LORD, the God of Israel."—Ezra 1:3)
וַיִּבֶן נֹחַ מִזְבֵּחַ לַיהוָה	("And Noah built an altar to the LORD."—Gen. 8:20)

The *heh* mater is lost, and the accent shifts to the pretonic position in the jussive forms. When the verb in question is also I-Guttural, the reduced vowel under the guttural consonant returns to a full vowel because it is now in a closed syllable:

יַעֲלֶה (Qal Imperf. 3ms of עלה) → יַ֫עַל (Qal Juss. 3ms of עלה)

→ וַיַּ֫עַל (Qal Narr. 3ms of עלה)

מִֽי־בָכֶ֣ם מִכָּל־עַמּ֗וֹ יְהוָ֣ה אֱלֹהָ֣יו עִמּ֔וֹ וְיַ֕עַל ("Whoever is among you from all his people, the LORD be with him, and let him go up."—Ezra 1:3)

וַיִּפְקֹ֖ד אֶת־הָעָ֑ם וַיַּ֨עַל ה֜וּא ("And he mustered the people and he went up."—Josh. 8:10)

This "short form" can be distinguished only in the 3ms and 3fs, since the וּ ending of the 3mp and the ֶינָה ending of the 3fp are not dropped.

יִכְלוּ֙ שֹׂטְנֵ֪י נַ֫פְשִׁ֥י ("May the ones who accuse me come to an end."—Ps. 71:13)

וַיִּבְנוּ־בַ֖יִת לְדָוִֽד ("And they built David a house."—2 Sam. 5:11)

C. Infinitive Construct. The **infinitive construct** of III-ה verbs ends in וֹת:

בְּנוֹת (Qal Inf. Const. of בנה)

גְּלוֹת (Qal Inf. Const. of גלה)

וַיֹּ֣אמֶר דָּוִ֗ד לִקְנ֨וֹת מֵעִמְּךָ֤ אֶת־הַגֹּ֙רֶן֙ לִבְנ֣וֹת מִזְבֵּ֔חַ לַיהוָ֑ה ("And David said, 'To buy the threshing floor from you to build an altar to the LORD.'"—2 Sam. 24:21)

וְלֹא־יַחְמֹ֥ד אִישׁ֙ אֶת־אַרְצְךָ֔ בַּעֲלֹֽתְךָ֗ לֵֽרָאוֹת֙ אֶת־פְּנֵי֙ יְהוָ֣ה אֱלֹהֶ֔יךָ ("No one will covet your land when you go up to appear before the face of the LORD your God."—Ex. 34:24)

לֹֽא־נִשְׁמַ֥ע בַּבַּ֖יִת בְּהִבָּנֹתֽוֹ ("It was not heard in the house while it was being built."—1 Kings 6:7)

D. Participles. The participles of III-ה verbs lose the ה of the root in all forms.

Qal Active Participle Paradigm

	Verbal Form	Suffix	Gloss
ms	בֹּנֶה	--	building/one who builds
fs	בֹּנָה	ָה	building/one who builds
mp	בֹּנִים	ִים	building/ones who build
fp	בֹּנוֹת	וֹת	building/ones who build

Because of the large difference between these forms and those of the strong verb, **the III-ה active participle forms must be memorized.**

Notes:

- Carefully note the similarities between the ms and fs forms of the active participle for III-ה verbs; the only difference is the final vowel.
- The alternative form of the feminine singular participle (the form בֹּנִיָּה) occurs, but rarely.

אֶבֶן מָאֲסוּ הַבּוֹנִים הָיְתָה לְרֹאשׁ פִּנָּה׃ ("The stone the builders rejected has become the cornerstone."—Ps. 118:22)

בֹּנֵי שְׁלֹמֹה וּבֹנֵי חִירוֹם ("Solomon's builders and Hiram's builders"—1 Kings 5:32)

Qal Passive Participle Paradigm

	Verbal Form	Suffix	Gloss
ms	בָּנוּי	--	one being built
fs	בְּנוּיָה	ָה	one being built
mp	בְּנוּיִים	ִים	ones being built
fp	בְּנוּיוֹת	וֹת	ones being built

Notes:

- Recall from 24.1 that most III-ה verbs were originally of III-י. The Qal passive participle form is regular once that change is recognized.

הַפָּר הַשֵּׁנִי הֹעֲלָה עַל־הַמִּזְבֵּחַ הַבָּנוּי	("The second bull had been offered up on the altar that had been built."—Judg. 6:28)
יְרוּשָׁלַם הַבְּנוּיָה כְּעִיר שֶׁחֻבְּרָה־לָּהּ יַחְדָּו׃	("Jerusalem, which is built as a city joined together."—Ps. 122:3)

E. Infinitive Absolute. The **infinitive absolute** of III-ה verbs is formed normally:

כִּי הַגִּלְגָּל גָּלֹה יִגְלֶה וּבֵית־אֵל יִהְיֶה לְאָוֶן	("for Gilgal will certainly go into exile, and Bethel will become nothing."—Amos 5:5)

24.5 Identifying "Missing" Root Letters

Unlike the gutturals (see chs. 22–23), the weakness of the III-ה verb creates a situation in which only two of the three root letters in the verb are evident in the inflected form:

Root	Inflected Form	Parsing
בנה	תִּבְנִי	Qal Imperf. 2fs of **בנה**, glossed as "you (fs) will build"
גלה	גָּלִיתִי	Qal Perf. 1cs of **גלה**, glossed as "I uncovered"

Both parsing and the use of a lexicon, however, require the identification of all three root letters.

At this point, if the removal of suffix and prefix letters results in only two evident root letters, there are three possible causes.

Possible Sources of "Missing" Root Letters
• The verbal root begins with *nun*
• The irregular verb לקח or הלך
• The verbal root ends with *heh*

Knowledge of both memory paradigms and vocabulary will help distinguish between these possibilities. Further, if the requisite entry does not exist in the lexicon (e.g.: you attempted to look up the root נבן, which does not exist), then you should reconsider and try other options.

24.6 The Hishtaphel

The Hishtaphel conjugation is used with only one verb in Biblical Hebrew, but that verb is important, since it is the verb glossed as "to bow down, do obeisance; to worship." Its root is debated, most likely being חוה, though other proposals are given.[2] Whatever the background, this verb is common, so it must become recognizable. As a final-*heh* verb, the endings should look familiar given the previous forms discussed in this chapter. The following forms occur in the Hebrew text:

Hishtaphel Perfect Paradigm

	Verbal Form	Suffix	Gloss
3ms	הִשְׁתַּחֲוָה	--	he worshiped
2ms	הִשְׁתַּחֲוִיתָ	תָ	you (ms) worshiped
1cs	הִשְׁתַּחֲוֵיתִי	תִי	I worshiped
3cp	הִשְׁתַּחֲווּ	וּ	they worshiped
2mp	הִשְׁתַּחֲוִיתֶם	תֶם	you (mp) worshiped

[2] The other major proposal, which has merit, suggests that the form is a Hithpael of the quadrilateral root (a root having four letters) שׁחוה. The debate over this root turns largely on whether one wishes to consider the Hebrew language more as a synchronic system or more in its diachronic development.

Hishtaphel Imperfect Paradigm

	Verbal Form	Prefix . . . Suffix	Gloss
3ms	יִשְׁתַּחֲוֶה	--- יִ	he will worship
2ms	תִּשְׁתַּחֲוֶה	--- תִּ	you (ms) will worship
1cs	אֶשְׁתַּחֲוֶה	--- אֶ	I will worship
3mp	יִשְׁתַּחֲווּ	וּ --- יִ	they (mp) will worship
2mp	תִּשְׁתַּחֲווּ	וּ --- תִּ	you (mp) will worship
1cp	נִשְׁתַּחֲוֶה	--- נִ	we will worship

וְאֶל־מֹשֶׁה אָמַר עֲלֵה אֶל־יְהוָה
אַתָּה וְאַהֲרֹן נָדָב וַאֲבִיהוּא
וְשִׁבְעִים מִזִּקְנֵי יִשְׂרָאֵל
וְהִשְׁתַּחֲוִיתֶם מֵרָחֹק׃

"And he said to Moses, 'Come up to the LORD, you and Aaron, Nadab and Abihu, and seventy of the elders of Israel, and worship from far off.'"—Ex. 24:1)

לֹא־תִשְׁתַּחֲוֶה לָהֶם וְלֹא תָעָבְדֵם
כִּי אָנֹכִי יְהוָה אֱלֹהֶיךָ אֵל קַנָּא

("You shall not bow down to them, nor shall you serve them, for I, the LORD your God, am a jealous God."—Ex. 20:5)

לֹא תִירְאוּ אֱלֹהִים אֲחֵרִים וְלֹא־
תִשְׁתַּחֲווּ לָהֶם וְלֹא תַעַבְדוּם וְלֹא
תִזְבְּחוּ לָהֶם

("You shall not fear other gods, nor shall you bow down to them, nor shall you serve them, nor shall you sacrifice to them."—2 Kings 17:35)

The Hishtaphel imperative, participle, narrative, and infinitive construct forms are all formed as would be expected from a final-ה verb:

Other Hishtaphel Forms

Imperative	fs	הִשְׁתַּחֲוִי	you (fs) worship
	mp	הִשְׁתַּחֲווּ	you (mp) worship
Participle	ms	מִשְׁתַּחֲוֶה	worshiper (ms)
	mp	מִשְׁתַּחֲוִים	worshipers (mp)
Narrative	3ms	וַיִּשְׁתַּחוּ	he worshiped
	2ms	וַתִּשְׁתַּחוּ	you (ms) worshiped
	3fp	וַתִּשְׁתַּחֲוֶיןָ	they (fp) worshiped
Infinitive Construct	הִשְׁתַּחֲוֹת		worshiping/to worship

וַיִּשְׁתַּחוּ אַבְרָהָם לִפְנֵי עַם הָאָרֶץ׃ ("And Abraham bowed down before the people of the land."—Gen. 23:12)

וַתִּגַּשׁ גַּם־לֵאָה וִילָדֶיהָ וַיִּשְׁתַּחֲווּ ("And Leah and her children also drew near, and they bowed down."—Gen. 33:7)

אֱלִילֵי כַסְפּוֹ וְאֵת אֱלִילֵי זְהָבוֹ
אֲשֶׁר עָשׂוּ־לוֹ לְהִשְׁתַּחֲוֹת ("The idols of silver and gold which they made to worship."—Isa. 2:20)

The ending וּ¯ does not necessarily indicate a plural form for this verb, as seen from the narrative 3ms and 2ms forms. Plural forms will end in ווּ¯, as seen in the perfect 3cp, the imperfect 3mp and 2mp, and the imperative mp.

24.7 Vocabulary

בָּכָה	to weep, wail
בָּנָה	to build
הָיָה	to be, become; to come to pass, occur, happen
חָיָה	to live, be alive
חַי	life
כָּלָה	to stop, come to an end, be finished
כִּלָּה	(Piel) to bring to an end, consume, destroy
כִּסָּה	(Piel) to cover, to conceal
הִכָּה	(Hiph.) to strike, to smite (from נכה)
הִשְׁתַּחֲוָה	to bow down, worship
עָלָה	to go up, ascend
הֶעֱלָה	(Hiph.) to bring up, make go up
עָנָה	to reply, answer; to give evidence, testify
עָשָׂה	to do, make
פָּנָה	to turn to one side, head in a direction; to turn to
צִוָּה	(Piel) to command, instruct
רָאָה	to see
הֶרְאָה	(Hiph.) to show
נִרְאָה	(Niph.) to appear, become visible
שָׁתָה	to drink

24.8 Language Exercises

A. Parse and gloss the following forms. Include the identification of the object suffix where appropriate.

הִשְׁתַּחֲוִ֫יתָ

נִגְלְתָה

עָשְׂתָה

עָלִית

יִשְׁתַּחֲווּ

עֲשִׂיתָ֫נִי

הִגָּלוֹת

עֲשֵׂה

וַיַּעֲלוּ

וַיִּשְׁתַּחוּ

מַעֲלִים

נַעֲלֶה

וָאַ֫עַשׂ

בְּנוֹתַ֫יִךְ

גָּלוּ

B. Translate the following and parse each verb and participle. Use your lexicon to look up the glosses for any words you do not know from your vocabulary.

Judg. 7:15–18

וַיְהִי֩ כִשְׁמֹ֨עַ גִּדְע֜וֹן אֶת־מִסְפַּ֧ר הַחֲל֛וֹם וְאֶת־שִׁבְר֖וֹ וַיִּשְׁתָּ֑חוּ וַיָּ֙שָׁב֙[3] אֶל־

מַחֲנֵ֣ה יִשְׂרָאֵ֔ל וַיֹּ֣אמֶר ק֔וּמוּ[4] כִּֽי־נָתַ֧ן יְהוָ֛ה בְּיֶדְכֶ֖ם אֶת־מַחֲנֵ֥ה מִדְיָֽן׃ וַיַּ֛חַץ

אֶת־שְׁלֹשׁ־מֵא֥וֹת הָאִ֖ישׁ שְׁלֹשָׁ֣ה רָאשִׁ֑ים וַיִּתֵּ֨ן שׁוֹפָר֤וֹת בְּיַד־כֻּלָּם֙ וְכַדִּ֣ים

רֵקִ֔ים וְלַפִּדִ֖ים בְּת֥וֹךְ הַכַּדִּֽים׃ וַיֹּ֣אמֶר אֲלֵיהֶ֔ם מִמֶּ֥נִּי תִרְא֖וּ וְכֵ֣ן תַּעֲשׂ֑וּ

וְהִנֵּ֙ה אָנֹכִ֥י בָא֙[5] בִּקְצֵ֣ה הַֽמַּחֲנֶ֔ה וְהָיָ֥ה כַאֲשֶׁר־אֶעֱשֶׂ֖ה כֵּ֥ן תַּעֲשֽׂוּן׃ וְתָקַעְתִּי֙

בַּשּׁוֹפָ֔ר אָנֹכִ֖י וְכָל־אֲשֶׁ֣ר אִתִּ֑י וּתְקַעְתֶּ֨ם בַּשּׁוֹפָר֜וֹת גַּם־אַתֶּ֗ם סְבִיבוֹת֙ כָּל־

הַֽמַּחֲנֶ֔ה וַאֲמַרְתֶּ֖ם לַיהוָ֥ה וּלְגִדְעֽוֹן׃

[3] Qal Narr. 3ms of שׁוב, glossed as “to return” (see ch. 26).

[4] Qal Imperative mp of קום, glossed as “to arise” (see ch. 26).

[5] Qal Part. ms of בוא, glossed as “to come, enter” (see ch. 26).

Judg. 2:11–15

וַיַּעֲשׂ֧וּ בְנֵֽי־יִשְׂרָאֵ֛ל אֶת־הָרַ֖ע בְּעֵינֵ֣י יְהוָ֑ה וַיַּעַבְד֖וּ אֶת־הַבְּעָלִֽים׃ וַיַּֽעַזְב֞וּ

אֶת־יְהוָ֣ה׀ אֱלֹהֵ֣י אֲבוֹתָ֗ם הַמּוֹצִ֣יא[6] אוֹתָם֮ מֵאֶ֣רֶץ מִצְרַיִם֒ וַיֵּֽלְכ֞וּ אַחֲרֵ֣י׀

אֱלֹהִ֣ים אֲחֵרִ֗ים מֵֽאֱלֹהֵ֤י הָֽעַמִּים֙ אֲשֶׁר֙ סְבִיבֽוֹתֵיהֶ֔ם וַיִּֽשְׁתַּחֲו֖וּ לָהֶ֑ם וַיַּכְעִ֖סוּ

אֶת־יְהוָֽה׃ וַיַּעַזְב֖וּ אֶת־יְהוָ֑ה וַיַּעַבְד֥וּ לַבַּ֖עַל וְלָעַשְׁתָּרֽוֹת׃ וַיִּֽחַר־אַ֤ף יְהוָה֙

בְּיִשְׂרָאֵ֔ל וַֽיִּתְּנֵם֙ בְּיַד־שֹׁסִ֔ים וַיָּשֹׁ֖סּוּ[7] אוֹתָ֑ם וַֽיִּמְכְּרֵ֞ם בְּיַ֤ד אוֹיְבֵיהֶם֙ מִסָּבִ֔יב

וְלֹֽא־יָכְל֣וּ[8] ע֔וֹד לַעֲמֹ֖ד לִפְנֵ֥י אוֹיְבֵיהֶֽם׃ בְּכֹ֣ל׀ אֲשֶׁ֣ר יָצְא֗וּ[9] יַד־יְהוָה֙

הָֽיְתָה־בָּ֣ם לְרָעָ֔ה כַּאֲשֶׁר֙ דִּבֶּ֣ר יְהוָ֔ה וְכַאֲשֶׁ֛ר נִשְׁבַּ֥ע יְהוָ֖ה לָהֶ֑ם וַיֵּ֥צֶר[10]

לָהֶ֖ם מְאֹֽד׃

---

[6] Hiph. Part. ms of יצא, glossed as "to bring out" (see ch. 27).

[7] Qal Narr. 3mp of שׁסס, glossed as "to plunder" (see ch. 28).

[8] Qal Perf. 3cp of יכל, glossed as "to be able" (see ch. 27).

[9] Qal Perf. 3cp of יצא, glossed as "to go out" (see ch. 27).

[10] Qal Narr. 3ms of צרר, glossed as "to be difficult" (see ch. 28).

Ex. 20:22–26

וַיֹּ֤אמֶר יְהוָה֙ אֶל־מֹשֶׁ֔ה כֹּ֥ה תֹאמַ֖ר אֶל־בְּנֵ֣י יִשְׂרָאֵ֑ל אַתֶּ֣ם רְאִיתֶ֔ם כִּ֚י מִן־

הַשָּׁמַ֔יִם דִּבַּ֖רְתִּי עִמָּכֶֽם: לֹ֥א תַעֲשׂ֖וּן אִתִּ֑י אֱלֹ֤הֵי כֶ֙סֶף֙ וֵאלֹהֵ֣י זָהָ֔ב לֹ֥א

תַעֲשׂ֖וּ לָכֶֽם: מִזְבַּ֣ח אֲדָמָה֮ תַּעֲשֶׂה־לִּי֒ וְזָבַחְתָּ֣ עָלָ֗יו אֶת־עֹלֹתֶ֙יךָ֙ וְאֶת־

שְׁלָמֶ֔יךָ אֶת־צֹאנְךָ֖ וְאֶת־בְּקָרֶ֑ךָ בְּכָל־הַמָּקוֹם֙ אֲשֶׁ֣ר אַזְכִּ֣יר אֶת־שְׁמִ֔י

אָב֥וֹא[11] אֵלֶ֖יךָ וּבֵרַכְתִּֽיךָ: וְאִם־מִזְבַּ֤ח אֲבָנִים֙ תַּֽעֲשֶׂה־לִּ֔י לֹא־תִבְנֶ֥ה אֶתְהֶ֖ן

גָּזִ֑ית כִּ֧י חַרְבְּךָ֛ הֵנַ֥פְתָּ[12] עָלֶ֖יהָ וַתְּחַלְלֶֽהָ[13]: וְלֹא־תַעֲלֶ֥ה בְמַעֲלֹ֖ת עַֽל־

מִזְבְּחִ֑י אֲשֶׁ֛ר לֹא־תִגָּלֶ֥ה עֶרְוָתְךָ֖ עָלָֽיו:

[11] Qal Imperf. 1cs of בוא, glossed as “to come, enter” (see ch. 26).

[12] Hiph. Perf. 2ms of נוף, glossed as “to wave, brandish” (see ch. 26).

[13] Piel Narr. 2ms of הלל, glossed as “to profane” (see ch. 28) plus 3fs suffix.

24.9 Exegetical Exercises—Euphemism

A. Translate this portion of Job 1:5:

כִּי אָמַר אִיּוֹב אוּלַי חָטְאוּ בָנַי וּבֵרֲכוּ אֱלֹהִים בִּלְבָבָם

B. Compare your translation to a major English translation such as the NIV or ESV. What differs?

This difference is a case of **euphemism**, in which a more polite word is substituted for the original word. For example, in English, "passed away" is a common euphemism for "died." Euphemisms are common in many languages, especially as terms for sex, certain diseases or bodily functions, and death. In this case the euphemism appears because no cantor or reader in a synagogue would want to even utter the words "curse God," so the phrase בֵּרֵךְ אֱלֹהִים (or בֵּרֵךְ יְהוָה) is substituted. Lexically, ברך has not changed meanings; it still indicates "to bless." But it is being used euphemistically to indicate cursing, not blessing. This is not as strange as it may sound; even in English we have a similar idiom. If we say that someone "blessed me out," it indicates a cursing, not a blessing. Job 1:5 is an example of euphemism in the Hebrew text of the OT.

C. Now consider a more challenging case. Translate Ruth 3:4:

וִיהִ֣י בְשָׁכְב֗וֹ וְיָדַ֙עַתְּ֙ אֶת־הַמָּק֙וֹם֙ אֲשֶׁ֣ר יִשְׁכַּב־שָׁ֔ם וּבָ֛את[14] וְגִלִּ֥ית מַרְגְּלֹתָ֖יו וְשָׁכָ֑בְתְּי[15]
וְהוּא֙ יַגִּ֣יד לָ֔ךְ אֵ֖ת אֲשֶׁ֥ר תַּעֲשִֽׂין׃

The debate around this verse centers on Naomi's instruction to Ruth—especially the commands indicated in the converted perfects of גלה and שכב. What exactly has Naomi instructed Ruth to do?

Residents of a town generally slept in that town for safety. But during the harvest time, the men slept out at the threshing floor to protect the grain from thieves. "Ladies of the night" (a euphemism, by the way) would visit the threshing floor to ply their trade. In the previous verses Naomi instructs Ruth to get cleaned up, to anoint herself with oil to smell nice, and to go out to the threshing floor at night. Then comes the instruction of verse 4.

1. Each of these three words (גָּלָה, רֶגֶל, and שָׁכַב) is potentially euphemistic.

   What is the meaning of גָּלָה in Leviticus 18 and 20, where it occurs twenty-four times? What is its meaning in Deuteronomy 23:1, 27:20, and Isaiah 22:8? (For more examples, consult TDOT II:479.)

   For רֶגֶל, what is the meaning in Exodus 4:25, Judges 3:24, 1 Samuel 24:4, and Isaiah 6:2?

---

[14] Qal Conv. Perf. 3fs of בוא, glossed as "to come, go" (see ch. 26).

[15] Use your BHS or BHQ to analyze the *Ketiv/Qere* of this form.

For שָׁכַב, what is the meaning in Genesis 19:33, 30:16, Deuteronomy 22:25, and 2 Samuel 11:4?

Based on these observations, consider the opinions of two commentators on this passage:

> The noun *marg'lātāw* in 3:4, 7, 8, 14, which is usually translated "feet" probably functions as a euphemism for the genitals, cf. Campbell, Ruth, pp. 121, 131–32. I should prefer that Campbell had left intact the ambiguity of this episode in the dark of night rather than conclude "that there was no sexual intercourse at the threshing floor" (p. 134).[16]

> This [common evangelical] perspective of sexual purity fails to find support in Scripture, because Ruth seeks an encounter with Boaz that many evangelical readers ignore: an interpretation generally supported by most biblical scholars who read the story with its historical and cultural context. . . . Two details in this narrative shatter the evangelical myth of sexual purity: the threshing floor as the place for sexual encounters, and the use of the term 'feet,' a literary euphemism for male genitalia. Look to most any study Bible, and you will see an explanation of this euphemism, widely accepted by Biblical scholars.[17]

On the other hand, consider these explanations from other commentators:

> To uncover Boaz's feet exposed them to the night air's increasing chill. Naomi cleverly figured that he would not awaken until aware of the discomfort, i.e., in the dead of night after other workers had either gone home or fallen asleep themselves.[18]

> *3:4 contains a statement that has become the object of great debate among rabbis of old and has continued to vex modern scholars: What*

[16] Phyllis Trible, *God and the Rhetoric of Sexuality* (Philadelphia: Fortress, 1986), 198.
[17] Kendra Weddle Irons and Melanie Springer Mock, *If Eve Only Knew* (St. Louis: Chalice, 2015), 22.
[18] Robert L. Hubbard, *Ruth*, NICOT (Grand Rapids: Eerdmans, 1988), 204.

> *did Naomi precisely advise Ruth when she bade her to "bare Boaz's 'legs'"?* . . . [T]he discussion . . . revolves around the meaning of *regel*, and the precise connotation of the verbs associated with *margelôt.* As is well known, *regel*, "foot," is used in the OT frequently enough as a euphemism for the sexual organs (BDB, 920). We could point out that the *pi``el* of *gālāh*, twice associated with our word, is often identified with the act of uncovering nakedness. . . . Nevertheless, there are enough exceptions to this usage of the *pi``el* of *gālāh* to caution us against rashly accusing Naomi of urging Ruth on to such acts of boldness. . . . I am in full agreement with Campbell (1975:121) who, along with other scholars, suggests that the "storyteller meant to be ambiguous and hence provocative."[19]

How is one to judge between these opinions when studying or preparing to teach Ruth 3? A general impression of the reliability or bias of the commentary series can help, but it is by no means a guarantee.

2. Note the following exegetical observations about the passage:

What is the particular word that relates to the root רגל?

Look it up in your lexicon. How many times does it occur?

Where outside this chapter does it occur?

[19] Jack Sasson, *Ruth: A New Translation with a Philological Commentary and a Formalist-Folklorist Interpretation*, 2nd ed. (Sheffield, UK: Sheffield Academic, 1989), 69–71.

To what part of the body does it refer in that context? Is it euphemistic?

Why might this word have been chosen by the author instead of רֶגֶל, which can clearly serve as a euphemism?

Consider the formulation of the word, with a *mem* prefix. Compare this word to מְרַאֲשׁוֹת, which also prefixes a *mem* to a noun indicating a part of the body. Look up מְרַאֲשׁוֹת in your lexicon. What is its root?

How many times does מְרַאֲשׁוֹת occur in the OT?

What does it mean in those instances?

How would this shed light on the nuance of meaning of מַרְגְּלוֹת?

3. Consider the broader context of the passage and the book:

Translate Boaz's immediate response to Ruth's request from verse 10a:

וַיֹּאמֶר בְּרוּכָה אַתְּ לַיהוָה בִּתִּי

Translate his elaboration in verse 11a:

וְעַתָּה בִּתִּי אַל־תִּֽירְאִי[20] כֹּל אֲשֶׁר־תֹּאמְרִי אֶֽעֱשֶׂה־לָּךְ כִּי יוֹדֵעַ כָּל־
שַׁעַר עַמִּי כִּי אֵשֶׁת חַיִל אָתְּ׃

Do a brief lexical review of the concept of חַיִל. What does this indicate about Boaz's perception of Ruth? How does that help inform the reader as to the actions that she did or did not take on the threshing floor?

Review chapter 4 in an English Bible. How do these actions accord with the two possibilities: (1) Ruth had sexual relations with Boaz at the threshing floor, and (2) she uncovered his physical feet?

[20] Qal Juss. 2fs of ירא, glossed as "to fear" (see ch. 27).

No doubt there are sexual overtones in this passage. Bush aptly states:

> Campbell (131) is indeed correct when he observes that it is quite incomprehensible that a Hebrew storyteller could use such terms all in the same context and not suggest to his audience that a set of sexually provocative circumstances confronts them. . . . However, he has depicted both of them throughout this narrative as people of unmatched integrity (cf. 2:1; 3:11) whose lives exhibit that faithful loyalty of relationships described by the Hebrew word חסד *ḥesed* (see 1:8; 2:20; 3:10), and so it is clear that his silence means to imply that they met this moment of choice with that same integrity.[21]

The takeaway: context always matters. In the process of learning Hebrew and developing more skill at detailed analysis, you must never forget that the ultimate reading of the whole composition controls the reading of the parts—something especially true in a book as carefully constructed as Ruth. In this case the detailed work of (2) points in the same direction as the overall contextual reading of the passage, giving a strong reason to support one side of this debate over the other.[22]

[21] Frederic W. Bush, *Ruth, Esther*, WBC (Waco, TX: Word, 1996), 155–56.
[22] For more detail, see Moshe Bernstein, “Two Multivalent Readings in the Ruth Narrative,” *JSOT* 50 (1991), 17.

כה (25) III-א Verbs

25.1 The Consonant א

The consonant א has no sound of its own, being an unvoiced glottal stop, the cessation of the airflow (see 1.1). When א takes a vowel, it is pronounced with the sound of that vowel. When it has no vowel, it becomes quiescent—it is not vocalized, even though the letter itself is still present in the text.

When א quiesces, a short vowel that precedes it is lengthened. If a quiescent א is the only letter between a vowel and a *begadkephat* letter, that following *begadkephat* letter will be pronounced as a spirant (losing the *dagesh lene*).

25.2 III-א Perfects

The perfect forms of III-א verbs use the same suffix endings as all other perfect forms, endings learned with the Qal perfect paradigm (see 3.2). The quiescence of the א from the root, however, causes the regular changes detailed in 25.1.

	Qal Perfect קטל	Qal Perfect מצא
3ms	קָטַל	מָצָא
3fs	קָֽטְלָה	מָֽצְאָה
2ms	קָטַ֫לְתָּ	מָצָ֫אתָ
2fs	קָטַלְתְּ	מָצָאת
1cs	קָטַ֫לְתִּי	מָצָ֫אתִי
3cp	קָֽטְלוּ	מָֽצְאוּ
2mp	קְטַלְתֶּם	מְצָאתֶם
2fp	קְטַלְתֶּן	מְצָאתֶן
1cp	קָטַ֫לְנוּ	מָצָ֫אנוּ

אַשְׁרֵ֣י אָ֭דָם מָצָ֣א חָכְמָ֑ה ("Blessed is the man who finds wisdom."—Prov. 3:13a)

וְקָרְא֤וּ לָהֶם֙ גְּב֣וּל רִשְׁעָ֔ה ("And they will be called a wicked land."—Mal. 1:4)

Though the א is usually present, it is occasionally omitted in spelling, as in:

חֲטוֹא = חֲטוֹ (Qal Inf. Const. of חטא, glossed as “to miss, to wrong, to sin”)

כִּֽי־הִרְבָּ֥ה אֶפְרַ֛יִם מִזְבְּחֹ֖ת לַחֲטֹ֑א (“Because Ephraim has multiplied altars for sin . . . .”—Hos. 8:11)

וָאֶחְשֹׂ֧ךְ גַּם־אָנֹכִ֛י אוֹתְךָ֖ מֵחֲטוֹ־לִ֑י (“And I held you back from sinning against me.”—Gen. 20:6)

The perfect forms of the derived stems show similar behavior, so the student who has memorized the Qal perfect paradigm for the strong verb and who pays attention to the tip-offs for the derived stems should be able to determine the parsing of each form:

	Qal Perfect מצא	Niphal Perfect מצא	Piel Perfect מצא	Pual Perfect מצא	Hithpael Perfect מצא	Hiphil Perfect מצא	Hophal Perfect מצא
3ms	מָצָא	נִמְצָא	מִצֵּא	מֻצָּא	הִתְמַצֵּא	הִמְצִיא	הֻמְצָא
3fs	מָֽצְאָה	נִמְצְאָה	מִצְּאָה	מֻצְּאָה	הִתְמַצְּאָה	הִמְצִ֫יאָה	הֻמְצְאָה
2ms	מָצָ֫אתָ	נִמְצֵ֫אתָ	מִצֵּ֫אתָ	מֻצֵּ֫אתָ	הִתְמַצֵּ֫אתָ	הִמְצֵ֫אתָ	הֻמְצָ֫אתָ
2fs	מָצָאת	נִמְצֵאת	מִצֵּאת	מֻצֵּאת	הִתְמַצֵּאת	הִמְצֵאת	הֻמְצָאת
1cs	מָצָ֫אתִי	נִמְצֵ֫אתִי	מִצֵּ֫אתִי	מֻצֵּ֫אתִי	הִתְמַצֵּ֫אתִי	הִמְצֵ֫אתִי	הֻמְצָ֫אתִי
3cp	מָֽצְאוּ	נִמְצְאוּ	מִצְּאוּ	מֻצְּאוּ	הִתְמַצְּאוּ	הִמְצִ֫יאוּ	הֻמְצְאוּ
2mp	מְצָאתֶם	נִמְצֵאתֶם	מִצֵּאתֶם	מֻצֵּאתֶם	הִתְמַצֵּאתֶם	הִמְצֵאתֶם	הֻמְצָאתֶם
2fp	מְצָאתֶן	נִמְצֵאתֶן	מִצֵּאתֶן	מֻצֵּאתֶן	הִתְמַצֵּאתֶן	הִמְצֵאתֶן	הֻמְצָאתֶן
1cp	מָצָ֫אנוּ	נִמְצֵ֫אנוּ	מִצֵּ֫אנוּ	מֻצֵּ֫אנוּ	הִתְמַצֵּ֫אנוּ	הִמְצֵ֫אנוּ	הֻמְצָ֫אנוּ

The *ṣere* of the Piel and Hithpael and the *ḥireq yod/ṣere* of the Hiphil do not lengthen, since they are already long vowels, but the *pataḥ* of the Qal, Niphal, Pual, and Hophal lengthens to *qameṣ*.

נִמְצְאוּ֙ חֲמֵ֣שֶׁת הַמְּלָכִ֔ים נֶחְבְּאִ֖ים בַּמְּעָרָ֥ה בְּמַקֵּדָֽה	("The five kings have been found, hidden in a cave in Makkedah."—Josh. 10:17)
וַאֲדֹנִיָּ֧ה בֶן־חַגִּ֛ית מִתְנַשֵּׂ֥א לֵאמֹ֖ר אֲנִ֣י אֶמְלֹ֑ךְ	("And Adonijah the son of Haggith raised himself up, saying, 'I will be king.'"—1 Kings 1:5)
עַל־חַטֹּ֤אות יָרָבְעָם֙ אֲשֶׁ֣ר חָטָ֔א וַאֲשֶׁ֥ר הֶחֱטִ֖יא אֶת־יִשְׂרָאֵ֑ל	("On account of the sins of Jeroboam which he sinned and which he caused Israel to sin"—1 Kings 15:30)

25.3 III-א Imperfects

The imperfect forms of III-א verbs use the same prefix and suffix endings as all other imperfect forms, endings learned with the Qal imperfect paradigm (see 5.1). The quiescence of the א from the root, however, creates the vowel lengthening detailed in 25.1.

	Qal Imperfect שׁלח	Qal Imperfect מצא
3ms	יִשְׁלַח	יִמְצָא
3fs	תִּשְׁלַח	תִּמְצָא
2ms	תִּשְׁלַח	תִּמְצָא
2fs	תִּשְׁלְחִי	תִּמְצְאִי
1cs	אֶשְׁלַח	אֶמְצָא
3mp	יִשְׁלְחוּ	יִמְצְאוּ
3fp	תִּשְׁלַ֫חְנָה	תִּמְצֶ֫ינָה
2mp	תִּשְׁלְחוּ	תִּמְצְאוּ
2fp	תִּשְׁלַ֫חְנָה	תִּמְצֶ֫ינָה
1cp	נִשְׁלַח	נִמְצָא

וְלֹא־יִקְרָא עָלֶיךָ אֶל־יְהוָה ("So that he will not cry out against you to the LORD"—1 Kings 1:5)

וּבַמִּדְבָּר אֲשֶׁר רָאִיתָ אֲשֶׁר נְשָׂאֲךָ יְהוָה אֱלֹהֶיךָ כַּאֲשֶׁר יִשָּׂא־אִישׁ אֶת־בְּנוֹ ("And in the wilderness, where you saw how the LORD your God carried you, just as a man carries his child"—Deut. 1:31)

The imperfect of the derived stems of III-א verbs shows the lengthening of *pataḥ* to *qameṣ* in the Pual and Hophal. The *ṣere* of the Niphal, Piel, and Hithpael is already long, so no change occurs in those stems:

	Qal Imperfect מצא	Niphal Imperfect מצא	Piel Imperfect מצא	Pual Imperfect מצא	Hithpael Imperfect מצא	Hiphil Imperfect מצא	Hophal Imperfect מצא
3ms	יִמְצָא	יִמָּצֵא	יְמַצֵּא	יְמֻצָּא	יִתְמַצֵּא	יַמְצִיא	יֻמְצָא
3fs	תִּמְצָא	תִּמָּצֵא	תְּמַצֵּא	תְּמֻצָּא	תִּתְמַצֵּא	תַּמְצִיא	תֻּמְצָא
2ms	תִּמְצָא	תִּמָּצֵא	תְּמַצֵּא	תְּמֻצָּא	תִּתְמַצֵּא	תַּמְצִיא	תֻּמְצָא
2fs	תִּמְצְאִי	תִּמָּֽצְאִי	תְּמַצְּאִי	תְּמֻצְּאִי	תִּתְמַצְּאִי	תַּמְצִ֫יאִי	תֻּמְצְאִי
1cs	אֶמְצָא	אֶמָּצֵא	אֲמַצֵּא	אֲמֻצָּא	אֶתְמַצֵּא	אַמְצִיא	אֻמְצָא
3mp	יִמְצְאוּ	יִמָּֽצְאוּ	יְמַצְּאוּ	יְמֻצְּאוּ	יִתְמַצְּאוּ	יַמְצִ֫יאוּ	יֻמְצְאוּ
3fp	תִּמְצֶ֫ינָה	תִּמָּצֶ֫אנָה	תְּמַצֶּ֫אנָה	תְּמֻצֶּ֫אנָה	תִּתְמַצֶּ֫אנָה	תַּמְצֶ֫אנָה	תֻּמְצֶ֫אנָה
2mp	תִּמְצְאוּ	תִּמָּֽצְאוּ	תְּמַצְּאוּ	תְּמֻצְּאוּ	תִּתְמַצְּאוּ	תַּמְצִ֫יאוּ	תֻּמְצְאוּ
2fp	תִּמְצֶ֫ינָה	תִּמָּצֶ֫אנָה	תְּמַצֶּ֫אנָה	תְּמֻצֶּ֫אנָה	תִּתְמַצֶּ֫אנָה	תַּמְצֶ֫אנָה	תֻּמְצֶ֫אנָה
1cp	נִמְצָא	נִמָּצֵא	נְמַצֵּא	נְמֻצָּא	נִתְמַצֵּא	נַמְצִיא	נֻמְצָא

The theme vowel of the 3fp and 2fp III-א imperfect forms changes to *segol* in all stems:

עַל שֵׁם אֲחֵיהֶם יִקָּרְאוּ בְּנַחֲלָתָם ("They will be called by the name of their brothers in their inheritance."—Gen. 48:6)

תִּתְחַטְּאוּ בַּיּוֹם הַשְּׁלִישִׁי וּבַיּוֹם הַשְּׁבִיעִי אַתֶּם וּשְׁבִיכֶם ("You shall purify yourselves and your captives on the third day and on the seventh day."—Num. 31:19)

25.4 Other III-א Forms

The imperative, infinitive construct, and infinitive absolute forms of III-א verbs are formed normally, e.g.:

מַצְּאִי	Piel Imperative fs of מצא
מְצֹא	Qal Inf. Const. of מצא
הַמְצֵא	Hiph. Inf. Abs. of מצא

וְלֹא־נָתַתִּי לַחֲטֹא חִכִּי ("I have not permitted my mouth to sin."—Job 31:30)

פְּרוּ וּרְבוּ וּמִלְאוּ אֶת־הַמַּיִם בַּיַּמִּים ("Be fruitful and multiply and fill the waters in the seas."—Gen. 1:22)

The participle forms of III-א verbs are also formed normally, with the exception of the fs participle. Where the fs participle would have taken the form --טֶּלֶת, that form is replaced by *ṣere* plus quiescent א:

מֹצֵאת	Qal Act. Part. fs of מצא
מְמַצֵּאת	Piel Part. fs of מצא
מַמְצֵאת	Hiph. Part. fs of מצא
מֻמְצֵאת	Hoph. Part. fs of מצא

אָ֛ז הָיִ֥יתִי בְעֵינָ֖יו כְּמוֹצְאֵ֥ת שָׁלֽוֹם׃ ("Then I was in his eyes like one who finds peace."—Song 8:10)

בְּנ֣וֹת עַמְּךָ֔ הַמִּֽתְנַבְּא֖וֹת מִלִּבְּהֶ֑ן וְהִנָּבֵ֖א עֲלֵיהֶֽן ("the daughters of your people, who prophesy out of their own hearts, prophesy against them."—Ezek. 13:17)

25.5 Vocabulary

בּוֹא	to come, enter
הִתְחַטָּא	(Hithp.) to purify oneself
חִטֵּא	(Piel) to cleanse from sin, purify; offer as a sin offering
חֵטְא	offense, sin, guilt
חָטָא	to miss, to wrong, to sin
טִמֵּא	(Piel) to defile, desecrate
טָמֵא	to become ritually unclean
מִלֵּא	(Piel) to fill, fulfill; endow; consecrate as priest
מַרְאֶה	seeing, appearance
מָלֵא	to be full, fulfilled; to fill up
מָצָא	to find; reach; obtain; achieve
נִטְמָא	(Niph.) to defile oneself
נָשָׂא	to lift up, carry, raise
קָרָא	to call, summon
שָׂנֵא	to hate

25.6 Language Exercises

A. Parse and gloss the following forms. Include the identification of the object suffix where appropriate.

נִקְרָא

שִׁלַּחְנוּ

יְחַטֵּא

וָאֶקְרָא

שְׂנֹא

הֶחֱטִיא

וַתִּמָּלֵא

מַשְׁלִיחַ

גְּלֵה

תֵּעָשֶׂה

קְרֻאִים

חָטָ֫אתִי

מִלֵּ֫אתָ

קְרָאתִ֫יךָ

נִגְלֵ֫יתִי

B. Translate the following and parse each verb and participle. Use your lexicon to look up the glosses for any words you do not know from your vocabulary.

Ex. 20:7–11 לֹ֥א תִשָּׂ֛א אֶת־שֵֽׁם־יְהוָ֥ה אֱלֹהֶ֖יךָ לַשָּׁ֑וְא כִּ֣י לֹ֤א יְנַקֶּה֙ יְהוָ֔ה אֵ֛ת אֲשֶׁר־יִשָּׂ֥א

אֶת־שְׁמ֖וֹ לַשָּֽׁוְא׃ זָכ֛וֹר֩ אֶת־י֥וֹם הַשַּׁבָּ֖ת לְקַדְּשֽׁוֹ׃ שֵׁ֤שֶׁת יָמִים֙ תַּעֲבֹ֔ד֮ וְעָשִׂ֖יתָ֮

כָּל־מְלַאכְתֶּֽךָ׃ וְי֙וֹם֙ הַשְּׁבִיעִ֔י שַׁבָּ֖ת לַיהוָ֣ה אֱלֹהֶ֑יךָ לֹ֣א־תַעֲשֶׂ֣ה כָל־

מְלָאכָ֡ה אַתָּ֣ה וּבִנְךָ֣־וּ֠בִתֶּךָ עַבְדְּךָ֨ וַאֲמָתְךָ֜ וּבְהֶמְתֶּ֗ךָ וְגֵרְךָ֙ אֲשֶׁ֣ר

בִּשְׁעָרֶֽיךָ׃ כִּ֣י שֵֽׁשֶׁת־יָמִים֩ עָשָׂ֨ה יְהוָ֜ה אֶת־הַשָּׁמַ֣יִם וְאֶת־הָאָ֗רֶץ אֶת־הַיָּם֙

וְאֶת־כָּל־אֲשֶׁר־בָּ֔ם וַיָּ֖נַח[1] בַּיּ֣וֹם הַשְּׁבִיעִ֑י עַל־כֵּ֗ן בֵּרַ֧ךְ יְהוָ֛ה אֶת־י֥וֹם

הַשַּׁבָּ֖ת וַֽיְקַדְּשֵֽׁהוּ׃

[1] Qal Narr. 3ms of נוח, glossed as “to rest” (see ch. 26).

Ex. 7:8–13

וַיֹּ֣אמֶר יְהוָ֔ה אֶל־מֹשֶׁ֥ה וְאֶֽל־אַהֲרֹ֖ן לֵאמֹֽר׃ כִּי֩ יְדַבֵּ֨ר אֲלֵכֶ֤ם פַּרְעֹה֙ לֵאמֹ֔ר

תְּנ֥וּ לָכֶ֖ם מוֹפֵ֑ת וְאָמַרְתָּ֣ אֶֽל־אַהֲרֹ֗ן קַ֧ח אֶֽת־מַטְּךָ֛ וְהַשְׁלֵ֥ךְ לִפְנֵֽי־פַרְעֹ֖ה יְהִ֥י

לְתַנִּֽין׃ וַיָּבֹ֨א[2] מֹשֶׁ֤ה וְאַהֲרֹן֙ אֶל־פַּרְעֹ֔ה וַיַּ֣עֲשׂוּ כֵ֔ן כַּאֲשֶׁ֖ר צִוָּ֣ה יְהוָ֑ה וַיַּשְׁלֵ֨ךְ

אַהֲרֹ֜ן אֶת־מַטֵּ֗הוּ לִפְנֵ֤י פַרְעֹה֙ וְלִפְנֵ֣י עֲבָדָ֔יו וַיְהִ֖י לְתַנִּֽין׃ וַיִּקְרָא֙ גַּם־פַּרְעֹ֔ה

לַחֲכָמִ֖ים וְלַֽמְכַשְּׁפִ֑ים וַיַּעֲשׂ֨וּ גַם־הֵ֜ם חַרְטֻמֵּ֥י מִצְרַ֛יִם בְּלַהֲטֵיהֶ֖ם כֵּֽן׃

וַיַּשְׁלִ֨יכוּ֙ אִ֣ישׁ מַטֵּ֔הוּ וַיִּהְי֖וּ לְתַנִּינִ֑ם וַיִּבְלַ֥ע מַטֵּֽה־אַהֲרֹ֖ן אֶת־מַטֹּתָֽם׃ וַיֶּחֱזַק֙

לֵ֣ב פַּרְעֹ֔ה וְלֹ֥א שָׁמַ֖ע אֲלֵהֶ֑ם כַּאֲשֶׁ֖ר דִּבֶּ֥ר יְהוָֽה׃

[2] Qal Narr. 3ms of בוא, glossed as "to come" (see ch. 26).

1 Kings
22:1–9

וַיֵּשְׁב֖וּ שָׁל֣שׁ שָׁנִ֑ים אֵ֤ין מִלְחָמָה֙ בֵּ֣ין אֲרָ֔ם וּבֵ֖ין יִשְׂרָאֵֽל׃ פ וַיְהִ֖י בַּשָּׁנָ֣ה

הַשְּׁלִישִׁ֑ית וַיֵּ֛רֶד[3] יְהוֹשָׁפָ֥ט מֶלֶךְ־יְהוּדָ֖ה אֶל־מֶ֥לֶךְ יִשְׂרָאֵֽל׃ וַיֹּ֤אמֶר מֶֽלֶךְ־

יִשְׂרָאֵל֙ אֶל־עֲבָדָ֔יו הַיְדַעְתֶּ֕ם כִּֽי־לָ֖נוּ רָמֹ֣ת גִּלְעָ֑ד וַאֲנַ֣חְנוּ מַחְשִׁ֔ים מִקַּ֣חַת

אֹתָ֔הּ מִיַּ֖ד מֶ֥לֶךְ אֲרָֽם׃ וַיֹּ֙אמֶר֙ אֶל־יְה֣וֹשָׁפָ֔ט הֲתֵלֵ֥ךְ אִתִּ֛י לַמִּלְחָמָ֖ה רָמֹ֣ת

גִּלְעָ֑ד וַיֹּ֤אמֶר יְהוֹשָׁפָט֙ אֶל־מֶ֣לֶךְ יִשְׂרָאֵ֔ל כָּמ֧וֹנִי כָמ֛וֹךָ כְּעַמִּ֥י כְעַמֶּ֖ךָ כְּסוּסַ֥י

כְּסוּסֶֽיךָ׃ וַיֹּ֥אמֶר יְהוֹשָׁפָ֖ט אֶל־מֶ֣לֶךְ יִשְׂרָאֵ֑ל דְּרָשׁ־נָ֥א כַיּ֖וֹם אֶת־דְּבַ֥ר

יְהוָֽה׃ וַיִּקְבֹּ֣ץ מֶלֶךְ־יִשְׂרָאֵ֣ל אֶת־הַנְּבִיאִים֮ כְּאַרְבַּ֣ע מֵא֣וֹת אִישׁ֒ וַיֹּ֣אמֶר

אֲלֵהֶ֗ם הַאֵלֵ֞ךְ עַל־רָמֹ֥ת גִּלְעָ֛ד לַמִּלְחָמָ֖ה אִם־אֶחְדָּ֑ל וַיֹּאמְר֣וּ עֲלֵ֔ה וְיִתֵּ֥ן

אֲדֹנָ֖י בְּיַ֥ד הַמֶּֽלֶךְ׃ וַיֹּ֙אמֶר֙ יְה֣וֹשָׁפָ֔ט הַאֵ֨ין פֹּ֥ה נָבִ֛יא לַיהוָ֖ה ע֑וֹד וְנִדְרְשָׁ֖ה

[3] Qal Narr. 3ms of ירד, glossed as “to go down” (see ch. 27).

מֵאוֹתוֹ׃ וַיֹּאמֶר מֶלֶךְ־יִשְׂרָאֵל׀ אֶל־יְהוֹשָׁפָט עוֹד אִישׁ־אֶחָד לִדְרֹשׁ אֶת־

יְהוָה מֵאֹתוֹ וַאֲנִי שְׂנֵאתִיו כִּי לֹא־יִתְנַבֵּא עָלַי טוֹב כִּי אִם־רָע מִיכָיְהוּ בֶּן־

יִמְלָה וַיֹּאמֶר יְהוֹשָׁפָט אַל־יֹאמַר הַמֶּלֶךְ כֵּן׃ וַיִּקְרָא מֶלֶךְ יִשְׂרָאֵל אֶל־

סָרִיס אֶחָד וַיֹּאמֶר מַהֲרָה מִיכָיְהוּ בֶן־יִמְלָה׃

25.7 Exegetical Exercises—Secondary Volitives

A. Translate Exodus 6:11 and parse each verb:

בֹּא[4] דַבֵּר אֶל־פַּרְעֹה מֶלֶךְ מִצְרָיִם וִישַׁלַּח[5] אֶת־בְּנֵי־יִשְׂרָאֵל מֵאַרְצוֹ׃

Look at your parsing of וִישַׁלַּח. Compare your translation to the various translation options for the imperfect given in 5.2. Which of them seem to fit this context? Which would you choose?

[4] Qal Imperative ms of בּוֹא, glossed as “to come, go” (see ch. 26).

[5] The *rule of shewa* is operative here (see 6.4).

B. Compare your choice to several major English translations. How do they treat this verb?

Exodus 6:11 is an example of a **secondary volitive**, a Hebrew construction that mainly expresses purpose. A secondary volitive construction occurs when a volitive form (cohortative, imperative, or jussive) is followed by a simple ו (as either וְ or וּ) plus an imperfect verbal form. In such a construction, the second verb (the simple ו plus imperfect) gives the reason for the initial volitive. This construction is typically translated into English as "so that . . . ," expressing the purpose of the initial command or wish.

Note the difference between a secondary volitive and a narrative form: a narrative form involves וַ־ plus doubling the first letter of a preterite form (see 12.1). A secondary volitive involves וְ־ (or וּ־) attached to the beginning of an imperfect form. While both are connected to prefixing verbal forms (see 5.1), they present *two separate verbal situations with nonoverlapping function.*

C. Translate the following verbal sequences and pay careful attention to the parsing of each verb. Mark each as either a secondary volitive sequence or a narrative sequence. Also note the difference between each form and a converted perfect (see 12.3).

Ex. 7:26 [Engl. 8:1]

וַיֹּאמֶר יְהוָה אֶל־מֹשֶׁה בֹּא[6] אֶל־פַּרְעֹה וְאָמַרְתָּ אֵלָיו כֹּה אָמַר יְהוָה

שַׁלַּח אֶת־עַמִּי וְיַעַבְדֻנִי׃

[6] Qal Imperative ms of בוא, glossed as "to come, go" (see ch. 26).

Num. 11:16 וַיֹּאמֶר יְהוָה אֶל־מֹשֶׁה אֶסְפָה־לִּי שִׁבְעִים אִישׁ מִזִּקְנֵי יִשְׂרָאֵל אֲשֶׁר יָדַעְתָּ

כִּי־הֵם זִקְנֵי הָעָם וְשֹׁטְרָיו וְלָקַחְתָּ אֹתָם אֶל־אֹהֶל מוֹעֵד וְהִתְיַצְּבוּ שָׁם

עִמָּךְ׃

Ex. 10:7a וַיֹּאמְרוּ עַבְדֵי פַרְעֹה אֵלָיו עַד־מָתַי יִהְיֶה זֶה לָנוּ לְמוֹקֵשׁ שַׁלַּח אֶת־

הָאֲנָשִׁים וְיַעַבְדוּ אֶת־יְהוָה

Gen. 27:9 לֶךְ[7]־נָא אֶל־הַצֹּאן וְקַח־לִי מִשָּׁם שְׁנֵי גְּדָיֵי עִזִּים טֹבִים וְאֶעֱשֶׂה אֹתָם

מַטְעַמִּים לְאָבִיךָ כַּאֲשֶׁר אָהֵב׃

1 Kings 1:4 וְהַנַּעֲרָה יָפָה עַד־מְאֹד וַתְּהִי לַמֶּלֶךְ סֹכֶנֶת וַתְּשָׁרְתֵהוּ וְהַמֶּלֶךְ לֹא יְדָעָהּ׃

Notice the importance of carefully observing these distinctions so that you do not miss the nuance of passages such as these.

---

[7] This is an imperative form that you would expect to be לֵךְ. What root letter is not evident in the form?

כו (26) Middle-Weak Verbs

26.1 The Consonants ו and י

Similar to ה and א, the consonants ו and י are weak. When they represent the middle letter of a Hebrew root, they often are not evident in the conjugated forms of the verb.[1] These roots are variously called *middle-weak*, *hollow*, *middle-*ו and *middle-*י, and II-ו and II-י.

The absence of these letters leaves it unclear from the conjugated form alone whether the verbal root is listed in the lexica as middle-ו or middle-י. For common words, knowledge of vocabulary will resolve this ambiguity, but for less common words you may be required to check both possible roots in a lexicon (middle-ו and middle-י) to determine which is the correct root.

Middle-weak verbs have three different vowel classes: *u*-class (e.g.: קוּם), *i*-class (e.g.: שִׂים), and *o*-class (e.g.: בּוֹא).

26.2 Middle-Weak Qal Perfects

The perfect forms of middle-weak verbs use the same suffix endings as all other perfect forms, endings learned with the Qal perfect paradigm (see 3.2). The weak middle root letter, however, disappears, leaving no obvious distinction between middle-ו and middle-י verbs in the perfect.

	Qal Perfect קטל	Qal Perfect קום	Qal Perfect שׂים	Qal Perfect בוא
3ms	קָטַל	קָם	שָׂם	בָּא
3fs	קָֽטְלָה	קָ֫מָה	שָׂ֫מָה	בָּ֫אָה
2ms	קָטַ֫לְתָּ	קַ֫מְתָּ	שַׂ֫מְתָּ	בָּ֫אתָ
2fs	קָטַלְתְּ	קַמְתְּ	שַׂמְתְּ	בָּאת
1cs	קָטַ֫לְתִּי	קַ֫מְתִּי	שַׂ֫מְתִּי	בָּ֫אתִי

[1] It is not clear that the *waw* and *yod* are true root letters, since these roots are likely biconsonantal—originating from two letter roots. Nonetheless, they are listed in the lexica with three letter roots (see 26.5).

3cp	קָֽטְלוּ	קָ֫מוּ	שָׂ֫מוּ	בָּ֫נוּ
2mp	קְטַלְתֶּם	קַמְתֶּם	שַׂמְתֶּם	בָּאתֶם
2fp	קְטַלְתֶּן	קַמְתֶּן	שַׂמְתֶּן	בָּאתֶן
1cp	קָטַ֫לְנוּ	קַ֫מְנוּ	שַׂ֫מְנוּ	בָּ֫אנוּ

The Qal perfect paradigm for קום must be memorized.

Notes:

- The typical form of the middle-weak perfect has a *qameṣ* for the first vowel of all third-person forms and a *pataḥ* for the first vowel of all second- and first-person forms. בוא, on the other hand, has a lengthened vowel in the first syllable of all forms because it is doubly weak, being both middle-ו and III-א. Similarly, the *dagesh lene* of the *taw* suffix is lost in the forms of בוא, as is typical of a III-א verb.
- The 3cp form of a middle-weak perfect is stressed on the first syllable. This enables the reader to distinguish it from a III-ה verb, in which the 3cp form is stressed on the final syllable. קָ֫מוּ is therefore a middle-weak form (from קום), while רָאוּ is a III-ה verb (from ראה).
- Middle-weak stative verbs will often show a different first vowel in the third-person forms:

מֵת	Qal Perf. 3ms of מות, glossed as "to die,"
טֹ֫בוּ	Qal Perf. 3cp of טוב, glossed as "to be good"

וְהִנֵּ֛ה קָ֥מָה אֲלֻמָּתִ֖י וְגַם־נִצָּ֑בָה	("And see, my sheaf arose and stood."—Gen. 37:7)
וְקַמְתִּ֣י עֲלֵיהֶ֔ם נְאֻ֖ם יְהוָ֣ה צְבָא֑וֹת	("'And I will rise up against them,' an oracle of the Lord of hosts."—Isa. 14:22)
וְאֶכְתֹּב֙ עַל־הַלֻּחֹ֔ת אֶת־הַדְּבָרִ֔ים אֲשֶׁ֥ר הָי֛וּ עַל־הַלֻּחֹ֥ת הָרִאשֹׁנִ֖ים אֲשֶׁ֣ר שִׁבַּ֑רְתָּ וְשַׂמְתָּ֖ם בָּאָרֽוֹן׃	("And I will write upon the tablets the words which were on the first tablets that you smashed, and you shall place them in the ark."—Deut. 10:2)
שָׂ֣מוּ שִׁקּֽוּצֵיהֶ֗ם בַּבַּ֛יִת אֲשֶׁר־נִקְרָא־שְׁמִ֥י עָלָ֖יו לְטַמְּאֽוֹ	("They have placed their vile things in the house which is called by my name to defile it."—Jer. 7:30)

וְעֵשָׂו אָחִיו בָּא מִצֵּידוֹ ("And Esau his brother came in from his hunting."—Gen. 27:30)

וְאַחַר בָּאוּ מֹשֶׁה וְאַהֲרֹן ("And afterwards Moses and Aaron went."—Ex. 5:1)

26.3 Middle-Weak Qal Imperfects

While the middle-weak perfect paradigm (above) shows no difference between middle-ו and middle-י forms, in the imperfect paradigm three different vowel patterns are evident.

	Qal Imperfect קטל	Qal Imperfect קום	Qal Imperfect שׂים	Qal Imperfect בוא
3ms	יִקְטֹל	יָקוּם	יָשִׂים	יָבוֹא
3fs	תִּקְטֹל	תָּקוּם	תָּשִׂים	תָּבוֹא
2ms	תִּקְטֹל	תָּקוּם	תָּשִׂים	תָּבוֹא
2fs	תִּקְטְלִי	תָּקוּמִי	תָּשִׂימִי	תָּבוֹאִי
1cs	אֶקְטֹל	אָקוּם	אָשִׂים	אָבוֹא
3mp	יִקְטְלוּ	יָקוּמוּ	יָשִׂימוּ	יָבוֹאוּ
3fp	תִּקְטֹלְנָה	תְּקוּמֶינָה	תְּשִׂימֶינָה	תְּבֹאֶינָה
2mp	תִּקְטְלוּ	תָּקוּמוּ	תָּשִׂימוּ	תָּבוֹאוּ
2fp	תִּקְטֹלְנָה	תְּקוּמֶינָה	תְּשִׂימֶינָה	תְּבֹאֶינָה
1cp	נִקְטֹל	נָקוּם	נָשִׂים	נָבוֹא

The Qal imperfect paradigm for קום must be memorized.

Notes:

- The vowel on the prefix letter is typically *qameṣ* in all forms except 3fp and 2fp, where it reduces to *shewa.* Other prefix vowels can occur, such as *ṣere*, but these are more rare.
- Though these three vowel classes are distinct, there is crossover between the types. A form such as יָשׂוּם can occur, even though the expected form would be יָשִׂים.
- The form תְּבֹאֶינָה (3fp/2fp imperfect of בוא) also occurs as תָּבוֹאנָה.

כִּי־יָקוּם בְּקִרְבְּךָ נָבִיא אוֹ חֹלֵם חֲלוֹם ("If a prophet or a dreamer of dreams arises in your midst"—Deut. 13:2)

יָשִׂים שָׂרֵי אֲלָפִים וְשָׂרֵי מֵאוֹת ("Will he make you commanders of thousands and commanders of hundreds?"—1 Sam. 22:7)

אַל־תִּירָא מֵרְדָה מִצְרַיְמָה כִּי־לְגוֹי גָּדוֹל אֲשִׂימְךָ שָׁם ("Do not be afraid to go down to Egypt, for I will make you a great nation there."—Gen. 46:3)

מִי אַתֶּם וּמֵאַיִן תָּבֹאוּ ("Who are you, and from where do you come?"—Josh. 9:8)

26.4 Middle-Weak Qal Participles

The Qal participle of middle-weak roots does not have the typical *ḥolem* vowel that marks almost all Qal participles (e.g.: קֹטֵל).

	Qal Participle קטל	Qal Participle קום
ms	קֹטֵל	קָם
fs	קֹטֶ֫לֶת	קָמָה
mp	קֹטְלִים	קָמִים
fp	קֹטְלוֹת	קָמוֹת

The Qal participle paradigm for קום must be memorized.

Notes:

- For middle-weak verbs, the Qal participle ms is identical to the Qal perfect 3ms. Context is required to distinguish between these forms.
- For middle-weak verbs, the Qal participle fs differs from the Qal perfect 3fs only in the placement of the accent. The fs participle is accented on the final syllable (שָׂמָה); the 3fs perfect is accented on the first syllable (שָׂ֫מָה).

כִּי־בֵן מְנַבֵּל אָב בַּת קָמָה בְאִמָּהּ ("For a son treats his father as a fool; a daughter rises up against her mother"—Mic. 7:6)

הוֹי הָאֹמְרִים לָרַע טוֹב וְלַטּוֹב רָע שָׂמִים חֹשֶׁךְ לְאוֹר וְאוֹר לְחֹשֶׁךְ שָׂמִים מַר לְמָתוֹק וּמָתוֹק לְמָר׃ ("Woe to the ones who speak good for evil and evil for good, and to the ones who place darkness for light and light for darkness, and to the ones who place bitter for sweet and sweet for bitter."—Isa. 5:20)

וְהִנֵּה עֵשָׂו בָּא וְעִמּוֹ אַרְבַּע מֵאוֹת אִישׁ ("And there was Esau, coming with four hundred men."—Gen. 33:1)

26.5 Other Middle-Weak Qal Forms

The infinitive construct of middle-weak verbs evidences its vowel class:

קוּם	Qal Inf. Const. of קום
דִּין	Qal Inf. Const. of דין
בּוֹא	Qal Inf. Const. of בוא

For this reason, the lexical forms of middle-weak verbs are the infinitive construct forms, not the 3ms perfect forms.[2]

וְלֹא־יָדַע בְּשִׁכְבָהּ וּבְקֻמָהּ ("And he did not know when she lay down or when she got up."—Gen. 19:35)

וְעֹמֵד לָדִין עַמִּים ("He stands to judge the peoples."—Isa. 3:13)

אוֹ הֲנִסָּה אֱלֹהִים לָבוֹא לָקַחַת לוֹ גוֹי מִקֶּרֶב גּוֹי ("Or has any god attempted to come to take for himself a nation from the midst of another nation?"—Deut. 4:34)

[2] As with most elements of language, this is not a hard-and-fast rule. For example, the infinitive construct of שׂים is typically written as שׂוּם.

The Qal infinitive absolute forms all contain the characteristic *ḥolem* vowel:

קוֹם Qal Inf. Abs. of קום

שׂוֹם Qal Inf. Abs. of שׂים

בּוֹא Qal Inf. Abs. of בוא

לְמַ֣עַן תֵּֽדְע֔וּ כִּ֗י ק֨וֹם יָק֧וּמוּ דְבָרַ֛י עֲלֵיכֶ֖ם לְרָעָֽה ("so that you may know that my words are certainly against you for evil"—Jer. 44:29)

שׂ֣וֹם תָּשִׂ֤ים עָלֶ֙יךָ֙ מֶ֔לֶךְ אֲשֶׁ֥ר יִבְחַ֛ר יְהוָ֥ה אֱלֹהֶ֖יךָ בּ֑וֹ ("You certainly may set a king whom the LORD your God will choose over yourself."—Deut. 17:15)

הֲב֣וֹא נָב֗וֹא אֲנִי֙ וְאִמְּךָ֣ וְאַחֶ֔יךָ לְהִשְׁתַּחֲוֺ֥ת לְךָ֖ אָֽרְצָה ("Will I and your mother and your brothers really come to bow down to the ground before you?"—Gen. 37:10)

The Qal narrative forms of middle-weak verbs show a retraction of the accent to the penultimate syllable:

וַיָּ֕קָם וַיֵּ֛לֶךְ אֶל־אֲרַ֥ם נַהֲרַ֖יִם אֶל־עִ֥יר נָחֽוֹר ("And he arose and went to Mesopotamia, to the city of Nahor."—Gen. 24:10)

וַיֹּ֣אכַל וַיֵּ֔שְׁתְּ וַיָּ֖קָם וַיֵּלַ֑ךְ וַיִּ֥בֶז עֵשָׂ֖ו אֶת־הַבְּכֹרָֽה ("And he ate and drank and rose up and left. And Esau despised his birthright."—Gen. 25:34)

וַיִּטַּ֞ע יְהוָ֧ה אֱלֹהִ֛ים גַּן־בְּעֵ֖דֶן מִקֶּ֑דֶם וַיָּ֣שֶׂם שָׁ֔ם אֶת־הָֽאָדָ֖ם אֲשֶׁ֥ר יָצָֽר׃ ("And the LORD God planted a garden in the east, in Eden, and there he placed the man he had formed."—Gen. 2:8)

וָאָב֨וֹא אֶל־הַגּוֹלָ֜ה תֵּ֣ל אָ֠בִיב הַיֹּשְׁבִ֤ים אֶֽל־נְהַר־כְּבָר֙ ("And I came to the exiles at Tel-Abib who were dwelling by the Chebar canal."—Ezek. 3:15)

The Qal imperative forms of middle-weak roots are formed normally:

וַיֹּאמֶר אֵלֶיהָ קוּמִי וְנֵלֵכָה וְאֵין עֹנֶה ("And he said to her, 'Get up so that we may go,' but there was no answer."—Judg. 19:28)

וַיֹּאמֶר יְהוָה אֶל־מֹשֶׁה עֲשֵׂה לְךָ שָׂרָף וְשִׂים אֹתוֹ עַל־נֵס ("And the LORD said to Moses, 'Make a snake for yourself, and place it on a pole.'"—Num. 3:8)

וַיֹּאמֶר יֵהוּא לָרָצִים וְלַשָּׁלִשִׁים בֹּאוּ הַכּוּם ("And Jehu said to the guards and officers, 'Go, strike them down.'"—2 Kings 10:25)

26.6 Middle-Weak Verbs in the Derived Stems

Middle-weak roots are rare in the Piel/Pual/Hithpael stems. Middle-weak roots do, however, commonly occur in the Hiphil and Hophal.

The Hiphil perfect of middle-weak roots is characterized by the typical *ḥireq yod* vowel of the Hiphil and by the addition of a *ḥolem waw* before any suffix that begins with a consonant. As in the Qal perfect of middle-weak roots, there is no difference in vowel pattern between middle-ו and middle-י verbs.

	Hiphil Perfect קטל	Hiphil Perfect קום
3ms	הִקְטִיל	הֵקִים
3fs	הִקְטִילָה	הֵקִימָה
2ms	הִקְטַלְתָּ	הֲקִימוֹתָ
2fs	הִקְטַלְתְּ	הֲקִימוֹת
1cs	הִקְטַלְתִּי	הֲקִימוֹתִי
3cp	הִקְטִילוּ	הֵקִימוּ
2mp	הִקְטַלְתֶּם	הֲקִימוֹתֶם
2fp	הִקְטַלְתֶּן	הֲקִימוֹתֶן
1cp	הִקְטַלְנוּ	הֲקִימוֹנוּ

Notes:

- The Hiphil's *ḥireq* prefix vowel lengthens to *ṣere* in the third-person forms, which reduces to a *ḥatep̄-pataḥ* in the first- and second-person forms.
- Adding the *ḥolem waw* before the consonantal suffix letters causes the *taw* to spirantize and lose its *dagesh lene*.
- Particularly with a III-א verb such as בוא, the *ḥolem waw* may not be present, e.g.: הֲבֵאתֶם and הֲבִיאוֹתֶם, which are both Hiphil perfect 2mp of בוא.

וַהֲקִמֹתִי אֶת־בְּרִיתִי בֵּינִי וּבֵינֶךָ וּבֵין זַרְעֲךָ אַחֲרֶיךָ ("And I will establish my covenant between myself and you and your descendants after you."—Gen. 17:7)

וַיִּקַּח דָּוִד מִיָּדָהּ אֵת אֲשֶׁר־הֵבִיאָה לוֹ ("And David received from her what she had brought to him."—1 Sam. 25:35)

In the Hiphil imperfect, all three vowel classes of middle-weak roots show the Hiphil's characteristic *ḥireq yod* vowel.

	Hiphil Imperfect קטל	Hiphil Imperfect קום	Hiphil Imperfect שׂים
3ms	יַקְטִיל	יָקִים	יָשִׂים
3fs	תַּקְטִיל	תָּקִים	תָּשִׂים
2ms	תַּקְטִיל	תָּקִים	תָּשִׂים
2fs	תַּקְטִילִי	תָּקִימִי	תָּשִׂימִי
1cs	אַקְטִיל	אָקִים	אָשִׂים
3mp	יַקְטִילוּ	יָקִימוּ	יָשִׂימוּ
3fp	תַּקְטֵלְנָה	תְּקִימֶינָה	תְּשִׂימֶינָה
2mp	תַּקְטִילוּ	תָּקִימוּ	תָּשִׂימוּ
2fp	תַּקְטֵלְנָה	תְּקִימֶינָה	תְּשִׂימֶינָה
1cp	נַקְטִיל	נָקִים	נָשִׂים

The only difference between the Qal imperfect and the Hiphil imperfect forms of middle-weak roots is the theme vowel (*ḥireq yod*, *ḥolem waw*, or *shureq* in the Qal and *ḥireq yod* in the Hiphil). For middle-weak roots with a *ḥireq yod* theme vowel in the Qal, the Qal and Hiphil imperfect forms will often be identical. Context will distinguish these forms.

וּבַחֲנֹת הַמִּשְׁכָּן יָקִימוּ אֹתוֹ הַלְוִיִּם ("And when the Tabernacle is to be pitched, the Levites shall raise it."—Num. 1:51)

וְהָיָה כָּל־הַדָּבָר הַגָּדֹל יָבִיאוּ אֵלֶיךָ וְכָל־הַדָּבָר הַקָּטֹן יִשְׁפְּטוּ־הֵם ("Let them bring every great matter to you, and let them judge for themselves every small matter."—Ex. 18:20)

The Hiphil imperative, infinitive construct, infinitive absolute, and participle are formed as expected. The typical *pataḥ* of these forms is lengthened to *qameṣ*.

	קטל	קום
Hiph. Imperative ms	הַקְטֵל	הָקֵם
Hiph. Inf. Const.	הַקְטִיל	הָקִים
Hiph. Inf. Abs.	הַקְטֵל	הָקֵם
Hiph. Part. ms	מַקְטִיל	מֵקִים

הָקֵם לְעַבְדְּךָ אִמְרָתֶךָ ("Confirm your word to your servant."—Ps. 119:38)

אֶרֶץ־כְּנַעַן אֲשֶׁר אֲנִי מֵבִיא אֶתְכֶם שָׁמָּה ("the land of Canaan, where I am bringing you."—Lev. 18:3)

The Hophal forms of middle-weak roots show a consistent *shureq* vowel in the perfect, imperfect, and participle:

	Hophal Perfect קוּם
3ms	הוּקַם
3fs	הוּקְמָה
2ms	הוּקַ֫מְתָּ
2fs	הוּקַמְתְּ
1cs	הוּקַ֫מְתִּי
3cp	הוּקְמוּ
2mp	הוּקַמְתֶּם
2fp	הוּקַמְתֶּן
1cp	הוּקַ֫מְנוּ

	Hophal Imperfect קוּם
3ms	יוּקַם
3fs	תּוּקַם
2ms	תּוּקַם
2fs	תּוּקְמִי
1cs	אוּקַם
3mp	יוּקְמוּ
3fp	תּוּקַ֫מְנָה
2mp	תּוּקְמוּ
2fp	תּוּקַ֫מְנָה
1cp	נוּקַם

	Hophal Participle קוּם
ms	מוּקָם
fs	מוּקֶ֫מֶת
mp	מוּקָמִים
fp	מוּקָמוֹת

וַיְהִ֞י בַּחֹ֧דֶשׁ הָרִאשׁ֛וֹן בַּשָּׁנָ֥ה הַשֵּׁנִ֖ית בְּאֶחָ֣ד לַחֹ֑דֶשׁ הוּקַ֖ם הַמִּשְׁכָּֽן׃

("In the first month, in the second year, on the first day of the month, the Tabernacle was set up."—Ex. 40:17)

בָּבֶ֥לָה יוּבָ֖אוּ וְשָׁ֣מָּה יִהְי֑וּ עַ֣ד י֧וֹם פָּקְדִ֣י אֹתָ֗ם

"They will be brought to Babylon and they will be there until the day I visit them."—Jer. 27:22)

וְנָֽתְנוּ־שָׁ֜מָּה הַכֹּהֲנִים֙ שֹׁמְרֵ֣י הַסַּ֔ף אֶֽת־כָּל־הַכֶּ֖סֶף הַמּוּבָ֥א בֵית־יְהוָֽה

("And the priests who guarded the entrance put all the money which was brought to the house of the LORD there."—2 Kings 12:10)

26.7 Identifying "Missing" Root Letters

Building on 24.5, if removing the suffix and prefix letters of a given form results in only two evident root letters, there are now four possible causes:

Possible Sources of "Missing" Root Letters
• The verbal root begins with *nun* • The irregular verb לקח or הלך • The verbal root ends with *heh* • The verbal root is middle-weak

Your knowledge of both memory paradigms and vocabulary will help distinguish between these possibilities. If the requisite entry does not exist in the lexicon, you should reconsider and try other options.

26.8 Vocabulary

בּוֹשׁ	to be ashamed
הֱבִישׁ	(Hiph.) to shame, put to shame; be ashamed
בִּין	to understand; perceive, consider
בֹּ֫שֶׁת	shame, shamefulness
הֵכִין	(Hiph.) to prepare, establish, make ready
נָכוֹנָה	(Niph.) to be established, steadfast, sure
מוּת	to die
הֵמִית	(Hiph.) to kill
נוּחַ	to rest
הֵנִיחַ	(Hiph.–A form) to cause to rest, pacify
הִנִּיחַ	(Hiph.–B form) to place, set, lay; to leave
סוּר	to turn aside, go off, retreat
הֵסִיר	(Hiph.) to remove
קוּם	to rise, get up, stand up
הֵקִים	(Hiph.) to set up, erect
רוּץ	to run
שׁוּב	to turn, return
הֵשִׁיב	(Hiph.) to bring or lead back; to repay
שִׂים	to set up, place, lay, establish

26.9 Language Exercises

A. Parse and gloss the following forms. Include the identification of the object suffix where appropriate.

תִּרְאוּ

סָ֫רָה

רָצוּ

רָ֫צוּ

תָּקֻ֫מוּ

יָסִיר

שַׁ֫בְנוּ

יָסֻר

וַיָּ֫קָם

שַׂמְתְּ

יָסוּר

ק֫וּמִי

וַיּוּשַׂם

תָּרִיץ

מֵשִׂים

B. Translate the following and parse each verb and participle. Use your lexicon to look up the glosses for any words you do not know from your vocabulary.

Gen. 43:1–3

וְהָרָעָב כָּבֵד בָּאָרֶץ׃ וַיְהִי כַּאֲשֶׁר כִּלּוּ לֶאֱכֹל אֶת־הַשֶּׁבֶר אֲשֶׁר הֵבִיאוּ

מִמִּצְרָיִם וַיֹּאמֶר אֲלֵיהֶם אֲבִיהֶם שֻׁבוּ שִׁבְרוּ־לָנוּ מְעַט־אֹכֶל׃ וַיֹּאמֶר אֵלָיו

יְהוּדָה לֵאמֹר הָעֵד הֵעִד בָּנוּ הָאִישׁ לֵאמֹר לֹא־תִרְאוּ פָנַי בִּלְתִּי אֲחִיכֶם

אִתְּכֶם׃

Ex. 20:18–21

וְכָל־הָעָם רֹאִים אֶת־הַקּוֹלֹת וְאֶת־הַלַּפִּידִם וְאֵת קוֹל הַשֹּׁפָר וְאֶת־הָהָר

עָשֵׁן וַיַּרְא הָעָם וַיָּנֻעוּ וַיַּעַמְדוּ מֵרָחֹק׃ וַיֹּאמְרוּ אֶל־מֹשֶׁה דַּבֵּר־אַתָּה עִמָּנוּ

וְנִשְׁמָעָה וְאַל־יְדַבֵּר עִמָּנוּ אֱלֹהִים פֶּן־נָמוּת׃ וַיֹּאמֶר מֹשֶׁה אֶל־הָעָם אַל־

תִּירָאוּ[3] כִּי לְבַעֲבוּר נַסּוֹת אֶתְכֶם בָּא הָאֱלֹהִים וּבַעֲבוּר תִּהְיֶה יִרְאָתוֹ

[3] Qal Juss. 2mp of ירא, glossed as “to fear” (see ch. 27).

עַל־פְּנֵיכֶם לְבִלְתִּי תֶחֱטָאוּ׃ וַיַּעֲמֹד הָעָם מֵרָחֹק וּמֹשֶׁה נִגַּשׁ אֶל־הָעֲרָפֶל

אֲשֶׁר־שָׁם הָאֱלֹהִים׃

וַיֹּאמֶר עוֹד אֱלֹהִים אֶל־מֹשֶׁה כֹּה־תֹאמַר אֶל־בְּנֵי יִשְׂרָאֵל יְהוָה אֱלֹהֵי Ex. 3:15–22

אֲבֹתֵיכֶם אֱלֹהֵי אַבְרָהָם אֱלֹהֵי יִצְחָק וֵאלֹהֵי יַעֲקֹב שְׁלָחַנִי אֲלֵיכֶם זֶה־

שְּׁמִי לְעֹלָם וְזֶה זִכְרִי לְדֹר דֹּר׃ לֵךְ וְאָסַפְתָּ אֶת־זִקְנֵי יִשְׂרָאֵל וְאָמַרְתָּ

אֲלֵהֶם יְהוָה אֱלֹהֵי אֲבֹתֵיכֶם נִרְאָה אֵלַי אֱלֹהֵי אַבְרָהָם יִצְחָק וְיַעֲקֹב

לֵאמֹר פָּקֹד פָּקַדְתִּי אֶתְכֶם וְאֶת־הֶעָשׂוּי לָכֶם בְּמִצְרָיִם׃ וָאֹמַר אַעֲלֶה

אֶתְכֶם מֵעֳנִי מִצְרַיִם אֶל־אֶרֶץ הַכְּנַעֲנִי וְהַחִתִּי וְהָאֱמֹרִי וְהַפְּרִזִּי וְהַחִוִּי

וְהַיְבוּסִי אֶל־אֶרֶץ זָבַת חָלָב וּדְבָשׁ׃ וְשָׁמְעוּ לְקֹלֶךָ וּבָאתָ אַתָּה וְזִקְנֵי

יִשְׂרָאֵ֜ל אֶל־מֶ֣לֶךְ מִצְרַ֗יִם וַאֲמַרְתֶּ֤ם אֵלָיו֙ יְהוָ֞ה אֱלֹהֵ֤י הָֽעִבְרִיִּים֙ נִקְרָ֣ה

עָלֵ֔ינוּ וְעַתָּ֗ה נֵֽלֲכָה־נָּ֞א דֶּ֣רֶךְ שְׁלֹ֤שֶׁת יָמִים֙ בַּמִּדְבָּ֔ר וְנִזְבְּחָ֖ה לַיהוָ֥ה

אֱלֹהֵֽינוּ׃ וַאֲנִ֣י יָדַ֔עְתִּי כִּ֠י לֹֽא־יִתֵּ֥ן אֶתְכֶ֛ם מֶ֥לֶךְ מִצְרַ֖יִם לַהֲלֹ֑ךְ וְלֹ֖א בְּיָ֥ד

חֲזָקָֽה׃ וְשָׁלַחְתִּ֤י אֶת־יָדִי֙ וְהִכֵּיתִ֣י אֶת־מִצְרַ֔יִם בְּכֹל֙ נִפְלְאֹתַ֔י אֲשֶׁ֥ר אֶֽעֱשֶׂ֖ה

בְּקִרְבּ֑וֹ וְאַחֲרֵי־כֵ֖ן יְשַׁלַּ֥ח אֶתְכֶֽם׃ וְנָתַתִּ֛י אֶת־חֵ֥ן הָֽעָם־הַזֶּ֖ה בְּעֵינֵ֣י מִצְרָ֑יִם

וְהָיָה֙ כִּ֣י תֵֽלֵכ֔וּן לֹ֥א תֵלְכ֖וּ רֵיקָֽם׃ וְשָׁאֲלָ֨ה אִשָּׁ֤ה מִשְּׁכֶנְתָּהּ֙ וּמִגָּרַ֣ת בֵּיתָ֔הּ

כְּלֵי־כֶ֛סֶף וּכְלֵ֥י זָהָ֖ב וּשְׂמָלֹ֑ת וְשַׂמְתֶּ֗ם עַל־בְּנֵיכֶם֙ וְעַל־בְּנֹ֣תֵיכֶ֔ם וְנִצַּלְתֶּ֖ם

אֶת־מִצְרָֽיִם׃

26.10 Exegetical Exercises—Hebrew Poetry

Section 10.10.A discussed the **bicolon**—the most common form of a line of Hebrew poetry. A typical line has an "A colon" and a "B colon." This division is usually marked by the Masoretic accentual system (see 11.8), but that system is different for three books known as "the three": Job, Psalms, and Proverbs.

Two prose clauses placed one after the other, however, do not make a line of poetry. Hebrew poetry is also terse, and it shows relaxed syntactic constraints. These features show up in several common ways.

A. Hebrew poetry tends to omit particles such as the definite direct object marker, definite article, prepositions, etc.:

יְהוָ֗ה בְּחָכְמָ֥ה יָֽסַד־אָ֑רֶץ כּוֹנֵ֥ן שָׁ֝מַ֗יִם בִּתְבוּנָֽה׃ ("The Lord founded [the] earth by wisdom; he established [the] heavens by understanding."—Prov. 3:19)

בֹּ֥זּוּ כֶ֛סֶף בֹּ֖זּוּ זָהָ֑ב ("Plunder [the] silver; plunder [the] gold."—Nah. 2:10a)

B. A word in one colon often does double duty and must be included in the translation of the other colon. This feature is called **gapping**. It is most common with verbs, but it can also occur with other words.

הָיְתָ֣ה יְהוּדָ֣ה לְקָדְשׁ֑וֹ יִ֝שְׂרָאֵ֗ל מַמְשְׁלוֹתָֽיו׃ ("Judah became his sanctuary, Israel [became] his dominion"—Ps. 114:2)

כִּ֤י ט֣וֹב סַ֭חְרָהּ מִסְּחַר־כָּ֑סֶף וּ֝מֵחָר֗וּץ תְּבוּאָתָֽהּ׃ ("Indeed her profit is better than a profit of silver and her yield [is better] than gold."—Prov. 3:14)

C. Singular construct forms occasionally add a *ḥireq*. Do not confuse this "linking *ḥireq*" with a 1cs possessive suffix.[4]

בְּנִ֣י אֲתֹנ֑וֹ ("the colt of a donkey"—Gen. 49:11)

דִּ֝בְרָתִ֗י מַלְכִּי־צֶֽדֶק ("the order of Melchizedek"—Ps. 110:4)

[4] Though this feature is rare, it can confuse the beginning student!

Translate the following lines of Hebrew poetry.

Ps. 3:3 רַבִּים֮ אֹמְרִ֪ים לְנַ֫פְשִׁ֥י

[Engl. 3:2]

אֵ֤ין יְֽשׁוּעָ֓תָה לּ֬וֹ בֵֽאלֹהִ֬ים

Mic. 6:2a שִׁמְע֤וּ הָרִים֙ אֶת־רִ֣יב יְהוָ֔ה

וְהָאֵתָנִ֖ים מֹ֣סְדֵי אָ֑רֶץ

Isa. 60:1 ק֥וּמִי א֖וֹרִי כִּ֣י בָ֣א אוֹרֵ֑ךְ

וּכְב֥וֹד יְהוָ֖ה עָלַ֥יִךְ זָרָֽח׃

Job 28:12 וְ֭הַֽחָכְמָה מֵאַ֣יִן תִּמָּצֵ֑א

וְאֵ֥י זֶ֝֗ה מְק֣וֹם בִּינָֽה׃

Prov. 9:5 לְ֭כוּ לַחֲמ֣וּ בְלַחֲמִ֑י

וּ֝שְׁת֗וּ בְּיַ֣יִן מָסָֽכְתִּי׃

כז (27) I-י Verbs

27.1 י as the First Root Letter

When the weak consonant י is the first letter of a verbal root, the suffixal forms such as the Qal perfect show no change. But when a prefix is added to the verbal root, changes occur. These changes can be understood by recognizing that I-י verbs historically come from two different sources.

Most I-י verbs were in fact historically not I-י but I-ו. At a later stage in the development of Hebrew, these original I-ו verbs were converted to I-י. For example, Arabic *walad* is the cognate for Hebrew יָלַד because Hebrew יָלַד was originally וָלַד. For original I-ו verbs, adding a verbal prefix often causes the original consonant ו to return.

Only seven or eight I-י verbs were originally I-י. These include יטב, יקץ, ינק, ילל, ימן, ישׁר, יבשׁ, and possibly ירשׁ.

27.2 I-י Perfect Forms

In the Qal and Piel/Pual perfect forms, the י is word-initial, so it shows no change. For example, the Qal perfect of ישׁב ("to sit, to dwell") matches the Qal perfect paradigm from 3.2.

	Qal Perfect קטל	Qal Perfect ישׁב
3ms	קָטַל	יָשַׁב
3fs	קָטְלָה	יָשְׁבָה
2ms	קָטַ֫לְתָּ	יָשַׁ֫בְתָּ
2fs	קָטַלְתְּ	יָשַׁבְתְּ
1cs	קָטַ֫לְתִּי	יָשַׁ֫בְתִּי
3cp	קָטְלוּ	יָשְׁבוּ
2mp	קְטַלְתֶּם	יְשַׁבְתֶּם
2fp	קְטַלְתֶּן	יְשַׁבְתֶּן
1cp	קָטַ֫לְנוּ	יָשַׁ֫בְנוּ

On the other hand, in the Niphal and Hiphil/Hophal perfect, adding the prefixed letter before the first root letter causes the י to change back to the original ו.

	Niphal Perfect ישׁב	Hiphil Perfect ישׁב	Hophal Perfect ישׁב
3ms	נוֹשַׁב	הוֹשִׁיב	הוּשַׁב
3fs	נוֹשְׁבָה	הוֹשִׁיבָה	הוּשְׁבָה
2ms	נוֹשַׁבְתָּ	הוֹשַׁבְתָּ	הוּשַׁבְתָּ
2fs	נוֹשַׁבְתְּ	הוֹשַׁבְתְּ	הוּשַׁבְתְּ
1cs	נוֹשַׁבְתִּי	הוֹשַׁבְתִּי	הוּשַׁבְתִּי
3cp	נוֹשְׁבוּ	הוֹשִׁיבוּ	הוּשְׁבוּ
2mp	נוֹשַׁבְתֶּם	הוֹשַׁבְתֶּם	הוּשַׁבְתֶּם
2fp	נוֹשַׁבְתֶּן	הוֹשַׁבְתֶּן	הוּשַׁבְתֶּן
1cp	נוֹשַׁבְנוּ	הוֹשַׁבְנוּ	הוּשַׁבְנוּ

פֶּן־אֲשִׂימֵךְ שְׁמָמָה אֶרֶץ לוֹא נוֹשָׁבָה	("Lest I make you a desolation, a land not inhabited"—Jer. 6:8)
וְהוּשַׁבְתֶּם לְבַדְּכֶם בְּקֶרֶב הָאָרֶץ	("And you are made to dwell alone in the midst of the land"—Isa. 5:8)
וַיֹּאמֶר יְהוָה אֵלַי שָׁמַעְתִּי אֶת־קוֹל דִּבְרֵי הָעָם הַזֶּה אֲשֶׁר דִּבְּרוּ אֵלֶיךָ הֵיטִיבוּ כָּל־אֲשֶׁר דִּבֵּרוּ	("And the LORD said to me, 'I have heard the sound of the words of this people which they have spoken to you. All which they have spoken is right.'"—Deut. 5:28)

27.3 I-י Imperfect Forms

Imperfect forms of I-י verbs have a prefix from the verbal paradigm that interacts with the י of the root. Two forms of the imperfect occur in the Qal: one in which the י of the root assimilates into the prefix, and one in which it is retained.

	Qal Imperfect קטל	Qal Imperfect ישׁב	Qal Imperfect יטב
3ms	יִקְטֹל	יֵשֵׁב	יִיטַב
3fs	תִּקְטֹל	תֵּשֵׁב	תִּיטַב
2ms	תִּקְטֹל	תֵּשֵׁב	תִּיטַב
2fs	תִּקְטְלִי	תֵּשְׁבִי	תִּיטְבִי
1cs	אֶקְטֹל	אֵשֵׁב	אִיטַב
3mp	יִקְטְלוּ	יֵשְׁבוּ	יִיטְבוּ
3fp	תִּקְטֹלְנָה	תֵּשַׁבְנָה	תִּיטַבְנָה
2mp	תִּקְטְלוּ	תֵּשְׁבוּ	תִּיטְבוּ
2fp	תִּקְטֹלְנָה	תֵּשַׁבְנָה	תִּיטַבְנָה
1cp	נִקְטֹל	נֵשֵׁב	נִיטַב

Notes:

- The typical *ḥireq* vowel of the imperfect prefix lengthens to a *ṣere* when the י of the root assimilates. When not reduced, the theme vowel is most often also *ṣere*, only occurring as *pataḥ* only in the 3fp and 2fp forms.
- The silent *shewa*—which usually occurs under the first root letter—typically does not occur in the Qal imperfect forms of I-י verbs that retain the י of the root. This is common because a silent *shewa* is frequently dropped when placed on a י (see 4.4).

בַּעֲב֗וּר תֵּשְׁבוּ֙ בְּאֶ֣רֶץ גֹּ֔שֶׁן ("in order that you may dwell in the land of Goshen"—Gen. 46:34)

וְהַֽנַּעֲרָ֗ה אֲשֶׁ֤ר תִּיטַב֙ בְּעֵינֵ֣י הַמֶּ֔לֶךְ תִּמְלֹ֖ךְ תַּ֣חַת וַשְׁתִּ֑י ("And may the young woman who is pleasing in the eyes of the king reign in the place of Vashti."—Esth. 2:4)

On the other hand, in the Niphal and Hiphil/Hophal imperfect, adding the prefix letter before the first root letter causes the י to change back to the original ו:

	Niphal Imperfect ישׁב	Hiphil Imperfect ישׁב	Hophal Imperfect ישׁב
3ms	יִוָּשֵׁב	יוֹשִׁיב	יוּשַׁב
3fs	תִּוָּשֵׁב	תּוֹשִׁיב	תּוּשַׁב
2ms	תִּוָּשֵׁב	תּוֹשִׁיב	תּוּשַׁב
2fs	תִּוָּשְׁבִי	תּוֹשִׁ֫יבִי	תּוּשְׁבִי
1cs	אִוָּשֵׁב	אוֹשִׁיב	אוּשַׁב
3mp	יִוָּשְׁבוּ	יוֹשִׁ֫יבוּ	יוּשְׁבוּ
3fp	תִּוָּשַׁ֫בְנָה	תּוֹשֵׁ֫בְנָה	תּוּשַׁ֫בְנָה
2mp	תִּוָּשְׁבוּ	תּוֹשִׁ֫יבוּ	תּוּשְׁבוּ
2fp	תִּוָּשַׁ֫בְנָה	תּוֹשֵׁ֫בְנָה	תּוּשַׁ֫בְנָה
1cp	נִוָּשֵׁב	נוֹשִׁיב	נוּשַׁב

Notes:

- The ו in the Niphal forms is a consonant, not a vowel, which can be seen in its taking a vowel pointing of its own. The *dagesh* in the ו is a *dagesh forte* due to the assimilation of the נ of the Niphal.
- The Niphal imperfect evidences the same *ṣere* vowel as the Qal imperfect of I-י verbs. The Hiphil and Hophal take the more standard theme vowel for each stem.

פֶּן־תִּוָּרֵשׁ אַתָּה וּבֵיתְךָ וְכָל־אֲשֶׁר־לָךְ	("lest you and your children and all who are yours be dispossessed."—Gen. 45:11)
כִּי־אַתָּה יְהוָה לְבָדָד לָבֶטַח תּוֹשִׁיבֵנִי	("for you alone, O LORD, make me dwell in security"—Ps. 4:9)
וְהָיָה הַטּוֹב הַהוּא אֲשֶׁר יֵיטִיב יְהוָה עִמָּנוּ וְהֵטַבְנוּ לָךְ	("And that good which the LORD will do for us, we will do for you."—Num. 10:32)

Piel/Pual/Hithpael I-י verbs form their imperfects normally, without any change of the י to ו, e.g.: יְיַסֵּר (Piel Imperf. 3ms of יסר, glossed as "to rebuke").

כָּל־עֵצְךָ וּפְרִי אַדְמָתֶךָ יְיָרֵשׁ הַצְּלָצַל׃ ("The locust will possess all your trees and the fruit of your soil."—Deut. 28:42)

The Qal imperfect of the common verb יכל ("to be able") has an irregular imperfect, appearing to follow a form similar to the Hophal imperfect:

	Qal Imperfect יכל
3ms	יוּכַל
3fs	תּוּכַל
2ms	תּוּכַל
2fs	תּוּכְלִי
1cs	אוּכַל
3mp	יוּכְלוּ
3fp	תּוּכַלְנָה*
2mp	תּוּכְלוּ
2fp	תּוּכַלְנָה*
1cp	נוּכַל

*This form is not Attested in Biblical Hebrew

וְכִסָּה אֶת־עֵין הָאָרֶץ וְלֹא יוּכַל לִרְאֹת אֶת־הָאָרֶץ ("And they will cover the land so that no one will be able to see the land."—Ex. 10:5)

וְנִלְחֲמוּ אֵלֶיךָ וְלֹא־יוּכְלוּ לָךְ כִּי־אִתְּךָ אֲנִי ("And they will fight against you, but they will not prevail over you, for I am with you."—Jer. 1:19)

וְאָנֹכִי לֹא אוּכַל לְהִמָּלֵט הָהָרָה ("But I am not able to flee to safety to the hills."—Gen. 19:19)

27.4 Other I-י Forms

I-י verbs form their Qal imperative, infinitive absolute, and participles normally:

רְשׁוּ Qal Imperative mp of ירשׁ, glossed as “to possess, dispossess”

יָשׁוֹב Qal Inf. Abs. of ישׁב, glossed as “to dwell”

יֹשְׁבוֹת Qal Act. Part. fp of ישׁב, glossed as “to dwell”

סְפוּ שָׁנָה עַל־שָׁנָה (“Add year upon year.”—Isa. 29:1)
וְאָנֹכִי יָשֹׁב־אֵשֵׁב עִם־הַמֶּלֶךְ לֶאֱכוֹל (“I certainly should sit with the king to eat.”—1 Sam. 20:5)

The Qal infinitive construct drops the initial י of the root and adds a ת. The vowel pattern of the I-י Qal infinitive construct is a double *segol*, and the stress is on the first syllable:

שֶׁבֶת Qal Inf. Const. of ישׁב, glossed as “to dwell”

עָרֶיךָ אֲשֶׁר יְהוָה אֱלֹהֶיךָ נֹתֵן לְךָ לָשֶׁבֶת שָׁם (“your cities, where the LORD your God is placing you to dwell”—Ps. 4:9)
אַתֶּם תִּירְשׁוּ אֶת־אַדְמָתָם וַאֲנִי אֶתְּנֶנָּה לָכֶם לָרֶשֶׁת אֹתָהּ (“You will possess their land, and I will give it to you to possess.”—Lev. 20:24)

Niphal and Hiphil/Hophal imperatives, infinitives (absolute and construct), and participles show the return of the original I-ו consonant, but they are otherwise formed normally:

הוֹשִׁיבוּ Hiph. Imperative mp of ישׁב, glossed as “to dwell”

הִוָּשֵׁב Niph. Inf. Const. or Abs. of ישׁב, glossed as “to dwell”

הוֹשֵׁב Hiph. Inf. Abs. of ישׁב, glossed as “to dwell”

נוֹשֶׁבֶת Niph. Part. fs of ישׁב, glossed as “to dwell”

מוּשָׁבִים Hoph. Part. mp of ישׁב, glossed as “to dwell”

קִרְאוּ־צ֑וֹם וְהוֹשִׁ֥יבוּ אֶת־נָב֖וֹת בְּרֹ֥אשׁ הָעָֽם	("Proclaim a fast and set Naboth at the head of the people."—1 Kings 21:9)
וּבְנֵ֣י יִשְׂרָאֵ֗ל אָֽכְלוּ֙ אֶת־הַמָּן֙ אַרְבָּעִ֣ים שָׁנָ֔ה עַד־בֹּאָ֖ם אֶל־אֶ֣רֶץ נוֹשָׁ֑בֶת	("And the people of Israel ate the manna for forty years, until they came to an inhabitable land."—Ex. 16:35)
הֵיטֵ֥ב אֵיטִ֖יב עִמָּ֑ךְ וְשַׂמְתִּ֤י אֶֽת־זַרְעֲךָ֙ כְּח֣וֹל הַיָּ֔ם אֲשֶׁ֥ר לֹא־יִסָּפֵ֖ר מֵרֹֽב	("I will certainly do good for you, and I will make your descendants like the sand of the sea, which cannot be counted for its abundance."—Gen. 32:13)

Piel/Pual/Hithpael imperatives, infinitives, and participles are formed normally, retaining the first consonant of the verbal root as a י:

מְיַסֵּר Piel Part. ms of יסר, glossed as "to rebuke"

27.5 Identifying "Missing" Root Letters

Building on 24.5 and 26.7, if the removal of suffix and prefix letters of a given form results in only two evident root letters, there are now five possible causes:

Possible Sources of "Missing" Root Letters
• The verbal root begins with *nun* • The irregular verb לקח or הלך • The verbal root ends with *heh* • The verbal root is middle-weak • In the imperfect, the verbal root may be I-י

Again, your knowledge of both memory paradigms and vocabulary will help you distinguish between these possibilities.

27.6 Vocabulary

יָדַע	to know (sometimes euphemistic for sex)
הוֹדִיעַ	(Hiph.) to make know, inform
דַּ֫עַת	knowledge
יָכֹל	to be able, capable of; succeed, prevail
יָלַד	to give birth, beget
יֶ֫לֶד	boy
יָסַף	to add; continue doing
הֹסִיף	(Hiph.) to add, increase, do again
יָצָא	to come/go out, set out
הוֹצִיא	(Hiph.) to bring out, lead out, cause to go out
יָרֵא	to fear, be afraid
יִרְאָה	fear
יָרֵא	(adj.) feared, fearful
יָרַד	to go down, descend
הוֹרִיד	(Hiph.) to bring down, cause to fall
יָרַשׁ	to take possession of; dispossess
יָשַׁב	to sit, sit down; to dwell, settle
יֹשֵׁב	inhabitant
נוֹתַר	(Niph.) to be left over
הוֹתִיר	(Hiph.) to leave over, be left over
הוֹשִׁיעַ	(Hiph.) to help, save, assist
נוֹשַׁע	(Niph.) to receive help

27.7 Language Exercises

A. Parse and gloss the following forms. Include the identification of the object suffix where appropriate.

יִוָּרֵשׁ

וַיִּיטְבוּ

וְהוֹרַדְתֶּם

יָשַׁ֫בְתָּ

רֵשׁ

הוּשַׁבְתֶּם

הַגִּיד

הוֹרַשְׁתֶּם

שֶׁ֫בֶת

יֵיטִיב

הוֹרִ֫ידוּ

יֵשְׁבוּ

רֶ֫שֶׁת

מוֹרִשָׁם

B. Translate the following and parse each verb and participle. Use your lexicon to look up the glosses for any words you do not know from your vocabulary.

Gen. 43:4–7

אִם־יֶשְׁךָ מְשַׁלֵּחַ אֶת־אָחִינוּ אִתָּנוּ נֵרְדָה וְנִשְׁבְּרָה לְךָ אֹכֶל׃ וְאִם־אֵינְךָ מְשַׁלֵּחַ

לֹא נֵרֵד כִּי־הָאִישׁ אָמַר אֵלֵינוּ לֹא־תִרְאוּ פָנַי בִּלְתִּי אֲחִיכֶם אִתְּכֶם׃ וַיֹּאמֶר

יִשְׂרָאֵל לָמָה הֲרֵעֹתֶם[1] לִי לְהַגִּיד לָאִישׁ הַעוֹד לָכֶם אָח׃ וַיֹּאמְרוּ שָׁאוֹל

שָׁאַל־הָאִישׁ לָנוּ וּלְמוֹלַדְתֵּנוּ לֵאמֹר הַעוֹד אֲבִיכֶם חַי הֲיֵשׁ לָכֶם אָח וַנַּגֶּד־לוֹ

עַל־פִּי הַדְּבָרִים הָאֵלֶּה הֲיָדוֹעַ נֵדַע כִּי יֹאמַר הוֹרִידוּ אֶת־אֲחִיכֶם׃

Judg. 3:12–14

וַיֹּסִפוּ בְּנֵי יִשְׂרָאֵל לַעֲשׂוֹת הָרַע בְּעֵינֵי יְהוָה וַיְחַזֵּק יְהוָה אֶת־עֶגְלוֹן מֶלֶךְ־

מוֹאָב עַל־יִשְׂרָאֵל עַל כִּי־עָשׂוּ אֶת־הָרַע בְּעֵינֵי יְהוָה׃ וַיֶּאֱסֹף אֵלָיו אֶת־בְּנֵי

[1] Hiph. Perf. 2mp of רעע, glossed as "to do evil, to treat badly" (see ch. 28).

עַמּ֖וֹן וַעֲמָלֵ֑ק וַיֵּ֗לֶךְ וַיַּךְ֙ אֶת־יִשְׂרָאֵ֔ל וַיִּֽירְשׁ֖וּ אֶת־עִ֥יר הַתְּמָרִֽים׃ וַיַּֽעַבְד֧וּ בְנֵֽי־

יִשְׂרָאֵ֛ל אֶת־עֶגְל֥וֹן מֶֽלֶךְ־מוֹאָ֖ב שְׁמוֹנֶ֥ה עֶשְׂרֵ֖ה שָׁנָֽה׃

וַיֶּאֱסֹ֧ף יְהוֹשֻׁ֛עַ אֶת־כָּל־שִׁבְטֵ֥י יִשְׂרָאֵ֖ל שְׁכֶ֑מָה וַיִּקְרָא֩ לְזִקְנֵ֨י יִשְׂרָאֵ֜ל וּלְרָאשָׁ֗יו Josh. 24:1–5

וּלְשֹֽׁפְטָיו֙ וּלְשֹׁ֣טְרָ֔יו וַיִּֽתְיַצְּב֖וּ לִפְנֵ֥י הָאֱלֹהִֽים׃ וַיֹּ֨אמֶר יְהוֹשֻׁ֜עַ אֶל־כָּל־הָעָ֗ם

כֹּֽה־אָמַ֣ר יְהוָה֮ אֱלֹהֵ֣י יִשְׂרָאֵל֒ בְּעֵ֣בֶר הַנָּהָ֗ר יָשְׁב֤וּ אֲבֽוֹתֵיכֶם֙ מֵֽעוֹלָ֔ם תֶּ֛רַח

אֲבִ֥י אַבְרָהָ֖ם וַאֲבִ֣י נָח֑וֹר וַיַּעַבְד֖וּ אֱלֹהִ֥ים אֲחֵרִֽים׃ וָ֠אֶקַּח אֶת־אֲבִיכֶ֤ם אֶת־

אַבְרָהָם֙ מֵעֵ֣בֶר הַנָּהָ֔ר וָאוֹלֵ֥ךְ אוֹת֖וֹ בְּכָל־אֶ֣רֶץ כְּנָ֑עַן וָאַרְבֶּ֙[2] אֶת־זַרְע֔וֹ וָֽאֶתֶּן־

לוֹ֙ אֶת־יִצְחָֽק׃ וָאֶתֵּ֣ן לְיִצְחָ֔ק אֶֽת־יַעֲקֹ֖ב וְאֶת־עֵשָׂ֑ו וָאֶתֵּ֨ן לְעֵשָׂ֜ו אֶת־הַ֤ר שֵׂעִיר֙

[2] Use your BHS or BHQ to analyze this *Ketiv*/*Qere*.

לָרֶשֶׁת אוֹתוֹ וְיַעֲקֹב וּבָנָיו יָרְדוּ מִצְרָיִם׃ וָאֶשְׁלַח אֶת־מֹשֶׁה וְאֶת־אַהֲרֹן וָאֶגֹּף

אֶת־מִצְרַיִם כַּאֲשֶׁר עָשִׂיתִי בְּקִרְבּוֹ וְאַחַר הוֹצֵאתִי אֶתְכֶם׃

Josh. 24:6–10

וָאוֹצִיא אֶת־אֲבוֹתֵיכֶם מִמִּצְרַיִם וַתָּבֹאוּ הַיָּמָּה וַיִּרְדְּפוּ מִצְרַיִם אַחֲרֵי

אֲבוֹתֵיכֶם בְּרֶכֶב וּבְפָרָשִׁים יַם־סוּף׃ וַיִּצְעֲקוּ אֶל־יְהוָה וַיָּשֶׂם מַאֲפֵל בֵּינֵיכֶם ׀

וּבֵין הַמִּצְרִים וַיָּבֵא עָלָיו אֶת־הַיָּם וַיְכַסֵּהוּ וַתִּרְאֶינָה עֵינֵיכֶם אֵת אֲשֶׁר־

עָשִׂיתִי בְּמִצְרָיִם וַתֵּשְׁבוּ בַמִּדְבָּר יָמִים רַבִּים׃ וָאָבִאה[3] אֶתְכֶם אֶל־אֶרֶץ

הָאֱמֹרִי הַיּוֹשֵׁב בְּעֵבֶר הַיַּרְדֵּן וַיִּלָּחֲמוּ אִתְּכֶם וָאֶתֵּן אוֹתָם בְּיֶדְכֶם וַתִּירְשׁוּ

אֶת־אַרְצָם וָאַשְׁמִידֵם מִפְּנֵיכֶם׃ וַיָּקָם בָּלָק בֶּן־צִפּוֹר מֶלֶךְ מוֹאָב וַיִּלָּחֶם

[3] Use your BHS or BHQ to analyze this *Ketiv/Qere*..

בְּיִשְׂרָאֵ֑ל וַיִּשְׁלַ֗ח וַיִּקְרָ֛א לְבִלְעָ֥ם בֶּן־בְּע֖וֹר לְקַלֵּ֥ל אֶתְכֶֽם׃ וְלֹ֥א אָבִ֖יתִי לִשְׁמֹ֣עַ

לְבִלְעָ֑ם וַיְבָ֤רֶךְ בָּרוֹךְ֙ אֶתְכֶ֔ם וָאַצִּ֥ל אֶתְכֶ֖ם מִיָּדֽוֹ׃

Josh. 24:11–13

וַתַּעַבְר֣וּ אֶת־הַיַּרְדֵּן֮ וַתָּבֹ֣אוּ אֶל־יְרִיחוֹ֒ וַיִּלָּחֲמ֣וּ בָכֶ֣ם בַּֽעֲלֵי־יְ֠רִיחוֹ הָֽאֱמֹרִ֨י

וְהַפְּרִזִּ֜י וְהַכְּנַעֲנִ֗י וְהַֽחִתִּי֙ וְהַגִּרְגָּשִׁ֔י הַחִוִּ֖י וְהַיְבוּסִ֑י וָאֶתֵּ֥ן אוֹתָ֖ם בְּיֶדְכֶֽם׃ וָאֶשְׁלַ֤ח

לִפְנֵיכֶם֙ אֶת־הַצִּרְעָ֔ה וַתְּגָ֤רֶשׁ אוֹתָם֙ מִפְּנֵיכֶ֔ם שְׁנֵ֖י מַלְכֵ֣י הָאֱמֹרִ֑י לֹ֥א בְחַרְבְּךָ֖

וְלֹ֥א בְקַשְׁתֶּֽךָ׃ וָאֶתֵּ֨ן לָכֶ֜ם אֶ֣רֶץ ׀ אֲשֶׁ֧ר לֹא־יָגַ֣עְתָּ בָּ֗הּ וְעָרִים֙ אֲשֶׁ֣ר לֹא־בְנִיתֶ֔ם

וַתֵּשְׁב֖וּ בָּהֶ֑ם כְּרָמִ֤ים וְזֵיתִים֙ אֲשֶׁ֣ר לֹא־נְטַעְתֶּ֔ם אַתֶּ֖ם אֹכְלִֽים׃

27.8 Exegetical Exercises—Theological Controversies

Using your lexicon, translate Proverbs 8:22–23.

22 יְהוָ֗ה קָ֭נָנִי רֵאשִׁ֣ית דַּרְכּ֑וֹ קֶ֖דֶם מִפְעָלָ֣יו מֵאָֽז׃

23 מֵ֭עוֹלָם נִסַּ֥כְתִּי מֵרֹ֗אשׁ מִקַּדְמֵי־אָֽרֶץ׃

Consider the translations of the ESV, NJPS, and NETS (New English Translation of the Septuagint).

ESV

22 The LORD possessed me at the beginning of his work,
the first of his acts of old.
23 Ages ago I was set up,
at the first, before the beginning of the earth.

NJPS

22 The LORD created me at the beginning of His course
As the first of His works of old.
23 In the distant past I was fashioned,
At the beginning, at the origin of the earth.

NETS

22 The LORD created me at the beginning of his work,
the first of his acts of long ago.
23 Ages ago I was set up
at the first, before the beginning of the earth.

Using your lexical tools, state how each translation would justify its translation of the verb קנה. Which choice do you think is correct? Why?

In the early fourth century A.D., the teachings of Arius (A.D. 250–336)—a presbyter from Alexandria, Egypt—became influential. Arius stressed the unified, eternal character of God and taught that the Son was subordinate to the Father. This ancient Arian doctrine was set to music:

> The uncreated God has made the Son
> A beginning of things created,
> And by adoption has God made the Son
> Into an advancement of himself.
> Yet the Son's substance is
> Removed from the substance of the Father:
> The Son is not equal to the Father,
> Nor does he share the same substance.
> God is the all-wise Father,
> And the Son is the teacher of his mysteries.
> The members of the Holy Trinity
> Share unequal glories.[4]

Arius's logic was this: "If the Father begat the Son, he that was begotten had a beginning of existence; hence it is clear that there was a time when the Son was not. It

[4] Robert Payne, *The Holy Fire: The Story of the Fathers of the Eastern Church* (Crestwood, NY: St. Vladimir's Seminary Press, 1980), 82–83, in Mark Noll, *Turning Points*, 3rd ed. (Grand Rapids: Baker, 2012), 45.

follows then of necessity that he had his existence from the non-existent."[5] The Council of Nicaea (A.D. 325) was convened and chaired by the Roman Emperor Constantine in response to Arianism. Athanasius (A.D. 296–373) was Arius's main opposition.

Proverbs 8:22–31 was especially important to Arius's position. Examine the broader context of Proverbs 8 in an English Bible. What equation was assumed by Arius and other Christians that causes them to read Proverbs 8:22–31 as speaking of Jesus?

Jews have, of course, used Proverbs 8 differently. The Midrash on Genesis states, "'Beginning' referring to the Torah, as in the verse, 'The Lord made me as the beginning of His way.'" Read Genesis 1:1. What word in Proverbs 8:22 is the source of the Midrash's connection?

Relate these conclusions back to the Arian controversy. How should you respond to Arius's use of Proverbs 8:32–33?

---

[5] Henry Bettenson, ed., *Documents of the Christian Church*, 2nd ed. (New York: Oxford University Press, 1963), 40, in Noll, *Turning Points*, 45.

כח (28) Geminate Verbs and Minor Stems

28.1 Geminate Roots

Geminate roots have identical second and third root letters, such as סָבַב ("to turn around, go around, encircle") and אָרַר ("to curse").[1] In many phonetic environments the third root consonant assimilates into the second, resulting in a *dagesh forte*, compensatory lengthening, or virtual doubling. A connecting vowel is also common in such forms, usually occurring between the root and the verbal ending.

28.2 Geminate Perfect Forms

In the Qal perfect, geminate roots show both the assimilation of the third root consonant and the connecting vowel וֹ in the first and second person forms.

	Qal Perfect קטל	Qal Perfect סבב	Qal Perfect ארר
3ms	קָטַל	סָבַב	אָרַר
3fs	קָֽטְלָה	סָֽבְבָה	אָֽרְרָה
2ms	קָטַ֫לְתָּ	סַבּ֫וֹתָ	אָר֫וֹתָ
2fs	קָטַלְתְּ	סַבּוֹת	אָרוֹת
1cs	קָטַ֫לְתִּי	סַבּ֫וֹתִי	אָר֫וֹתִי
3cp	קָֽטְלוּ	סָֽבְבוּ	אָֽרְרוּ
2mp	קְטַלְתֶּם	סַבּוֹתֶם	אָרוֹתֶם
2fp	קְטַלְתֶּן	סַבּוֹתֶן	אָרוֹתֶן
1cp	קָטַ֫לְנוּ	סַבּ֫וֹנוּ	אָר֫וֹנוּ

The Qal perfect paradigm for סבב must be memorized.

Notes:

- The assimilation of the third root consonant occurs in the first- and second-person forms but *not* in the third-person forms.

[1] The terminology is from the Latin *geminus*, meaning "twin." (Hence the constellation Gemini.)

- Compensatory lengthening and virtual doubling occur as expected.
- The connecting vowel וֹ causes the spirantization of the *taw* of the suffix and the loss of its silent *shewa* in the 2fs form.
- Geminate verbs are relatively inconsistent in their written forms. Both the second and third root letters may be repeated in a first- or second-person form, and the third-person forms may show gemination only through the *dagesh forte*. The connecting vowel is usually present where indicated by the paradigm, but it can be omitted.

וְסַבֹּתֶם אֶת־הָעִיר	("And you shall march around the city."—Josh. 6:3)
חֶבְלֵי שְׁאוֹל סַבֻּנִי	("The cords of Sheol surrounded me."—2 Sam. 22:6)
וְשִׁלַּחְתִּי בָכֶם אֶת־הַמְּאֵרָה וְאָרוֹתִי אֶת־בִּרְכוֹתֵיכֶם וְגַם אָרוֹתִיהָ	("And I will send upon you the curse, and I will curse your blessings, and indeed I have cursed it."—Mal. 2:2)

The Hiphil and Niphal perfect forms of geminate verbs show a similar tendency toward a connecting vowel וֹ in all first- and second-person forms.

	Qal Perfect	Hiphil Perfect	Niphal Perfect
	סבב	סבב	סבב
3ms	סָבַב	הֵסֵב	נָסַב
3fs	סָֽבְבָה	הֵסֵבָּה	נָסַבָּה
2ms	סַבּוֹתָ	הֲסִבּוֹתָ	נְסַבּוֹתָ
2fs	סַבּוֹת	הֲסִבּוֹת	נְסַבּוֹת
1cs	סַבּוֹתִי	הֲסִבּוֹתִי	נְסַבּוֹתִי
3cp	סָֽבְבוּ	הֵסֵבּוּ	נָסַבּוּ
2mp	סַבּוֹתֶם	הֲסִבּוֹתֶם	נְסַבּוֹתֶם
2fp	סַבּוֹתֶן	הֲסִבּוֹתֶן	נְסַבּוֹתֶן
1cp	סַבּוֹנוּ	הֲסִבּוֹנוּ	נְסַבּוֹנוּ

Notes:

- The gemination of the second root letter is not indicated in the 3ms form of the Hiphil or Niphal.
- The first vowel in the Niphal perfect forms is typically *qameṣ* (when it does not reduce), though *ḥireq* also occurs.
- The presence of a guttural for the geminate consonant can produce an *a*-class vowel, which is expected with gutturals. These gutturals can also cause the *ḥireq* of the second- and first-person forms to lengthen to a *ṣere*.

כִּי שִׂמְּחָם יְהוָה וְהֵסֵב לֵב מֶלֶךְ־אַשּׁוּר עֲלֵיהֶם (“For the LORD made them glad and he turned the heart of the king of Assyria toward them.”—Ezra 6:22)

וְנָסַב הַגְּבוּל מִבַּעֲלָה יָמָּה אֶל־הַר שֵׂעִיר (“And the boundary circles from Baalah to the west to Mount Seir.”—Josh. 15:10)

Geminate roots are not common in the Piel/Pual/Hithpael stems. When they occur, the doubling of the second root letter prevents the assimilation of the third root letter, as in הִלַּלְתָּ (Piel Perf. 2ms of הלל). Such forms are therefore regular.

מִן־הָאֲדָמָה אֲשֶׁר אֵרְרָהּ יְהוָה (“from the ground which the LORD has cursed”—Gen. 5:29)

כִּי חִלֵּל יְהוּדָה קֹדֶשׁ יְהוָה אֲשֶׁר אָהֵב (“for Judah has profaned the sanctuary of the LORD, which he loves”—Mal. 2:11)

The call from Books IV and V of the Psalter הַלְלוּ יָהּ is a Piel imperative of הלל, plus יָהּ (a shortened form of the divine name). The expected doubling of the second root letter is prevented by the vocal *shewa* that follows it. The English translation “Hallelujah” reflects the Greek transcription ἁλληλουϊά, which preserves the doubling.

הַלְלוּ יָהּ הַלְלוּ אֶת־יְהוָה מִן־הַשָּׁמַיִם הַלְלוּהוּ בַּמְּרוֹמִים׃ (“Praise the LORD. Praise the LORD from the heavens; praise him upon the heights.”—Ps. 148:1 [Engl. 148:2])

28.3 Geminate Imperfect Forms

In the Qal imperfect, geminate roots show the assimilation of the root consonant only in forms with a suffix.

	Qal Imperfect קטל	Qal Imperfect סבב	Qal Alternative Imperfect סבב	Qal Imperfect תמם
3ms	יִקְטֹל	יָסֹב	יִסֹּב	יֵתַם
3fs	תִּקְטֹל	תָּסֹב	תִּסֹּב	תֵּתַם
2ms	תִּקְטֹל	תָּסֹב	תִּסֹּב	תֵּתַם
2fs	תִּקְטְלִי	תָּסֹ֫בִּי	תִּסֹ֫בִּי	תֵּתַ֫מִּי
1cs	אֶקְטֹל	אָסֹב	אֶסֹּב	אֵתַם
3mp	יִקְטְלוּ	יָסֹ֫בּוּ	יִסֹ֫בּוּ	יֵתַ֫מּוּ
3fp	תִּקְטֹ֫לְנָה	תְּסֻבֶּ֫ינָה	תִּסֻבֶּ֫ינָה	תְּתַמֶּ֫ינָה
2mp	תִּקְטְלוּ	תָּסֹ֫בּוּ	תִּסֹ֫בּוּ	תֵּתַ֫מּוּ
2fp	תִּקְטֹ֫לְנָה	תְּסֻבֶּ֫ינָה	תִּסֻבֶּ֫ינָה	תְּתַמֶּ֫ינָה
1cp	נִקְטֹל	נָסֹב	נִסֹּב	נֵתַם

The Qal imperfect paradigm for סבב must be memorized.

Notes:

- Adding an object suffix will cause gemination to be shown by a *dagesh forte*, unless the geminate letter is a guttural.
- In any imperfect form without a suffix, there is no obvious clue that the form is geminate. When parsing an unfamiliar form, after other options have been ruled out you should consider the possibility of a geminate root.
- Three different vowel patterns are possible: *qameṣ-ḥolem*, *ḥireq-ḥolem*, and *ṣere-pataḥ*.
- The alternative geminate Qal imperfect form resembles a I-*nun* verb, as the *dagesh forte* is placed in the first root letter. When parsing such forms, if no root beginning with *nun* is given in the lexicon, you should consider the possibility of a geminate root.

וְחוּט֙ שְׁתֵּים־עֶשְׂרֵ֣ה אַמָּ֔ה יָסֹ֖ב אֶת־הָעַמּ֥וּד	("A measuring cord of twelve cubits went around the pillar."—1 Kings 7:15)
הַיָּ֣ם רָ֭אָה וַיָּנֹ֑ס הַ֝יַּרְדֵּ֗ן יִסֹּ֥ב לְאָחֽוֹר׃	("The sea looked and fled; the Jordan turned back."—Ps. 114:3)

In the Hiphil and Niphal imperfect, geminate roots again show the assimilation of the root consonant only in forms with a suffix.

	Qal Imperfect קטל	Hiphil Imperfect סבב	Niphal Imperfect סבב
3ms	יִקְטֹל	יָסֵב	יִסַּב
3fs	תִּקְטֹל	תָּסֵב	תִּסַּב
2ms	תִּקְטֹל	תָּסֵב	תִּסַּב
2fs	תִּקְטְלִי	תָּסֵ֫בִּי	תִּסַּ֫בִּי
1cs	אֶקְטֹל	אָסֵב	אֶסַּב
3mp	יִקְטְלוּ	יָסֵ֫בּוּ	יִסַּ֫בּוּ
3fp	תִּקְטֹלְנָה	תְּסִבֶּ֫ינָה	תִּסַּבֶּ֫ינָה
2mp	תִּקְטְלוּ	תָּסֵ֫בּוּ	תִּסַּ֫בּוּ
2fp	תִּקְטֹלְנָה	תְּסִבֶּ֫ינָה	תִּסַּבֶּ֫ינָה
1cp	נִקְטֹל	נָסֵב	נִסַּב

Notes:

- The Hiphil imperfect of geminate roots follows a *qameṣ-ṣere* vowel pattern—except for 3fp and 2fp forms.
- The Niphal imperfect of geminate roots follows a *ḥireq-pataḥ* vowel pattern—except for the *segol* in the 1cs form. The assimilation of *nun* occurs as expected. A *ḥolem* can occur in place of the *pataḥ* as the second vowel.
- Adding an object suffix will again cause gemination to be shown by a *dagesh forte* unless the geminate letter is a guttural.
- If the first letter of a Niphal form is a guttural, compensatory lengthening will occur.

נִבְנֶה אֶת־הֶעָרִים הָאֵלֶּה וְנָסֵב חוֹמָה וּמִגְדָּלִים	("Let us build these cities so that we may surround them with walls and towers."—2 Chron. 14:6)
יִהְיֶה־שָׁמָּה הָרוּחַ לָלֶכֶת יֵלֵכוּ לֹא יִסַּבּוּ בְּלֶכְתָּן	("And where the spirit went, they went; they did not turn as they went."—Ezek. 1:12)

As with the perfect verbs, geminate verbs in the Piel/Pual/Hithpael stems are regular in form:

עִם־גִּבּוֹר תָּמִים תִּתַּמָּם	("With the blameless you prove yourself blameless."—2 Sam. 22:26)

28.4 Other Geminate Forms

The imperative forms of geminate verbs are formed as expected by removing the imperfect prefix and (in the case of the Hiphil and Niphal) adding *heh*:

סֹב	Qal Imperative ms of סבב
הָחֵל	Hiph. Imperative ms of חלל
הִסַּב	Niph. Imperative ms of סבב

Caution must be taken because these forms are easily confused with I-*nun* and middle-weak forms. Knowledge of the imperfect forms should allow identification of geminate imperatives.

וַיֹּאמֶר הַמֶּלֶךְ לְדוֹיֵּג סֹב אַתָּה וּפְגַע בַּכֹּהֲנִים	("And the king said to Doeg, 'You turn and strike down the priests.'"—1 Sam. 22:18)
לֹא תַעֲלֶה הָסֵב אֶל־אַחֲרֵיהֶם	("Do not go up; go around to their rear."—2 Sam. 5:23)
נָתַתִּי בְיָדְךָ אֶת־סִיחֹן מֶלֶךְ־חֶשְׁבּוֹן הָאֱמֹרִי וְאֶת־אַרְצוֹ הָחֵל רָשׁ	("I have given Sihon the king of Heshbon, the Amorite, and his land into your hand. Begin to take possession."—Deut. 2:24)

The participle forms of geminate roots may be regular like סבב, or they may indicate gemination by the *dagesh forte* like תמם. Hiphil and Niphal participles show their typical *mem* and *nun* prefixes.

	Qal Participle סבב	Qal Participle תמם	Hiphil Participle סבב	Niphal Participle סבב
ms	סֹבֵב	תַּם	מֵסֵב	נָסָב
fs	סֹבֶ֫בֶת	תַּמָּה	מְסִבָּה	נְסַבָּה
mp	סֹבְבִים	תַּמִּים	מְסִבִּים	נְסַבִּים
fp	סֹבְבוֹת	תַּמּוֹת	מְסִבּוֹת	נְסַבּוֹת

מְצָאֻ֙נִי֙ הַשֹּׁ֣מְרִ֔ים הַסֹּבְבִ֖ים בָּעִ֑יר ("The watchmen who go around the city found me."—Song 3:3)

הִנְנִ֣י מֵסֵב֩ אֶת־כְּלֵ֨י הַמִּלְחָמָ֜ה אֲשֶׁ֣ר בְּיֶדְכֶ֗ם ("See, I am about to turn back the weapons of war which are in your hands."—Jer. 21:4)

כִּ֣י הִנֵּ֡ה בָעִיר֩ אֲשֶׁ֨ר נִֽקְרָא־שְׁמִ֜י עָלֶ֗יהָ אָנֹכִי֙ מֵחֵ֣ל לְהָרַ֔ע ("For, see, in the city which is called by my name I am beginning to work disaster."—Jer. 25:29)

The infinitive forms of geminate roots show the typical shortening of the construct form (versus the absolute form in the Qal and Niphal).

	Qal Infinitives סבב	Hiphil Infinitives סבב	Niphal Infinitives סבב
Abs.	סָבוֹב	הָסֵב	הִסּוֹב
Const.	סֹב	הָסֵב	הִסֵּב

While the infinitive construct form does not typically show its gemination, adding a suffix will result in the indication of gemination via a *dagesh forte*:

רַב־לָכֶם סֹב אֶת־הָהָר הַזֶּה	("Enough of you traveling around this hill country!"—Deut. 2:3)
עַד־תֹּם כָּל־הַדּוֹר אַנְשֵׁי הַמִּלְחָמָה מִקֶּרֶב הַמַּחֲנֶה	("until all the generation, the men of war, perished from the midst of the camp."—Deut. 2:14)
עַד־תֻּמָּם מֵעַל הָאֲדָמָה אֲשֶׁר־נָתַתִּי לָהֶם וְלַאֲבוֹתֵיהֶם	("until they perish from the land which I gave to them and to their fathers"—Jer. 24:10)

28.5 Identifying "Missing" Root Letters

Building on 27.5, if the removal of suffix and prefix letters in a given form results in only two evident root letters, there are now six possible causes:

Possible Sources of "Missing" Root Letters

- The verbal root begins with *nun*
- The irregular verb לקח or הלך
- The verbal root ends with *heh*
- The verbal root is middle-weak
- In the imperfect, the verbal root may be I-י
- The root may be geminate

Again, your knowledge of both memory paradigms and vocabulary will help you distinguish between these possibilities.

One more note is necessary: geminate roots are often confused with other weak verb formations in the pointing of the Hebrew text (e.g.: the alternative form of the Qal imperfect). Unless you are dealing with a common word you know from your vocabulary, it is best to consider a geminate root only once the other options have been exhausted.

28.6 Minor Stems

While this grammar has introduced all of the major stems, other verbal forms are found in the Hebrew text.

The most common of these occur when a middle-weak root is placed in the D-stem (the doubling stem; typically the Piel/Pual/Hithpael). Since doubling the weak consonant in a middle-weak root is problematic, forms such as the Polel, Polal, and Hithpolel replace the typical Piel, Pual, and Hithpael:

אֲקוֹמֵם	Polel Imperf. 1cs of קום
מִתְקוֹמָמָה	Hithpolel Part. fs of קום

וְחָרְבוֹתֶיהָ אֲקוֹמֵם	("And I will raise up its ruins."—Isa. 44:26)
הַצִּילֵנִי מֵאֹיְבַי ׀ אֱלֹהָי מִמִּתְקוֹמְמַי תְּשַׂגְּבֵנִי׃	("Deliver me from my enemies, my God; protect me from the ones rising up against me."—Ps. 59:2)

Other rare forms may be from more minor patterns or the occasional use of a root with four root letters. For example, הִתְמַהְמָהְנוּ ("we delayed"—Gen. 43:10) is typically treated as a Hithpalpel perfect 1cp of מהה ("to harry, hesitate, delay"). For such forms you should consult a reference grammar.

28.7 Vocabulary

חִלֵּל	(Piel) to profane
הֵחֵל	(Hiph.) to profane; begin (from חלל)
נִחַל	(Niph.) to be defiled (from חלל)
כּוֹנֵן	(Polel) to set up, establish
נוּס	to flee
סָבַב	to turn oneself around, reverse; to go around; to encircle
הֵסֵב	(Hiph.) to make go around; cause to travel or wander
רָם	to be high
הֵרִים	(Hiph.) to make high
רוֹמֵם	(Polel) to bring up, aloft
תְּרוּמָה	contribution, offering

28.8 Language Exercises

A. Parse and gloss the following forms. Include the identification of the object suffix where appropriate.

סָֽבְבוּ

תָּֽמּוּ

סֹ֫בִּי

וַיִּ֫גֶל

אָרוֹר

הוּקַם

וַיָּ֫שֶׁם

תַּתֵּם

וַנָּ֫סָב

נִגְלְתָה

יָהֵל

הֲסִבֹּתָ

מֵשִׂים

B. Translate the following and parse each verb and participle. Use your lexicon to look up the glosses for any words you do not know from your vocabulary.

Judg. 1:1–8

וַיְהִי אַחֲרֵי מוֹת יְהוֹשֻׁעַ וַיִּשְׁאֲלוּ בְּנֵי יִשְׂרָאֵל בַּיהוָה לֵאמֹר מִי יַעֲלֶה־לָּנוּ אֶל־

הַכְּנַעֲנִי בַּתְּחִלָּה לְהִלָּחֶם בּוֹ׃ וַיֹּאמֶר יְהוָה יְהוּדָה יַעֲלֶה הִנֵּה נָתַתִּי אֶת־

הָאָרֶץ בְּיָדוֹ׃ וַיֹּאמֶר יְהוּדָה לְשִׁמְעוֹן אָחִיו עֲלֵה אִתִּי בְגוֹרָלִי וְנִלָּחֲמָה

בַּכְּנַעֲנִי וְהָלַכְתִּי גַם־אֲנִי אִתְּךָ בְּגוֹרָלֶךָ וַיֵּלֶךְ אִתּוֹ שִׁמְעוֹן׃ וַיַּעַל יְהוּדָה וַיִּתֵּן

יְהוָה אֶת־הַכְּנַעֲנִי וְהַפְּרִזִּי בְּיָדָם וַיַּכּוּם בְּבֶזֶק עֲשֶׂרֶת אֲלָפִים אִישׁ׃ וַיִּמְצְאוּ

אֶת־אֲדֹנִי בֶזֶק בְּבֶזֶק וַיִּלָּחֲמוּ בוֹ וַיַּכּוּ אֶת־הַכְּנַעֲנִי וְאֶת־הַפְּרִזִּי׃ וַיָּנָס אֲדֹנִי

בֶזֶק וַיִּרְדְּפוּ אַחֲרָיו וַיֹּאחֲזוּ אֹתוֹ וַיְקַצְּצוּ אֶת־בְּהֹנוֹת יָדָיו וְרַגְלָיו׃ וַיֹּאמֶר

אֲדֹנִי־בֶזֶק שִׁבְעִים ׀ מְלָכִים בְּהֹנוֹת יְדֵיהֶם וְרַגְלֵיהֶם מְקֻצָּצִים הָיוּ מְלַקְּטִים

תַּ֣חַת שֻׁלְחָנִ֔י כַּאֲשֶׁ֣ר עָשִׂ֔יתִי כֵּ֥ן שִׁלַּם־לִ֖י אֱלֹהִ֑ים וַיְבִיאֻ֥הוּ יְרוּשָׁלִַ֖ם וַיָּ֥מָת שָֽׁם׃

וַיִּלָּחֲמ֤וּ בְנֵי־יְהוּדָה֙ בִּיר֣וּשָׁלִַ֔ם וַיִּלְכְּד֣וּ אוֹתָ֔הּ וַיַּכּ֖וּהָ לְפִי־חָ֑רֶב וְאֶת־הָעִ֖יר

שִׁלְּח֥וּ בָאֵֽשׁ׃

1 Kings 1:1–5

וְהַמֶּ֤לֶךְ דָּוִד֙ זָקֵ֔ן בָּ֖א בַּיָּמִ֑ים וַיְכַסֻּ֙הוּ֙ בַּבְּגָדִ֔ים וְלֹ֥א יִחַ֖ם לֽוֹ׃ וַיֹּ֧אמְרוּ ל֣וֹ עֲבָדָ֗יו

יְבַקְשׁ֞וּ לַאדֹנִ֤י הַמֶּ֙לֶךְ֙ נַעֲרָ֣ה בְתוּלָ֔ה וְעָֽמְדָה֙ לִפְנֵ֣י הַמֶּ֔לֶךְ וּתְהִי־ל֖וֹ סֹכֶ֑נֶת

וְשָׁכְבָ֣ה בְחֵיקֶ֔ךָ וְחַ֖ם לַאדֹנִ֥י הַמֶּֽלֶךְ׃ וַיְבַקְשׁוּ֙ נַעֲרָ֣ה יָפָ֔ה בְּכֹ֖ל גְּב֣וּל יִשְׂרָאֵ֑ל

וַֽיִּמְצְא֗וּ אֶת־אֲבִישַׁג֙ הַשּׁ֣וּנַמִּ֔ית וַיָּבִ֥אוּ אֹתָ֖הּ לַמֶּֽלֶךְ׃ וְהַֽנַּעֲרָ֖ה יָפָ֣ה עַד־מְאֹ֑ד

וַתְּהִ֨י לַמֶּ֤לֶךְ סֹכֶ֙נֶת֙ וַתְּשָׁ֣רְתֵ֔הוּ וְהַמֶּ֖לֶךְ לֹ֥א יְדָעָֽהּ׃ וַאֲדֹנִיָּ֧ה בֶן־חַגִּ֛ית מִתְנַשֵּׂ֥א

לֵאמֹ֖ר אֲנִ֣י אֶמְלֹ֑ךְ וַיַּ֣עַשׂ ל֗וֹ רֶ֚כֶב וּפָ֣רָשִׁ֔ים וַחֲמִשִּׁ֥ים אִ֖ישׁ רָצִ֥ים לְפָנָֽיו׃

Josh. 6:12–17

וַיַּשְׁכֵּ֥ם יְהוֹשֻׁ֖עַ בַּבֹּ֑קֶר וַיִּשְׂא֥וּ הַכֹּהֲנִ֖ים אֶת־אֲר֥וֹן יְהוָֽה׃ וְשִׁבְעָ֨ה הַכֹּהֲנִ֜ים

נֹשְׂאִ֗ים שִׁבְעָ֞ה שׁוֹפְר֣וֹת הַיֹּבְלִ֘ים לִפְנֵ֣י אֲר֣וֹן יְהוָ֗ה הֹלְכִ֤ים הָלוֹךְ֙ וְתָקְע֖וּ

בַּשּׁוֹפָר֑וֹת וְהֶחָלוּץ֙ הֹלֵ֣ךְ לִפְנֵיהֶ֔ם וְהַֽמְאַסֵּ֗ף הֹלֵךְ֙ אַחֲרֵי֙ אֲר֣וֹן יְהוָ֔ה הָוֹלֹ֖ךְ[2]

וְתָק֖וֹעַ בַּשּׁוֹפָרֽוֹת׃ וַיָּסֹ֨בּוּ אֶת־הָעִ֜יר בַּיּ֤וֹם הַשֵּׁנִי֙ פַּ֣עַם אַחַ֔ת וַיָּשֻׁ֖בוּ הַֽמַּחֲנֶ֑ה כֹּ֥ה

עָשׂ֖וּ שֵׁ֥שֶׁת יָמִֽים׃ וַיְהִ֣י ׀ בַּיּ֣וֹם הַשְּׁבִיעִ֗י וַיַּשְׁכִּ֙מוּ֙ כַּעֲל֣וֹת הַשַּׁ֔חַר וַיָּסֹ֧בּוּ אֶת־

הָעִ֛יר כַּמִּשְׁפָּ֥ט הַזֶּ֖ה שֶׁ֣בַע פְּעָמִ֑ים רַ֚ק בַּיּ֣וֹם הַה֔וּא סָבְב֥וּ אֶת־הָעִ֖יר שֶׁ֥בַע

פְּעָמִֽים׃ וַיְהִי֙ בַּפַּ֣עַם הַשְּׁבִיעִ֔ית תָּקְע֥וּ הַכֹּהֲנִ֖ים בַּשּׁוֹפָר֑וֹת וַיֹּ֨אמֶר יְהוֹשֻׁ֤עַ אֶל־

הָעָם֙ הָרִ֔יעוּ כִּֽי־נָתַ֧ן יְהוָ֛ה לָכֶ֖ם אֶת־הָעִֽיר׃ וְהָיְתָ֨ה הָעִ֥יר חֵ֛רֶם הִ֥יא וְכָל־

---

[2] Consult your BHS or BHQ to interpret the *Ketiv*/*Qere* reading.

אֲשֶׁר־בָּ֖הּ לַֽיהוָ֑ה רַ֣ק רָחָ֞ב הַזּוֹנָ֗ה תִּֽחְיֶ֗ה הִ֚יא וְכָל־אֲשֶׁ֣ר אִתָּ֣הּ בַּבַּ֔יִת כִּ֣י

הֶחְבְּאַ֔תָה אֶת־הַמַּלְאָכִ֖ים אֲשֶׁ֥ר שָׁלָֽחְנוּ׃

28.9 Exegetical Exercises—The Text-Critical Apparatus

In both BHS and BHQ the bottom of the page is occupied by the text-critical apparatus,[3] where the editors of individual books make text-critical observations or suggestions. Both BHS and BHQ provide the text of the Leningrad Codex, the oldest complete manuscript of the Hebrew text. Unlike a Greek NT, which draws on the combination of many manuscripts and fragments for its text, BHS and BHQ reproduce the Leningrad Codex even though—like all extant copies—it contains flaws.

Observations on the text and suggestions for alternative readings are made in the apparatus. These are editorial judgments and comments, and not every text-critical note is a suggested change. Some editors of biblical books are more apt to suggest changes than others, but in all cases they attempt to include information relevant to the question, even if they believe the text of Leningrad to be superior to the alternatives.

Both BHS and BHQ include a key to the apparatus, with a comprehensive list of signs and abbreviations. You will find this key in the front of your BHS or BHQ. The key to the signs (*sigla*) indicates how the various textual witnesses are noted in the apparatus. If you are using BHQ, the apparatus includes English language commentary. If you are using BHS, the apparatus commentary is in Latin; you will have to consult the English key to the Latin terms, which is also bound at the front of the volume. Find and familiarize yourself with each necessary key.

[3] See 2.11.

Translate Judges 1:21 from your Hebrew text:

In BHS the word יֹשֵׁב is marked by a superscript [a], indicating a textual note. In BHQ the note is marked by the word יֹשֵׁב in the apparatus, following the number 21. Use the key in your BHS or BHQ to determine the meaning of each symbol or word in the note. Write the meaning in the chart below:

BHS Symbol/Word	Meaning
nonn	
Mss	
Q^{Or}	
יֹשְׁבֵי	Have יֹשְׁבֵי
cf	
27[a]	Note a on v. 27

BHQ Symbol/Word	Meaning
G	
V	
I	
pl	
S	
T	
(assim-ctext)	

What does the textual note communicate? Write a prose summary of the content of the note.

Given the content, do you think that the Leningrad text preserves the best reading of this word in Judges 1:21, or was the text originally יֹשְׁבֵי? Why?

Using your key, summarize the content of the following notes in a prose summary. In each case, do you think the text of the Leningrad Codex as presented in BHS or BHQ is the best approximation of the original text, or do you think the note provides ample evidence that the best approximation of the original text would require a change to the Leningrad text? Why?

- Judges 5:3, note a-a (BHS) / note on אָנֹכִי לַיהוָה (BHQ)

  Summarize the content of the critical apparatus note:

  Do you believe this provides evidence that the Leningrad Codex does not accurately preserve the original text? Why or why not?

- Judges 16:14, note a (BHS) / note on וַתִּתְקַע (BHQ)

  Summarize the content of the critical apparatus note:

  Do you believe this provides evidence that the Leningrad Codex does not accurately preserve the original text? Why or why not?

Blank Parsing Grids

Verb Parsing Grid

Form to Parse	Verbal Stem	Conjugation	Person	Gender	Number	Root	Gloss

Blank Parsing Grids

Noun Parsing Grid

Form to Parse	Gender	Number	Lexical Form	Gloss

Hebrew-English Glossary

א

אָב	6	(masc.) father (pl.: אָבוֹת)
אבד		
אָבַד	3	to die, perish; become lost; go astray
הֶאֱבִיד	16	(Hiph.) to exterminate, wipe out
אֶ֫בֶן	7	stone
אבר		
אִבַּד	16	(Piel) to destroy
אָדוֹן	2	lord, master; the Lord
אָדָם	1	man, mankind; Adam
אהב		
אָהַב	3	to love
אֹ֫הֶל	7	tent
אוֹ	2	(conj.) or
אָ֫וֶן	20	wickedness, sin, injustice; disaster
אוֹר	18	daylight, dawn; light
אוֹת	20	sign, standard; (miraculous) event; mark (of seasons)
אָז	9	then, at that time
אֹ֫זֶן	19	ear
אָח	6	brother (pl.: אַחִים)
אָחוֹת	9	sister
אחז		
אָחַז	15	to seize, grasp
אֲחֻזָּה	15	possession, property; landed property
אַחֵר	19	other, later, following
אַחַר / אַחֲרֵי	8	(prep. or adv.) after, behind
אֵי / אַיֵּה	8	where?
אֹיֵב	4	enemy
אֵיךְ / אֵיכָה	8	how? (also used as an exclamation "How!")
אַ֫יִל	9	ram; ruler, mighty one
אַיִן	8	there is not/are not (particle of nonexistence)
אִישׁ	6	man, husband; person (pl.: אֲנָשִׁים)
אַךְ	9	(adv.) surely; only; however, but
אכל		
אָכַל	3	to eat, feed
אֶל	1	(prep.) to, toward
אֵל	1	god; God
אִם	1	(conj.) if
אֵם	9	mother
אַמָּה	4	forearm, cubit

Hebrew-English Glossary

אמן		
נֶאֱמַן	22	(Niph.) to be reliable, faithful, trustworthy; to be permanent
הֶאֱמִין	22	(Hiph.) to believe, have trust in
אָמֵן	2	"surely!"
אמר		
אָמַר	3	to say
אֱמֶת	11	truth, trustworthiness, faithfulness
אסף		
אָסַף	22	to gather, bring in
נֶאֱסַף	22	(Niph.) to assemble, gather together
אסר		
אָסַר	16	to bind, capture, confine
אַף	9	(conj.) also, even
אַף	16	nose, nostrils; anger (forms dual instead of plural)
אֲרוֹן	4	ark, money chest
אֲרִי / אַרְיֵה	20	lion
אֶ֫רֶז	20	cedar
אֹ֫רֶךְ	20	length
אֶ֫רֶץ	1	earth, ground; land; country
אֵשׁ	1	fire
אִשָּׁה	6	woman, wife (pl.: נָשִׁים)
אֲשֶׁר	6	the relative pronoun (who, whom, which, that, where)
אֵת / אֶת	2	an untranslatable particle that can be used to mark the definite
אֵת / אֶת	8	(prep.) with

ב

בֶּ֫גֶד	17	garment, cloak, covering
בְּהֵמָה	9	cattle, domestic animals; beasts
בוא		
בּוֹא	25	to come, enter
בושׁ		
בּוֹשׁ	26	to be ashamed
הֵבִישׁ	26	(Hiph.) to shame, put to shame; be ashamed
בָּחוּר	22	young man
בחר		
בָּחַר	22	to choose
בטח		
בָּטַח	5	to trust; have confidence
בֶּ֫טֶן	20	belly, internal organs; womb

Hebrew-English Glossary

בֵּין	8	(prep.) between
בין		
בִּין	26	to understand; perceive, consider
בַּ֫יִת	6	(masc.) house (pl.: בָּתִּים)
בכה		
בָּכָה	24	to weep, wail
בְּכוֹר	10	firstborn
בָּמָה	9	hill, high place
בֵּן	6	son (pl.: בָּנִים)
בנה		
בָּנָה	24	to build
בַּ֫עַד	9	behind; through, out of; round about; for the benefit of
בַּ֫עַל	16	lord, master, owner; husband; Baal
בער		
בָּעַר	22	to burn, blaze; to consume, burn up
בִּעֵר	22	(Piel) to kindle, to light
בָּקָר	10	herd, cattle
בֹּ֫קֶר	10	morning, tomorrow
בקשׁ		
בִּקֵּשׁ	14	(Piel) to seek, search for; discover, find
בַּרְזֶל	21	iron
בְּרִית	15	covenant
ברך		
בֵּרֵךְ	22	(Piel) to bless
בְּרָכָה	22	blessing
בָּרוּךְ	22	(Qal Pass. Part.) blessed
בָּשָׂר	9	skin, flesh, meat
בֹּ֫שֶׁת	26	shame, shamefulness
בַּת	6	daughter (pl.: בָּנוֹת)
בְּתוֹךְ	8	(prep.) in the middle of, in the midst of

ג

גאל		
גָּאַל	5	to redeem, reclaim
גְּבוּל	7	boundary, territory
גִּבּוֹר	21	hero, champion, warrior
גָּדוֹל	11	great
גדל		
גָּדַל	3	to grow up, become strong, become great

Hebrew-English Glossary

גּוֹי	2	people, nation (pl. = nations other than Israel)
גּוֹרָל	21	lot
גלה		
גָּלָה	23	to uncover, reveal; to go into exile
גִּלָּה	23	(Piel) to uncover, disclose, reveal, expose
הֶגְלָה	23	(Hiph.) to deport, take into exile
גַּם	1	also, even; as well as
גֵּר	11	stranger, alien (protected citizen)

ד

דָּבָר	1	word; thing, affair, matter
דבק		
דָּבַק	17	to stick to
הִדְבִּיק	17	(Hiph.) to overtake; cause to stick
דבר		
דִּבֶּר	14	(Piel) to say, speak
דֶּלֶת	21	door
דָּם	1	blood
דַּעַת	27	knowledge
דֹּר	10	generation, lifetime
דרך		
דָּרַךְ	15	to tread, trample
דֶּרֶךְ	15	(fem.) way, road
דרשׁ		
דָּרַשׁ	17	to seek, turn to; inquire, consult

ה

הֶבֶל	17	breath, vanity, idols
הוה		
הִשְׁתַּחֲוָה	24	to bow down, worship
היה		
הָיָה	24	to be, become; to come to pass, occur, happen
הֵיכָל	21	palace, temple
הלך		
הָלַךְ	3	to go, walk
הלל		
הִלֵּל	22	(Piel) to praise; eulogize
הִתְהַלֵּל	22	(Hithp.) to boast
הִנֵּה	8	"behold" (particle of immediacy – often untranslated)

הַר	1	hill, hill country, mountain
הַרְבֵּה	2	much, many; (adv.) very much
הרג		
הָרַג	22	to kill, slay

ו

וְ or וּ	2	(conj.) and; but

ז

זבח		
זָבַח	5	to slaughter, sacrifice
זֶ֫בַח	6	sacrifice
זָהָב	4	gold
זכר		
זָכַר	3	to remember, call to mind
הִזְכִּיר	16	(Hiph.) to make known, mention; to profess, praise
זָכָר	21	man, male; male animal
זמר		
זִמֵּר	19	(Piel) to sing
זעק		
זָעַק	14	to cry, cry for help
זָקֵן	2	old
זְרוֹעַ	21	arm, forearm; power, force, help
זרע		
זָרַע	15	to sow
זֶ֫רַע	15	seed, offspring, descendants

ח

חֹ֫דֶשׁ	17	new moon, month
חוֹמָה	9	wall
חוּץ	9	outside
חזק		
חָזַק	3	to be strong, become strong, have courage
חִזֵּק	20	(Piel) to make firm or strong; strengthen
הֶחֱזִיק	20	(Hiph.) to seize, grasp, hold on to
הִתְחַזֵּק	20	(Hithp.) to show courage; prove oneself strong
חָזָק	2	firm, hard; strong, powerful
חַי	1	living, alive
חַי	24	life

Hebrew-English Glossary

חיה		
חָיָה	24	to live, be alive
חַיִל	4	power, strength
חָכָם	21	skillful, shrewd, wise
חָכְמָה	21	wisdom, skill, shrewdness
חלל		
נִחַל	28	(Niph.) to be defiled
חִלֵּל	28	(Piel) to profane
הֵחֵל	28	(Hiph.) to profane; begin
חֲלוֹם	21	dream
חֵמָה	10	heat, rage, wrath, poison
חֵן	13	grace, charm, favor
חטא		
חָטָא	25	to miss, to wrong, to sin
חִטֵּא	25	(Piel) to cleanse from sin, purify; offer as a sin offering
הִתְחַטָּא	25	(Hithp.) to purify oneself
חֵטְא	25	offense, sin, guilt
חַטָּאת	11	sin, sin offering
חנה		
חָנָה	23	to encamp
חֶסֶד	17	loyalty, faithfulness, goodness, graciousness
חפץ		
חָפֵץ	15	to enjoy; to feel inclined
חֵפֶץ	15	joy, delight
חֲצִי	16	half, half the height, middle
חָצֵר	9	court, enclosure (of a building); unwalled village
חֹק	23	prescription, rule, law, regulation
חֻקָּה	23	statute
חֶרֶב	7	sword
חרם		
הֶחֱרִים	22	(Hiph.) to put under the ban, devote to destruction
חשב		
חָשַׁב	5	to think, assume, plan
חֹשֶׁךְ	15	darkness

ט

טוֹב	2	good
טוֹבָה	13	good things, goodness
טָהוֹר	13	pure, clean

טמא		
טָמֵא	25	to become ritually unclean
נִטְמָא	25	(Niph.) to defile oneself
טִמֵּא	25	(Piel) to defile, desecrate
טָמֵא	11	unclean, ceremonially unclean

י

יָד	7	hand, forearm
ידע		
יָדַע	27	to know (sometimes euphemistic for sex)
הוֹדִיעַ	27	(Hiph.) to make know, inform
ידה		
הוֹדוּ	23	(Hiph.) to praise God, give thanks, confess one's sin
יוֹם	2	day, daylight
יוֹם	6	previous vocabulary – day (pl.: יָמִים)
יוֹמָם	2	(adv.) daily, by day
יטב		
יָטַב	23	to go well; be pleasing
הֵיטִיב	23	(Hiph.) to do well with (someone); treat well
יַיִן	9	wine
יכל		
יָכֹל	27	to be able, capable of; succeed, prevail
ילד		
יָלַד	27	to give birth, beget
יֶלֶד	27	boy
יָם	1	sea, lake
יָמִין	10	right side, right hand, south
יסף		
יָסַף	27	to add; continue doing
הֹסִיף	27	(Hiph.) to add, increase, do again
יצא		
יָצָא	27	to come/go out, set out
הוֹצִיא	27	(Hiph.) to bring out, lead out, cause to go out
ירא		
יָרֵא	27	to fear, be afraid
יָרֵא	27	(adj.) feared, fearful
יִרְאָה	27	fear
ירד		
יָרַד	27	to go down, descend
הוֹרִיד	27	(Hiph.) to bring down, cause to fall

Hebrew-English Glossary

ירשׁ		
יָרַשׁ	27	to take possession of; dispossess
יֵשׁ	8	there is/are (particle of existence)
יֹשֵׁב	27	inhabitant
יְשׁוּעָה	11	help, salvation, deliverance
ישׁב		
יָשַׁב	27	to sit, sit down; to dwell, settle
ישׁע		
נוֹשַׁע	27	(Niph.) to receive help
הוֹשִׁיעַ	27	(Hiph.) to help, save, assist
יָשָׁר	21	straight, level, smooth; proper, right, just
יתר		
נוֹתַר	27	(Niph.) to be left over
הוֹתִיר	27	(Hiph.) to leave over, be left over
יֶתֶר	11	remainder, excess

כ

כבד		
כָּבֵד	5	to be heavy, weigh heavily upon; be honored
כָּבֵד	5	heavy, thick, oppressing
כָּבוֹד	4	glory, splendor, reputation
כֶּבֶשׂ	17	young ram
כֹּה	2	(adv.) here; now; thus
כֹּהֵן	21	priest
כון		
הֵכִין	26	(Hiph.) to prepare, establish, make ready
כּוֹנֵן	28	(Polel) to set up, establish
כֹּחַ	17	power, strength, property
כִּי	9	that, since, because, for, although, surely
כִּי אִם־	9	but, surely; except, unless, only
כלה		
כָּלָה	24	to stop, come to an end, be finished
כִּלָּה	24	(Piel) to bring to an end, consume, destroy
כְּלִי	2	vessel; instrument; weapon
כֵּן	2	(adv.) thus, so; then, afterwards
כָּנָף	10	wing, skirt, edge
כִּסֵּא	18	seat, throne, chair
כסה		
כִּסָּה	24	(Piel) to cover, to conceal

כֶּ֫סֶף	7	silver, money
כעס		
כָּעַס	17	to be irritated, vexed
הִכְעִיס	17	(Hiph.) to irritate; provoke to anger
כַּף	10	palm, sole
כפר		
כִּפֶּר	14	(Piel) to atone, appease, make amends
כַּפֹּ֫רֶת	14	atonement cover (on the ark)
כרת		
כָּרַת	3	to cut; cut off, exterminate (with בְּרִית = to make a covenant)
נִכְרַת	19	(Niph.) to be cut off, exterminated; to disappear
הִכְרִית	19	(Hiph.) to exterminate; cut off
כשל		
כָּשַׁל	15	to stumble, stagger
כתב		
כָּתַב	18	to write

ל

לֹא	1	no, not
לֵב	4	heart, mind, will (alt. spelling = לֵבָב)
לְבַד	10	except, apart from, beside
לְבוּשׁ	5	garment
לבשׁ		
לָבַשׁ	5	to put on, clothe
לְבִלְתִּי	13	not
לחם		
נִלְחַם	19	(Niph.) to fight
לֶ֫חֶם	6	bread, food
לַ֫יְלָה	9	night
לכד		
לָכַד	5	to catch, overthrow
לָכֵן	1	(adv.) therefore
למד		
לָמַד	12	to learn
לִמֵּד	14	(piel) to teach
לָ֫מָּה / לָמָה	9	why?
לְמַ֫עַן	8	(prep.) on account of, for the sake of
לִפְנֵי	8	(prep.) before, in front of

Hebrew-English Glossary

לקח		
לָקַח	3	to take, seize, grasp
לִקְרַאת	16	opposite, contrary to (prep. + inf. const.)
לָשׁוֹן	10	tongue, gulf
מְאֹד	1	(adv.) very, exceedingly

מ

מאס		
מָאַס	14	to refuse, reject
מִגְדָּל	18	tower, watchtower
מִגְרָשׁ	18	pasture land belonging to a city
מִדְבָּר	7	desert, wilderness, steppe
מַדּוּעַ	5	why, on what account?
מַה	8	what?
מוֹעֵד	20	meeting, assembly; meeting place, time; festival
מות		
מוּת	26	to die
הֵמִית	26	(Hiph.) to kill
מָוֶת	10	death, dying
מִזְבֵּחַ	5	altar
מִזְמוֹר	19	psalm, song
מִזְרָח	15	sunrise, east
מַחֲנֶה	11	camp, army
מַטֶּה	11	stick, staff; tribe
מִי	8	who/whom?
מַיִם	4	water (always dual)
מכר		
מָכַר	13	to sell, betray to others
מלא		
מָלֵא	25	to be full, fulfilled; to fill up
מִלֵּא	25	(Piel) to fill, fulfill; endow; consecrate as priest
מָלֵא	2	full, filled, full of
מַלְאָךְ	1	angel, messenger
מְלָאכָה	18	business, work; handiwork, craftsmanship
מְלוּכָה	18	kingdom
מִלְחָמָה	11	battle, war
מלך		
מָלַךְ	3	to rule, reign, be king; become king
מֶלֶךְ	11	king, ruler
מַלְכוּת	18	royal dominion, kingship

מַמְלָכָה	11	dominion, kingdom
מִן	1	(prep.) from
מִנְחָה	4	gift, present, offering
מִסְפָּר	5	number, quantity
מַ֫עַל	8	(prep.) above
מְעַט	21	a little, a trifle
מַעֲשֶׂה	4	work, labor, deed
מצא		
מָצָא	25	to find; reach; obtain; achieve
מִצְוָה	4	command, commandment
מִצְרַיִם	6	Egypt
מִקְדָּשׁ	7	holy place, sanctuary
מָקוֹם	4	place, location
מִקְנֶה	13	property, livestock; possessions
מַרְאֶה	25	seeing, appearance
משׁח		
מָשַׁח	15	to smear with liquid, anoint
מָשִׁיחַ	15	anointed one
מִשְׁכָּן	12	abode, the tabernacle
משׁל		
מָשַׁל	13	to rule
מִשְׁפָּחָה	7	extended family, clan
מִשְׁפָּט	11	decision, judgment; law
מִשְׁתֶּה	11	banquet, feast

נ

נָא	8	particle of address (untranslated)
נְאֻם	9	an oracle of
נבא		
נִבָּא	19	(Niph.) to be in a prophetic trance, behave like a prophet
נבט		
הִבִּיט	17	(Hiph.) to look; consider; accept
נָבִיא	5	prophet
נֶ֫גֶב	10	south, arid terrain
נגד		
הִגִּיד	16	(Hiph.) to tell, announce, inform
נִגְלָה	23	(Niph.) to expose oneself, reveal oneself; be exposed
נֶ֫גֶד	2	(prep.) opposite, in front of, before
נגע		
נָגַע	5	to touch, strike

Hebrew-English Glossary

נֶ֫גַע	6	plague, affliction
נגשׁ		
נָגַשׁ	5	to approach, draw near, step forward
נָהָר	10	river
נוח		
נוּחַ	26	to rest
הֵנִיחַ	26	(Hiph. - A form) to cause to rest, pacify
הִנִּיחַ	26	(Hiph. - B form) to place, set, lay; to leave
נוס		
נוּס	28	to flee
נַ֫חַל	10	wadi, seasonal stream
נַחֲלָה	18	inheritance; inalienable, hereditary property
נחם		
נִחַם	22	(Niph.) to regret, be sorry, repent; to console oneself
נִחַם	22	(Piel) to comfort, console
נְחֹ֫שֶׁת	18	bronze, copper
נָטָה	23	to reach out, hold out, stretch out; to bow down
נכה		
הִכָּה	24	(Hiph.) to strike, to smite (from נכה)
נָכוֹנָה	26	(Niph.) to be established, steadfast, sure
נכר		
נִכַּר	17	(Piel) to deface
הִכִּיר	17	(Hiph.) to investigate; to recognize; to know, acknowledge
נָכְרִי	17	a foreigner
נסע		
נָסַע	5	to tear out, pull up; to journey further on
נַ֫עַר	7	young man, servant
נַעֲרָה	7	young (unmarried) girl, female attendant
נפל		
נָפַל	5	to fall
נֶ֫פֶשׁ	7	throat, neck, self, soul
נצל		
נִצַּל	19	(Niph.) to be saved
הִצִּיל	19	(Hiph.) to tear out, remove, take away; to rescue, snatch, deliver
נִצֵּל	19	(Piel) to rob; to deliver, save
נָשִׂיא	4	leader, chieftain
נשׂא		
נָשָׂא	25	to lift up, carry, raise
נשׂג		
הִשִּׂיג	17	(Hiph.) to overtake, reach; to be sufficient

נתן		
נָתַן	3	to give, set, put

ס

סבב		
סָבַב	28	to turn oneself around, reverse; to go around; to encircle
הֵסֵב	28	(Hiph.) to make go around; cause to travel or wander
סָבִיב	5	surrounding, on all sides (noun = surroundings)
סגר		
סָגַר	13	to shut
סוּס	4	horse
סוּסָה	4	mare
סור		
סוּר	26	to turn aside, go off, retreat
הסיר	26	(Hiph.) to remove
ספר		
סָפַר	5	to count, record
סִפֵּר	18	(Piel) to count; to make known; to report, tell
סֵ֫פֶר	6	something written, scroll, letter

ע

עבד		
עָבַד	3	to serve, work
עֶ֫בֶד	11	servant, slave
עֵ֫בֶר	14	bank, edge; other side
עֲבוֹדָה	11	work, service; worship
עבר		
עָבַר	3	to pass over, pass by, move through
עַד	8	(prep.) until, as far as
עֵד	18	testimony, witness
עֵדָה	20	assembly; throng, gang; community
עוֹד	11	again; still, as long as
עוֹלָם	2	long time, duration; eternity
עָוֹן	15	misdeed, sin, iniquity; guilt
עוֹף	21	flying creature; bird
עֹז	16	might, strength
עזב		
נֶעֱזַב	22	(Niph.) to be abandoned

Hebrew-English Glossary

עזר		
עָזַר	13	to help, assist, aid
עֵ֫זֶר	13	help, assistance
עִיר	4	city, town (fem.; pl. = עָרִים)
עַל	8	(prep.) on, upon, on account of, over
עַל־דְּבַר	8	(prep.) because, on account of
עַל־כֵּן	14	therefore
עלה		
עָלָה	24	to go up, ascend
הֶעֱלָה	24	(Hiph.) to bring up, make go up
עֹלָה	4	burnt offering
עַם	7	people, clan
עִם	8	(prep.) with
עמד		
עָמַד	3	to stand, stand before
עַמּוּד	4	pillar, tent pole
ענה		
עָנָה	24	to reply, answer; to give evidence, testify
עָנִי	13	poor, wretched, needy, afflicted
עָפָר	10	dust, soil
עֵץ	7	tree, timber, wood (collective noun)
עֵצָה	13	advise, plan
עֶ֫צֶם	10	bone
עֶ֫רֶב	10	sunset, evening
ערך		
עָרַךְ	13	to lay out, set in rows; get ready; draw up a battle line
עשׂה		
עָשָׂה	24	to do, make
עֵת	20	point in time, occasion, time
עַתָּה	20	now

פ

פֶּה	7	mouth, opening
פֶּן	2	(conj.) lest, so that not
פנה		
פָּנָה	24	to turn to one side, head in a particular direction; to turn to
פָּנִים	11	front, face
פַּ֫עַם	10	step, pace; time

פקד		
פָּקַד	3	to visit, appoint, inspect
פַּר	18	bull, steer
פְּרִי	20	fruit
פרשׂ		
פָּרַשׂ	15	to spread out, stretch over; stretch out one's hands
פתח		
פָּתַח	14	to open
פִּתַּח	14	(Piel) to untie, let loose, set free
פֶּ֫תַח	11	opening, entrance, door

צ

צֹאן	2	flocks, herds (collective noun)
צָבָא	16	military service, campaign; military men, troops; heavenly warriors
צַדִּיק	20	innocent, righteous, just, upright
צֶ֫דֶק	20	equity, what is right, loyalty, salvation, well-being
צְדָקָה	20	honesty, justice, entitlement, just cause
צוה		
צִוָּה	24	to command, instruct
צוּר	4	rock
צָפוֹן	20	north
צַר	21	enemy
צָרָה	18	need, distress, anxiety

ק

קבר		
קָבַר	12	to bury
קֶ֫בֶר	12	grave
קבץ		
קָבַץ	6	to gather together, collect, assemble
קדשׁ		
קָדַשׁ	6	to be holy
קִדֵּשׁ	18	(Piel) to make something holy; to dedicate or consecrate
הִקְדִּישׁ	18	(Hiph.) to mark as holy or consecrated
הִתְקַדֵּשׁ	20	(Hithp.) to keep oneself consecrated; to be sanctified
קָדוֹשׁ	6	holy
קֹ֫דֶשׁ	6	something holy, holiness, pl.: votive offerings
קָהָל	19	contingent, assembly
קוֹל	2	voice, sound, noise

Hebrew-English Glossary

קום		
קוּם	26	to rise, get up, stand up
הֵקִים	26	(Hiph.) to set up, erect
קטר		
קִטֵּר	14	(Piel) to make a sacrifice, make something go up in smoke
קְטֹרֶת	14	incense
קרא		
קָרָא	25	to call, summon
קרב		
קָרַב	12	to draw near, approach
הִקְרִיב	18	(Hiph.) to bring near; to offer a sacrifice
קֶרֶב	12	entrails, inner parts
קָרְבָּן	12	offering, gift
קָרוֹב	12	nearby, close

ר

ראה		
רָאָה	24	to see
נִרְאָה	24	(Niph.) to appear, become visible
הֶרְאָה	24	(Hiph.) to show
רֹאשׁ	1,6	head, top, chief (pl.: רָאשִׁים)
רִאשׁוֹן	9	first
רַב	21	numerous, many; much; great
רֹב	21	quantity, fullness; wealth; plenty
רבה		
רָבָה	23	to be(come) numerous
הִרְבָּה	23	(Hiph.) to make numerous
רֶגֶל	21	foot, leg
רדף		
רָדַף	6	to pursue, follow
נִרְדַּף	19	(Niph.) to vanish, disappear
רוּחַ	16	breeze, wind, breath; spirit
רום		
רָם	28	to be high
הֵרִים	28	(Hiph.) to make high
רוֹמֵם	28	(Polel) to bring up, aloft
רוץ		
רוּץ	26	to run
רֹחַב	21	breadth, width, expanse

רָחוֹק	17	far
רחץ		
רָחַץ	13	to wash, bathe
רחק		
רָחַק	17	to be distant
הִרְחִיק	17	(Hiph.) to remove (make distant)
רכב		
רָכַב	13	to ride, mount
רֶ֫כֶב	13	chariot
רַע	13	evil, wickedness, misfortune
רֵעַ	10	friend, companion
רָעָב	16	hunger, famine
רעה		
רָעָה	23	to feed, graze, pasture
רֹעֶה	12	shepherd
רַק	18	only
רָשָׁע	20	guilty

שׂ

שׂבע		
שָׂבַע	13	to eat or drink one's fill, satisfy oneself
שָׂ֫דֶה	7	field, pasture, arable land
שׂים		
שִׂים	26	to set up, place, lay, establish
שׂכל		
הִשְׂכִּיל	17	(Hiph.) to make wise, give insight; understand, be prudent
שׂמח		
שָׂמַח	16	to rejoice, be glad
שִׂמַּח	16	(Piel) to gladden, make merry
שִׂמְחָה	16	joy
שׂנא		
שָׂנֵא	25	to hate
שָׂפָה	19	lip, edge, language
שַׂר	7	king's representative, prince, head, leader
שׂרף		
שָׂרַף	12	to burn

Hebrew-English Glossary

שׁ

שאל		
שָׁאַל	16	to ask
שאר		
נִשְׁאַר	19	(Niph.) to remain, be left
הִשְׁאִיר	19	(Hiph.) to leave over, spare, allow to survive
שְׁאֵרִית	19	remnant, remainder
שֵׁבֶט	19	stick, rod, staff; tribe
שבע		
נִשְׁבַּע	23	(Niph.) to swear
הִשְׁבִּיעַ	23	(Hiph.) to make someone swear
שבר		
שָׁבַר	12	to break, break down
שֶׁבֶר	12	breaking, break; collapse
שבת		
שָׁבַת	15	to cease, stop
שַׁבָּת	15	Sabbath
שוב		
שׁוּב	26	to turn, return
הֵשִׁיב	26	(Hiph.) to bring or lead back; to repay
שחט		
שָׁחַט	15	to slaughter
שחת		
שִׁחֵת	23	(Piel) to ruin, destroy
הִשְׁחִית	23	(Hiph.) to ruin, destroy, annihilate, wipe out
שִׁיר	13	song
שכב		
שָׁכַב	11	to lie down, to have sex
שכח		
שָׁכַח	14	to forget
שכם		
הִשְׁכִּים	16	(Hiph.) to get up early, do something early
שכן		
שָׁכַן	12	to dwell, reside
שָׁכֵן	12	resident, neighbor
שָׁלוֹם	12	prosperity, success; welfare; peace
שלח		
שָׁלַח	3	to send, send out, stretch out
שִׁלַּח	14	(Piel) to let go free; expel

שׁלך		
הִשְׁלִיךְ	16	(Hiph.) to throw, to cast
שׁלם		
שָׁלֵם	12	to be completed, ready; to be healthy, unharmed; to keep peace
שִׁלַּם	18	(Piel) to make intact, complete; to make restitution; to recompense,
שָׁלֵם	12	(adj.) whole, untouched, undivided
שֶׁ֫לֶם	12	salvation or peace offering
שָׁם	1	(adv.) there; then
שֵׁם	7	name, reputation
שָׁמַ֫יִם	4	heaven, sky (always dual)
שֶׁ֫מֶן	10	oil, fat
שׁמע		
שָׁמַע	3	to hear, listen, obey
שׁמר		
שָׁמַר	3	to guard, watch over
שֶׁ֫מֶשׁ	19	sun
שַׁ֫עַר	7	gate
שׁפט		
שָׁפַט	3	to judge (mainly military sense), pass judgment, rule
שׁפך		
שָׁפַךְ	12	to pour, shed blood; to pour out; to heap up
שֶׁ֫קֶר	15	lie
שׁרת		
שֵׁרֵת	22	(Piel) to serve, minister
שׁתה		
שָׁתָה	24	to drink

ת

תָּ֫וֶךְ	7	midst
תְּהִלָּה	22	praise, song of praise
תּוֹעֵבָה	21	abomination, abhorrence
תּוֹרָה	18	law, direction, instruction, rule
תַּ֫חַת	8	(prep.) under
תָּמִיד	19	lasting, continually
תְּפִלָּה	13	prayer
תְּרוּמָה	28	contribution, offering

Index of Authors

Index of Subjects

Index of Subjects

Index of Scripture

(Exegetical Exercises Only)